Lecture Notes in Artificial Intelligence   1047

Subseries of Lecture Notes in Computer Science
Edited by J.G. Carbonell and J. Siekmann

Lecture Notes in Computer Science

Edited by G. Goos, J. Hartmanis and J. van Leeuwen

Springer

Berlin
Heidelberg
New York
Barcelona
Budapest
Hong Kong
London
Milan
Paris
Santa Clara
Singapore
Tokyo

Elżbieta Hajnicz

Time Structures

Formal Description
and Algorithmic Representation

 Springer

Series Editors

Jaime G. Carbonell
School of Computer Science
Carnegie Mellon Universtiy
Pittsburgh, PA 15213-3891, USA

Jörg Siekmann
University of Saarland
German Research Center for Artificial Intelligence (DFKI)
Stuhlsatzenhausweg 3, D-66123 Germany

Author

Elżbieta Hajnicz
Polish Academy of Sciences, Institute of Computer Science
ul. Ordona 21, PL-01-237 Warszawa, Poland

Cataloging-in-Publication data applied for

Die Deutsche Bibliothek - CIP-Einheitsaufnahme

Hajnicz, Elżbieta:
Time structures : formal description and algorithmic
representation / Elżbieta Hajnicz. - Berlin ; Heidelberg ; New
York ; Barcelona ; Budapest ; Hong Kong ; London ; Milan ;
Paris ; Santa Clara ; Singapore ; Tokyo : Springer, 1996
  (Lecture notes in computer science ; 1047 : Lecture notes in artificial
  intelligence)
  ISBN 3-540-60941-5
NE: GT

CR Subject Classification (1991): I.2, F.4.1

ISBN 3-540-60941-5 Springer-Verlag Berlin Heidelberg New York

© Springer-Verlag Berlin Heidelberg 1996
Printed in Germany

Typesetting: Camera-ready by author
SPIN 10512635   06/3142 – 5 4 3 2 1 0   Printed on acid-free paper

Preface

The notion of time: the mystery of time passing, the eternal circle of the seasons, of birth, life, and death, the evanescence of what we experience, remembering past things and future misgivings and prospects—all that has fascinated people for ages. The nature of time has been contemplated by philosophers. The reason is that its role is fundamental both in science and in everyday life. We do not all even realize when and how frequently we use this notion. The modern sciences, particularly physics and astronomy, are based on the parameter of time.

Given all this, it is evident that the notion of time plays an important role in artificial intelligence, especially in planning robot activity, natural language processing, and time-varying scenes analysis. In all these disciplines, many experimental and practical algorithmic solutions, as well as formal, logical descriptions and analyses, have been presented. These two approaches are not separate, since many representations and reasoning algorithms are logic-based.

The important characteristic of the notion of time with regard to its applications is that its treatment does not depend on a particular use, and is very specific and different from the treatment of other parameters. On the contrary, description and representation of time strictly depend on the assumptions concerning its structure: whether it is composed of points or of intervals and how these individuals are organized in a particular order.

Thus it seems justified to consider the notion of time separately from its applications and from other parameters utilized in them.

This book is intended to discuss different time structures and their properties from various perspectives. The logical description of time (both by means of classic and modal logics) is a broad discipline itself. The book contains a comprehensive presentation of logical theories of various time structures (point- and interval-based). These theories may be used as a basis for logic-based representations.

On the other hand, there are many representation and reasoning algorithms concerning time. They differ in their expressive power and their algorithmic characteristics (e.g. time and space complexity). Several of them are presented in this book. They are often used in concrete applications from various disciplines.

All these logical theories and algorithmic representations concern specified time structures. Thus these approaches are not independent: they are connected by corresponding time structures. This work aims to show these connections between classic (first order) theories of time structures, modal logic of corresponding structures, and their algorithmic representations. To make this relationship complete, a formalisation of Allen's famous algorithm is presented (which can be applied for various structures of time), as well as its translation to modal logics. Note that a logical characterization of algorithmic solutions, which are not logic-based, is really helpful.

Thus this book contains a comprehensive analysis of logical description and algorithmic representation of time structures, and will be interesting for many people working on or studying computer science and artificial intelligence.

I am very grateful to Prof. Leonard Bolc, Prof. Andrzej Szałas, Dr Witold Bartol and all my colleagues from the Man-Machine Communication Group at the Institute of Computer Science, Polish Academy of Sciences for their helpful comments and discussions. Without their help and support I would probably not have managed to write this book.

This research was supported in part by the Polish Committee for Scientific Research KBN under grant 3 070069 1 01.

November 1995   E. Hajnicz

Contents

1. Introduction

Temporal information plays a very important role in communication between people as well as in many specialized domains of human activity. Therefore, work on artificial intelligence also comprises research on representing and reasoning about temporal interdependencies.

All the work concerning time performed in the area of artificial intelligence, especially that on algorithmization, is aimed at applications in the basic domains of artificial intelligence. Notions concerning time are used, for instance, in planning robot activity, natural language processing and time-varying scenes analysis.

However, before we apply any notion, we should think about its meaning and structure. We should then answer a fundamental question, what is time composed of (philosophical considerations whether time is a real being or not do not have much significance for us).

Therefore, in order to formally describe the reality changing in time (together with complicated notions concerning time) as well as to represent information about this reality in concrete applications, an analysis of problems directly related to time and its structure is indispensable—formal description as well as algorithmic representation of time structures are needed.

As in the case of space, where it is believed that it appears only where matter occurs and these notions are inseparable, time (time passing, as a matter of fact) takes place only where events occur. Because of that many researchers [van Benthem, 1983; Kowalski & Sergot, 1986; Eberle, 1988] consider time composed of events and describe event structures. Nevertheless, in considerations concerning space scientists often treat matter as something that occurs in space (e.g. in metric space). Analogously, in the case of time we can treat events as something occurring in time and consider time as a more basic notion. In this paper we want to describe time in such an abstract manner. Then we can assume that time is composed of points or intervals.

In both cases we should consider how the above individuals form time. An obvious property of time that we all experience is its passing. McTaggart (1908; 1927) formulates two opposite concepts of time, calling them A-series and B-series. In his own words, dynamic A-series is *the series of positions which runs from the far past through the near past to the present, and then from the present through the near future to the far future.* The static B-series is *the series of positions which runs from earlier to later.* A-series can be treated as a representation of time experienced from the inside; time is described in this way by modal tense logics. On the other hand B-series represent time viewed from the outside. Then time forming individuals appear in a certain order. The first (and higher) order predicate calculus is best suited for such kind of description of time. Then it is necessary to study this order, i.e. consider and describe different temporal structures. The next question is whether individuals form linear, backward linear or partial order. Sometimes it is also important whether this order is dense or discrete, whether structures are infinite or not. In chapter 2 we present some well-known time descriptions in the first order predicate calculus, whereas in chapter 3 in modal tense logics. Moreover, we try to describe the same classes of time structures in both ways. This is inasmuch as the semantics of modal tense logics is based on structures described in the first order predicate calculus.

Point time and interval time were very often related. Intervals were defined as sets of points (e.g. van Benthem, 1983) or pairs of points (e.g. Shoham, 1987). There also exist examples of defining points in interval structures [Allen & Hayes, 1987; van Benthem, 1983]. As a result we obtain a method for transforming point structures into interval ones and *vice versa*. We sketch this issue in chapter 2.

From the artificial intelligence point of view, formal solutions have an auxiliary character only, ordering knowledge about a particular domain. On the other hand, significant role is played by algorithmic solutions that make possible a representation of knowledge about the domain and drawing from it suitable conclusions, needed in particular applications. For this reason, several algorithms of reasoning about time are presented in chapter 4. Special attention is paid to Allen's (1983) constraint propagation algorithm, as it makes it possible to represent different time structures, in particular those formally described in chapter 2.

Though we have differentiated two directions in investigations on time— logical description of time and algorithms for reasoning about time—we do not want to suggest that these two directions are entirely independent. After all, a good formal description of a domain is very useful for an effective algorithmic representation. Such relations often go further—a formal description of an algorithmic solution is created. In chapter 5 we present a formalization of Allen's algorithm based on formal descriptions of time structures presented in chapter 2 (for different time structures). Eventually, in chapter 6 this formalization is related to the appropriate modal logics. Thus, this book presents a comprehensive approach to the problem of time description and representation based on existing investigations on time in artificial intelligence.

However, before we discuss different time structures, we sketch the most important notions concerning time and their basic applications, in order to make more explicit the aim of choosing for consideration exactly these time structures and not other ones.

1.1 Basic time notions

In order to use time in the artificial intelligence framework, a description of some individuals functioning in time is necessary. These primitives are needed in all the applications of time in artificial intelligence, and actually they do not depend on formalism used for their description, even though a method of representation depends on it.

Though different authors use different terminology, we can assume that such basic primitives are facts, events and processes. In this section we want to describe these notions.

1.1.1 Facts

Facts are individuals presenting a state of a described world, a represented reality. This notion is connected with everything which is static, permanent, invariant in the represented reality. We use a term *fact* after [McDermott, 1982]. Allen (1983) uses the term *property*, as facts most often describe properties of described objects, e.g. *The cupboard was high, made of light wood and it had curved doors.* On the other hand, however, a sentence *The cupboard was standing in a corner of the room, near a window*, describes a fact, too, even though we can hardly call it a property of the cupboard.

McDermott considers facts holding at single time moments (world states). In each state some facts hold and other do not. He also considers facts holding in time intervals (seen as sets of states). Evidently, a fact holds in a certain interval, if it holds in all the states composing this interval. Two special facts are distinguished: *always*—the set of all the states and *never*—the empty set of states.

In contrast, Allen (1984) only speaks of properties holding in intervals—this is obvious, as there are no points in his logic. He makes instead a strong assumption that if a property holds in any time interval, then it holds in all its subintervals.

Both Allen and McDermott consider conjunction, disjunction and negation of facts.

The essence of facts is that they cannot be changed by themselves, but such a change has to be caused by some event. Nevertheless McDermott claims that certain facts, some time period after they appear stop autonomously or at least we loose knowledge whether it still holds or not. For instance, if we leave a car on a parking, then we return a few days later being almost sure that it is still there. But returning several years later we can only hope that we will find the car in the right place, but we are sure of nothing. 120 years after someone's birth we can safely assume that he is dead knowing nothing about the circumstances of his death. McDermott calls such a time period the *lifetime* of a fact. The fact lifetime is certainly a characteristic feature of the fact. Nevertheless, most of the authors assume that facts can only undergo changes after an occurrence of an appropriate event, in other words, they treat the lifetime of all the facts as infinite.

1.1.2 Events

If we think of facts as a static image of the world, then we can treat events as a dynamic image of the world. Events happen, and their occurrences break the immobility of the world, initiate changes in it, i.e. in facts holding in it.

Most events cause changes in facts. There also exist "neutral" events that do not have any effects (e.g. *a few runs around the house*), but actually such events are not interesting from the artificial intelligence point of view, and they are usually ignored.

The simplest example of such a treatment of facts and events led McCarthy & Hayes (1969) to create *situation calculus*. In contrast to facts, events (actions) are not represented in it directly, but they constitute transition functions between situations (equivalents of world states) as a cause for change in facts. Events are provided with sets of preconditions that have to hold in an initial situation in order to enable the event to occur (a question of feasibility of actions) and a set of effects (postconditions) that should hold in a destination situation.

Georgeff (1987) suggests an interesting extension of the situation calculus. Namely, he finds that treating events as transition relations on situations instead of transition functions makes it possible to represent simultaneous events. Then it is not possible to assume that no fact that has not been influenced by the event can undergo change. Instead of this, the author introduces a requirement that if a fact has undergone a change then there exists an event responsible for it.

Georgeff did not call changing facts by events causality, but he considered causing some events by other ones (in the same situation or in its successor). Evidently, such a relationship occurs only when appropriate conditions are satisfied.

Another example of operating on instantaneous events is [Kahn & Gorry, 1977]. The authors pay less attention to interdependencies between events and facts, and focus on the problem of time passing between events and the problem of incomplete knowledge on the time of occurrence of these events.

However, genuine events are not instantaneous. Not only they last for a certain period of time, but they often have their structure, phases. The fact that events extend in time has its far-reaching implications—several events can occur more or less simultaneously, which can influence their course as well as their effects. Because of that many authors accept that events occur in time intervals.

Allen (1984) static properties not only with events, but with the general class of *occurrences*. He distinguished two subclasses among occurrences—*events* and *processes*. In Allen's opinion, a characteristic feature of events is that they have one culmination point and univocal effects.

Allen defines an interval of event occurrence as the smallest relevant interval. Thus any event occurs in the exactly one interval. As a matter of fact, there exist repeatable events, e.g. if we consider the event *Chris threw a ball to Kate*, then he can repeat this action many times. This raises the problem of distinguishing individual <u>event tokens</u> from <u>event types</u> [McDermott, 1982; Haugh, 1987].

In fact, Allen considers event types and he imposes a condition that if any event occurs in a particular interval, then it occurs in none of its subintervals. Haugh (1987) suggests a stronger condition, namely he demands that intervals of occurrence of an event be disjoint. Shoham (1987) calls this property of intervals *solidity*.

Allen also presents a definition of composed events, e.g. events occurring several times in a particular time interval, sequences of several events or simultaneous occurrences of several events.

Also McDermott (1982) regards events as occurring in intervals, not in points. He suggests to treat an event (actually an event type) as the set of all the intervals of its occurrence.

Similarly as in the case of facts, McDermott defines an event *never* that never occurs—it is an empty set of intervals. In contrast, there is no event *always*, since events cannot (at least intuitively) have an infinite duration—on the contrary, their duration is short in comparison with duration of facts.

1.1.3 Actions

Among events we can distinguish *actions*, i.e. events consciously performed by living agents, typically human. Evidently some events are not actions, e.g. *a flash of lightening* is not an action.

An action is called by McDermott (1982) *an entity, the doing of which by an agent is an event*, whereas Allen (1984) speaks of an action caused by an agent, which results in a certain event. In our opinion, the difference between these two definitions is purely superficial.

McDermott treats some actions as primitive ones. These actions are defined directly, together with their preconditions, effects, durations etc. Moreover, he also considers some special actions, such as allowing, avoiding, or preventing an occurrence of an event. McDermott gives an example of an agent, who has to prevent a heroine from being mashed by a train. Sometimes there is no possibility to perform a particular action; then the result of performing it is the event *never*.

Allen considers some composite actions, too. He focuses on the problem of generating one action by another. Generation of actions consists mainly in that one action constitutes a way of performing the other. Allen presents an example of John playing the piano in order to wake up Sue. We have here the action of *playing the piano* performed by John. The event resulting from this action is the reason for Sue's *waking up*. But John <u>wanted</u> to wake up Sue, so he performed the action of waking her up **by** playing the piano (and not, for instance, by screaming loudly or by shaking her).

Contrary to these mentioned above, typical composite actions consist of several actions performed simultaneously or sequentially, and each of them can be treated independently from the other ones.

Shoham (1989) claims that viewing actions as simple causality gives them the character of implication enriched by a temporal parameter. In his opinion an **action** is associated with making a certain choice among several courses of events. This choice is temporally asymmetric—it depends on the past and does not depend on the future (though it can depend on expectations concerning the future). Moreover, actions can only affect the future. An action depends on agent's free will—anything that can be predicted is not an action. On the other hand, depending on the possessed knowledge, one observer can recognize a particular event as a conscious action, and the second as an independent event.

1.1.4 Processes

The last notion we want to consider is a *process*. Processes are in some sense an intermediate notion between events and facts. They undoubtedly belong to the dynamic image of the world, since they cause changes, "are happening". However, changes are made by processes in a gradual, continuous, often slow and imperceptible way. In contrast, changes caused by events are sudden and discrete.

Continuity of an occurrence of a process is expressed by allowing it to be occurring in subintervals of the considered interval. Allen (1984) requires that if a process is occurring over a particular interval, it must also be occurring over at least one of its subintervals. In contrast to facts, processes need not be occurring over all the subintervals of their occurrence intervals. An excellent example of such a process is *a car ride round a city with breaks for stops on traffic lights*.

With this definition of a process, one could assume that a particular process has been occurring in a much longer (in fact, in an arbitrarily long) time interval than it actually has. In order to avoid such a situation, we can demand that a process is occurring in some initiating and some terminating subintervals of its occurrence interval.

Evidently, there exist processes which occur in all the subintervals of each of their occurrence intervals. They are called *continuous processes*. An example of such a process is *an apple falling down*. Such processes cannot be distinguished from facts in a purely temporal way—they are *temporally homogenous*. The only difference is that such a process causes changes in the world (an apple changes its position). Such changes are also called *continuous* [Raulefs, 1987].

Many event classes are closely related to appropriate process classes. For instance, with the above process of *an apple falling down* the event of *the apple falling down from a tree to the ground* is connected. Then the event occurrence interval is the maximal interval the process has been occurring in.

It is sometime possible that a process has been occurring while the corresponding event has not been realized. Allen presents an example of John *walking from home to the store* who changed his mind and returned home. However, there is an inverse dependence: if an event has occurred, then the relevant process has been occurring (if only such a connection exists).

We can also differentiate a process from an event by counting, how many times the event has occurred. In the case of processes this makes no sense.

Certainly, some processes are not related to any events. Examples of such processes are living organisms growing old or the decay of rocks.

Allen also points out the fact that there exist actions that do not result in events, but in processes, e.g. *John is running*. He calls actions resulting in events *performances* and actions resulting in processes *activities*.

Let us now return to McDermott's concept of a *lifetime*. It seems that we deal with two different cases here. If a fact lifetime is connected with a loss of knowledge on whether the fact still holds, then it results from a big likelihood that an event interrupting the fact has occurred. This applies to the example of *a car left on a parking*. On the other hand, if a fact lifetime is connected with an assumption of its termination, then it results from a process directly related to the fact and occurring simultaneously with it. In the case of human (or animal) life, this is the process of growing old, which leads to the event of death (which can occur earlier because of an illness, an accident etc.), whereas in the case of a rock, the process of decay is accompanied by a process of decrease in volume, up to complete disappearance. Therefore, processes can cause changes in facts, other processes (rock decay causes decrease in volume) or even events (growing old causes death). It seems evident that events can cause processes.

An important class of processes is that of *physical processes*. It contains the movement of objects, the flow of liquids, changes of temperature etc. These processes are continuous, temporally homogenous. In physics, such processes are characterized by differential equations representing changes of appropriate physical parameters. However, real processes have a structure, which allows to draw conclusions without any quantitative information. For instance, if we put on a stove a kettle filled with water, then some time later the water will boil. If, moreover, the kettle has a whistle, then it will be whistling to inform us that the water is boiling [Forbus, 1984].

We can also look at processes in a different, somehow opposite way to that discussed above. Namely, we can treat them as long sequences of small events, the effects of which are perceived globally as continuous changes. An example of such processes are *historical processes*. Most of events composing them do not deserve the name of *historical events*, nevertheless they influence the course of history. Similarly, individual events of *wave break on a beach* constitute a process of *waves breaking on the beach*. We cannot say about such processes that they are occurring over at least one subinterval of any its occurrence interval. We can, however, make a simplifying assumption that the minimal interval of occurrence of such a process consists of the union of two successive occurrence intervals of component events.

Processes treated as sequences of events or actions are considered by Georgeff (1987) in the framework of a generalized situation calculus. For each such process he distinguishes a set of its internal facts. These facts can be influenced only by events of the process, i.e. they are not sensitive to outside events. Events composing a process are connected by causal interdependencies. A process can also be composed of actions (e.g. a manufacturing process). In this case pre- and prevail-conditions of actions can only be internal facts. Such a process can consist of events and actions repeated infinitely many times. The author also considers conjunctions (a simultaneous performance of two or more processes) and disjunctions of processes.

1.2 Time notions in artificial intelligence

The notion of time is widely used in artificial intelligence. We will discuss its application in basic fields of interest of artificial intelligence.

1.2.1 Planning

One of the important subjects artificial intelligence deals with is planning actions needed to achieve a particular goal. Usually these actions are to be performed by an agent (robot).

The general schema of the planning problem is the following: We have a certain initial situation and a certain goal to achieve. The goal can be treated as a set of conditions imposed on a destination situation—conditions to achieve. Moreover, we have a set of actions. There is a set of *preconditions* for an action, which must hold before or during the action is performed (depending on the solution) and a set of *effects* resulting from the performance of the actions. If preconditions of an action do not hold, their satisfaction can constitute a subgoal to achieve—a hierarchy of goals is considered [Fikes & Nillson, 1971].

In early planners world states are instantaneous, actions do not occupy time, and there are no simultaneous actions. Moreover, there exists exactly one agent and there are no independent events. In later works, solutions eliminating the above restrictions as well as solving other problems have been discussed.

Hendrix (1973) points out that actions not only can influence the occurrence of facts (i.e. a change of a static world state), but they can also initiate or terminate continuous processes (e.g. *turning on the water* causes *a container to be filled with water*). Processes can also end autonomously, e.g. *overflow of a container being filled with water*. The important thing is that processes as well as actions have their direct and indirect effects enabling other actions to be performed and influencing other processes [Forbus, 1989; Hogge, 1987].

Schmolze (1986) states that physical processes occur if and only if their enabling conditions are satisfied. We can see a noticeable difference between processes and actions. In the case of actions, satisfaction of their preconditions only represents a potential possibility of their performance. Moreover, some processes not only change properties of objects, but also influence their existence. Good examples of such situations are *melting and freezing of water*, or some *cooking activities* as *making coffee, baking cakes* etc. We mean here that properties of objects change to such an extent that we recognize it as a transformation of the objects.

Many authors [Sacerdoti, 1977; Levi, 1988; Hertzberg & Hotz, 1989] suggest not to determine any order on the performance of actions as long as this is not necessary. To accept this we need partially ordered time structures. Cheng & Irani (1987; 1989) remark that in such a case it is important to represent ordering constraints on actions explicitly, in order to exclude situations violating these constraints. An example of such a situation is the necessity of performing an action which disturbs the effects of another earlier action (e.g. *washing clothes* should precede *their drying*). Dean (1985) concludes that in the case of non-sequential plan generation all the desired conditions (preconditions and effects) should be protected. Therefore, there is a need for monitoring to check whether the conditions are disturbed by new actions. In such a case, the plan should be corrected. Another way of protection is to prevent the occurence of some facts in certain intervals [Hogge, 1988]. A comprehensive comparison of representing plans as total orders and partial orders can be found in Minton et al. (1992).

Miller et al. (1985) point out that the duration of individual activities play an important role in planning. It sometimes depends on the order of their performance. Thus optimisation of the time of task realization imposes additional constraints on the order of actions. Similar questions are considered in [Huber & Becker, 1988; Levi, 1988].

Hayes (1989) shows that joining different operations (i.e. performing them more or less simultaneously) makes plans more efficient. Hence we should aim at performing actions simultaneously, whenever possible. Georgeff (1989) remarks that if actions are to be performed simultaneously, preconditions for separate, individual actions are not sufficient. For instance, having two blocks A and B, it is not sufficient that their upsides be free to be able to perform actions "put A on B" and "put B on A" simultaneously. For actions performed simultaneously, effects of some actions should not disturb the preconditions of the remaining ones. In the case of simultaneous actions, Sandewall & Ronnquist (1986) suggest to consider prevail-conditions besides pre- and post-conditions.

Pednault (1988) notices that effects of some actions are context-dependent. He therefore divides preconditions of actions into two groups, primary preconditions which are indispensable to perform an action and secondary preconditions, defining the context in which these actions produce particular effects. The need for operating on actions with conditional effects is also raised by Peberthy & Weld (1992).

A long series of problems is related to planning in an unpredictable, dynamic environment. In this case we are not able to predict everything in a plan. Hence, monitoring of each action is indispensable (whether preconditions are satisfied and effects achieved), and in the case of failure correction mechanisms should be applied. Typically this consists in restarting planning, starting from the new situation [Doyle et al., 1986].

Morgenstern (1987) points out that in the case of a complex, underspecified environment the design of a plan is not based on exact knowledge of the conditions of its execution. Sometimes learning how to perform a particular action can be part of a plan.

Schoppers (1987) analyses the planning of robot actions in totally unpredictable environment. We have a well determined goal, but we do not know the initial situation. Actions may not achieve their intended effects, and effects once achieved may be destroyed. The design of a *universal* plan is needed; it has the form of a *decision tree*. The root of the tree represents the goal to be) achieved. If it is already satisfied, there is nothing to do. If not, other relevant conditions enabling performance of actions leading to the goal are checked. Each path in the tree constitutes a classic linear plan.
Reactive planning is also considered by Firby (1987) and Tychonievitch et al. (1989).

Georgeff & Lansky (1987) analyse robot action planning for a set of several goals to be achieved. In their opinion, goals represent expected behaviour of an environment rather than static properties of the world. Hence, they are expressed as conditions on particular sequences of world states. Goals can have different priorities, so when a new higher-priority goal appears, the actually executed one can be abandoned or interrupted.

In order to plan acting in an unpredictable environment more efficiently, a possibility of preventing some other agents' actions or external events with undesirable effects on our plan is needed. Allen & Koomen (1983) remark that an event we want to prevent has to be somehow represented in a plan. This requires a possibility of representing genuine non-linear time, an *open future*, i.e. admitting that a particular event may occur or not. Note, that in the above considerations non-linearity only means that the order of events need not be necessarily known in advance.

Haas (1992) indicates that in reactive planning reasoning about the past (the near past, i.e. the time that has passed since a known situation) is crucial, as we want to know what may undergo change.

Badaloni & Berati (1994) show that in may situations, it is useful to plan at different levels of abstraction, hence to use different time granularity.

The above considerations refer to the problem of generating (synthesis of) plans intended to achieve a particular goal. However, the inverse situation is also possible—a certain sequence of actions has been performed and we want to know why, for what sake and following what strategy they have been performed [Kautz & Allen, 1986; Kautz, 1987, Song & Cohen, 1991]. This can be useful for story understanding, carrying on conversations (in order to identify interlocutor's strategy) etc. We often want to apply such an analysis to be able to predict subsequent actions. Also in this case the order of actions need not be completely determined and simultaneous actions are allowed. Moreover, an observed action (or set of actions) can sometimes occur in several different plans. And the necessity of drawing conclusions from partial information (a subset of actions designed in the plan should also be taken into account.

1.2.2 Natural language processing

The occurrence of a time parameter in natural language sentences is unquestionable. In most languages, a sentence is provided with a tense determining the time of occurrence of an event described in the sentence relative to the speech point. It was these dependencies in natural language sentences that inspired Prior (1967) to elaborate his tense logic. He introduced two famous modal operators P—at least once in the *past* and F—at least once in the *future*. These operators allow to express not only basic dependencies, but also such complicated tenses as *past perfect, future perfect* or *future in the past*.

A very famous and often cited in literature [Hornstein, 1977; Man-Kam Yip, 1985; Song & Cohen, 1988] approach is that of Reichenbach (1966). The author uses three evaluation points for a sentence—the speech point (S), the event point (E) and the reference point (R). A tense of a sentence is characterized by the mutual position of these points on the time-axis (there exist 13 different such positions assuming that these points can coincide). Song & Cohen (1988) claim that only 7 English tenses (from among 16) can be differentiated by this method.

Man-Kam Yip (1985) discusses how to extend such a structure of basic tenses to be able to represent sentences containing temporal adverbials (*now, yesterday, tomorrow*), temporal connectives (*when, before, after*) and reported speech.

Song & Cohen (1988) classify occurrences described by sentences of a story as *facts* (called *states* by them), *processes* and *events*. This differentiation is based on the parsing of a sentence (mainly on its tense). They extend Reichenbach's approach by treating E as interval and allowing some different reference points R.

Moens & Steedman (1988) and Blackburn et al., (1994) analyse problems concerning the English present perfect tense. They show that Reichenbachian representation does not explain why the present perfect is awkward in combination with stative, process and point expressions:

Example
The following present perfect sentences are awkward:

The house has been empty.	(stative expression)
I have worked in the garden.	(process expression)
The star has twinkled.	(point expression)

In contrast to Reichenbach, Hwang & Schubert (1994) suggest that representing simple tense (past, present and future), perfect aspect and progressiveness as separate, composable entities, leeds to an uniform representation, which turns out to be especially convenient in the presence of time adverbials.

Kahn & Gorry (1977) focus on imprecise formulation characteristic for a natural language, such as *3 or 4 days later, about 2 hours ago, for several years, during a few weeks*.

Merkel (1988) considers *temporal frame-adverbial phrases*. These are expressions concerning time periods events occur in. Such phrases are categorized as *deictic, calendar* and *dependent*, and each of them is labeled by +, = or − depending on direction (e.g. *previous week* is an anterior deictic phrase, and *now* is a simultaneous deictic phrase). Some expressions can have complex character.

Example
Next week on Monday, at 6 p.m.

These expressions are based on a hierarchy Year, Month, Day, Hour, Minute, Second. There also exists Weeks that do not match this hierarchy, as months are not divided into weeks.

The author also analyses a problem relative to the adverb *next* (*previous*). For instance, *next Wednesday* is the nearest Wednesday on Thursday and Friday and the second nearest on Monday and Tuesday. The meaning of this term between weeks, on Saturday and Sunday, is ambiguous, and it can have two interpretations—different people can have different impressions.

Merkel formulates a correctness rule for these phrases. They are correct if individual terms form a chain in the hierarchy, i.e. there are no gaps between them. For instance, correct phrases are *May 24th, in 2 weeks and 3 days*, and incorrect ones are *in 1987 at 9:15, in 2 months and 3 hours*. Nevertheless, this rule also allows senseless formulations, e.g. *in 1987 a month ago*.

Applications of natural language analysis in artificial intelligence can be divided into three groups: conversation with a system user in natural language, discourse analysis (story understanding) and translations from one language into another.

For the sake of discourse analysis, Hirschman & Story (1981) introduce a convention of *narrative time progression* assuming that time does not move backward unless this is univocally stated. Certainly, the basic information still consists of the tense of sentences and other linguistic denominators of time implying mutual position of events (e.g. *during, after, then, now*) or their duration.

Eberle (1988) points out that in a sequence of sentences, subsequent sentences can be not only a continuation, but also an elaboration of the preceding sentences.

Example
> *George wrote a program. He logged in, opened his file and began writing and correcting, using his papers.*

Moreover, he observes that an order of events is sometimes not determined at the moment of analysis and can be specified by additional information contained in the subsequent sentences.

Example
From the text:
> *George took the plane to Frankfurt. Then he took the train to Stuttgart. As he was hungry, he bought a sandwich at the station.*

we are not able to deduce whether George bought his sandwich in Frankfurt or in Stuttgart. This can follow from the subsequent sentences:
> *Then he boarded the train.*

or
> *Then he phoned his wife to say that he had arrived.*

In the case of German there are additional complications, as the aspect of verbs is sometimes not uniquely determined, and additional information is needed to decide whether the culmination of an event has actually been reached.

Hobs & Agar (1981) call attention to the fact that in order to understand a story (or a conversation between people) one should understand the strategy of utterance, for which a recognition of author's goal and plan is needed. Planning proceeds on two levels—there exists a goal of utterance and goals and strategies of agents described in it. Thus, for understanding a text (especially its temporal structure), a recognition of plans used by interlocutors (or the author of a text) is needed. This also concerns conversations with a system user, but in this case the system should try to recognize user's plan and adopt its own strategy of utterance to it.

Richards et al. (1989) analyse, besides the problem of tenses, many other problems relative to time expressions in natural languages; some of them are specific of English. The main of them are adverbial phrases *at 5 o'clock, 3 days before* etc., negation and the perfective aspect of verbs. They pay special attention to indexicals—*now, today, tomorrow, last year*, which can have special character In the case of reported speech.

Example

In a sentence:

George always said that he would be rich tomorrow.

the term *tomorrow* can be related to the moment of the formulation of this statement about George as well as to each George's utterance.

The next issue that is carefully analysed in this work are temporal dependences in subordinate complex sentences. The authors show that tenses in subject relative clauses are generally independent of tenses in superordinate clauses. In reported speech, however, tenses in oblique clauses are generally subordinate to tenses in superordinate position. In the case of subordinate clause in object position, often two different interpretations exist.

In natural language processing, *temporal quantifiers* (such as *always, never, twice*) are very important, too. The authors show that such quantifiers seem to have a certain anaphoric use.

Example

Considering sentences:

George has had a headache 5 times last week.

He took an aspirin twice.

we know not only that George took an aspirin last week, but that he took it in two cases of headache.

The authors also consider other cases of *temporal anaphoras*, in particular temporal connectives such as *later* or *two days before*. The connective *before* seems to be particularly interesting, since in special cases it can have a modal character.

Example

In sentences:

George stopped the car before he hit the tree.

George managed to stop the car before he hit the tree.

George probably avoided hitting the tree. This problem does not appear in sentences:

George washed his hands before he sat at the table.
George managed to get into the lift before its doors closed.

Di Maio & Zanardo (1994) show that it makes sense to establish temporal comparison among different (and incompatible) courses of affairs.

In the case of machine translation, problems concerning time are also very important. Meya & Vidal (1988) show that translations of temporal expressions are not just simple mappings of tense, aspect and temporal adverbials from a source language to a target one. Therefore, a semantic representation of statements is essential (similarly as in the above applications of natural language processing). This representation should take into account *verb classification, deictic dependencies* between events and other reference points (e.g. the speech point) including distances and aspect. For instance, differences concerning aspect are sometimes expressed in Spanish by different verbs. Eventually, such an intermediate representation can be translated into a target language.
A similar subject is discussed in [van Eynde, 1988].

1.2.3 Time-varying scene analysis

Scene analysis is based on the analysis of individual images—there is no temporal factor in it. Identification of the objects of an image has a great importance here [Matsujama & Hwang, 1985; Bajcsy et al., 1985; Burns & Kitchen, 1987; Fisher, 1987]. The next question is the analysis of motion, change, by comparison of subsequent images of a sequence. Asada & Tsuji (1985) suggest selecting moving objects from a motionless background. In some cases, the environment are motionless, but the camera is moving [Lucas & Kenade, 1985; Barron et al., 1987; Ayache & Lustman, 1987; Ayache & Faugeras, 1987].

Burger & Bhanu (1987) describe a system in which a camera placed on a moving vehicle observes the environment in which other objects are moving. Thus a change in a sequence of images results from the both motions. The aim of the system is to find an interpretation of a scene, i.e. to determine the trajectory of the camera, to identify moving objects and to determine their trajectories. Finally the system creates a 3-dimensional model of the environments.

At this level, time is treated as a physical, metric parameter, analogous to space parameters.

In works discussed above, two crucial operations are performed—identification of objects on fixed images and identification of their trajectories in time. From our point of view, however, the most interesting factor is the process of recognizing abstract, "meaningful" events occurring in a analysed sequence of images, using the above data. Such events, after their identification, can be represented and manipulated in several ways—e.g. they can be described in natural language.

Neumann (1984a; 1984b) and Novak (1985) have worked on this subject. In their solution, a crossroad of two streets had been filmed from a stationary camera. There is a motionless background (buildings, street lamps, pavements etc.), which is known and represented in the system in advance. The moving objects are cars, cyclists, pedestrians etc.

The authors distinguish two main types of events: *primitive* (temporally homogeneous) and *composite* ones. It is possible to differentiate distinct phases of composite events, arranged in some specified order.

Example

We present here a model of an event of one car *overtaking* another; it appears in the papers quoted above.

All the events listed in the model body are primitive. Obviously, we assume implicitly that the beginning of an event precedes its ending.

Events understood in such a way fall under the definition of processes. Clearly, primitive events correspond to temporally homogenous processes.

head:	(OVERTAKE	OBJ1	OBJ2	T1	T2)
body:	(MOVE	OBJ1	T1	T2)	
	(MOVE	OBJ2	T1	T2)	
	(APPROACH	OBJ1	OBJ2	T1	T3)
	(BEHIND	OBJ1	OBJ2	T1	T3)
	(BESIDE	OBJ1	OBJ2	T3	T4)
	(IN_FRONT_OF	OBJ1	OBJ2	T4	T2)
	(PRECEDE	OBJ1	OBJ2	T4	T2)

The authors also assume a possibility a conversation about the scene under consideration. Thus, it is possible to obtain answers to questions concerning events occurring in it. Natural language statements are directly connected with event models (by *deep cases*); besides objects taking part in an event, the background is also taken into account (where is an object moving from and to, where has an event occurred, what are its circumstances—accompanying events etc.). On the other hand, the order of event occurrence is important for the generation of a description of the whole scene.

Andre at al. (1988) consider a similar topic. Namely, they analyse an image sequences representing a fragment of a football match and they identify events occurring in it. In contrast to the previous solution, a scene description (a report of the match) is generated during its course (as it is in real life). Thus, there appear additional problems with an identification of events that have not been finished yet, and with selection of events to be reported, depending on their importance. In the extreme case, an event description should be interrupted when something much more important is happening (e.g. a goal).

1.2.4 Temporal databases

The basic and probably the widest area of application of computer science are databases. Therefore in many of them, like in everyday life, time is a usefull, or sometimes even indispensable parameter. However, time is a very specific notion. Treating it as any other parameter strongly limits the expressive power of a representation. Therefore, an important class of databases are *temporal databases*, in which time has a special status.

In traditional databases, only current knowledge (from temporal point of view) is stored, or time is treated as an ordinary parameter. First attempts to incorporate changes into databases consisted in considering updates as starting and/or finishing moments of dependencies being stored. Lee et al. (1985) call it *a database treated as its history of update transactions, each marked with the time the update occurred* (using computer clock). Therefore starting and finishing moments are added to each dependency, marking moments when it was inserted and deleted.

Kowalski & Sergot (1985) pay attention to the fact that dependencies need not be introduced to a database in the same moment as they really started or finished, or even in the same order as they happen in the real world. Instead of typical updates, they use events (having their time of occurence) that start and/or finish specified dependencies (facts) (one or more). Moreover, information already stored in a database can be incomplete, as in the example:

Mary was hired as a lecturer on 10 May 1970.
Mary left as a professor on 1 October 1980.
where an event (one or more) changing Mary's rank should occur.

Since databases represent information about the world, it is not surprising that their entries can have fact-like or event-like character. This should be somehow encoded in the representation. Kowalski & Sergot (1985) consider facts and (pointwise) events. The problems connected with these notions are similar to those encounterd in other applications.

Typically, databases set some constraints on a form of their entries, corresponding to general a knowledge about a represented domain. In the case of temporal databases, such constraints can have form od causal rules.

Mays (1983) distinguishes actual and potential data w.r.t. the current content of a database. For instance, the question:

Is Kitty in Norfolk?

can be answered:

> *Yes, she is.*

or

> *No, but she was on May, 10.*

if they correspond to the current content of the database, or

> *No, shall I let you know when she is?*

if there is a possible future with Kitty being in Norfolk (according to the database constraints). Evidently, possibility of giving such an answer needs a monitoring mechanism in the system. In contrast, the questions like:

> *Is New York less than 50 miles from Philadelphia?*

can be answered only *Yes* or *No*, as they concern time-independent dependencies.

A general form of queries Mays considers is as follows:

> *Could it have been the case that* p *?*   (counterhistoricals)

and

> *Might it ever be the case that* p *?*   (futurities).

The author proposes a rich modal temporal language for representing constraints and queries for his database.

Böhlen & Marti (1994) notice that representing facts from their start to their finish (i.e. taking into account only maximal intervals of their occurence) we should remember that no overlapping or even meeting intervals of validity of the same fact can be represented together. The authors call this feature *temporal irreducibility*. The representation of Kowalski & Sergot is similar in this respect. Note, that this feature has nothing to do with *solidity* of events. The *temporal homogeneity* of facts is represented here by the notion of *snapshot*, A snapshot contains all dependencies valid at a given moment of time (i.e. those which have already started, whereas are not yet finished).

Böhlen & Marti differentiate *temporally grouped* and *temporally ungrouped* data models. In the first one, time is connected with every single object, while in the second—with the whole dependency.

Katsuno & Mendelzon (1991) widely discuss a difference between an *update* and a *revision* of a database. An *update* conssist in bringing the database up to date when the desribed world changes (e.g. as a result of a performed action). A *revision* is used when we obtain new information about the static world, i.e. our knowledge about the world changes, not the world itself. Therefore new data may contradict old ones. The authors formally describe both classes of modifications and differences between them.

Typically, there are three levels dinstinguished in databases: *phisical, conceptual* and *external.* Chomicki (1994) suggests to split the conceptual level (in the context of temporal databases) into *abstract* and *concrete* level. An abstract temporal database captures the formal, representation-independent meaning of a temporal database. A concrete temporal database provides a specific, finite representation for it in terms of a specific temporal data model. This also concerns query languages.

Kabanza et al. (1990) present how to incorporate infinite temporal data (i.e. dependencies holding infintely many times, for instance *every Tuesday*) into temporal databases.

Many problems concerning temporal databases can also be found in other applications of time (choosing time points or intervals as a base of representation, defining hierarchy of time units, using causal rules etc.). An up to date survey of the subject can be found in [McKenzie & Snodgrass, 1991; Snodgrass, 1992; Baudinet et al., 1993; Chomicki, 1994].

1.2.5 Program specification and verification

The idea of describing programs properties by means of a temporal logic is based on the observation that program executions constitute sequences of actions performed in some order. Thus a typical logic used for this is based on discrete time structures infinite only to the future.

Earlier solutions were based on linear point structures [Gabbay et al., 1980; Manna & Pnueli, 1981; 1982; Kröger, 1985]. Now branching [Lamport, 1980; Ben-Ari et al., 1983; Emerson, 1991; Kwiatkowska et al., 1994], partially ordered [Pinter & Wolper, 1984; Kornatzky & Pinter, 1986; Penczek, 1994] and interval-based [Moszkowski & Manna, 1984; Schwartz et al., 1984; Hansen & Chaochen, 1991; Kutty et al., 1994] structures are usually considered. Branching time structures are often thoughed of as better suited for non-deterministic programs. A comparison of linear and branching time representations can be found in [Emerson & Halpern, 1986; Grumberg & Kurshan, 1994].

Most of the papers concern specification and verification of concurrent programs (i.e. several concurrent processes), with sequential programs treated as "special case". A parallel execution of a concurrent program is modelled by considering its possible sequentializations, called an *interleaving model*; partially ordered structures enables representing concurrent programs without such sequentializations.

In this domain, modal temporal logics (tense logics) are prefered to logics based on the first order predicate calculus. To represent a program in a temporal logic, we need propostional variables to represent its variables ("memory") and additional variables to represent a state of each process (pointing at an action to be executed next). In advanced logics object variables are used, too [Andréka et al., 1995]. On the semantic level, each time point contain a description of an appropriate total state of the program.

A fundamental classification of program properties [e.g. Gabbay et al., 1980; Kröger, 1985] is as follows:

- Safety (invariance) properties,
- Liveness (eventuality) properties.

The main invariance property is *partial correctnes*. This means that if a precondition P holds upon the start of a computation of a program and the computation terminates, then a postcondition Q holds upon termination. Other invariant conditions are *mutual exclusion*, determining that two processes can never fall into a specified critical sections together, *general safety* stating that whenever a program executes a specified action, its preconditions are satisfied (e.g. it never divides by 0), and *deadlock freedom* guaranteeing that in every non-terminating state of a program it is possible to perform an action.

More complicated invariance properties require some formulas to be performed in a given order [Kröger, 1985].

The main eventuality property is *total correctness*. It says that if a precondition P holds upon the start of a computation of a program, then the computation terminates and a postcondition Q holds upon termination. Its subnotion is the condition of *termination* itself. Other eventuality properties are: an *accessibility* of one program state from another, *livelock freedom* preventing any process from infinitly waiting for entering a critical section, and *fairness*, stating that a process cannot be active infinitely often without ever being chosen. Gabbay et al. (1980) discuss a wide class of the last property.

In the recent years, specifying and veryfing real-time properties of programs [Abadi & Lamport, 1991; Alur et al., 1991; Emerson, 1991; Hansen & Chaochen, 1991; Sørensen et al., 1994] on the one hand, and object-based systems [Fiadero & Maibaum, 1994] on the other hand, stir up great interest. Mokkedem & Méry (1994) analyse the so-called modular reasoning about concurrent programs. This is useful for systematic design of a concurrent program, i.e. enables its verification during design.

The discipline of temporal logics of programs is so rich, that the above notes can be treated only as exemplary.

It follows from the many examples of applications of the time factor presented above that it is advisable to have temporal reasoning algorithms enabling representation of alternative or even exclusive event courses on one hand, and metric dependencies between time moments on the other hand. This is the reason why we believe that it is useful to consider here non-linear as well as metric time structures in both formal and algorithmic approaches.

2. Description of time structures in the first order predicate calculus

To be able to describe different time structures and their properties, a certain formalism is needed. The basic logical formalism is the first order predicate calculus.

We would like to recall here some basic information concerning the first order predicate calculus relative to the problems to be presented later in the text. Since in our considerations function symbols will not be necessary, we will use a limited version of the calculus. The alphabet consists of a countable set of *individual variables* Z, a set of n-ary *predicate symbols* and standard logical operators. The set of all the *well-formed formulas* $\mathcal{F}$ is defined by means of the above symbols. A *theory* $\mathcal{T}$ is any chosen set of formulas, called *specific axioms*. Typically, we choose first a particular set of predicate symbols (called *primitive notions*), and the specific axioms of the theory $\mathcal{T}$ contain only predicate symbols from this set. With a theory $\mathcal{T}$ we associate the set of all logical consequences of its specific axioms.

Thus we have described a syntactic level of the first order predicate calculus, and now we want to present its semantic level. An *interpretation* is an ordered couple $\mathcal{I} = \langle D, m \rangle$, where D is a non-empty set (a *domain*), and m is a function assigning a mapping from D^n to $\{0, 1\}$ to each n-ary predicate symbol. A *valuation v* is a function assigning a value from D to each individual variable from Z. Standard rules for interpreting logical symbols ensure that an interpretation and a valuation assign to each formula from $\mathcal{F}$ its logical value. If it is 1, then the interpretation $\mathcal{I}$ and the valuation v *satisfy* the formula. If for each valuation v, $\mathcal{I}$ and v satisfy a formula, then we can say that the interpretation $\mathcal{I}$ satisfies the formula.

When we consider any particular theory $\mathcal{T}$, it is sufficient that the function m interpret predicate symbols, which are its primitive notions. An interpretation satisfying all the specific axioms of a given theory is called a *model* of this theory. Soundness of the first order predicate calculus ensures that such an interpretation satisfies all the logical consequences of the specific axioms of the theory under consideration.

In the works concerned with ontology of time (e.g. van Benthem, 1983) the order is often reversed—time structures, i.e. *a totality of temporal individuals arranged in a temporal "order"* [van Benthem, 1983, p. xi], are defined first. Only then a logical description of the structures, characterizing their properties, is given. As a result, however, theories are defined with the considered time structures being their models.

In the following sections we present a first order description of point and interval structures, and a comparison of different approaches.

2.1 Point structures

Temporal structures for time consisting of points are constructed by means of the precedence relation $<$. Therefore, a point structure $\mathfrak{T}$ is an ordered couple $\langle T, < \rangle$, where T is a nonempty set of time points and $<$ is a precedence relation over T. Such a temporal structure is axiomatized by properties:

- transitivity $\forall x, y \ (x < y \ \& \ y < z \ \rightarrow \ x < z)$
- irreflexivity $\forall x \ \neg(x < x)$

From these two axioms we can derive the property of antisymmetry $\forall x, y \ (x < y \ \rightarrow \ \neg(x < y))$. In this way we obtain the basic theory T_P describing a class of structures with a partial order. Furthermore, we can obtain the theory T_L describing linear structures by adding an axiom:

- linearity $\forall x, y \ (x < y \ \lor \ x = y \ \lor \ y < x)$,

or the theory T_B describing branching (backward linear) structures by adding an axiom:

- backward linearity $\forall x, y \ (x < z \ \& \ y < z \ \rightarrow \ x < y \ \lor \ x = y \ \lor \ y < x)$.

Evidently, there exist many other properties of point structures; in particular, van Benthem (1983) presents axiomatizations for structures based on sets of moments isomorphic to $\mathbf{Z}$, $\mathbf{Q}$ and $\mathbf{R}$. Among these properties the most important ones are those stating whether we have to do with a discrete or dense order. This can be imposed by the following axioms:

- discreteness $\forall x, y \ (x < y \ \rightarrow \ \exists z \ (x < z \ \& \ \neg\exists u \ (x < u \ \& \ u < z)))$
  $\forall x, y \ (x < y \ \rightarrow \ \exists z \ (z < y \ \& \ \neg\exists u \ (z < u \ \& \ u < y)))$,
- density $\forall x, y \ (x < y \ \rightarrow \ \exists z \ (x < z \ \& \ z < y))$.

Another way of axiomatizating point structures consists in replacing the strong precedence relation $<$ by its weak counterpart $\leq$. This implies the replacement of the axiom of irreflexivity by the axiom of weak antisymmetry $\forall x, y \ (x \leq y \ \& \ y \leq x \ \rightarrow \ x = y)$ and with a small modification of other axioms. The differences between these two approaches are insignificant, and we can hardly consider them as essentially different axiomatizations. As there are no other, really competing descriptions of time structures, there is no need for comparison.

2.1.1 Non-linear point time structures

In this work, we want to focus one attention on problems that appear when the condition of linearity of a structure is abandoned. This specific situation is often underestimated. Point time causes seemingly no problems—we have to do with either backward linear or partial order. However, when one speaks about non-linear time, they often use a notion of *branching point*. This is such a point that some points preceding or succeding it are not collinear. Unfortunately, there are possible structures in which there is no branching point in the area of fork of branches. Consider a structure which is *dense* before it branches, so there is not last point preceding non-collinear points located on two branches (see fig. 2.1. (a)). We can imagine a *discrete* structure without branching point, such a structure is presented in fig. 2.1. (b).

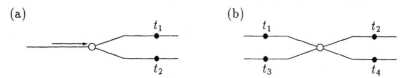

Fig. 2.1. Structures without branching point

- fork $\forall t, t'\ (t\ !\ t'\ \&\ \exists t''\ (t'' < t\ \&\ t'' < t')\ \rightarrow$

$$\exists t''\ (t'' < t\ \&\ t'' < t' \forall \bar{t}\ (\bar{t} < t\ \&\ \bar{t} < t'\ \rightarrow\ \bar{t} < t'')),$$

$$\forall t, t'\ (t\ !\ t'\ \&\ \exists t''\ (t < t''\ \&\ t' < t'')\ \rightarrow$$

$$\exists t''\ (t < t''\ \&\ t' < t'' \forall \bar{t}\ (t < \bar{t}\ \&\ t' < \bar{t}\ \rightarrow\ t'' < \bar{t}))).$$

The problem with an area of fork of branches is discussed in detail in [Hajnicz, 1996].

Other problems appear when we distinguish dates among moments of time. The term *date* is usually associated with the calendar dating—year, month and day number. This corresponds for instance to dating of historical events. Vilain (1982) and McDermott (1982) treat dates as points; in this work we follow their approach.

Date is a time specification that is chronologically stable [Rescher & Urquhardt, 1971]. In practice, the method of denoting dates is strict and univocally determined. For instance, we can consider dates with formats YYYY.MM.DD or hh:mm:ss. It is important that a precedence relation between two dates be univocally determined; certainly, two dates cannot be placed on two different branches. On the other hand, the same date can occur on several (all) branches of a structure (event courses), so the problem of its identity appears. Hence, we cannot connect dates with branches at all. This fact was noticed by McDermott (1982). He considered a date line disjoint with the main time structure. Dates form a linear order: if two dates are not equal, then one of them is earlier. McDermott uses the many-sorted first order predicate calculus. We have to do with two main sorts (McDermott defines also other sorts)—simple points (called *world states*) and dates. As a result, we have two mutually related time structures. The main one is a backward linear order (possibly also a partial order), and the second is a linear order. McDermott defines a function which to each world state assigns the date of its occurrence. Certainly, this function preserves order. This approach is very restrictive, because it assumes that we know the time of occurrence of each world state (thus of each event, too). In practice, this assumption is sometimes too optimistic—it is after all possible that we know only the approximate time of occurrence of an event (see, for instance, Kahn & Gorry, 1977). However, if we give up this rigorous assumption, some additional precedence relations will be necessary to establish positions of world states relative to dates. So, we can say that we have the following complex time structure $\mathfrak{T} = \langle T, D, <_{tt}, <_{dd}, <_{td}, <_{dt} \rangle$, where T is a set of time moments (world states), D is a set of dates, $<_{tt}$—a backward linear (partial) order over T, $<_{dd}$—a linear order over D, whereas $<_{td}$ and $<_{dt}$ are precedence relations linking the above two orders. Because of the latter two relations some additional axioms, which can be called *quasi-transitivity*, are needed:

- $t_1 <_{tt} t_2$ & $t_2 <_{td} d$ $\rightarrow$ $t_1 <_{td} d$,

- $d_1 <_{dd} d_2$ & $d_2 <_{dt} t$ $\rightarrow$ $d_1 <_{dt} t$,

- $d <_{dt} t_1$ & $t_1 <_{tt} t_2$ $\rightarrow$ $d <_{dt} t_2$,

- $d_1 <_{dt} t$ & $t <_{td} d_2$ $\rightarrow$ $d_1 <_{dd} d_2$,

- $t <_{td} d_1$ & $d_1 <_{dd} d_2$ $\rightarrow$ $t <_{td} d_2$,

- $t_1 <_{td} d$ & $d <_{dt} t_2$ $\rightarrow$ $t_1 \neq t_2$ & $\neg(t_2 <_{tt} t_1)$.

•Obviously, positions of states relative to dates are univocal ("quasi-linear"). The last axiom is different from the other ones because of the non-linearity of the structure $\mathfrak{T}$ (see fig. 2.2).

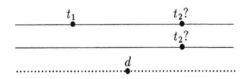

Fig. 2.2. Possible mutual positions between two points t_1 and t_2, when
$t_1 <_{td} d$ and $d <_{dt} t_2$

The solution presented above is less elegant than that suggested by McDermott. Instead of two separate structures connected by a morphism we have to do with one complicated structure, provided with a very complicated system of relationships between individuals. Moreover, we cannot express simultaneousness of a world state and a date (certainly, this cannot be simple equality) in this language. To make this possible, further extension of the theory is needed.

We may say that we have two subsequent new theories T_{PD} = { transitivity, antisymmetry, quasi-transitivity } and T_{BD} = { transitivity, antisymmetry, backward linearity, quasi-transitivity }.

There also exists a solution more closely related to McDermott's approach. Instead of one function assigning a date of a world state occurrence, we would define two functions D_L and D_R designating bounds on the time of the state occurrence. If these functions are equal, we have to do with McDermott's case.

In this situation, it is more difficult to state interdependencies between the considered orders. It is clear that if $t_1 <_t t_2$, then $D_L(t_1) <_d D_R(t_2)$. However, a stronger condition can be imposeed: $D_L(t_1) <_d D_L(t_2)$ and $D_R(t_1) <_d D_R(t_2)$.

It should also be mentioned that this solution involves renouncement of our initial assumption that the first order predicate calculus is considered without function symbols.

A special case of temporal partial order is constituted by *relativistic time*. In Einstein's Special Theory of Relativity, time and space are viewed as forming the 4-dimensional *Lorentz space*, which may be coordinated by 3 spatial coordinates x, y and z, and one time coordinate t. They are related by *Lorentz invariant* $x^2 + y^2 + z^2 - c^2 t^2$, where c is the speed of light. For the sake of simplicity, we reduce space to one dimension and assume units such that $c = 1$. Such a simplification is often made by authors engaged in the subject [van Benthem, 1983; Rodriguez et al., 1991; Rodriguez, 1993]. In this special case redescription is possible by rotating the whole space clockwise over 45 degrees. The resulting structure is equivalent to $R \times R$ (see fig. 2.3), in which coordinates cannot be distinguished, and the precedence relation is simply:

$$(x, y) < (u, v) \quad \equiv_{def} \quad x < u \ \& \ y < v.$$

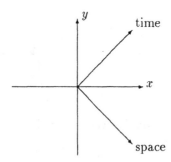

Fig. 2.3. Two-dimensional representation of relativistic space-time

Note, that the considered order is neither left nor right linear. But there exist other properties characterizing this structure (suggested by van Benthem):

- $\forall x, y \, ((\neg(x < y) \, \& \, \neg(y < x)) \rightarrow (x \, L \, y \, \vee \, y \, L \, x \, \vee \, \forall z \, ((\neg(x < z) \, \& \, \neg(z < x) \, \& \, \neg(y < z) \, \& \, \neg(z < y)) \rightarrow (Bxyz \, \vee \, Byzx \, \vee \, Bzxy))))$

- $\forall x, y \, \exists z \, (x < z \, \& \, y < z)$

  $\forall x, y \, \exists z \, (x < z \, \& \, y < z)$

where $x \, L \, y \, \equiv_{def} \, \neg(x < y) \, \& \, \forall z \, (y < z \, \rightarrow \, x < z)$ means "connectability by the speed of light", and $Bxyz \, \equiv_{def} \, \forall u \, ((y < u \, \& \, z < u) \, \rightarrow \, x < u) \, \& \, \forall u \, ((u < y \, \& \, u < z) \, \rightarrow \, u < x)$ means "betweennes".

Rodriguez et al. (1991) consider also relativity in the case of interval time, but we will not discuss it here.

2.1.2 Metric point time structures

Time structures presented earlier were based on the assumption that moments occur in time in a certain order, but distances between them are not important. In fact, however, moments occur in time at certain distances, time passing is measurable, and in addition, this information is of big practical importance in many applications. So, in this section we shall discuss metric time—we present metric point structures.

Time distances between points

Time distances play an important role in the information concerning the position of points in time. They are represented by a certain number of specified units. The most common units are *years, months, days, hours, minutes* and *seconds*; these units were considered in our system described in [Hajnicz, 1989b]. Units of this kind constitute a hierarchy, and usually each unit of a higher level is composed of a certain number of units of a lower one. If the considered sequence of units is finite, then the corresponding set of time distances is discrete. If, on the other hand, the sequence of units is infinite, the set of time distances is dense. An interesting approach to an infinite sequence of units has been described by Ladkin (1987).

The simplest sequence of units is that composed of one element (e.g. day, minute). In this case, the set of distances is isomorphic to the set of non-negative integers $\mathbf{Z}^+$ unless fractional distances are admitted (e.g. *half an hour*)—otherwise the set of distances can be viewed as isomorphic to the set of non-negative rationals $\mathbf{Q}^+$ or even to the set of non-negative reals $\mathbf{R}^+$.

It should also be noted that a distance can consist of several different units (components of value 0 can be omitted), but at least one component is needed (even 0). On the other hand, it can happen that a number of units of some level exceeds the unit of a higher level; such formulations are often used in natural language.

Example
Let us consider a sequence of units composed of hour, minute and second. For this sequence the following time distances can be defined: *2 hours 40 minutes, 30 minutes, 90 minutes, 0 minutes, 2 hours 5 minutes 20 seconds, 1 hour 20 seconds,* etc.

A notion of time distance is a basis for introducing a metric point structure.

DEFINITION
A metric point structure $\mathfrak{T}$ is an ordered quadruple $\langle T, C, <, \delta \rangle$, where T is a set of time points, C is a set of distances between time points, $<$ is a strict linear order over T and δ is a metric over T.
A metric is a function $\delta: T \times T \longrightarrow C$ such that:

1. $\delta(t_1, t_2) = 0$ iff $t_1 = t_2$,

2. $\delta(t_1, t_2) = \delta(t_2, t_1)$,

3. $\delta(t_1, t_2) + \delta(t_2, t_3) \geq \delta(t_1, t_3)$.

The above conditions imply an additional important property of a metric, namely that $\delta(t_1, t_2) \geq 0$. As $<$ is a strict linear order, such a metric over T can be defined.

To make the above definition of a metric correct, C has to be an additive set, i.e. $C = \langle C, 0, +, \geq \rangle$, where $+$ is an addition operation over C, 0 is its neutral element and $\geq$ is an ordering relation over C. We will not characterize this set more precisely. For singleton unit sequences it is isomorphic to the set of natural numbers $\mathbf{N}$, if we allow distances composed of total units, and to the set of rational numbers $\mathbf{Q}^+$, if we allow fractional distances. For other sequences of units it is usually possible to establish equivalence classes of equal distances and, as a result, to obtain sets isomorphic to $\mathbf{N}$ or $\mathbf{Q}^+$. Some problems caused by a sequence of units *year, month, day* are outlined in section 4.3.3.

Now we should relate metrization and ordering of a structure. It is rather clear that they cannot be treated independently.

Example
Let us consider the structure presented in fig. 2.4, where points A, B, C, D are placed on the time-axis at one second distances. Arrows show a precedence relation $<$. If it were a typical point structure, the arrows would suggest that points occur in time in the succession A, C, B, D. Unfortunately, in such a situation the distance between B and D would be 1 s, whereas the distance between points B and C would be 2s. Actually, the case is just the opposite.

Fig. 2.4. Inconsistency between ordering of points and their metrization

Therefore, a metric point structure is axiomatized by the theory T_L extended by an axiom:

- consistency $\forall x, y, z \ (x < y \ \& \ y < z \ \rightarrow \ \delta(x, y) + \delta(y, z) = \delta(x, z))$

with a metric δ satisfying the above conditions. This theory will be denoted by T_M.

Also in the case of metric point time it is possible to distinguish *dates* among points. It should be noted that *dates* are closely related to *distances*, e.g. the same units are used in both cases. It is after all impossible to measure distances between dates of format hh:mm:ss in days! We speak of date formats, and we do not speak of distance formats, because the notation for dates is much more rigorous. There exist distances such as *90 minutes* or even *1 hour 200 seconds*, but certainly no dates such as *00:90:00* or *1:00:200* exist! In a date, all elements of a format should occur, and some of them can only assume strictly determined values.

It is important that not only the ordering of any two dates, but also a distance between them is univocally determined, depending only on a choice of dates. There is still the question whether <u>all</u> points from T are dates or not. In the case of finite sequences of units this problem is not artificial, as we have to do with a point structure, whereas actually *days* or even *seconds* last (exactly 1 s), so dates constitute a discrete structure with successive dates located at a unit distance. Then some other points can occur between two successive dates. This is possible only when we allow fractional distances. Otherwise, we are not able to determine a distance between these points. So, in this case either <u>all</u> points from T are dates or δ is a partial function.

There is another way of presenting dates (see e.g. Augustynek, 1972), similar to McDermott's approach mentioned above. We distinguish a particular moment t_0 in a set of moments T.

DEFINITION
Let D be a set of dates disjoint from the set of time moments T. A *coordinate system* is a function $c: T \longrightarrow D$ such that it assigns to each point $t \in T$ its *coordinate* $c(t) \in D$ in the following way:

1. $c(t) = 0$ iff $t = t_0$
2. $c(t) = \delta(t, t_0)$ iff $t_0 < t$
3. $c(t) = -\delta(t, t_0)$ iff $t < t_0$

The moment t_0 is called the *origin of coordinates*. Thus, a set of dates $D \subseteq C \cup C^-$, where $C^- = \{-o \mid o \in C\}$. We have not written $D = C \cup C^-$, because not all distances, as we have stated, can form dates. This would be true in the case of a singleton unit sequence. As a result, we obtain a structure $\mathfrak{T} = \langle T, C, D, <, \delta, c \rangle$.

The choice of the moment t_0 is arbitrary. In practice, it is the beginning of an era (e.g. the birth of Christ for YYYY.MM.DD format or the hour 00:00:00 for hh:mm:ss format).

In the case of time we are used to refer to a coordinate system as a *calendar*. Formally, this is a very elegant definition of a calendar. However, it holds true only for one-element date formats. The reason for this is that, in practice, only the "main" unit is negative for points on the negative semi-axis, the remaining ones are positive. For instance, the date of Julius Caesar stabbing is March 15th, 44 B.C. It can be written as $-44.(+)03.(+)15$. Undoubtedly this is not a proper notation for distances!

2.1.3 Cyclic time structures

In most philosophical and physical research an assumption is made that time forms a line (or possibly a tree). There is also, however, a different idea with time forming a circle, related to the idea of perpetual returns. If in the future a moment occurs at which the world will look and behave in the same way as it does now, then we can say that it is the same moment of time. According to the attributive conception of time [Augustynek, 1972; 1979] it has to be so. This conception assumes that time is an attribute of the reality: a time moment is defined as an equivalence class of simultaneous events (instantaneous physical events). If we also accept extreme determinism (with which the idea of perpetual returns has close connections!), then the repetition of one moment leads to the repetition of all other time moments in the same order and with the same distances. We thus just have to do with cyclic time.

In the case of cyclic time, the precedence relation $<$ looses, in fact, its meaning: everything has already happened and everything will happen. Therefore $<$ ceases to be an irreflexive and antisymmetric relation. On the other hand, transitivity becomes a trivial property—each time moment precedes any other. Therefore, to be able to differentiate cyclic time from a total chaos, we need metrization of time.

DEFINITION
A distance δ between two points x, y of cyclic time $\mathfrak{T}$ $(x, y \in T)$ is the length of the shorter arc linking these two points on a circle [Augustynek, 1972].

Therefore, if we assume that the time structure under consideration forms a circle of length $2S$, then $\delta(x, y) \in [0, S]$. The distance defined in such a way satisfies all conditions of a metric formulated in the previous section. Certainly, the distance measure units are arbitrary.

Even though the precedence relation $<$ does not satisfy the conditions required of the ordering relation, we can define a relation $<^*$ of local precedence that "locally" satisfies these conditions.

DEFINITION

A metric cyclic point time structure $\mathfrak{T}$ is an ordered tuple $\langle T, C, <, <^*, \delta, S \rangle$, where T is a set of time moments, C is a set of distances between time points, $<$ is a "global" order over T, $<^*$ is a "local" order over T, δ is a metric over T, and S is the length of the semicircle.

For each point $x \in T$ there exists exactly one point $x^* \in T$ such that $\delta(x, x^*) = S$. These two points divide the circle into two semi-circles. We are not able to determine which of them is earlier, and this is the effect of the locality of the relation $<^*$. Now we can axiomatize the above structure by the following properties:

- totality $\forall x, y \ (x < y)$,
- local antisymmetry $\forall x, y \ (x <^* y \ \rightarrow \ \neg(y <^* x))$,
- local linearity $\forall x, y \ ((x \neq y \ \& \ x \neq y^*) \ \rightarrow \ (x <^* y \ \lor \ y <^* x))$,
- local transitivity $\forall x, y, z \ ((\delta(x, y) + \delta(y, z) < S) \ \rightarrow$
  $$(x <^* y \ \& \ y <^* z \ \rightarrow \ x <^* z)),$$
- consistency $\forall x, y, z \ ((\delta(x, y) + \delta(y, z) < S) \ \rightarrow$
  $$(x <^* y \ \& \ y <^* z \ \rightarrow \ \delta(x, y) + \delta(y, z) = \delta(x, z))).$$

The condition of local transitivity ensures the transitivity of the relation $<^*$ within the limits of one semi-circle—this is exactly what its locality depends on. The same concerns the condition of consistency. Note, that these conditions can be formulated in metric structures only. A theory based on the above axioms will be referred to as $\mathcal{T}_{MC}$.

In such a structure it is possible to define a local coordinate system with an origin t_0. Its definition would be the same as in the previous section, but with the local precedence relation $<^*$. In consequence, we would not be able to determine $c(t_0^*)$.

2.1.4 Defining intervals in point structures

Intuitively, an interval seems to be a more complicated individual then a point, so we often encounter operations on point structures, with intervals defined from points. Therefore, before we describe interval structures, where intervals are primitive individuals, we will try to define them in a point time structure $\mathfrak{T} = \langle T, < \rangle$. There are two ways of defining intervals in point structures: as sets of points and as pairs of points. Both cases involve convex intervals only.

Intervals treated as sets of points are considered, e.g. by van Benthem (1983) and McDermott (1982).

DEFINITION

Let $\mathfrak{T}$ be a point time structure with partial order. A subset X of T is *convex*, if $\forall x, y, z \ (x, z \in X \ \& \ x < y \ \& \ y < z \ \rightarrow \ y \in X)$. A *convex interval structure* CONV($\mathfrak{T}$) is $\langle I, \subseteq, < \rangle$, where

(i) I is a set of non-empty convex subsets of T,

(ii) $\subseteq$ is the usual set-theoretic inclusion relation,

(iii) $<$ is defined in the following way:

$$X < Y \equiv_{def} \forall x, y \ (x \in X \ \& \ y \in Y \ \rightarrow \ x < y).$$

Theorem 2.1.4.1. A convex interval structure defined in such a way satisfies all axioms of the theory $\mathcal{T}_K$ introduced in section 2.2.1.

The proof of this theorem can be found in [van Benthem, 1983].

Van Benthem presented also a more complicated definition of unconvex intervals, but we will not consider it here.

On the other hand, intervals treated as pairs of points are discussed e.g. by Kahn & Gorry (1977), Shoham (1987), Halpern & Shoham (1991) and Venema (1988; 1990).

DEFINITION

Let $\mathfrak{T}$ be a point time structure with linear order. A *time interval* $X = \langle x, y \rangle$ is any pair of points $x, y \in T$ such that $x < y$. A *convex interval structure* PAIR($\mathfrak{T}$) is $\langle J, \parallel, \subseteq_B, \subseteq_E \rangle$, where:

(i) J is the set of all time intervals over T,

(ii) $\parallel$ is defined in the following way:

for each $x, y, z \in T$ such that $\langle x, y \rangle, \langle y, z \rangle \in J$ we have $\langle x, y \rangle \parallel \langle y, z \rangle$,

(iii) $\subseteq_B$ is defined in the following way:

for every $x, y, z \in T$ such that $\langle x, y \rangle, \langle x, z \rangle \in J$ we have $\langle x, y \rangle \subseteq_B \langle x, z \rangle$.

(iv) $\subseteq_E$ is defined in the following way:

for every $x, y, z \in T$ such that $\langle y, z \rangle, \langle x, z \rangle \in J$ we have $\langle y, z \rangle \subseteq_E \langle x, z \rangle$.

If we limit ourselves to the items (i) and (ii) in the above definition, then we will consider a structure $\langle J, \parallel \rangle$. Then the following theorem is satisfied:

Theorem 2.1.4.2. A convex interval structure defined in such a way satisfies all axioms of the theory $\mathcal{T}_A$ introduced in section 2.2.2.

Time structures, in which $\langle x, x \rangle$ are treated as a time interval, can be considered, too. To do this the strict precedence relation $<$ has to be replaced by its unstrict counterpart $\leq$ in the above definitions.

With the above definitions, we can use intervals in point time structures.

2.2 Interval structures

Contrary to the case of points, interdependencies between intervals can be described in different ways—intervals can form different structures. In this section, we shall present some well-known axiomatizations of interval structures based on the first order predicate calculus.

2.2.1 The classic axiomatization

The most famous interval structure, presented for instance in [van Benthem, 1983] is $\Im = \langle I, <, \subseteq \rangle$, where I is a nonempty set of time intervals, $<$ is a precedence relation over I and $\subseteq$ is the inclusion relation over I. Since the theories based on primitives $<$ and $\subseteq$ are the earliest and most discussed (not only in connection with AI), they will be called *classic*. Axiomatization of such a structure is much more complicated than that of point structures.

Let the set of variables for classic theories be Z_C. Then we can define the set of well-formed formulas $\mathcal{F}_C$ as the smallest set such that if $x, y \in Z_C$, then $x < y$, $x \subseteq y \in \mathcal{F}_C$ and for each $\alpha, \beta \in \mathcal{F}_C$ and $x \in Z_C$ the following holds: $\neg \alpha \in \mathcal{F}_C$, $\alpha \rightarrow \beta \in \mathcal{F}_C$ and $\forall x\, \alpha(x) \in \mathcal{F}_C$.

The basic axiomatization of interval temporal structures, presented by van Benthem, is as follows (abbreviations of names of properties are taken from van Benthem):

- P_TRANS $\forall x, y, z\ (x < y\ \&\ y < z\ \rightarrow\ x < z)$,
- P_IRREF $\forall x\ \neg(x < x)$,
- I_TRANS $\forall x, y, z\ (x \subseteq y\ \&\ y \subseteq z\ \rightarrow\ x \subseteq z)$,
- I_REF $\forall x\ (x \subseteq x)$,
- I_ANTIS $\forall x, y\ (x \subseteq y\ \&\ y \subseteq x\ \rightarrow\ x = y)$,
- MON $\forall x, y\ (x < y\ \rightarrow\ \forall z\ (z \subseteq x\ \rightarrow z < y))$
              $\forall x, y\ (x < y\ \rightarrow\ \forall z\ (z \subseteq y\ \rightarrow x < z))$,
- $CONJ$ $\forall x, y\ (\exists u\ (u \subseteq x\ \&\ u \subseteq y)\ \rightarrow\ \exists z\ (z \subseteq x\ \&\ z \subseteq y\ \&$
              $\forall u\ (u \subseteq x\ \&\ u \subseteq y\ \rightarrow\ u \subseteq z)))$.

The basic theory consisting of these axioms will be referred to as T_{CB}.

In the formalization of Allen's (1983) interval calculus, presented in [Hajnicz, 1991], interval structures also had to satisfy the following axioms (presented by van Benthem, too):

- LIN $\forall x, y\ (x < y\ \vee\ \exists u\ (u \subseteq x\ \&\ u \subseteq y)\ \vee\ y < x)$,
- $FREE$ $\forall x, y\ (\forall z\ (z \subseteq x\ \rightarrow\ \exists u\ (u \subseteq z\ \&\ u \subseteq y))\ \rightarrow\ x \subseteq y)$,
- $CONV$ $\forall x, y, z\ (x < y\ \&\ y < z\ \rightarrow\ \forall u\ (x \subseteq u\ \&\ z \subseteq u\ \rightarrow\ y \subseteq u))$,

but they did not have to satisfy *CONJ* (conjunction). Certainly, *LIN* (linearity) has to be satisfied, as Allen's interval calculus concerns the position of intervals on the time-axis; if we renounce it, we obtain a kind of a partial order. We can also consider a backward linear order, replacing the axiom *LIN* by:

- *L_LIN* $\forall x, y, z \ (x < z \ \& \ y < z) \ \rightarrow$

$$(x < y \ \lor \ \exists u \ (u \subseteq x \ \& \ u \subseteq y) \ \lor \ y < x)).$$

Moreover, in the analysis of different properties of interval structures the following axioms can be formulated (also considered by van Benthem):

- *NEIGH* $\forall x, y \ (x < y \ \rightarrow \ \exists z \ (x < z \ \& \ \forall u \ \neg(x < u \ \& \ u < z)))$
  $\forall x, y \ (y < x \ \rightarrow \ \exists z \ (z < x \ \& \ \forall u \ \neg(z < u \ \& \ u < x)))$,

- *DISJ* $\forall x, y \ (\exists u \ (x \subseteq u \ \& \ y \subseteq u) \ \rightarrow \ \exists z \ (x \subseteq z \ \& \ y \subseteq z \ \&$
  $\forall v \ (x \subseteq v \ \& \ y \subseteq v \ \rightarrow \ z \subseteq v)))$,

- *DIR* $\forall x, y \ \exists z \ (x \subseteq z \ \& \ y \subseteq z)$,

- *SUCC* $\forall x \ \exists y \ (x < y) \qquad \forall x \ \exists y \ (y < x)$,

- *MOND* $\forall x, y, z \ (x < z \ \& \ y < z \ \rightarrow \ \exists v \ (x \subseteq v \ \& \ y \subseteq v \ \&$
  $v < z \ \& \ \forall u \ (x \subseteq u \ \& \ y \subseteq u \ \rightarrow \ v \subseteq u)))$
  $\forall x, y, z \ (z < x \ \& \ z < y \ \rightarrow \ \exists v \ (x \subseteq v \ \& \ y \subseteq v \ \&$
  $z < v \ \& \ \forall u \ (x \subseteq u \ \& \ y \subseteq u \ \rightarrow \ v \subseteq u)))$.

MOND (duration monotonicity) makes sense only when *DISJ* (disjunction) and *DIR* (directedness) are satisfied, and it obviously implies these properties.

Many theories can be defined on the basis of the above axioms. For our needs concerning a comparison with Allen & Hayes's and Tsang's theories, we distinguish the theory $\mathcal{T}_C = \{$ *P_TRANS, P_IRREF, I_TRANS, I_REF, I_ANTIS, MON, CONJ, CONV, LIN, FREE, NEIGH, DISJ, DIR, SUCC, MOND* $\}$. Van Benthem presents theories, which axiomatize the interval temporal structures INT($\mathbf{Z}$) and INT($\mathbf{Q}$).

Now let us consider properties of these axioms and interdependencies between them.

Lemma 2.2.1.1. The formula $x < y \ \rightarrow \ \neg(x \subseteq y) \ \& \ \neg(y \subseteq x)$ is a theorem of the classic theory $\mathcal{T}_C$.
The proof of this theorem can be found in [Hajnicz, 1995a]

Convexity, monotonicity and freedom are seemingly obvious properties of intervals and ordering relations on them. Nevertheless, it was only monotonicity that van Benthem included in the basic theory $\mathcal{T}_{CB}$. Also Ladkin (1986) considers the notion of unconvex intervals (intervals "with holes"). However, convexity is such an evident, intuitive property of intervals that it is often assumed implicitly.

For instance, van Benthem, even though he considers convexity explicitly, has not indicated that *LIN, MON* and *FREE* imply *CONV!*

Lemma 2.2.1.2. The axioms *LIN, MON* and *FREE* imply the axiom *CONV.* The proof of this theorem can be found in [Hajnicz, 1995a]

Therefore, we can use this definition of linearity only for structures of convex intervals, though, on the other hand, unconvex intervals can also form a kind of linear order (see fig. 2.5), which of course, is more complicated than that of convex intervals.

Fig. 2.5. An example of the position of unconvex intervals on a linear time-axis

Certainly, we are able to characterize such generalized linearity, by means of the following axiom:

- LIN^* $\forall x, y \; \forall x', y' \; (x' \subseteq x \; \& \; y' \subseteq y \; \rightarrow \; \exists x'', y'' \; (x'' \subseteq x' \; \& \; y'' \subseteq y' \; \& \; (x'' < y'' \; \vee \; \exists u \; (u \subseteq x'' \; \& \; u \subseteq y'') \; \vee \; y'' < x'')))$.

The above formula is very complicated. However, a simpler condition $\forall x, y \; \forall x', y' \; (x' \subseteq x \; \& \; y' \subseteq y \; \rightarrow \; (x' < y' \; \vee \; \exists u \; (u \subseteq x' \; \& \; u \subseteq y') \; \vee \; y' < x')))$ is too strong (it is stronger than the original axiom *LIN*), whereas a condition $\forall x, y \; \exists x', y' \; (x' \subseteq x \; \& \; y' \subseteq y \; \& \; (x' < y' \; \vee \; \exists u \; (u \subseteq x' \; \& \; u \subseteq y') \; \vee \; y' < x')))$ is to weak, as it treats such intervals as x and y from fig. 2.13 (d) and (e) as being collinear. Note, that the original axiom *LIN* treats such intervals x and y from fig. 2.13 (b) and (c) as collinear, too. Thus LIN^* is weaker than *LIN* where it is needed and it is stronger than *LIN* where it is needed.

2.2.2 Allen & Hayes's axiomatization

Allen & Hayes (1985), in an attempt to formalize common-sense reasoning about time define an interval temporal structure $\mathcal{J} = \langle J, \| \rangle$, where J is a nonempty set of temporal intervals and $\|$ is a binary relation of meeting of intervals from J.

Let the set of variables for Allen & Hayes's theories be Z_A. Then we can define the set of well-formed formulas $\mathcal{F}_A$ as the smallest set such that if $x, y \in Z_A$, then $x < y$, $x \subseteq y \in \mathcal{F}_A$ and for each $\alpha, \beta \in \mathcal{F}_A$ and $x \in Z_A$ the following holds: $\neg \alpha \in \mathcal{F}_A$, $\alpha \rightarrow \beta \in \mathcal{F}_A$ and $\forall x \; \alpha(x) \in \mathcal{F}_A$.

Allen & Hayes axiomatize the above structure as follows:

- **M1** $\forall i,j \ (\exists k \ (i \parallel k \ \& \ j \parallel k) \ \rightarrow \ \forall l \ (i \parallel l \ \leftrightarrow \ j \parallel l)),$
- **M2** $\forall i,j \ (\exists k \ (k \parallel i \ \& \ k \parallel j) \ \rightarrow \ \forall l \ (l \parallel i \ \leftrightarrow \ l \parallel j)),$
- **M3** $\forall i,j,k,l \ ((i \parallel j \ \& \ k \parallel l) \ \rightarrow i \parallel l \qquad \text{XOR}$

$$\exists m \ (i \parallel m \ \& \ m \parallel l) \qquad \text{XOR} \qquad \exists n \ (k \parallel n \ \& \ n \parallel j)),$$

- **M4** $\forall i \ (\exists j,k \ (j \parallel i \ \& \ i \parallel k),$
- **M5** $\forall i,j \ (i \parallel j \ \rightarrow$

$$\exists k,l,m \ ((k \parallel i \ \& \ i \parallel j \ \& \ j \parallel l) \ \& \ (k \parallel m \ \& \ m \parallel l)).$$

Axioms M1 and M2 determine the uniqueness of the meeting places of intervals, axiom M3 determines the linearity of the order of meeting places of intervals (see fig. 2.6), axiom M4 determines the infinity of time together with the assumption that no interval is infinite, and axiom M5 establishes the existence of the union for any pair of intervals (see fig. 2.7).

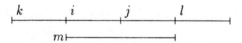

Fig. 2.6. Three possible orders of pairs of meeting intervals

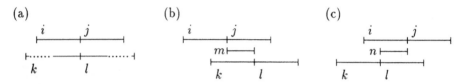

Fig. 2.7. Existence of the union of two meeting intervals

The above axioms form the theory $T_{A^\circ} = \{$ M1, M2, M3, M4, M5 $\}$.

In their next paper Allen & Hayes (1987) replace axioms M1 and M2 by one axiom:

- **M1'** $\forall i,j,k,l \ (i \parallel j \ \& \ i \parallel k \ \& \ l \parallel j \ \rightarrow \ l \parallel k),$

and they add a new axiom:

- **M6** $\forall i,j,k,l \ (i \parallel k \ \& \ k \parallel j \ \& \ i \parallel l \ \& \ l \parallel j \ \rightarrow \ k = l)$

imposing the uniqueness of intervals with fixed "endings" (meeting places). So, we get a second theory $T_A = \{$ M1', M3, M4, M5, M6 $\}$. Because axioms M1 and M1' are equivalent (see below), these theories differ only in the presence of axiom M6.

The above axiomatization ensures the validity of the basic properties of the relation of meet of intervals.

Lemma 2.2.2.1. Axiom M1' is equivalent to axioms M1 and M2. Moreover, axioms M1 and M2 are equivalent to each other.
The proof of this lemma can be found in [Hajnicz, 1995a].

Lemma 2.2.2.2. Axioms M1–M5 ensure that
  (i) $\forall i \ \neg(i \parallel i)$,
  (ii) $\forall i, j \ (i \parallel j \ \rightarrow \ \neg \exists k \ (i \parallel k \ \& \ k \parallel j))$,
  (iii) $\forall i, j \ (i \parallel j \ \rightarrow \ \neg(j \parallel i))$,
i.e. the relation $\parallel$ is irreflexive, anti-transitive and antisymmetric. The proof of these properties can be found in [Tsang, 1986].

Ladkin (1986) claims that axiom M5 is redundant, since it follows from axioms M3 and M4. Unfortunately this is not true. We show this on an example of a simple structure of cyclic time $\{i, j, k\}$, where $i \parallel j \ \& \ j \parallel k \ \& \ k \parallel i$.

Theorem 2.2.2.1. The above structure satisfies axioms M1–M4 and does not satisfy axiom M5.
The proof of this theorem can be found in [Hajnicz, 1995a].

Thus M3 stands for a linearity axiom only in presence of M5; actually it excludes branching time, but does not exclude cyclic time. However, we can consider only cyclic structures with all intervals lying on one semicircle (i.e. with their lengths not greater than S). Thus we can say that M3 itself forces local transitivity only (see section 2.1.3).

The aim of Allen & Hayes was to formalize human intuition rather than to create a minimal theory. It is worth considering, however, whether all Allen & Hayes's axioms are "minimal", indispensable. Axiom M4 gives rise to special doubts. First, a set of intervals need not be infinite. Second, exclusion of infinite intervals is not obvious. For instance, McDermott (1982) assumes the existence of an infinite fact *always*. A problem appears only for structures that have a beginning or an end—it is possible that a union of an interval at the end of such a structure with some other interval meeting it does not exist. However, if we replaced M4 by its weaker counterpart:

  • **M4'** $\forall i \ \exists j \ (i \parallel j) \ \vee \ \exists i \ \forall j \ (i \neq j \ \rightarrow \ j \parallel i \ \vee \ \exists k \ (j \parallel k \ \& \ k \parallel i)$
       $\forall i \ \exists j \ (j \parallel i) \ \vee \ \exists i \ \forall j \ (i \neq j \ \rightarrow \ i \parallel j \ \vee \ \exists k \ (i \parallel k \ \& \ k \parallel j)$,

then we would force each structure with one or two ends to have at each of its ends exactly one guard-interval preceding (succeeding) all other intervals, for which the required property of existence of a union would hold without any problem.

Certainly, it is not necessary for a union of any two meeting intervals to exist. Nevertheless, removing axiom M4 from the theory would open the way for degenerate structures, i.e. structures such that some (or even all) intervals in them have no meet with any other interval. To avoid this we can introduce a variant of M4 even weaker than M4':

  • **M4"** $\forall i \ \exists j \ (i \parallel j \ \vee \ j \parallel i)$.

It turns out that M4" and M5 imply M4.

Lemma 2.2.2.3. Axioms M4" and M5 imply axiom M4.
The proof of this theorem can be found in [Hajnicz, 1995a].

There is no doubt, however, that the removal of axiom M3 would weaken the theory too much, since M3 not only concerns linearity, but also imposes some other important constraints on a structure (e.g. it is used in the proof of lemma 2.2.2.2.). Therefore we can take $\mathcal{T}_{AB} = \{$ M1, M3, M4" $\}$ to be the weakest basic theory of the considered axiomatization (M4" is included because a linearity condition together with the existence of isolated intervals looks strange).

While discussing classic theories we have paid much attention to the question of convexity of intervals. Unfortunately, this property cannot be considered in any axiomatization based exclusively on the relation of meet of intervals $\|$. This relation only allows to determine a mutual position of endings of intervals, and does not refer to their insides. Allen & Hayes assume implicitly that intervals are convex "by nature" (in other words their axiomatization concerns only the class of structures of convex intervals.). This is evidenced by the way primitive relations of Allen's (1983) interval calculus (e.g. the *during* relation) are defined in Allen & Hayes's theory. Actually, it means treating intervals not as primitive notions, but (implicitly) as pairs of points—their beginnings and ends.

Therefore, if intervals were treated as really primitive notions, Allen & Hayes's axiomatization would not impose their convexity. We show it on an example of a particular structure of unconvex intervals:
$$\mathcal{J} = \{\ \langle m,n \rangle,\ \| :\ m,n \in Z,\ m < n,\ \langle m,n \rangle = \{x : m \leq x \leq m+1\}\ \cup$$
$$\{x : n-1 \leq x \leq n\},\ \langle m_1,n_1 \rangle \parallel \langle m_2,n_2 \rangle\ \Rightarrow\ n_1 = m_2\ \}.$$
Such intervals are composed of one part if $n \leq m+2$, and they are composed of two parts, if $n > m+2$. Thus it is a structure of unconvex intervals.

Theorem 2.2.2.2. The structure $\mathcal{J}$ defined above satisfies the axioms of Allen & Hayes's theory $\mathcal{T}_A$.
The proof of this theorem can be found in [Hajnicz, 1995a].

Note that for a similar structure of convex intervals:
$$\mathcal{J}' = \{\ \langle m,n \rangle,\ \| : m,n \in Z,\ \langle m,n \rangle = \{x : m \leq x \leq n\},\ m < n,$$
$$\langle m_1,n_1 \rangle \parallel \langle m_2,n_2 \rangle\ \Longleftrightarrow\ n_1 = m_2\ \},$$
(i.e. INT($\mathbf{Z}$)) the proof would be identical. This follows from the very fact that the relation of meet of intervals gives no chance to "look inside them". Moreover, in the class of structures with the relation of meet of intervals $\|$ the structures $\mathcal{J}$ and $\mathcal{J}'$ are isomorphic!

On the other hand, the lack of the convexity condition in Allen & Hayes's theory suggests that M3 is a linearity axiom satisfied also in structures of unconvex intervals. However, a more thorough examination of the axiom shows that it is true only when axiom M6 is satisfied. Otherwise we can imagine another structure of (convex!) intervals with integer endpoints, with two such intervals for every pair of points.

$$\mathcal{J}'' = \{ \langle m, n \rangle^i, \| : m, n \in Z, m < n, i = 1 \vee i = 2,$$
$$\langle m_1, n_1 \rangle^i \| \langle m_2, n_2 \rangle^j \iff n_1 = m_2 \}.$$

Theorem 2.2.2.3. The structure $\mathcal{J}''$ defined above satisfies the axioms of Allen & Hayes's theory $\mathcal{T}_{A^\circ}$.

The proof of this theorem is identical to the proof of theorem 2.2.2.2. Certainly intervals considered there should have upper indices, but these are not used in the proof. This is due to the fact that the relation of meeting of intervals holds independently of the values of these indices.

It is obvious that a structure of this kind, made up of two often osculating axes, can be recognized as degenerate—it depends only on our "agreement" whether we treat these intervals as lying on different axes or as simultaneous intervals. On the other hand, we have no overlapping relation to determine whether the intervals are simultaneous or not.

2.2.3 Tsang's axiomatization

A third, different axiomatization of interval structures is that of Tsang (1986; 1987). Tsang uses an approach suggested by Kamp (1979; 1980), often used in the analysis of time structure of natural language texts. This axiomatization is based on a temporal structure $\mathfrak{G} = \langle G, <, \mathcal{O} \rangle$, where G is a nonempty set of temporal intervals, $<$ is a precedence relation over G and $\mathcal{O}$ is an overlapping relation over G. Thus, Tsang's axiomatization, like the classic one, is based on two relations, and $\mathcal{O}$, like $\subseteq$, is used to "look inside intervals". These two relations are similar to some extent, and that is why Tsang's approach seems to be closer to the classic approach than to that of Allen & Hayes, though Tsang himself claims that his approach is equivalent to Allen & Hayes's proposal.

Let the set of variables for Tsang's theories be denoted by Z_T. Then we can define the set of well-formed formulas $\mathcal{F}_T$ as the smallest set such that if $x, y \in Z_T$, then $x < y$, $x \mathcal{O} y \in \mathcal{F}_T$ and for each $\alpha, \beta \in \mathcal{F}_T$ and $x \in Z_T$ the following holds: $\neg \alpha \in \mathcal{F}_T$, $\alpha \rightarrow \beta \in \mathcal{F}_T$ and $\forall x\, \alpha(x) \in \mathcal{F}_T$.

For this structure Kamp suggests the following axiomatization:

- **E1** $\forall x, y\, (x < y \ \rightarrow \ \neg(y < x))$ ANTISYM $(<)$,
- **E2** $\forall x, y, z\, (x < y \ \& \ y < z \ \rightarrow \ x < z)$ TRANS $(<)$,
- **E3** $\forall x, y\, (x \mathcal{O} y \ \rightarrow \ y \mathcal{O} x)$ SYM $(\mathcal{O})$,
- **E4** $\forall x\, (x \mathcal{O} x)$ REF $(\mathcal{O})$,
- **E5** $\forall x, y\, (x < y \ \rightarrow \ \neg(x \mathcal{O} y))$ SEP,

- **E6** $\forall x, y, z, u \ (x < y \ \& \ y \mathcal{O} z \ \& \ z < u \ \rightarrow \ x < u)$,

- **E7** $\forall x, y \ (x < y \ \lor \ x \mathcal{O} y \ \lor \ y < x)$ LIN.

So we can speak of an original Kamp's theory $\mathcal{T}_{TB} = \{\text{E1, E2, E3, E4, E5,}$
E6, E7$\}$. We will call $\mathcal{T}_{TB}$ a *basic* theory since it forms a basis for Tsang's
considerations. In order to obtain equivalence of his description with Allen &
Hayes's theory $\mathcal{T}_A$. Tsang defines the following additional axioms:

- **E8** $\forall x \ \exists y \ (y < x \ \& \ \neg \exists u \ (y < u \ \& \ u < x))$,

- **E9** $\forall x \ \exists y \ (x < y \ \& \ \neg \exists u \ (x < u \ \& \ u < y))$,

- **E10** $\forall x, y \ (x \mathcal{O} y \ \rightarrow \ \exists z \ (z \ in \ x \ \& \ z \ in \ y \ \&$ INTERSECTION
  $\qquad\qquad \forall u \ (u \ in \ x \ \& \ u \ in \ y \ \rightarrow \ u \ in \ z)))$,

- **E11** $\forall x, y \ \exists z \ (x \ in \ z \ \& \ y \ in \ z \ \&$ UNION
  $\qquad\qquad \forall u \ (u < x \ \& \ u < y \ \rightarrow \ u < z) \ \&$
  $\qquad\qquad \forall u \ (x < u \ \& \ y < u \ \rightarrow \ z < u))$,

where $x \ in \ y =_{def} \forall u \ (u \mathcal{O} x \rightarrow u \mathcal{O} y)$.
So, the basis for our further considerations on the comparison of Tsang's concepts
with other theories will be provided by the theory $\mathcal{T}_T = \{$ E1, E2, E3, E4, E5,
E6,E7, E8, E9, E10, E11 $\}$. Tsang also considers theories without the linearity
axiom E7.

Unfortunately, the definition of the relation *in* given above is too weak to
describe the real inclusion relation.

Example
Let us imagine a structure as that presented in fig. 2.8 (the figure contains
only a fragment of the structure). Its relations $<$ and $\mathcal{O}$ are defined in a
natural way. Then we have $x \mathcal{O} y \ \& \ x \mathcal{O} z \ \& \ y \mathcal{O} z$. The remaining intervals
either overlap all of the intervals x, y, z or none of them. As a result, we have
$x \ in \ y$, $x \ in \ z$, $y \ in \ x$, $y \ in \ z$, $z \ in \ x$ and $z \ in \ y$. Eventually, each of these intervals
can be, accordingly to axioms E10 and E11, a union as well as an intersection
of any pair of these intervals. This certainly contradicts intuition, what follows
from the fact that this structure does not have a "real" intersection of intervals
x and y, or from the definition of the relation *in*, which is not antisymmetric.

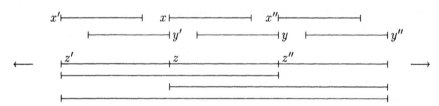

Fig. 2.8. An example of a structure disproving the definition of the relation *in*

As it turns out, it is possible to add an axiom to Tsang's theory so that the above structure is no more a model of the resulting theory. We can formulate it in the following way:

- **E12** $\forall x, y \, (\forall u \, (u \mathcal{O} x \leftrightarrow u \mathcal{O} y) \rightarrow x = y)$.

As a result, we obtain theory a $\mathcal{T}_{T'} = \mathcal{T}_T \cup \{ \text{E12} \}$.

In the above example, the properties $\forall u \, (u \mathcal{O} x \leftrightarrow u \mathcal{O} y)$, $\forall u \, (u \mathcal{O} x \leftrightarrow u \mathcal{O} z)$ and $\forall u \, (u \mathcal{O} y \leftrightarrow u \mathcal{O} z)$ holds for the structure presented in fig. 2.8. Hence by E12 we have $x = y = z$. Therefore, it is not a model of the theory $\mathcal{T}_{T'}$.

Note that the absence of antisymmetry of the relation of interval inclusion (axiom E12 is equivalent to the formula $\forall x, y \, (x \text{ in } y \And y \text{ in } x \rightarrow x = y)$, so it can be interpreted in such a way) in Tsang's theory is a conscious decision: Tsang considers event structures, not interval structures, and in the same time interval several different events can occur. Unfortunately, as we have shown, this assumption leads to other, undesirable effects.

It shoud be mentioned here that Tsang's linearity axiom is identical with the classic linearity axiom, hence Tsang <u>imposes</u> the convexity axiom on intervals. Therefore, the equivalence of Tsang's theory $\mathcal{T}_T$ and Allen & Hayes's theory $\mathcal{T}_{A\circ}$ can be considered only in the class of structures of convex intervals.

A more precise analysis of these problems will be presented in the next section when the above theories are compared.

2.2.4 Comparison of axiomatizations of interval structures

Having various presentations of interval temporal structures, their comparison becomes necessary. Such a comparison including Allen & Hayes's theory, the classic theory (axiomatization presented by van Benthem for $INT(Q)$) and his own [Ladkin & Maddux, 1987] has been performed by Ladkin (1987). He enriched Allen & Hayes's theory $\mathcal{T}_A$ by adding an axiom imposing density of meeting places of intervals. The resulting theory is an axiomatization of the interval structure $INT(Q)$. Van Benthem proved it to be countably categorical; so all the three axiomatizations of this structure are logically equivalent.

In [Hajnicz, 1995a] we performed such a comparison in a more straightforward way, by defining translations between the theories under consideration and thus examining the interpretability of one of the theories in the other. First, we presented the following translations between Allen & Hayes's theory $\mathcal{T}_A$ and the classic theory $\mathcal{T}_C$:

Let $\varrho \colon Z_A \longrightarrow Z_C$ be a function transforming the set of variables of Allen & Hayes's theories to the set of variables of the classic theories. We define a function $\xi \colon \mathcal{F}_A \longrightarrow \mathcal{F}_C$ such that:

$$\xi(i \parallel j) = \varrho(i) < \varrho(j) \And \forall x \, \neg(\varrho(i) < x \And x < \varrho(j)).$$

It is clear that $i, j \in Z_A$, $x \in Z_C$. The other formulas are translated in the obvious way. In what follows, we will not differentiate the standard logical symbols in both theories—their meaning is the same and the context is always clearly defined.

Let $\varrho': Z_C \longrightarrow Z_A$ be a function transforming the set of variables of the classic theories to the set of variables of Allen & Hayes's theories. We define a function $\xi': \mathcal{F}_C \longrightarrow \mathcal{F}_A$ such that:

$$\xi'(x < y) = \varrho'(x) \parallel \varrho'(y) \vee \exists i \, (\varrho'(x) \parallel i \,\&\, i \parallel \varrho'(y)),$$

$$\xi'(x \subseteq y) = \exists i, j \, (i \parallel \varrho'(y) \,\&\, \varrho'(y) \parallel j \,\&\, (i \parallel \varrho'(x) \vee \exists k \, (i \parallel k \,\&\, k \parallel \varrho'(x)) \,\&\,$$
$$(\varrho'(x) \parallel j \vee \exists k \, (\varrho'(x) \parallel k \,\&\, k \parallel j)).$$

Evidently, $x, y \in Z_C$, $i, j, k \in Z_A$.

In the discussed work we have also introduced the translations between Tsang's theory $\mathcal{T}_T$ and the classic theory $\mathcal{T}_C$ (see below). These theories are much more similar to each other than the theories $\mathcal{T}_A$ and $\mathcal{T}_C$—the precedence relation $<$ is the same for both of them. Consequently, some axioms are also identical or very similar.

Let $\sigma: Z_T \longrightarrow Z_C$ be a function transforming the set of variables of Tsang's theories to the set of variables of the classic theories. We define a function $\zeta: \mathcal{F}_T \longrightarrow \mathcal{F}_C$ such that:

$$\zeta(x < y) = \sigma(x) < \sigma(y),$$

$$\zeta(x \,\mathcal{O}\, y) = \exists u \, (u \subseteq \sigma(x) \,\&\, u \subseteq \sigma(y)).$$

Evidently, $x, y \in Z_T$, $u \in Z_C$. Since the meaning of the precedence relation is the same in both theories, it will be denoted by the same symbol in both theories—the context is always clear.

Let $\sigma': Z_C \longrightarrow Z_T$ be a function transforming the set of variables of the classic theories to the set of variables of Tsang's theories. We define a function $\zeta': \mathcal{F}_C \longrightarrow \mathcal{F}_T$ such that:

$$\zeta'(x < y) = \sigma'(x) < \sigma'(y),$$

$$\zeta'(x \subseteq y) = \forall u \, (u \,\mathcal{O}\, \sigma'(x) \rightarrow u \,\mathcal{O}\, \sigma'(y)),$$

where $x, y \in Z_C$, $u \in Z_T$.

On the other hand, Tsang (1986) has constructed translations between Allen & Hayes's theory $\mathcal{T}_{A^\circ}$ and his own theory $\mathcal{T}_T$ by defining the relation $\parallel$ in the theory $\mathcal{T}_T$ in the following way:

$$x \parallel y \iff_{def} x < y \,\&\, \neg\exists z \, (x < z \,\&\, z < y),$$

which is identical to the translation of this formula into the classic theory presented above. Moreover, Tsang defines the relations $<$ and $\mathcal{O}$ in the theory $\mathcal{T}_{A^\circ}$ in the following way:

$$x < y \iff_{def} x \parallel y \vee \exists z \, (x \parallel z \,\&\, z \parallel y),$$

$$x \,\mathcal{O}\, y \iff_{def} \neg(x < y) \,\&\, \neg(y < x).$$

The definition of the relation $<$ is identical with its counterpart in the translation of the classic theory $\mathcal{T}_C$ into Allen & Hayes's theory $\mathcal{T}_A$. On the other hand, the definition of the relation $\mathcal{O}$ is based on the definition of the relation $<$ and on axiom E7.

A comparison of Allen & Hayes's theory and Tsang's (actually Kamp's) theory from the philosophical point of view is performed in [Lin, 1991].

[Hajnicz, 1995a] and [Tsang, 1986] provide theorems which show that for each pair of the above theories translations of all the axioms of one theory are satisfied in all models of the other. The result is that all the three theories are mutually interpretable. Actually, we have to do with two sets of theories, depending on whether they contain the axioms $LANTIS$, M6 and E12 respectively or not (in other words, whether we consider interval or event structures). Mutual interpretability holds for both sets.

Moreover, we showed in [Hajnicz, 1995a] that if $\varrho'(\varrho(i)) = i$ for $i \in Z_A$, $\varrho(\varrho'(x)) = x$, for $x \in Z_K$, $\sigma'(\sigma(x)) = x$ for $x \in Z_T$ and $\sigma(\sigma'(x)) = x$ for $x \in Z_K$, then $\xi'(\xi(i \parallel j)) \leftrightarrow i \parallel j$, $\xi(\xi'(x < y)) \leftrightarrow x < y$, $\xi(\xi'(x \subseteq y)) \leftrightarrow x \subseteq y$, $\zeta(\zeta'(x \subseteq y)) \leftrightarrow x \subseteq y$ and $\zeta'(\zeta(x \mathcal{O} y)) \leftrightarrow x \mathcal{O} y$ holds.

Since Tsang's translations between theories implicitly, with relations of one theory being defined in the other, it is difficult to show that these translations are mutually correct with respect to these relations (as it has been done before). The author does not do it anyway, whereas he concludes that the theories $\mathcal{T}_T$ and $\mathcal{T}_{A\circ}$ are equivalent.

The above result is surprising in so far as considerations described in sections presenting the respective theories suggest fundamental differences in their expressive power, especially in Allen & Hayes's theory compared with the other theories. This inconsistency is apparent. In fact, translations of particular relations eliminate these differences, because they contain the corresponding restrictions.

First, the translations of Allen & Hayes's relation $\parallel$ into the classic and Tsang's theories are based on the relation $<$ only, and they ignore the relation $\subseteq$ or $\mathcal{O}$ (i.e. relations which "look inside intervals"). Second, the translation of the classic relation $\subseteq$ does not correspond to the genuine character of this relation. This results from the same phenomenon, namely that Allen & Hayes's theory considers only endpoints, meet points of intervals, without "looking inside intervals". However, to make "looking inside intervals" unnecessary we had to restrict ourselves to the class of convex interval structures. Moreover, the linearity of a structure is also indispensable for the correctness of this translation, and not only because of the fact that Allen & Hayes consider linear structures. The inadequacy of the translation in non-linear or unconvex interval structures is shown in fig. 2.9. This stems from the fact that in order to prove the appropriate theorems it is necessary to have the axiom LIN satisfied (which consequently means also that the axiom *CONV* has to be satisfied). On the other hand, in these proofs the axioms *L_TRANS* and *L_REF*, i.e. those involving "looking inside intervals", have not been used.

Unfortunately, there is no possibility to define a more adequate translation of the relation $\subseteq$ into Allen & Hayes's theory.

(a)   (b)

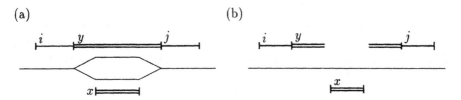

Fig. 2.9. The translation of the relation $\subseteq$ into Allen & Hayes's theory
versus properties of interval time structures

Since the inclusion relation $\subseteq$ does not occur in the translation $\xi(x \parallel y)$ of Allen & Hayes's theory into the classic theory, it does not occur in the formula $\xi(\xi'(x \subseteq y))$, either. Thus, it is possible to treat this formula as a definition of the inclusion relation, adequate only for linear structures of convex intervals. It can be said that we consider a translation of a theory with one relation, namely with the precedence relation $<$.

As for the definition of the relation $\mathcal{O}$ in Allen & Hayes's theories, it depends on the satisfaction of axiom E7. Hence, the translation assumes that both the linearity and the convexity condition in the described structures are satisfied. However, though Allen & Hayes's theory <u>imposes</u> the linearity condition, it <u>does not impose</u> (as we have noted several times) the condition of convexity of intervals. Thus the translation makes sense only for structures of convex intervals. On the other hand, defining a direct translation of the formula $x \mathcal{O} y$ would not help to avoid the problems, because they are intrinsic features of Allen & Hayes's theory and they have also appeared when the translation of the classic theory into Allen & Hayes's theory was defined. We can say, however, that the above translation has been defined for a theory with one predicate $<$, because the translation of the predicate $\mathcal{O}$ is <u>defined</u> by means of it. It seems to be particularly risky to base a translation on an axiom which is meant to be removed—and Tsang did just this. But, on the other hand, as in the case of theories T_C and T_A, the translations make sense only for linear structures of convex intervals.

Thus we have to do with two axiomatizations of linear time structures of convex intervals based on the relation $<$ (with the relations $\subseteq$ and $\mathcal{O}$ defined within them), and with one axiomatization based on the relation $\parallel$. These three theories are mutually interpretable in each other and can be treated as equivalent.

This problem, of course, does not appear when classic theories are compared with Tsang's theories. These theories are really similar, and we can speak of their equivalence, although there is no mutual correspondence between the respective axioms.

Venema (1988) proposes a modification of the structure $\mathfrak{J}$ that eliminates limitations discussed above. Namely, he suggests relations "looking inside intervals" corresponding to the idea of this structure. He defines a structure $\mathfrak{J} = \langle J, \parallel, \subset_B, \subset_E \rangle$, where J is a set of intervals, $\parallel$ is a relation of meet of intervals over J, and $\subset_B$ and $\subset_E$ are relations of initial (terminal) inclusion over J. The author considers interval time structures in which the condition of atomicity is satisfied. In this case the relation $\parallel$ can be defined by the relations $\subset_B$ and $\subset_E$ in the following way:

$$i \parallel j \quad \equiv_{def} \quad \exists k \, (k \subset_E i \ \& \ k \subset_B j \ \& \ \forall l \, \neg(l \subset_B k \ \lor \ l \subset_E k))$$

Therefore we obtain a structure $\mathfrak{J} = \langle J, \subset_B, \subset_E \rangle$. Venema axiomatizes this structure in the following way:

- **V1** $\forall x, y, z \, (x \subset_* y \ \& y \subset_* z \ \to \ x \subset_* z)$,

- **V2** $\forall x, y, z \, (x \subset_* z \ \& y \subset_* z \ \to \ (x \subset_* y \ \lor \ x = y \ \lor \ y \subset_* x))$,

- **V3** $\forall x \, (\neg \exists z \, (z \subset_* x) \ \lor \ \exists y \, (y \subset_* x \ \& \ \neg \exists z \, (z \subset_* y)))$,

- **V4** $\forall x \, (\neg \exists y \, (z \subset_B x) \ \leftrightarrow \ \neg \exists y \, (z \subset_E x))$,

- **V5** $\forall x, y, z \, (x \subset_B y \ \& \ x \subset_E z \ \to \ \exists! u \, (y \subset_E u \ \& \ z \subset_B u))$,

- **V6** $\forall x, y, z \, (x \subset_E y \ \& \ y \subset_B z \ \to \ \exists! u \, (x \subset_B u \ \& \ u \subset_E z))$,

- **V7** $\forall x, y, z \, (x \subset_B y \ \& \ y \subset_E z \ \to \ \exists! u \, (x \subset_E u \ \& \ u \subset_B z))$,

- **V8** $\forall x, y \, \neg(x \subset_B y \ \& \ x \subset_E y)$,

where $\subset_* = \subset_B$ or $\subset_E$. On the other hand, in the case of linear time structures of convex intervals, we can define $\subset_B$ and $\subset_E$ by $\parallel$, so we can obtain Allen & Hayes's (1985) structure $\mathfrak{J} = \langle J, \parallel \rangle$:

$$i \subset_B j \quad \equiv_{def} \quad \exists k, l, m \, ((k \parallel i \ \& \ i \parallel m \ \& \ m \parallel l) \ \& \ (k \parallel j \ \& \ j \parallel m)),$$

$$i \subset_B j \quad \equiv_{def} \quad \exists k, l, m \, ((k \parallel m \ \& \ m \parallel i \ \& \ i \parallel l) \ \& \ (k \parallel j \ \& \ j \parallel m)).$$

The above definitions correspond to the definitions of the relations *starts* and *finishes* suggested by Allen & Hayes (see section 5.1). They are similar to definitions of the inclusion relation $\subseteq$ or the overlap relation $\mathcal{O}$ by the relation $<$ and they have similar shortcomings.

Certainly, one could try to compare Venema's theory and the classic or Tsang's theories. For instance, a translations between the classic and Venema's theories would be based on the following dependencies:

$$\bar{\xi}(x < y) \quad = \quad \xi(x < y),$$

$$\bar{\xi}(x \subseteq y) \quad = \quad \varrho(x) \subset_B \varrho(y) \ \lor \ \varrho(x) = \varrho(y) \ \lor \ \varrho(x) \subset_E \varrho(y) \ \lor$$
$$\exists i \ (\varrho(x) \subset_B i \ \& \ i \subset_E \varrho(y)),$$

$$\bar{\xi}'(i \parallel j) \quad = \quad \xi'(i \parallel j),$$

$$\bar{\xi}'(i \subset_B j) \quad = \quad \varrho'(i) \subseteq \varrho'(j) \ \& \ \exists x \ (x \subseteq \varrho'(j) \ \& \ \varrho'(i) < x) \ \&$$
$$\forall y \ (y \subseteq \varrho'(j) \ \rightarrow \ \neg(y < \varrho'(i))),$$

$$\bar{\xi}'(i \subset_E j) \quad = \quad \varrho'(i) \subseteq \varrho'(j) \ \& \ \exists x \ (x \subseteq \varrho'(j) \ \& \ x < \varrho'(i)) \ \&$$
$$\forall y \ (y \subseteq \varrho'(j) \ \rightarrow \ \neg(\varrho'(i) < y)).$$

Also in this case, translations link together precedence relations and inclusion relations separately. It is difficult, however, to compare these approaches, since we do not have in our disposal mutually adequate sets of axioms.

In Tsang's opinion, the main advantage of his theory over Allen & Hayes's is that Allen & Hayes's axiom M3 contains much more than the linearity, so non-linear structures cannot be described in this theory. However, the translation of the classic theory into Tsang's theory shows that also E7 implies the validity of several other properties (even though not as much as M3). And a direct expression of these properties often requires the use of an auxiliary relation *in*. Even Tsang in his considerations sometimes claims that two overlapping intervals have a common subinterval, so in fact he does not treat the relation $\mathcal{O}$ as primitive.

Finally, we think that the precedence relation $<$ and the inclusion relation $\subseteq$ characterize the nature of intervals in the most natural way. Therefore, the classic theories are best to describe interval temporal structures. We should also note that the classic approach contains many more different axioms, and thus it permits a description of many more different classes of structures, thus being the most flexible one. One should note that the removal of the linearity axiom *LIN* results in the lest harm to the characteristics of a structure (the more so as van Benthem considers the convexity condition *CONV* separately). Therefore, in our further considerations involving an abandonment of the linearity condition, we will use the classic approach.

2.2.5 Non-linear interval time structures

It follows from the above considerations that a description of interval time is much more complex than a description of point time. We have discussed this problem in [Hajnicz, 1991c; 1995b]. It turns out that for interval time it is not enough to discard the linearity condition to make the axiomatization of a structure satisfy the requirements imposed on interval time structures in artificial intelligence. That is why we will carry out a detailed analysis of this problem in this section. It will be based on the classic approach, since we have shown above that discarding the linearity axiom involves the lest cost.

The proofs of all theorems from this section can be found in [Hajnicz, 1995b].

The basic assumption made in this section is that a time structure forms a universe of intervals—time units, in which certain facts can be true or false and certain events may occur. Obviously, the existence of an interval without an event occurring in it is possible, but the mutual position of intervals must not be such that it would <u>make no sense</u> for an event or fact to occur in any of these intervals. Therefore, an interval is acceptable only if an event or a fact <u>can</u> occur in it. This issue has also been pointed out by Tsang [1987].

Before we present new axioms we want to recall that we consider a structure $\Im = \langle I, <, \subseteq \rangle$, where I is a set of time intervals, $<$ is a precedence relation over I and $\subseteq$ is the inclusion relation over I.

Since we discuss non-linear structures, we will often consider intervals that do not lie on the same branch. To express this fact we will use, besides the basic relations $<$ and $\subseteq$, the following auxiliary relation representing this property:

$$x \, ! \, y \quad \equiv_{def} \quad \neg(x < y \; \lor \; \exists u \, (u \subseteq x \; \& \; u \subseteq y) \; \lor \; y < x).$$

The axioms presented in section 2.2.1 do not imply that an interval cannot lie on two different branches (see fig. 2.10 and 2.11). Such situations contradict the intuitive understanding of an interval and the definition of an interval as a pair of points or a convex set of points (see section 2.1.4). To eliminate these degenerate situations, we would need an axiom stating that any two intervals included in another interval must be collinear (must lie on the same branch). This property will be called *normality*.

- $NORMAL \quad \forall x, y, z \, ((x \subseteq z \; \& \; y \subseteq z) \; \rightarrow$
$$x < y \; \lor \; \exists u \, (u \subseteq x \; \& \; u \subseteq y) \; \lor \; y < x)$$

The above condition, which states that any two intervals contained in any other intervals should lie on the same branch, is independent of the theory $\mathcal{T}_{CB}$, because all the axioms of the theory are satisfied in such structures as those presented in fig. 2.12.

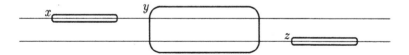

Fig. 2.10. Mutual position of intervals, with one interval lying
      on two branches

(a)   (b)

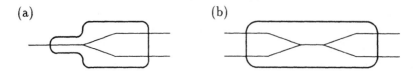

Fig. 2.11. Intervals with at least one fragment lying exactly on one branch

Fig. 2.12. An example of a model of the theory $\mathcal{T}_B$
not satisfying the *normality* condition

If we accepted the intuitive meaning of an interval as a pair or a set of points, we should be able to represent such mutual positions of intervals, as presented in fig. 2.13 (items (c) and (e) concern the partial order only).

However, let us now consider the semantics of the interval positions presented in fig. 2.13 (b) and (c), if these intervals were treated as time of occurrence of events or facts (the cases (d) and (e) are similar). In this situation, in a certain course of events there would exist events that begin but do not finish (or *vice versa*), i.e. they suddenly stop mid-way. This means that the event has no culmination point (or no starting point, which is even more absurd). So, it is not an event at all. On the other hand, for facts (or processes) such a situation would mean that, in one course of events, at the moment of branching, there is a cause for a fact to become true (or false), and in another course of events no such cause exists. The problem is discussed in detail in [Hajnicz, 1995b].

(a)   (b)   (c)

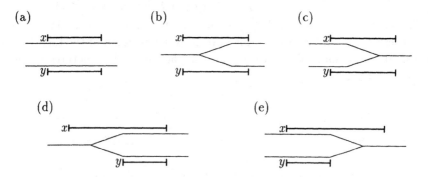

Fig. 2.13. Possible positions of *normal* intervals in non-linear time

Moreover, from the purely temporal point of view, we really do not know how to interpret the mutual position of intervals x and z in fig. 2.14 (a). Neither they are positioned on different branches, nor x precedes z. We strongly object to an identification of x with its subinterval collinear with z. In conclusion, we do not want to consider such intervals as presented in fig. 2.13 (b), (c), (d) and (e) at all.

What we want is to eliminate situations when two intervals lie "partially" on one common branch and "partially" on two different branches. Thus, their subintervals should also lie on the same branch. It would seem that a condition excluding such positions can be formulated in the following way:

$$\forall x, y\ (\exists u\ (u \subseteq x\ \&\ u \subseteq y) \quad \to \quad \forall z, v\ ((z \subseteq x\ \&\ v \subseteq y) \to$$
$$(z < v \ \lor\ \exists u\ (u \subseteq z\ \&\ u \subseteq v) \ \lor\ v < z))).$$

Unfortunately, this condition is too strong, as it entails (together with I_REF) the axiom $NORMAL$.

Theorem 2.2.5.1. The condition $\forall x, y\ (\exists u\ (u \subseteq x\ \&\ u \subseteq y) \quad \to \quad \forall z, v\ ((z \subseteq x\ \&\ v \subseteq y) \quad \to \quad (z < v \ \lor\ \exists u\ (u \subseteq z\ \&\ u \subseteq v) \ \lor\ v < z)))$ entails the *normality* axiom.

Proof

Consider any structure $\mathfrak{S} = \langle I,\ <,\ \subseteq \rangle$. Consider any $u \in I$ and any $x = u$, $y = u$. Then by I_REF we have $u \subseteq x$ and $u \subseteq y$. Consider any $v, z \in I$ such that $v \subseteq x$ and $z \subseteq y$. Then the premise of the considered condition is satisfied, hence $z < v \lor \exists u\ (u \subseteq z\ \&\ u \subseteq v) \lor v < z$. The above conclusion was obtained for any $z, v, u \in I$ such that $z \subseteq u$ and $v \subseteq u$. Therefore $NORMAL$ is satisfied.

∎

On the other hand, the above condition is too weak to exclude the situations presented in fig. 2.13 (d) and (e), and with more precision in fig. 2.14.

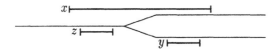

Fig. 2.14. An interval lying in the area of bifurcation of branches

As we cannot impose the condition on subintervals, let us impose it on the intervals:

$$\forall x, y\ (\exists z\ (z \subseteq x\ \&\ (z < y \ \lor\ z \subseteq y \ \lor\ y < z) \quad \to$$
$$(x < y \ \lor\ \exists u\ (u \subseteq x\ \&\ u \subseteq y) \ \lor\ y < x)).$$

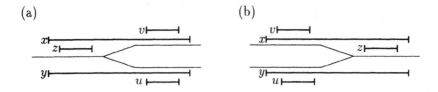

Fig. 2.15. Characteristics of intervals lying in the area of a fork of branches

In the above formula we used $u \subseteq y$ instead of $\exists w \, (w \subseteq u \, \& \, w \subseteq y)$, because then $w \subseteq x$ (by *L_TRANS*), so w satisfies the original condition. Thus this is an equivalent and simpler formulation. It turns out that this condition is sufficient to exclude situations presented in fig. 2.15, since it is not satisfied by the intervals x, u, z and y, v, z. Note that this figure already contains the situation presented in fig. 2.14.

By examining the considered condition one can see that it is trivially satisfied for $u \subseteq y$. And for the remaining two cases the condition is somewhat too weak, as it admits some redundant positions of intervals. Thus, eventually, this property, called *solidity*, can be re-written in the form of the following two formulas:

- *SOLID* $\forall x, y, z \, (z \subseteq x \, \& \, y < z \quad \rightarrow \quad (y < x \, \lor \, \exists u \, (u \subseteq x \, \& \, u \subseteq y)))$

  $\forall x, y, z \, (z \subseteq x \, \& \, z < y \quad \rightarrow \quad (x < y \, \lor \, \exists u \, (u \subseteq x \, \& \, u \subseteq y)))$.

Unfortunately, the above axiom is satisfied if we assume that $x < y$ in fig. 2.14. To exclude such unproper precedence of intervals, we need an additional axiom:

- *P_PROPER* $\forall x, y \, (\forall z \, (z \subseteq y \quad \rightarrow \quad \exists u, v \, (u \subseteq x \, \& \, v \subseteq z \, \& \, u \, ! \, v)) \quad \rightarrow$

  $x, y \, (x \, ! \, y)$.

It should be mentioned here that those authors who consider intervals in non-linear structures of point time (e.g. McDermott [1982] who treats intervals as sets of points, or Shoham [1987] who treats them as pairs of points) do not take the condition of *solidity* into account. In both cases the "correct" convex intervals do not have to satisfy this condition. We do not know of any papers on non-linear time, in which intervals are treated as primitive individuals.

The axiom *SOLID* implies very important properties. First, it ensures that subintervals of intervals lying on different branches cannot be collinear.

Theorem 2.2.5.2. The axiom *SOLID*, together with the axiom *L_TRANS*, imply satisfaction of the formula $\forall x, y \, (x \, ! \, y \quad \rightarrow \quad \forall z \, (z \subseteq x \quad \rightarrow \quad z \, ! \, y))$.

Moreover, it follows from the above theorem that two intervals having collinear subintervals are themselves collinear. This is an important property, since we have rejected the situation presented in fig. 2.10, where an interval can lie on two different branches (so it can be a subinterval of one interval on one branch and of another interval on the other branch).

Corollary The axiom *SOLID* together with the axiom *I_TRANS* imply satisfaction of the formula $\forall i, j, k, l\ ((k \subseteq i\ \&\ l \subseteq j\ \&\ (k < l\ \vee\ \exists u\ (u \subseteq k\ \&\ u \subseteq l)\ \vee\ l < k))\ \rightarrow\ (i < j\ \vee\ \exists u\ (u \subseteq i\ \&\ u \subseteq j)\ \vee\ j < i))$.

Since we have decided to reject positions of intervals such as those presented in fig. 2.13 (b), (c), (d) and (e), we need another way of representing intervals lying in a bifurcation of branches. In our opinion, the only possible solution is to accept creatures such as those presented in fig. 2.11 as time intervals. Note that these creatures <u>are</u> convex sets of points, so they conform to the traditional interpretation of intervals as convex sets of points.

Therefore, the axiom *NORMAL* is not always considered, which contradicts "geometrical" definitions of an interval. Actually, this only proves the fact that time is a very specific notion, and the "geometrical" approach can be applied to it only to a limited degree. Nevertheless, we definitely reject the situation represented in fig. 2.10. Notice that the structure presented there is not transitive—we have $\neg(x < z)$. *Transitivity* is so fundamental property of the order (and the precedence relation $<$ <u>is</u> an order) that we are unwilling to abandon it.

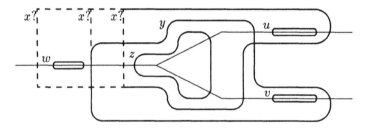

Fig. 2.16. A paradoxical position of intervals in the area of bifurcation
        of branches

We have mentioned that the position of intervals presented in fig 2.14 contradicts the assumption that events and facts occur in intervals. However, it is not obvious whether this also concerns the situation presented in fig. 2.16. Typically, events have their characteristic durations, and it is difficult to imagine them lasting shorter on one branch and longer on the other (the more so that they begin in the same situation). In the case of facts the situation is different. It can happen that in one course of events an event terminating the occurrence of a certain fact appears earlier than in another course of events. So, theoretically, one should not exclude such a possibility.

On the other hand, we should notice that when the intervals x and y from fig. 2.16 do not begin at the same moment, the axiom $CONV$ rules out the structure presented there. For instance, if $w \subseteq x$ & $u \subseteq x$ & $w < y$ & $y < u$ holds (with the standard meaning of the inclusion relation $\subseteq$), then by $CONV$ we have $y \subseteq x$, which does not take place in fig. 2.16. So, we do not want the situation when the intervals x and y begin (end) at the same moment to be an exception. Moreover, one should also admit that the statement $u \subseteq x$ & $y < u$ & $x < v$ & $v \subseteq y$ looks strange. We exclude this situation by introducing an axiom of *ordinariness*. However, if we wanted to allow such situations as presented in fig. 2.16, we would need a different condition of *convexity* or a different notion of inclusion.

- $ORDINAR$ $\forall x, y \; (\exists u \; (u \subseteq x \; \& \; y < u) \;\; \rightarrow \;\; \forall v \; (v \subseteq y \;\; \rightarrow \;\; \neg(x < v)))$

               $\forall x, y \; (\exists u \; (u \subseteq x \; \& \; u < y) \;\; \rightarrow \;\; \forall v \; (v \subseteq y \;\; \rightarrow \;\; \neg(v < x)))$

The situation presented in fig. 2.10 is not possible, because P_TRANS imposes that if $x < y$ & $y < z$ then $x < z$. This does not suffice, however, to completely exclude situations similar to that presented in fig. 2.17, when the interval x appears at the beginning or at the end of a structure. Since we require that a certain part of each interval lie on a single branch, the subinterval lying on that branch is collinear with all the subintervals of the considered interval. It could seem that this property can be formulated as follows:

$$\forall x \; \exists y \; (y \subseteq x \; \& \; \forall z \; (z \subseteq x \;\; \rightarrow \;\; (y < z \; \vee \; \exists u \; (u \subseteq y \; \& \; u \subseteq z) \; \vee \; z < y))).$$

Unfortunately, this condition is trivially satisfied by $y = x$. As we allow only situations like those presented in fig. 2.11, the required property can be represented by the formula:

$$\forall x \; \exists y \; (y \subseteq x \; \& \; \forall u, v \; (u \subseteq x \; \& \; v \subseteq x \; \& \; u \;!\; v \;\; \rightarrow$$
$$(y < u \; \& \; y < v \; \vee \; u < y \; \& \; v < y)).$$

The interval y will be called *the interval embedding the interval* x, and the property—*embedment* of the interval x.

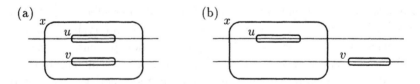

Fig. 2.17. Inadmissible positions of intervals on two branches

Unfortunately, though the above formula excludes the situation presented in fig. 2.17 (a), it does not exclude the situation presented in fig. 2.17 (b). Thus we have to formulate the axiom in a stronger form, separating different cases (see fig. 2.18):

- *EMBED* $\forall x \,\exists y \,(y \subseteq x \,\&\, \forall \, u, v \,(u \,!\, v \quad \rightarrow$
$$(u \subseteq x \,\&\, v \subseteq x \;\rightarrow\; y < u \,\&\, y < v \,\lor\, u < y \,\&\, v < y) \,\&$$
$$(u \subseteq x \,\&\, v < x \;\rightarrow\; u < y \,\&\, v < y) \;\&$$
$$(u \subseteq x \,\&\, x < v \;\rightarrow\; y < u \,\&\, y < v))).$$

This axiom is evidently satisfied when the *normality* condition holds (as then no u, v satisfy the antecedent of the implication), so it should be considered only in those theories which do not include the *normality* condition.

Theorem 2.2.5.3. Each subinterval of an interval *embedding* a particular interval is also its *embedding interval.*

Theorem 2.2.5.4. If y is an interval *embedding* the interval x, then for any interval z such that $\exists u \,(u \subseteq x \,\&\, u \subseteq z)$ we have $\neg(y \,!\, z)$, for any interval z such that $z < x$ we have $z < y$, and for any interval z such that $x < z$ we have $y < z$.

It turns out that when the condition of *normality* is abandoned for non-linear structures, two of the properties of linear time considered by van Benthem (see section 2.2.1) as basic do not hold. The first such property is the condition of *monotonicity*, which can be seen in fig. 2.18.

(a)   (b)

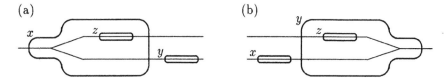

Fig. 2.18. Structures not satisfying the condition of *normality*

Therefore, the axiom of *monotonicity* should be replaced by its weaker form:

- *WMON* $\forall x, y, z \,(x < y \,\&\, z \subseteq x \quad \rightarrow \quad (z < y \,\lor\, y \,!\, z))$
$$\forall x, y, z \,(x < y \,\&\, z \subseteq y \quad \rightarrow \quad (x < z \,\lor\, x \,!\, z)).$$

An at least partial satisfaction of the condition *MON* depends, on the other hand, on the satisfaction of the axiom *L_LIN*. Looking carefully at fig. 2.18 one can note that the axiom *NORMAL* is satisfied in it, in spite of the fact that intervals shown there do not look "normally". In fact, only structures satisfying the axioms *NORMAL* and *MON* are entirely *normal* structures. Certainly, there is a possibility of strengthening the axiom *NORMAL* in such a way that, together with *WMON*, it would entail *MON* (see Hajnicz, 1991c; 1995b], but actually there is no reason for this. The existing axiom is sufficient for our purposes, because *MON* belongs to $\mathcal{T}_B$.

It turns out that the basic property of interval structures, i.e. that none of two overlapping intervals can precede the other one (this property follows from the *monotonicity* of structures) is preserved.

Theorem 2.2.5.5. The axioms *P_IRREF, I_REF* and *WMON* imply that for any $i, j \in I$ if there exists $k \in I$ such that $k \subseteq i$ and $k \subseteq j$, then $\neg(i < j)$.

Moreover, we can state that all *normal* structures are *ordinary*.

Theorem 2.2.5.6. The axioms *NORMAL* and *MON* entail the axiom *ORDINAR*.

The second axiom which does not hold is *CONJ*. An example of a structure that does not (and <u>cannot</u>) satisfy it is presented in fig. 2.20. As in the case of *monotonicity*, we define a weaker axiom. It would not be adequate to call it *weak conjunction*, since the conjunction of intervals x and y from the figure simply does not exist. So, we call it *branch conjunction*.

- $BCONJ \quad \forall x, y, u \, (u \subseteq x \, \& \, u \subseteq y \; \rightarrow$
  $$\exists z \, (z \subseteq x \, \& \, z \subseteq y \, \& \, u \subseteq z \, \&$$
  $$\forall v \, (v \subseteq x \, \& \, v \subseteq y \, \& \, \neg(v \,!\, u) \; \rightarrow \; v \subseteq z)))).$$

Theorem 2.2.5.7. The axioms *NORMAL* and *BCONJ* imply the axiom *CONJ*.

Theorem 2.2.5.8. The axioms *L_LIN* and *BCONJ* together with the axioms *P_IRREF, I_TRANS, CONV, WMON* and *EMBED* imply the axiom *CONJ*. satisfied. ∎

On the other hand, if we renounced from the *transitivity* condition (changing it into $(x < y \, \& \, y < z) \; \rightarrow \; (x < z \; \vee \; x \,!\, z)$) and the *embedment* condition, i.e. if we accepted the situations presented in figs. 2.9 and 2.16, the axiom *CONJ* would hold (though it would not be implied by *BCONJ* in any way).

In general, the above axioms cover the problems connected with an axiomatization of non-linear structures. But actually there is one question left open, namely that concerning filling in time.

Let us consider the structure presented in fig. 2.19. The situation seems to agree with intuition. But on the other hand, as the event y took place in a certain course of events, time has passed, too. This passing of time should occur in the other course of events (expressed in the picture by a certain length of the branch). In real world, time is densely filled with events, and thus with intervals. In the case of interval time we can hardly speak of a typical condition of *density*, but time passing with no intervals in it is not possible. As we have mentioned in the introduction, time passing is often treated as a derivative of the change itself and of the events causing it. The fact that the structure presented in fig. 2.19 contains no event following x on the lower branch can be caused either by our ignorance on what has happened, or by the limitations of our field of view due to which we overlook events leave out during this period of time for being insignificant. However, such a situation can be thought of as artificial. All the time something is happening to any object or agent considered in a particular domain (even if it is in rest). It is hardly possible to have no information about any of them. Moreover, the intervals z and u are treated as adjacent (as there are no other intervals between them on the branch), which is contrary to intuition.

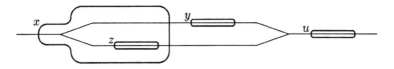

Fig. 2.19. A structure with time passing with no events

In order to avoid this undesirable situation, we add one more condition, which we call *filling* of time.

$$\forall x, y, z \ (x < y \ \& \ z \subseteq x \ \& \ y \ ! \ z \quad \rightarrow \quad \exists u \ (x < u \ \& \ y \ ! \ u)$$
$$\forall x, y, z \ (y < x \ \& \ z \subseteq x \ \& \ y \ ! \ z \quad \rightarrow \quad \exists u \ (u < x \ \& \ y \ ! \ u)$$

In contrast, the absence of an interval on the upper branch seems to be justified—the interval x itself fills time in. However, we decided to impose the existence of such an interval for the sake of uniformity of the solution. As a result, we obtain formulas:

- *FILL* $\forall x, y, z \ (x < y \ \& \ z \subseteq x \ \& \ y \ ! \ z \quad \rightarrow$
  $$\exists u, v \ (x < u \ \& \ z < u \ \& \ y \ ! \ u \ \& \ v < y \ \& \ v \subseteq x \ \& \ z \ ! \ v))$$
  $\forall x, y, z \ (y < x \ \& \ z \subseteq x \ \& \ y \ ! \ z \quad \rightarrow$
  $$\exists u, v \ (u < x \ \& \ u < z \ \& \ y \ ! \ u \ \& \ y < v \ \& \ v \subseteq x \ \& \ z \ ! \ v)).$$

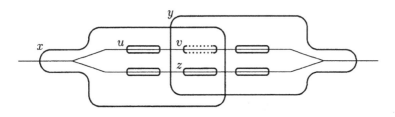

Fig. 2.20. A non-typical overlapping of intervals

The theorem 2.2.5.2. implies that it is impossible for two intervals to overlap on one branch (i.e. to have a common subinterval) and to occur one after the other on another branch. Nevertheless, the structure presented in fig. 2.20 satisfies all the axioms (except *normality*) formulated so far (even after deleting the interval v from it), though on the upper branch there exists no interval being a common subinterval of both x and y. But the interval x cannot precede the interval y on the upper branch! So, we must introduce one more kind of filling related to overlapping of intervals.

$$\forall x, y, z, u \ (z \subseteq x \ \& \ z \subseteq y \ \& \ u \subseteq x \ \& \ u \ ! \ z \quad \rightarrow$$
$$\exists v \ (v \subseteq x \ \& \ v \subseteq y \ \& \ v \ ! \ z \ \& \ \neg(v \ ! \ u)))$$

The above condition is evidently too strong, as its premise is satisfied for any interval x having two subintervals z and u lying on different branches; additionally, we assume $y = z$, hence $z \subseteq y$. Eventually, we formulate the condition by two formulas:

- *OFILL* $\forall x, y, z, u \ (z \subseteq x \ \& \ z \subseteq y \ \& \ u \subseteq x \ \& \ u < y \ \& \ u \ ! \ z \quad \rightarrow$
$$\exists v \ (v \subseteq x \ \& \ v \subseteq y \ \& \ u < v \ \& \ v \ ! \ z)))$$
$\forall x, y, z, u \ (z \subseteq x \ \& \ z \subseteq y \ \& \ u \subseteq x \ \& \ y < u \ \& \ u \ ! \ z \quad \rightarrow$
$$\exists v \ (v \subseteq x \ \& \ v \subseteq y \ \& \ v < u \ \& \ v \ ! \ z))).$$

We also have to consider two situations involving time filling on branches. These situations are actually less motivated then those presented above. However, in this section we want to describe theories of exactly the same structures as those which can be represented by means of the algorithm presented in section 4.3.5. We waive the introduction of several non-typical primitive relations between intervals such that their "linear" mutual positions are different on different branches. Positions of this kind can be quite well motivated in many situations, but for the sake of uniformity with the algorithmical approach (which will be especially important while formalizing the algorithm in section 5.8) we will formulate the remaining filling axioms. An example of the first situation of this kind is presented in fig. 2.21. The structure in the figure satisfies all the previous axioms (even the axiom *FILL* as for the intervals x, y and u it is satisfied by u!). Nevertheless, the situation when two intervals are adjacent on one branch and not on the other is not typical. In order to exclude such a situation we need an axiom for filling time in *between* intervals:

- *BFILL* $\forall x, y, z, u \ (x < z \ \& \ z < y \ \& \ u \subseteq x \ \& \ u < y \ \& \ z \ ! \ u \quad \rightarrow$
$$\exists v \ (x < v \ \& \ v < y \ \& \ u < v \ \& \ z \ ! \ v))$$
$\forall x, y, z, u \ (x < z \ \& \ z < y \ \& \ u \subseteq y \ \& \ x < u \ \& \ z \ ! \ u \quad \rightarrow$
$$\exists v \ (x < v \ \& \ v < y \ \& \ v < u \ \& \ z \ ! \ v)).$$

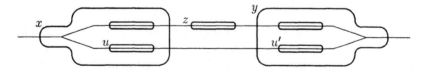

Fig. 2.21. Intervals meeting each other on one of the branches

(a)   (b)

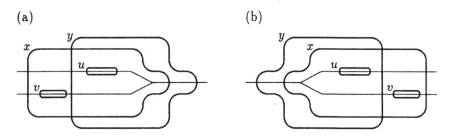

Fig. 2.22. Nonuniform ending of intervals on two branches

An example of the second situation is presented in fig. 2.22. In fig. 2.22 (a) we have two overlapping intervals, and the interval x, beginning earlier, contains a subinterval which precedes the interval y on one branch and does not precede it on the other branch (and the axiom $FILL$ is satisfied by any interval preceding x and noncollinear with v). This means that these intervals begin simultaneously on a one branch (as there exists no interval determining time passing) and do not begin simultaneously on the other branch. The situation is somehow similar to the situation involving the axiom of *ordinariness*, but nevertheless it is not subsumed by it. Therefore we formulate an axiom of *filling endings*, which excludes this situation, (together with its counterpart from fig. 2.22 (b)).

- $EFILL$ $\forall x, y, z, u \, (z \subseteq x \, \& \, z \subseteq y \, \& \, u \subseteq x \, \& \, u < y \, \& \, u \, ! \, z \quad \rightarrow$
  $\exists v \, (v \subseteq x \, \& \, v < y \, \& \, v < z \, \& \, v \, ! \, u))$
  $\forall x, y, z, u \, (z \subseteq x \, \& \, z \subseteq y \, \& \, u \subseteq x \, \& \, y < u \, \& \, u \, ! \, z \quad \rightarrow$
  $\exists v \, (v \subseteq x \, \& \, y < v \, \& \, z < v \, \& \, v \, ! \, u))$

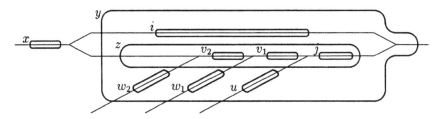

Fig. 2.23. A fragment of an infinite structure not satisfying the axiom $BEFILL$

The last situation is the less intuitive one. At the first sight the following $BEFILL$ axiom should result from the previous axioms. In reality this is not the case, though. The appropriate counterexample is presented in [Hajnicz, 1991c]. A fragment of an infinite structure not satisfying the axiom BEFILL, while it satisfies all the previous axioms is presented in fig. 2.23. Since this property excludes meet of an interval with a non-ending subinterval of its neighbour, it can be understood as a union of *filling* time in *between* intervals and on their *endpoints*.

- BEFILL $\quad \forall x, y, z \ (x < y \ \& \ \neg(x \ ! \ z) \ \& \ \exists u \ (u \subseteq y \ \& \ u < z) \quad \rightarrow$
  $\exists v \ (x < v \ \& \ v \subseteq y \ \& \ v < z))$
  $\forall x, y, z \ (y < x \ \& \ \neg(x \ ! \ z) \ \& \ \exists u \ (u \subseteq y \ \& \ z < u) \quad \rightarrow$
  $\exists v \ (v < x \ \& \ v \subseteq y \ \& \ z < v))$

It turns out that if we accepted the condition of *normality*, there would be no need to consider any of the axioms concerning time filling, as then they are automatically satisfied.

Theorem 2.2.5.9. The axiom *NORMAL* implies satisfaction of the axiom *FILL*.

Theorem 2.2.5.10. The axiom *NORMAL* implies satisfaction of the axiom *OFILL*.

Since the premises of the axiom *EFILL* are the same as those of the axiom *OFILL*, the above proof ensures that *NORMAL* also implies *EFILL*.

Theorem 2.2.5.11. The axiom *NORMAL* implies satisfaction of the axiom *BFILL*.

Theorem 2.2.5.12. The axiom *NORMAL* together with the axiom *MON* implies satisfaction of the axiom *BEFILL*.

The situations related to the axioms *OFILL* and *BFILL*, presented in figs. 2.19 and 2.20, can occur only in partially ordered structures.

Theorem 2.2.5.13. The axiom *L_LIN* together with the axioms *EMBED, FILL, P_TRANS* and *CONV* implies the axiom *OFILL*.

Theorem 2.2.5.14. The axiom *L_LIN* together with the axiom *FILL* implies the axiom *BFILL*.

Finally, we put forward four basic theories of non-linear interval time, depending on whether one considers a *partial* or a *left linear* order and whether the discussed structures are supposed to be *normal* or not:

T_P = { *P_TRANS, P_IRREF, I_TRANS, I_REF, I_ANTIS, FREE, CONV, WMON, BCONJ, SOLID, P_PROPER, ORDINAR, EMBED, FILL, OFILL, BFILL, EFILL, BEFILL* },

T_{PN} = { *P_TRANS, P_IRREF, I_TRANS, I_REF, I_ANTIS, FREE, CONV, MON, CONJ, SOLID, P_PROPER, NORMAL* },

T_{LL} = { *P_TRANS, P_IRREF, I_TRANS, I_REF, I_ANTIS, FREE, CONV, WMON, CONJ, SOLID, P_PROPER, ORDINAR, EMBED, FILL, EFILL, L_LIN* },

T_{LN} = { *P_TRANS, P_IRREF, I_TRANS, I_REF, I_ANTIS, FREE, CONV, MON, CONJ, SOLID, P_PROPER L_LIN, NORMAL* }.

Notice that the above theories contain neither the linear theory $\mathcal{T}_C$ nor the basic theory $\mathcal{T}_{CB}$. So, the difference does not consist merely in the obvious abandon of the linearity axiom LIN. Most of the axioms listed in these theories (and also other axioms, e.g. those considered by van Benthem) can be added to the above theories, producing the theories that describe structures with more specific properties. The axioms like $NEIGH$ or $SUCC$ were not included in the above theories, as in our opinion they are less important. Moreover, it is significant that they do not need to be satisfied in structures represented by means of the algorithm from sections 4.3.5 and 5.8. However, it should be noticed that the axiom DIR cannot be satisfied in the theories $\mathcal{T}_{PN}$ and $\mathcal{T}_{LN}$, since the axioms $NORMAL$ and $SOLID$ together exclude the existence of a common superinterval of any non-collinear intervals. On the contrary, we cannot require the satisfaction of the axioms MON and $CONJ$, belonging to the basic theory $\mathcal{T}_B$, in structures that do not satisfy the axiom $NORMAL$. Only the theories $\mathcal{T}_{PN}$ and $\mathcal{T}_{LN}$ (containing the condition of *normality*) subsume the basic theory $\mathcal{T}_B$.

It is worth mentioning here that $SOLID$ is a specific property resulting from the role ascribed to time intervals in artificial intelligence. In contrast, $NORMAL$ is an important property of intervals treated "geometrically" (and its possible absence results just from the specificity of the domain). The absence of the property of *normality* in the analysis carried out by van Benthem indicates clearly that only linear structures were considered, and the consequences of abandoning the axiom of *linearity* had not been thoroughly analysed. This is all the more important as $NORMAL$ implies all the other properties considered in this paper, except $SOLID$, of course. Moreover, the classic property $CONJ$ is lost only if the condition of *normality* is missing.

In section 2.1.4 we have presented definitions of intervals as convex sets or pairs of points. It is obvious that intervals defined in such a way need not satisfy the condition of *solidity*. On the other hand, the definition of intervals as pairs of points seems to impose the condition of *normality*. It is so in the case of the *left linear* order. Consider, however, the situation presented in fig. 2.24. If the interval u were treated as a pair of points, we could assume it to contain both the upper branch and the lower branch of time, and then the structure (without the interval v) would not be *normal*, but it would be *solid* instead. Obviously, adding any interval with one of its endings positioned on any branch (e.g. the interval v) would cause a loss of this property. However, it seems to us that the researchers who represent intervals as pairs of points have a different approach in mind. On the other hand, if we imposed the condition of *normality*, we would not be able to state on which branch (the upper or the lower one) the interval u lies. Moreover, it follows from fig. 2.24 that in such] partially ordered structures the axiom of *convexity* of intervals $CONV$ need not be satisfied, even though these are structures of convex intervals (the assumption that the interval u lies on the same branch as the interval y would eliminate non-linearity of the structure, unless there were another interval on the lower branch).

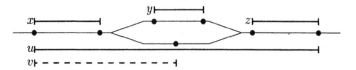

Fig. 2.24. A structure not satisfying the conditions *CONV* and *SOLID*

2.2.6 Defining points in interval structures

In literature, we can find not only examples of intervals defined in point structures, but also examples of points defined in interval structures. In this section we want to present three methods for defining points in interval structures that are somehow complementary with respect to the considerations in section 2.1.4.

A method for defining intervals in a structure $\mathfrak{I} = \langle I, <, \subseteq \rangle$ was considered by van Benthem (1983). Among axioms considered by him that have been omitted in section 2.2.1 there is a condition of *atomicity* concerning the existence of indivisible intervals:

- *ATOM* $\forall x \, \exists y \, (y \subseteq x \, \& \, \forall z \, (z \subseteq y \, \rightarrow \, z = y))$.

DEFINITION
Let $\mathfrak{I}$ be a structure satisfying the axioms of the theory $\mathcal{T}_{CB}$ extended by the axiom *ATOM*. A *time point* is any *atomic* interval, i.e. $x \in I$ is a point if $\forall y \in I \, (y \subseteq x \, \rightarrow \, y = x)$. A point structure ATOM($\mathfrak{I}$) is $\langle T, < \rangle$, where:

(i) $T \subseteq I$ is a set of atoms in I,

(ii) $<$ is the precedence relation of $\mathfrak{I}$ restricted to T.

Theorem 2.2.6.1. A point structure ATOM($\mathfrak{I}$) defined in such a way satisfies all axioms of the theory $\mathcal{T}_L$ presented in section 2.1.
The proof of this theorem can be found in [van Benthem, 1983].

Another method for defining points in interval structures was suggested by Ladkin (1987) for the structure $\mathfrak{J} = \langle J, \parallel \rangle$. Namely, in this structure he defined an equivalence relation for two pairs of meeting intervals (where a pair of meeting intervals p and q is denoted by $[p, q]$) : $[p, q] \sim [r, s]$ iff $p \parallel q \, \& \, r \parallel s \, \& \, p \parallel s$, where $p, q, r, s \in J$.

Lemma 2.2.6.1. The relation $\sim$ defined in such a way is an equivalence relation.

DEFINITION
A *point* is an equivalence class (for a pair of meeting intervals $[p, q]$ denoted as $[\![p, q]\!]$) of the relation $\sim$. A linear point structure MEET($\mathfrak{J}$) is $\langle J_{/\sim}, \prec \rangle$, where:

(i) $J_{/\sim}$ is the set of equivalence classes of the relation $\sim$ for the set of intervals J from the structure $\mathfrak{J}$,

(ii) $\prec$ is a precedence relation defined in the following way (see fig. 2.6 (b)):

$$[\![p,q]\!] \prec [\![r,s]\!] \equiv_{def} \exists u \; ([p,q] \sim [p,u] \; \& \; [r,s] \sim [u,s]).$$

Theorem 2.2.6.2. A point structure MEET($\mathfrak{J}$) defined in such a way satisfies all axioms of the theory $\mathcal{T}_L$ presented in section 2.1.
The proofs of this theorem as well as of the above lemma can be found in [Ladkin, 1987].

A third method for defining points out from intervals for the structure $\mathfrak{G} = \langle G, <, \mathcal{O} \rangle$ can be found in [Lin, 1991]. He defines points as clusters of overlapping intervals.

DEFINITION
Let $\mathfrak{G}$ be an interval time structure satisfying the axioms of the theory $\mathcal{T}_T$. A set X constitutes a *point*, if it is a maximal set such that for every $i, j \in X$ we have $i \, \mathcal{O} \, j$. A point structure OVERLAP($\mathfrak{G}$) is $\langle T, \prec \rangle$, where:

(i) T is a subset of 2^G composed of all sets satisfying the above condition,

(ii) $\prec$ is a precedence relation defined in the following way

$$X < Y \quad \equiv_{def} \quad \exists i \in X \; \exists j \in Y \; i < j.$$

If an interval is a member of a point, then the interval is said to be *going on* at the point. Evidently an interval can be a member of several points. Two overlapping intervals must have at least one point in common.

Theorem 2.2.6.3. A point structure OVERLAP($\mathfrak{G}$) defined in such a way satisfies all axioms of the theory $\mathcal{T}_L$ presented in section 2.1.
The proof of this theorem can be found in [Lin, 1991].

Note that individuals defined in the structures MEET($\mathfrak{J}$) and OVERLAP($\mathfrak{G}$), like individuals defined in structures CONV($\mathfrak{T}$) and PAIR($\mathfrak{T}$) in section 2.1.4, are new individuals that do not occur in original structures. In contrast, in the structure ATOM($\mathfrak{S}$) we consider a particular subset of elements of the original structure. Moreover, in the structure MEET($\mathfrak{J}$) we consider equivalence classes, whereas in the structure OVERLAP($\mathfrak{G}$) sets of intervals constituting points need not be disjoint. Thus in these cases we have to do with quite different definition processes.

On the other hand, in section 2.1.4 we presented two methods of definition for the same point structure (resulting in two different interval structures), whereas in this section we have considered definitions of points in three different interval structures (resulting in isomorphic point structures).

3. Modal temporal logics and description of time structures

Just as the first order predicate calculus, modal temporal logics can be used to describe formally time structures as well as to represent time-dependent knowledge. Seemingly one can have an impression that they are rather intended for this second task—we have to do with modal operators determining temporal dependencies between propositions or predicates. Actually, however, even though on the syntactic level the classic tense logics correspond to McTaggartian dynamic A-series, on the semantic level they correspond to static B-series [Ladkin, 1986b]. This is so because theorems have to be valid at all time moments, hence no moment can be distinguished. Therefore, temporal knowledge representation systems based on tense logics [Orłowska, 1981; 1982; Mays, 1983] use not only general axioms characterizing dependencies between predicates being represented, but they also use concrete time structures containing particular facts. Certainly, such structures must be models of the considered theory, which enables reasoning based on a particular logic.

In contrast, for describing time structures we use propositional modal temporal logic. Then all the theorems have to be valid not only at all time moments for a given valuation, but for every valuation of all propositional variables. For this very reason axioms characterize general properties of the considered structures. In this chapter we will focus on this last aspect of modal temporal logics. However, there exist a very rich literature on different aspects of modal temporal logics, especially concerning completeness and dicidability of various modal temporal languages (cf. [Gabbay et al., 1994]).

However, before we turn to discuss different modal temporal logics, we want to dedicate a few words to standard modal logics. We discuss them on the propositional level and with a single modality. The alphabet of the considered logic consists of a countable set of predicates $\mathbf{P}$, a set of standard logical connectives $(\neg, \rightarrow)$ and a modal operator $\Box$ ("necessary"). A modal operator $\Diamond$ is defined as $\neg\Box\neg$.

The most famous semantics for modal logics is the so-called *possible worlds semantics* of Kripke (1959; 1963). In this approach, a model is an ordered triple $\mathfrak{M} = \langle W, R, m \rangle$, where W is a set of possible worlds, $R \subseteq W^2$ is an *access relation* over W, and m is an *interpretation*, i.e. a function assigning a logical value 1 or 0 to each proposition $p \in \mathbf{P}$ and each world $w \in W$ (in other words m assigns to each proposition p the set of all these worlds in which it is satisfied). Logical connectives are interpreted in the standard way, and $\Box\varphi$ is satisfied in a world $w \in W$ if φ is satisfied in every world w' such that $w \, R \, w'$.

The main axiom for modal logics is $\Box(A \rightarrow B) \rightarrow (\Box A \rightarrow \Box B)$, This axiom, together with the rule of inference $A/\Box A$, constitutes the deductive system **K**. Subsequent axioms are connected with properties of the access relation R: the axiom $\Box A \rightarrow A$ ensures its reflexivity, the axiom $\Box A \rightarrow \Box\Box A$ ensures its transitivity, and the axiom $A \rightarrow \Box\Diamond A$ is responsible for its symmetry. These axioms added consecutively to the system **K** constitute systems **T**, **S4** and **S5**, respectively.

There also exist multimodal logics; then for every pair of operators "necessary" and "possible" a separate access relation is introduced.

3.1 Point time

As it was in the case of describing time in the first order predicate calculus, we start considering modal temporal logics by considering point time. However, in contrast to that case, there exist now various possibilities for a description of time structures, as there exist many different modal temporal operators.

3.1.1 Classical priorean instant tense logic

The most famous modal temporal logic is *instant tense logic* introduced by Prior (1957; 1967). The term *tense logic* originates from the fact that this logic has been used for determining the tense of sentences (determining the moment of occurrence of an event described by the sentence in relation to the moment of speech); the term *instant* was added by van Benthem in order to differentiate it from *extended tense logic* based on intervals.

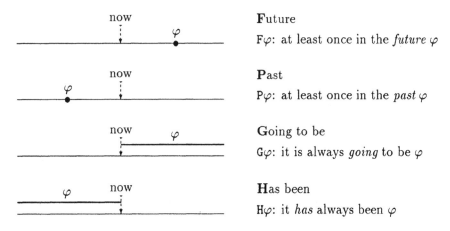

now $\quad\quad\varphi$	**Future**
	$F\varphi$: at least once in the *future* φ
now	**Past**
φ	$P\varphi$: at least once in the *past* φ
now $\quad\varphi$	Going to be
	$G\varphi$: it is always *going* to be φ
$\varphi\quad$ now	**H**as been
	$H\varphi$: it *has* always been φ

Fig. 3.1. A graphical interpretation of temporal operators

Prior's main idea is a temporal interpretation of modal operators, i.e. treating the access relation between possible worlds as a time precedence relation. As a result, the modal operators $\Box$, $\Diamond$ are replaced by temporal operators F—possible in the future and G—necessary in the future, going to be. Moreover, they were complemented by their counterparts in the past: P—possible in the past and H— necessary in the past, has been. A graphical interpretation of these operators is presented in fig. 3.1.

Now we present priorean instant tense logic in a formal way.

<u>Alphabet</u>

- a nonempty, countable set of propositional variables X,

- logical connectives $\neg$, $\rightarrow$,

- time operators G, H.

DEFINITIONS

$$\varphi \vee \psi \quad \equiv_{def} \quad \neg\varphi \rightarrow \psi,$$
$$\varphi \mathrel{\&} \psi \quad \equiv_{def} \quad \neg(\varphi \rightarrow \neg\psi),$$
$$\varphi \leftrightarrow \psi \quad \equiv_{def} \quad \neg((\varphi \rightarrow \psi) \rightarrow \neg(\psi \rightarrow \varphi)),$$
$$F\varphi \quad \equiv_{def} \quad \neg G\neg\varphi,$$
$$P\varphi \quad \equiv_{def} \quad \neg H\neg\varphi.$$

The set of well-formed formulas is the smallest set $\mathcal{G}$ such that:

- $X \subseteq \mathcal{G}$,

- if $\varphi, \psi \in \mathcal{G}$, then $\neg\varphi$, $\varphi \rightarrow \psi$, $G\varphi$, $H\varphi \in \mathcal{G}$.

<u>Semantics</u>

The semantics of the considered logic is based on the point time structure $\mathfrak{T} = \langle T, < \rangle$ described in section 2.1.

DEFINITIONS

A function $V \colon X \longrightarrow 2^T$ is called a *valuation*. An ordered triple $M = \langle T, <, V \rangle$ is called a *model*.

We define satisfaction of a formula φ in a model M at a moment t (notation: $M \models \varphi\,[t]$) in the following way:

$M \models p[t]$	iff	$t \in V(p)$,
$M \models \neg\varphi[t]$	iff	$M \not\models \varphi[t]$,
$M \models (\varphi \rightarrow \psi)[t]$	iff	if $M \models \varphi[t]$, then $M \models \psi[t]$,
$M \models G\varphi[t]$	iff	$M \models \varphi[t']$ holds for every t' such that $t < t'$,
$M \models H\varphi[t]$	iff	$M \models \varphi[t']$ holds for every t' such that $t' < t$.

Let φ be any formula from $\mathcal{G}$ and $M = \langle \mathfrak{T}, V \rangle$ be any model. We say that $M \models \varphi$ if $M \models \varphi[t]$ holds for every $t \in T$. We say that $\mathfrak{T} \models \varphi$ if $M \models \varphi$ holds for every valuation V.

Let S be any set of formulas. We say that $S \models \varphi$ if $\mathfrak{T} \models \varphi$ holds for any structure $\mathfrak{T}$ such that $\mathfrak{T} \models S$.

Axiomatization

First we present an axiomatization of the basic deductive system for instant tense logic K_t. The name of the system indicates that it is a counterpart of the basic (minimal) deductive system K for modal logics.

Axioms

- $\varphi \to (\psi \to \varphi)$,
- $(\varphi \to (\psi \to \chi)) \to ((\varphi \to \psi) \to (\varphi \to \chi))$,
- $(\neg\varphi \to \neg\psi) \to (\psi \to \varphi)$,
- $G(\varphi \to \psi) \to (G\varphi \to G\psi)$,
- $H(\varphi \to \psi) \to (H\varphi \to H\psi)$,
- $\varphi \to GP\varphi$,
- $\varphi \to HF\varphi$.

Rules of inference

- $$\dfrac{\varphi,\ \varphi \to \psi}{\psi},$$

- $$\dfrac{\varphi}{G\varphi},$$

- $$\dfrac{\varphi}{H\varphi}.$$

DEFINITION

A formula φ is K_t-*derivable* from a set of formulas S (notation: $S \vdash_{K_t} \varphi$), if there exists a finite sequence of formulas ending with φ such that each formula in the sequence either is an axiom from K_t or belongs to S or is derived from the preceding formulas by an application of some rule of inference.

Van Benthem (1983) shows that the above axiomatization ensures soundness and completeness of priorean instant tense logic with the considered semantics.

Theorem 3.1.1.1. For any set of formulas S we have $S \vdash_{K_t} \varphi$ iff $S \models \varphi$ holds.

Since this is a basic axiomatization, it does not impose any conditions onto time structures. Thus, it does not even impose that time should form an order. In order to impose additional conditions onto structures we need to formulate additional axioms. Unfortunately, some properties of point time structures (even basic ones presented in section 2.1) cannot be formulated in the considered logic. Now we will list axioms being counterparts of the ones presented in section 2.1.

- transitivity $Gp \rightarrow GGp$,
- irreflexivity   is not tense-logically definable,
- linearity   is not tense-logically definable,
  left linearity $Pp \rightarrow H(Pp \lor p \lor Fp)$,
  right linearity $Fp \rightarrow G(Pp \lor p \lor Fp)$,
- discreteness $H(Hp \rightarrow p) \rightarrow (PHp \rightarrow Hp)$
                   $G(Gp \rightarrow p) \rightarrow (FGp \rightarrow Gp)$,
- density $GGp \rightarrow Gp$.

As we can see, irreflexivity (and antisymmetry) of precedence relation is not tense-logically definable. Van Benthem (1983) gives a proof for this. The whole subsequent analysis is performed for the class of structures that constitute a strict partial order. Linearity is not tense-logically definable, either—we have left and right linearity instead. This property is obviously weaker—structures composed of several "parallel" linear axes are allowed. We do not want to suggest that tense logic is weaker than the first order predicate calculus—it is possible to define some second order properties in it (see e.g. [van Benthem, 1983]).

3.1.2 Additional operators for structure specification

Temporal structures can be characterized not only by appropriate axioms, but also using different temporal operators. The temporal logic presented above has been extended several times by various operators, specifying properties of structures.

Such a basic operator for discrete time structures is the operator *next*, together with its counterpart for the past—the operator *previous*. They are used mainly, though not exclusively, in temporal logics of programs. The operator *next* is differently denoted in different works, e.g. it is sometimes denoted by X [Gabbay et al., 1980; Mays, 1983]. In this work we will use a popular denotation ○ [Abadi & Manna, 1985; Lichtenstain et al., 1985], and ✻ for the operator *previous*. Therefore, our alphabet is enriched by the two new temporal operators.

Semantics
In the case of a logic of programs, the semantics is usually based on a special structure representing an execution sequence. Nevertheless, we will found the semantics of this enriched logic on the same point time structure $\mathfrak{T} = \langle T, < \rangle$ as before. Thus we have only to define satisfaction in a model $M = \langle T, <, V \rangle$ of formulas with the new operators.

$M \models \bigcirc\varphi[t]$ iff $M \models \varphi[t']$ holds for every t' such that
$\qquad\qquad\qquad\qquad t < t'$ & $\forall t''$ $(t < t'' \rightarrow t' < t'')$,

$M \models *\varphi[t]$ iff $M \models \varphi[t']$ holds for every t' such that
$\qquad\qquad\qquad\qquad t' < t$ & $\forall t''$ $(t'' < t \rightarrow t'' < t')$.

In the case of linear structures (or even quasi-linear ones, i.e. structures that are both left and right linear), we should replace the term "for all" by the term "exists". Such a formulation would be better since the above notation hides a trap—in a dense structure a formula $\bigcirc\varphi$ (or $*\varphi$) defined in such a way is satisfied at every time point t, and we would prefer it to be satisfied at none. Therefore, the operators $\bigcirc$ and $*$ play their specification role only in the class of linear (quasi-linear) structures.

Axiomatization
Evidently, introduction of new operators requires some new axioms that characterize them. Two new rules of inference are needed, too.

Axioms
- $\bigcirc(\varphi \rightarrow \psi) \rightarrow (\bigcirc\varphi \rightarrow \bigcirc\psi)$,
- $*(\varphi \rightarrow \psi) \rightarrow (*\varphi \rightarrow *\psi)$,
- $G\varphi \leftrightarrow \bigcirc\varphi$ & $\bigcirc G\varphi$,
- $H\varphi \leftrightarrow *\varphi$ & $*H\varphi$.

Rules of inference

- $\dfrac{\varphi}{\bigcirc\varphi}$,

- $\dfrac{\varphi}{*\varphi}$.

Mays (1983) presents an extreme example of characterizing time structures by means of additional operators. He introduces a multitude of operators for description of branching time. These operators have a doubly modal character— they quantify both over the precedence relation and over branches. As we have to do with branching time, this double modality concerns only future operators. Mays introduces the following operators: AG—every always, AF—every eventually, EG—some always, EF—some eventually, H—always past and P—sometime past. As we can see, the future operators consist of two symbols: the first one quantifies over branches (and resembles "typical" quantifiers), the second one quantifies over time (and resembles "typical" modal operators). Eventually, the new set of well-formed formulas is the smallest set $\mathcal{G}$ such that:

- $X \subseteq \mathcal{G}$,
- if $\varphi, \psi \in \mathcal{G}$, then $\neg\varphi$, $\varphi \rightarrow \psi$, $AG\varphi$, $EG\varphi$, $H\varphi \in \mathcal{G}$.

DEFINITIONS

$$\begin{aligned}
\text{EF}\varphi &\equiv_{def} \neg\text{AG}\neg\varphi, \\
\text{AF}\varphi &\equiv_{def} \neg\text{AG}\neg\varphi, \\
\text{P}\varphi &\equiv_{def} \neg\text{H}\neg\varphi.
\end{aligned}$$

<u>Semantics</u>

Let $\mathfrak{T} = \langle T, < \rangle$ be any point time structure, and $\text{M} = \langle T, <, V \rangle$ be any model based on this structure (for a certain valuation V). Unfortunately, the above notions are not sufficient to define satisfiability of Mays' formulas in such a structure. We will also need the notion of *branch*. Note, that it is analogous to the notion of *chronicle* used by McDermott (1982).

DEFINITION

A *branch* is any subset $B \subseteq T$ such that:

$$\forall t, t' \in B \ (t < t' \ \vee \ t = t' \ \vee \ t' < t) \quad \&$$

$$\forall t \in T \ (\forall t' \in B \ ((t < t' \ \vee \ t = t' \ \vee \ t' < t) \ \rightarrow \ t \in B)).$$

The notion of branch is used to define satisfiability of a formula φ in a model M at a moment t.

$$\begin{aligned}
&\text{M} \models p[t] &&\text{iff} &&t \in V(p), \\
&\text{M} \models \neg\varphi[t] &&\text{iff} &&\text{M} \not\models \varphi, \\
&\text{M} \models (\varphi \ \rightarrow \ \psi)[t] &&\text{iff} &&\text{if } \text{M} \models \varphi[t], \text{ then } \text{M} \models \psi[t], \\
&\text{M} \models \text{AG}\varphi[t] &&\text{iff} &&\text{for every branch } B \text{ and for every } t' \in B \\
& && &&\text{such that } t < t' \text{ we have } \text{M} \models \varphi[t'], \\
&\text{M} \models \text{EG}\varphi[t] &&\text{iff} &&\text{there exists a branch } B \text{ such that for every} \\
& && &&t' \in B \text{ such that } t < t' \text{ we have } \text{M} \models \varphi[t'], \\
&\text{M} \models \text{H}\varphi[t] &&\text{iff} &&\text{for every } t' \text{ such that } t' < t \text{ we have } \text{M} \models \varphi[t'].
\end{aligned}$$

Actually, Mays (1983) considers discrete branching time, so he also considers operators next and previous besides the above ones. Clearly, we have two operators next: **AX**—every next and **EX**—some next, while there is only one operator previous—**L**. Now we have to establish the semantics of these additional operators. In fact, **EX**φ can be defined as $\neg\text{AX}\neg\varphi$.

$$\begin{aligned}
&\text{M} \models \text{AX}\varphi[t] &&\text{iff} &&\text{for every } t' \text{ such that } t < t' \ \& \ \forall t'' \ (t < t'' \ \rightarrow \ t' < t'') \\
& && &&\text{we have } \text{M} \models \varphi[t'], \\
&\text{M} \models \text{L}\varphi[t] &&\text{iff} &&\text{for } t' \text{ such that } t' < t \ \& \ \forall t'' \ (t'' < t \ \rightarrow \ t'' < t') \\
& && &&\text{we have } \text{M} \models \varphi[t'].
\end{aligned}$$

There is no need to use the notion of branch here, since every moment has at most one successor (predecessor) on each branch.

Mays (1983) does not present an axiomatization of his logic. Such an axiomatization would be extremely large because of the number of operators he introduces.

There also exist logics of branching time (in the area of temporal logics of programs) with separate operators quantifying over precedence relation and over branches [Emerson & Halpern, 1986; Katz, 1994; Grumberg & Kurshan, 1994]. Thus only one new operator A (with its dual A defined from it) is added to the set of ordinary tense operators.

3.1.3 Operators "Since" and "Until"

Among the most important and famous temporal operators are the operators "Since" and "Until". They are often used as operators complementing priorean tense logic. However, we decided to discuss them separately because of their great importance and because they can be used to define priorean operators. Thus we have a second independent modal temporal logic. Certainly, it is somehow similar to the one discussed before and it is connected with the same time structure. The considered operators will be denoted as S and U. Both are binary—their graphical interpretation is presented in fig. 3.2.

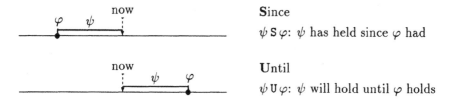

Since

$\psi \, S \, \varphi$: ψ has held since φ had

Until

$\psi \, U \, \varphi$: ψ will hold until φ holds

Fig. 3.2. Graphical interpretation of the operators "Since" and "Until"

One can wonder why the above operators, seemingly describing formulas holding in time intervals, are considered in point structures. In fact, however, only one of the formulas is considered in a time interval—the interval between two time points. Thus, the semantics of the operators is evidently connected with the point time structure. We shall now discuss the temporal logic of the operators "Since" and "Until" in details.

<u>Alphabet</u>

- a nonempty, countable set of propositions X,
- logical connectives $\neg$, $\rightarrow$,
- time operators S, U.

DEFINITIONS

$$
\begin{array}{llll}
H\varphi & \equiv_{def} & \neg(true \, S \, \neg\varphi), & H'\varphi & \equiv_{def} & \varphi \, S \, true, \\
G\varphi & \equiv_{def} & \neg(true \, U \, \neg\varphi), & G'\varphi & \equiv_{def} & \varphi \, U \, true, \\
P\varphi & \equiv_{def} & true \, S \, \varphi, & P'\varphi & \equiv_{def} & \neg(\neg\varphi \, S \, true), \\
F\varphi & \equiv_{def} & true \, U \, \varphi, & F'\varphi & \equiv_{def} & \neg(\neg\varphi \, U \, true),
\end{array}
$$

where $true \equiv_{def} p \lor \neg p$.

The set of well-formed formulas is the smallest set $\mathcal{G}$ such that:

- $X \subseteq \mathcal{G}$,
- if $\varphi, \psi \in \mathcal{G}$, then $\neg\varphi$, $\varphi \rightarrow \psi$, $\varphi S \psi$, $\varphi U \psi \in \mathcal{G}$.

In the above definitions, besides "standard" operators H, G, P, F, we have defined the operators $H'\varphi$ meaning that φ has been uninterruptedly for some (short) time, $G'\varphi$ meaning that φ is going to be uninterruptedly for some time, $P'\varphi$ meaning that φ has been arbitrarily recently, and $F'\varphi$ meaning that φ will be arbitrarily soon. These specific operators, somehow dual to the "standard" H, G, P, F can be found in Burgess (1982a).

Semantics
As we have just mentioned, the semantics of this logic will be also based on the point time structure $\mathfrak{T} = \langle T, < \rangle$ described in section 2.1. The notions of a valuation V and a model M are defined in the same way as in section 3.1.1. We define satisfaction of a formula φ in a model M at a moment t (notation: $M \models \varphi[t]$) in the following way:

$M \models p[t]$	iff	$t \in V(p)$,
$M \models \neg\varphi[t]$	iff	$M \not\models \varphi$,
$M \models (\varphi \rightarrow \psi)[t]$	iff	if $M \models \varphi[t]$, then $M \models \psi[t]$,
$M \models \psi S \varphi[t]$	iff	there exists t' such that $t' < t$ and $M \models \varphi[t']$ and for every t'' such that $t' < t''$ & $t'' < t$ we have $M \models \psi[t'']$,
$M \models \psi U \varphi[t]$	iff	there exists t' such that $t < t'$ and $M \models \varphi[t']$ and for every t'' such that $t < t''$ & $t'' < t''$ we have $M \models \psi[t'']$.

The notions of satisfiability of a formula in a model and in a structure are defined in the same way as in section 3.1.1.

Axiomatization
Let $\mathcal{K}_0$ be the class of all the structures $\mathfrak{T}$ such that $<$ is a linear order in them. An axiomatization of the logic of the operators "Since" and "Until" for this class of point time structures was suggested by Burgess (1982a) (with a somewhat different notation). He called the corresponding deductive system $\mathcal{S}_0$.

Axioms

- $\varphi \rightarrow (\psi \rightarrow \varphi)$,
- $(\varphi \rightarrow (\psi \rightarrow \chi)) \rightarrow ((\varphi \rightarrow \psi) \rightarrow (\varphi \rightarrow \chi))$,
- $(\neg\varphi \rightarrow \neg\psi) \rightarrow (\psi \rightarrow \varphi)$,
- $G(\varphi \rightarrow \psi) \rightarrow (\chi U \varphi \rightarrow \chi U \psi)$,
- $H(\varphi \rightarrow \psi) \rightarrow (\chi S \varphi \rightarrow \chi S \psi)$,
- $G(\varphi \rightarrow \psi) \rightarrow (\varphi U \chi \rightarrow \psi U \chi)$,

- $H(\varphi \rightarrow \psi) \rightarrow (\varphi S \chi \rightarrow \psi S \chi)$,
- $(\chi \,\&\, \varphi U \psi) \rightarrow \varphi U (\psi \,\&\, \varphi S \chi)$,
- $(\chi \,\&\, \varphi S \psi) \rightarrow \varphi S (\psi \,\&\, \varphi U \chi)$,
- $(\varphi U \psi \,\&\, \neg(\chi U \psi)) \rightarrow \psi U (\psi \,\&\, \neg \chi)$,
- $(\varphi S \psi \,\&\, \neg(\chi S \psi)) \rightarrow \psi S (\psi \,\&\, \neg \chi)$,
- $\varphi U \psi \rightarrow (\varphi \,\&\, \varphi U \psi) U \psi$,
- $\varphi S \psi \rightarrow (\varphi \,\&\, \varphi S \psi) S \psi$,
- $\varphi U (\varphi \,\&\, \varphi U \psi) \rightarrow \varphi U \psi$,
- $\varphi S (\varphi \,\&\, \varphi S \psi) \rightarrow \varphi S \psi$,
- $(\varphi U \psi \,\&\, \chi U \zeta) \rightarrow ((\varphi \,\&\, \chi) U (\psi \,\&\, \zeta) \vee (\varphi \,\&\, \chi) U (\psi \,\&\, \chi) \vee (\varphi \,\&\, \chi) U (\varphi \,\&\, \zeta))$,
- $(\varphi S \psi \,\&\, \chi S \zeta) \rightarrow ((\varphi \,\&\, \chi) S (\psi \,\&\, \zeta) \vee (\varphi \,\&\, \chi) S (\psi \,\&\, \chi) \vee (\varphi \,\&\, \chi) S (\varphi \,\&\, \zeta))$.

Rules of inference

- $$\dfrac{\varphi, \ \varphi \rightarrow \psi}{\psi},$$

- $$\dfrac{\varphi}{G\varphi},$$
- $$\dfrac{\varphi}{H\varphi}.$$

DEFINITION
A formula φ is S_0–derivable (notation: $\vdash_{S_0} \varphi$), if there exists a finite sequence of formulas ending with φ such that each formula in the sequence either is an axiom from S_0 or is derived from the preceding formulas by an application of some rule of inference.

The author does not present any reason for the introduction of the same rules of inference as in the classic tense logic, instead of the more natural for the considered logic rules $\varphi, \psi \,/\, \psi U \varphi$. Perhaps this facilitates the proof method. Burgess (1982a) proves soundness and completeness of the considered logic in the class of linear structures.

Theorem 3.1.3.1. $\vdash_{S_0} \varphi$ holds if and only if $M \models \varphi$ holds for every model $M = \langle \mathfrak{T}, V \rangle$ such that $\mathfrak{T} \in \mathcal{K}_0$.

Reynolds (1994) presents a sound and complete axiomatization of the logic for integer time, and Venema (1992) presents such an axiomatization over natural numbers.

3.1.4 Metric tense logic

Metric tense logic was introduced by Prior (1967). Here we intend to continue his approach. Analogously as for the description of metric time in the first order predicate calculus, we have to consider a set of distances between points $\mathcal{C} = \langle C, 0, + \rangle$. We will use operators G_n, H_n, F_n and P_n (where $n \in \mathcal{C}$) instead of the operators G, H, F and P.

Alphabet

- a nonempty, countable set of propositions X,

- logical connectives $\neg$, $\rightarrow$,

- time operators G_n, H_n.

DEFINITIONS
The basic definitions are the same as in section 3.1.1, additionally we have to define the following metric operators:

$$F_n\varphi \quad \equiv_{def} \quad \neg G_n \neg \varphi,$$
$$P_n\varphi \quad \equiv_{def} \quad \neg H_n \neg \varphi.$$

The set of well-formed formulas is the smallest set $\mathcal{G}$ such that:

- $X \subseteq \mathcal{G}$,

- if $\varphi, \psi \in \mathcal{G}$, then $\neg\varphi$, $\varphi \rightarrow \psi$, $G_n\varphi$, $H_n\varphi \in \mathcal{G}$.

Semantics

In this case the semantics will be based on the metric point time structure $\mathfrak{T} = \langle T, \mathcal{C}, <, \delta \rangle$ presented in section 2.1.2. Thus for simplicity we assume that the set of distances is the same on the syntactic and semantic level. This is because we do not want to increase the number of symbols used.

DEFINITIONS
A function $V \colon X \longrightarrow 2^T$ is called a *valuation*. An ordered tuple $M = \langle T, \mathcal{C}, <, \delta, V \rangle$ is called a *model*.
We define satisfaction of a formula φ in a model M at a moment t (notation: $M \models \varphi\,[t]$) in the following way:

$$M \models p\,[t] \qquad \text{iff} \quad t \in V(p),$$
$$M \models \neg\varphi\,[t] \qquad \text{iff} \quad M \not\models \varphi[t],$$
$$M \models (\varphi \rightarrow \psi)\,[t] \quad \text{iff} \quad \text{if } M \models \varphi[t], \text{ then } M \models \psi\,[t],$$

$M \models G_n\varphi\,[t]$ iff   for every t' such that $t < t'$ & $\delta(t,t') = n$
$\qquad\qquad\qquad\qquad\qquad\qquad M \models \varphi\,[t']$ holds,

$M \models H_n\varphi\,[t]$ iff   for every t' such that $t' < t$ & $\delta(t,t') = n$
$\qquad\qquad\qquad\qquad\qquad\qquad M \models \varphi\,[t']$ holds.

The notions of satisfiability of a formula in a model and in a structure are defined in the same way as in section 3.1.1.

Axiomatization

In the following axiomatization the classic propositional calculus axioms are assumed, even though they are not listed.

Axioms

- $F_0\varphi \rightarrow \varphi$,
- $F_n(\varphi \rightarrow \psi) \rightarrow (F_n\varphi \rightarrow F_n\psi)$,
- $F_nF_m\varphi \rightarrow F_{(n+m)}\varphi$,
- $F_nP_m\varphi \rightarrow F_{(n-m)}\varphi$ for $n > m$,
- $F_nP_m\varphi \rightarrow P_{(m-n)}\varphi$ for $n < m$,
- $P_0\varphi \rightarrow \varphi$,
- $P_n(\varphi \rightarrow \psi) \rightarrow (P_n\varphi \rightarrow P_n\psi)$,
- $P_nP_m\varphi \rightarrow P_{(n+m)}\varphi$,
- $P_nF_m\varphi \rightarrow P_{(n-m)}\varphi$ for $n > m$,
- $P_nF_m\varphi \rightarrow F_{(m-n)}\varphi$ for $n < m$.

Rules of inference

Besides *modus ponens* we consider the following two rules of inference:

- $$\frac{\varphi}{G_n\varphi},$$
- $$\frac{\varphi}{H_n\varphi}.$$

For infinite linear time $G_n = F_n$ and $H_n = P_n$ holds, since for every moment t there exists exactly one moment t' satisfying the required condition. Therefore, in this case we can leave out the above definitions, and add the following conditions to the set of axioms:

- $F_n\neg\varphi \rightarrow \neg F_n\varphi$,
- $P_n\neg\varphi \rightarrow \neg P_n\varphi$.

On the other hand, in order to metrize non-linear time structures, δ has to be a partial function.

Since Prior (1967) considers quantifying over distances, he can define the operators G, H, F, P in the language obtained, e.g. $F \equiv_{def} \exists n\, F_n\varphi$. However, we have renounced this, possibly because we do not want to mix elements of the first order logic with propositional logic. Thus, the only solution is to add these operators directly to the language. The resulting language is the union of the above language and the one presented in section 3.1.1. The semantics is also the same—a metric point structure is a point structure. As for the axiomatization, we have to enrich the union of both axiomatizations by the following axioms connecting them:

- $F_n\varphi \rightarrow F\varphi$,   for $n > 0$
- $P_n\varphi \rightarrow P\varphi$ for $n > 0$.

Prior (1967) also considers the possibility of introducing dates into a metric time structure. In order to do this we need not only a set of distances $\mathcal{C}$, but also a set of dates $D \subseteq C \cup C^-$ (see section 2.1.2). Our alphabet is now enriched by a new operator B_d, where $d \in D$. Moreover we define $D_d = \neg B_d \neg$.

Semantics

Let $\mathfrak{T} = \langle T, \mathcal{C}, D, <, \delta, c \rangle$ be a metric time structure with dates (as presented in section 2.1.2), and let the ordered tuple $M = \langle T, \mathcal{C}, D, <, \delta, c, V \rangle$ be a model, where V is defined as before. Satisfaction of a formula φ in a model M at a moment t will be now defined only for the new operator, the rest remains unchanged.

$$M \models B_d \varphi[t] \quad \text{iff} \quad \text{for every } t' \text{ such that } c(t') = d \text{ we have } M \models \varphi[t'].$$

Axiomatization

The axioms concerning the "old" operators remain unchanged, we have only to consider axioms connected with the operator D_d and one new rule of inference.

- $B_d(\varphi \rightarrow \psi) \rightarrow (B_d\varphi \rightarrow B_d\psi)$,
- $F_n D_d \varphi \rightarrow D_d \varphi$, $P_n D_d \varphi \rightarrow D_d \varphi$,
- $D_d F_n \varphi \rightarrow D_{(d+n)}\varphi$, $D_d P_n \varphi \rightarrow D_{(d-n)}\varphi$,
- $\dfrac{\varphi}{B_d\varphi}$.

As we can see, the operators B_d and D_d are neither past nor future, and their validity does not depend on the moment of evaluation of a formula—it depends only on a particular date. Also the possibility of adding dates and distances should be remarked—this is not surprising, because dates are viewed as specific distances. But actually *dates* are not *distances*, even though they are closely related to them: a sum of two distances is a distance, a sum of a date and a distance is a date, and two dates cannot be added. More information about adding dates and distances, especially for the format RR.MM.DD, can be found in [Hajnicz, 1988; 1991b].

The operators introduced above can be used to describe cyclic metric time. Then their semantics based on the structure $\mathfrak{T} = \langle T, \mathcal{C}, <, <^*, \delta, S \rangle$ is similar as before, but we use the relation $<$ for the operators G, H (as before), and the relation $<^*$ for the operators G_n, H_n. Obviously, $n \in [0, S)$.

Axiomatization

The main difference characterizing cyclic time is its axiomatization. We will only list the axioms differentiating both situations, without the obvious ones.

Axioms

- $G\varphi \rightarrow H\varphi$,
- $F_n F_m \varphi \rightarrow F_{(n+m)}\varphi$ if $n + m < S$,

- $P_n P_m \varphi \rightarrow P_{(n+m)} \varphi$ if $n + m < S$,
- $F_n F_m \varphi \rightarrow P_{(2S-n-m)} \varphi$ if $n + m > S$,
- $P_n P_m \varphi \rightarrow F_{(2S-n-m)} \varphi$ if $n + m > S$.

The first of the above axioms concerns the totality of the order $<$, whereas the others refer to the locality of the order $<^*$.

Another interesting modal temporal logic based on a metric structure was suggested by Rescher & Urquhardt (1971). It is directly related to McTaggartian A-series, as it contains the notions of the near and far past and the near and far future.

<u>Alphabet</u>

- a nonempty, countable set of propositions X,
- logical connectives $\neg$, $\rightarrow$,
- time operators G°, $G^\star$ H°, $H^\star$.

DEFINITIONS

The basic definitions are the same as in section 3.1.1, additionally we have to define the following metric operators:

$$F^\circ \varphi \quad \equiv_{def} \quad \neg G^\circ \neg \varphi,$$
$$F^\star \varphi \quad \equiv_{def} \quad \neg G^\star \neg \varphi,$$
$$P^\circ \varphi \quad \equiv_{def} \quad \neg H^\circ \neg \varphi,$$
$$P^\star \varphi \quad \equiv_{def} \quad \neg H^\star \neg \varphi.$$

the set of well-formed formulas is the smallest set $\mathcal{L}$ such that:

- $X \subseteq \mathcal{L}$,
- if $\varphi, \psi \in \mathcal{L}$, then $\neg \varphi$, $\varphi \rightarrow \psi$, $G^\circ \varphi$, $G^\star \varphi$, $H^\circ \varphi, H^\star \varphi \in \mathcal{L}$.

<u>Semantics</u>

Also in this case the semantics will be based on the metric point time structure $\mathfrak{T} = \langle T, \mathcal{C}, <, \delta \rangle$ presented in section 2.1.2.

DEFINITIONS

A valuation is a function $U : X \longrightarrow 2^T$. Moreover, we choose two arbitrary constants $c, C \in \mathcal{C}$. A model is an ordered tuple $M = \langle T, \mathcal{C}, c, C, <, \delta, U \rangle$. We define satisfaction of a formula φ in a model M at a moment t (notation: $M \models \varphi [t]$) in the following way:

$M \models p [t]$	iff	$t \in U(p)$,
$M \models \neg \varphi [t]$	iff	$M \not\models \varphi [t]$,
$M \models (\varphi \rightarrow \psi) [t]$	iff	if $M \models \varphi [t]$, then $M \models \psi [t]$,
$M \models G^\circ \varphi [t]$	iff	for every t' such that $t < t'$ & $\delta(t, t') < c$ $M \models \varphi[t']$ holds,

$$M \models G^\star\varphi\,[t] \qquad \text{iff} \quad \text{for every } t' \text{ such that } t < t' \ \& \ \delta(t,t') > C$$
$$M \models \varphi[t'] \text{ holds,}$$

$$M \models H^\circ\varphi\,[t] \qquad \text{iff} \quad \text{for every } t' \text{ such that } t' < t \ \& \ \delta(t,t') < c$$
$$M \models \varphi[t'] \text{ holds,}$$

$$M \models H^\star\varphi\,[t] \qquad \text{iff} \quad \text{for every } t' \text{ such that } t' < t \ \& \ \delta(t,t') > C$$
$$M \models \varphi[t'] \text{ holds.}$$

The notions of satisfiability of a formula in a model and in a structure are defined in the same way as in section 3.1.1.

It should be noted here that the above semantics depends essentially on the choice of the constants c and C. If $c < C$, then it is possible that neither $F^\circ\varphi[t]$ nor $F^\star\varphi[t]$ is satisfied. On the other hand, if $C < c$, then it is possible that both $F^\circ\varphi[t]$ and $F^\star\varphi[t]$ are satisfied. Therefore, the best possibility seems to admit $c = C$ (and one of the relevant inequalities to be nonstrict).

3.2 Interval time

We consider now a description of interval time structures by means of modal temporal logics. In contrast to point time, we now have a more restricted choice of operators, and hence a smaller number of possibilities to describe time structures than in the case of time structures described by means of the first order predicate calculus. The reason for this is probably a greater stress laid on points than on intervals. Nevertheless, we present here two completely different modal logics of interval time and we try to compare them.

While considering modal logics of interval time, attention is often paid to the dependency between the satisfaction of a formula in a particular interval and its satisfaction in subintervals of this interval, which is related to the so-called *homogeneity* of time (e.g. Burgess, 1982b). Since this has no connection with the choice of time structures, we will not take this dependency into account.

3.2.1 Extended tense logic

Van Benthem (1983) presents an extension of the priorean tense logic which enables description of interval time structures. Obviously, the operators G, H, F and P concern the precedence relation $<$ and preserve their meaning; however the logic is enriched by two operators concerning the relation $\subseteq$—van Benthem uses symbols $\square$ and $\lozenge$. We present this logic now.

Alphabet

- a nonempty, countable set of propositions X,
- logical connectives $\neg$, $\rightarrow$,
- time operators G, H, $\square$.

DEFINITIONS

Definitions presented in section 3.1.1 preserve their validity. Moreover we define:

$$\Diamond\varphi \quad \equiv_{def} \quad \neg\Box\neg\varphi.$$

The set of well-formed formulas is the smallest set $\mathcal{G}$ such that:

- $X \subseteq \mathcal{G}$,
- if $\varphi, \psi \in \mathcal{G}$, then $\neg\varphi$, $\varphi \rightarrow \psi$, $G\varphi$, $H\varphi$, $\Box\varphi \in \mathcal{G}$.

A graphical presentation of the above operators can be found in fig. 3.3.

<u>Semantics</u>

The semantics of the considered logic is based on the interval time structure $\mathfrak{I} = \langle I, <, \subseteq \rangle$ described in section 2.2.1.

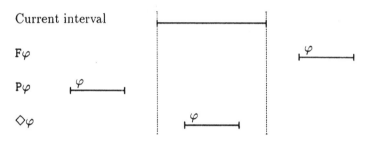

Fig. 3.3. Graphical interpretation of the classic interval operators

DEFINITIONS

A function $V : X \longrightarrow 2^I$ is called a *valuation*. An ordered quadruple $M = \langle I, <, \subseteq, V \rangle$ is called a *model*.

We define satisfaction of a formula φ in a model M in an interval i (notation: $M \models \varphi\,[i]$) in the following way:

$$
\begin{array}{lll}
M \models p\,[i] & \text{iff} & i \in V(p), \\
M \models \neg\varphi\,[i] & \text{iff} & M \not\models \varphi\,[i], \\
M \models (\varphi \rightarrow \psi)\,[i] & \text{iff} & \text{if } M \models \varphi\,[i], \text{ then } M \models \psi\,[i], \\
M \models G\varphi\,[i] & \text{iff} & M \models \varphi\,[j] \text{ holds for every } j \text{ such that } i < j, \\
M \models H\varphi\,[i] & \text{iff} & M \models \varphi\,[j] \text{ holds for every } j \text{ such that } j < i, \\
M \models \Box\varphi\,[i] & \text{iff} & M \models \varphi\,[j] \text{ holds for every } j \text{ such that } j \subseteq i.
\end{array}
$$

Let φ be any formula in $\mathcal{G}$ and let $M = \langle \mathfrak{I}, V \rangle$ be any model. We can that $M \models \varphi$ if $M \models \varphi[t]$ holds for every $i \in I$. We say that $\mathfrak{I} \models \varphi$, if $M \models \varphi$ holds for every valuation V.

Let S be any set of formulas. We say that $S \models \varphi$ if $\mathfrak{I} \models \varphi$ holds for any structure $\mathfrak{I}$ such that $\mathfrak{I} \models S$.

Axiomatization

As in the case of points, we present first an axiomatization of the basic deductive system for extended tense logic. In this case, too, it is a modification of the deductive system **K** for modal logic. This is in fact the same axiomatization, with basic information on the operator $\Box$ added.

Axioms

- $\varphi \rightarrow (\psi \rightarrow \varphi)$

- $(\varphi \rightarrow (\psi \rightarrow \chi)) \rightarrow (\varphi \rightarrow \psi) \rightarrow (\varphi \rightarrow \chi)),$

- $(\neg\varphi \rightarrow \neg\psi) \rightarrow (\psi \rightarrow \varphi),$

- $G(\varphi \rightarrow \psi) \rightarrow (G\varphi \rightarrow G\psi),$

- $H(\varphi \rightarrow \psi) \rightarrow (H\varphi \rightarrow H\psi),$

- $\Box(\varphi \rightarrow \psi) \rightarrow (\Box\varphi \rightarrow \Box\psi),$

- $\varphi \rightarrow GP\varphi,$

- $\varphi \rightarrow HF\varphi.$

Rules of inference

- $$\frac{\varphi, \ \varphi \rightarrow \psi}{\psi},$$

- $$\frac{\varphi}{\Box\varphi},$$

- $$\frac{\varphi}{G\varphi},$$

- $$\frac{\varphi}{H\varphi}.$$

The above axiomatization can be viewed as minimal. Then the relations $<$ and $\subseteq$ should be considered fully independent, as it is often the case for "typical" modal logics, e.g. logics with knowledge operators. But in such circumstances the relations $<$ and $\subseteq$ loose their meaning. This was the reason for van Benthem to include axioms corresponding to those describing the basic properties of the structure $\mathfrak{S}$ into the minimal deductive system K_i for extended tense logic.

- *I_TRANS* $\Box p \rightarrow \Box\Box p,$

- *I_REF* $\Box p \rightarrow p,$

- *I_ANTIS*   is not tense-logically definable,

- *MON* $Pp \rightarrow \Box Pp$

             $Fp \rightarrow \Box Fp.$

Now we formulate the remaining axioms presented in section 2.2.1 in the extended tense logic (using the same denotations). As in the case of points, this is not always possible. Some of them are identical as in the previous section.

- *P_TRANS* $\mathrm{G}p \;\to\; \mathrm{GG}p$,
- *P_IRREF*   is not tense-logically definable,
- *CONJ*   is not tense-logically definable,
- *CONV* $\Diamond \mathrm{F}(\Box p \,\&\, q) \;\to\; (\mathrm{F}p \,\vee\, \Diamond q)$,

              $\Diamond \mathrm{P}(\Box p \,\&\, q) \;\to\; (\mathrm{P}p \,\vee\, \Diamond q)$,
- *FREE*   is not tense-logically definable,
- *NEIGH** $(p \,\&\, \Box q) \;\to\; \mathrm{FH}(\mathrm{F}p \,\vee\, \Diamond q)$,

              $(p \,\&\, \Box q) \;\to\; \mathrm{PG}(\mathrm{P}p \,\vee\, \Diamond q)$,
- *DISJ*   is not tense-logically definable,
- *DIR* $(\mathrm{F}p \,\&\, \mathrm{F}q) \;\to\; \mathrm{F}(\Diamond p \,\&\, \Diamond q)$,

              $(\mathrm{P}p \,\&\, \mathrm{P}q) \;\to\; \mathrm{P}(\Diamond p \,\&\, \Diamond q)$,
- *SUCC* $\mathrm{G}p \;\to\; \mathrm{F}p$,

              $\mathrm{H}p \;\to\; \mathrm{P}p$,
- *LIN*   is not tense-logically definable,

  L_LIN $\mathrm{P}(p \,\&\, \Box q) \,\&\, \mathrm{P}(r \,\&\, \Box s) \;\to$

              $\mathrm{P}(q \,\&\, s) \,\vee\, \mathrm{P}(p \,\&\, \mathrm{P}r) \,\vee\, \mathrm{P}(r \,\&\, \mathrm{P}p)$,

  R_LIN $\mathrm{F}(p \,\&\, \Box q) \,\&\, \mathrm{F}(r \,\&\, \Box s) \;\to$

              $\mathrm{F}(q \,\&\, s) \,\vee\, \mathrm{F}(p \,\&\, \mathrm{F}r) \,\vee\, \mathrm{F}(r \,\&\, \mathrm{F}p)$.

Not all of the axioms presented above are direct counterparts of those presented in section 2.2.1. For instance, *NEIGH** corresponds directly to its prototype only in infinite structures (satisfying *SUCC*); *DIR*, *L_LIN* and *R_LIN* are modifications of the original axioms, too. We have presented here formulations used by van Benthem; *left* and *right linearity* can be formulated in a simpler way:

- *L_LIN* $\mathrm{P}\Box p \;\to\; \mathrm{H}(\mathrm{P}p \,\vee\, \Diamond p \,\vee\, \mathrm{F}p)$,
- *R_LIN* $\mathrm{F}\Box p \;\to\; \mathrm{G}(\mathrm{P}p \,\vee\, \Diamond p \,\vee\, \mathrm{F}p)$.

The logic presented above can be further enriched with two additional operators inverse of $\Box$ and $\Diamond$ with respect to the relation $\subseteq$ (in the same way as the operators H, P are inverse of the operators G, F with respect to the relation $<$). The new operators will be denoted as $\boxtimes$, $\oplus$, respectively. Thus our alphabet is added by the operator $\boxtimes$, and we define $\oplus\varphi \;\equiv_{def}\; \neg\boxtimes\neg\varphi$. The definition of satisfiability of a formula has to be enlarged by:

     $\mathrm{M} \models \boxtimes\varphi[i]$ iff $\mathrm{M} \models \varphi[j]$ holds for every j such that $i \subseteq j$, whereas the axiomatization of the basic deductive system must be enlarged by three axioms and one rule of inference:

- $\boxtimes(\varphi \rightarrow \psi) \rightarrow (\boxtimes\varphi \rightarrow \boxtimes\psi)$,

- $\varphi \rightarrow \Box\lozenge\!\!\!\!\diagup\varphi$,

- $\varphi \rightarrow \boxtimes\lozenge\varphi$,

- $$\frac{\varphi}{\boxtimes\varphi}.$$

The enlarged logic certainly has a greater expressive power—we are able to express in it some statements that were not expressible in the original language. In particular, this concerns the above axioms—in what follows we present formulas closer to the original ones than those presented before or describing for the first time a particular property. Unfortunately, some properties still cannot be expressed, which is not so much surprising anyway.

- *FREE* $(\lozenge p \rightarrow \lozenge(p \And \lozenge\!\!\!\!\diagup q)) \rightarrow (\Box\neg p \vee \lozenge\!\!\!\!\diagup q)$,

- *DIR* $(\mathrm{P}p \vee \lozenge\!\!\!\!\diagup p \vee \mathrm{F}p) \rightarrow \lozenge\!\!\!\!\diagup\lozenge p$,

- *L_LIN* $\mathrm{P}p \rightarrow \mathrm{H}(\mathrm{P}p \vee \lozenge\!\!\!\!\diagup p \vee \mathrm{F}p)$,

- *R_LIN* $\mathrm{F}p \rightarrow \mathrm{G}(\mathrm{P}p \vee \lozenge\!\!\!\!\diagup p \vee \mathrm{F}p)$.

3.2.2 Halpern & Shoham's modal logic of time intervals

The next modal temporal logic we want to discuss in this chapter is the logic introduced by Halpern & Shoham (1991). It is completely different from the one presented above—it contains none of the operators described in the previous section.

Alphabet

- a nonempty, countable set of propositions Y,

- logical connectives $\neg$, $\rightarrow$,

- time operators $[B]$, $[E]$, $[A]$, $[\bar{B}]$, $[\bar{E}]$, $[\bar{A}]$.

DEFINITIONS
The basic definitions are the same as those presented in section 3.1.1. Moreover we define:
$$\langle R\rangle\varphi \equiv_{def} \neg[R]\neg\varphi, \text{ where } R = B, E, A, \bar{B}, \bar{E}, \bar{A}.$$
A graphical presentation of the above operators can be found in fig. 3.4.

The set of well-formed formulas is the smallest set $\mathcal{H}$ such that:

- $Y \subseteq \mathcal{H}$,

- if $\varphi, \psi \in \mathcal{H}$, then $\neg\varphi$, $\varphi \rightarrow \psi$, $[A]\varphi$, $[B]\varphi$, $[E]\varphi$, $[\bar{A}]\varphi$, $[\bar{B}]\varphi$, $[\bar{E}]\varphi \in \mathcal{G}$.

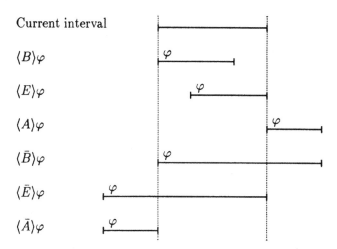

Fig. 3.4. Graphical interpretation of Halpern & Shoham's modal operators

Halpern & Shoham (1991) also use the above operators to define a set of derived operators, corresponding to other mutual positions of intervals in linear time. We will not define them separately, though the corresponding positions of intervals are presented in fig. 3.5. As a result, we obtain the same positions as those represented by the set of primitive relations between intervals for Allen's (1983) constraint propagation algorithm (discussed in section 4.3.4).

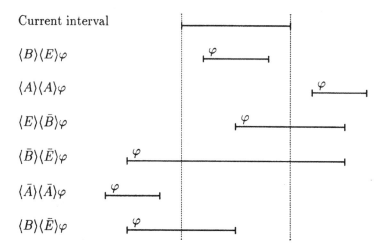

Fig. 3.5. Graphical interpretation of Halpern & Shoham's derived operators

Semantics

The original Halpern & Shoham's semantics is formulated for time intervals defined as pairs of points in a point structure. Let $\mathfrak{T} = \langle T, < \rangle$ be a point structure. We will not consider the interval structure PAIR($\mathfrak{T}$) presented in section 2.1.4, but we will rather consider an interval-point structure $\mathfrak{S} = \langle T, J, < \rangle$, where J is a set of intervals as defined in section 2.1.4.

DEFINITIONS

A function $U : Y \longrightarrow 2^J$ is called a *valuation*. An ordered quadruple $\mathfrak{M} = \langle T, J, <, U \rangle$ is called a *model*.
We define satisfaction of a formula φ in a model $\mathfrak{M}$ in an interval $\langle t_1, t_2 \rangle$ (notation: $\mathfrak{M} \models \varphi\,[\langle t_1, t_2 \rangle]$) in the following way:

$$\mathfrak{M} \models p\,[\langle t_1, t_2 \rangle] \qquad \text{iff} \qquad \langle t_1, t_2 \rangle \in U(p),$$

$$\mathfrak{M} \models \neg\varphi\,[\langle t_1, t_2 \rangle] \qquad \text{iff} \qquad \mathfrak{M} \not\models \varphi\,[\langle t_1, t_2 \rangle],$$

$$\mathfrak{M} \models (\varphi \rightarrow \psi)\,[\langle t_1, t_2 \rangle] \qquad \text{iff} \qquad \text{if } \mathfrak{M} \models \varphi\,[\langle t_1, t_2 \rangle], \text{ then } \mathfrak{M} \models \psi\,[\langle t_1, t_2 \rangle],$$

$$\mathfrak{M} \models [A]\,\varphi\,[\langle t_1, t_2 \rangle] \qquad \text{iff} \qquad \mathfrak{M} \models \varphi\,[\langle t_2, t_3 \rangle] \text{ holds for every } t_3 \in T \text{ such that } t_2 < t_3,$$

$$\mathfrak{M} \models [B]\,\varphi\,[\langle t_1, t_2 \rangle] \qquad \text{iff} \qquad \mathfrak{M} \models \varphi\,[\langle t_1, t_3 \rangle] \text{ holds for every } t_3 \in T \text{ such that } t_1 \leq t_3 \ \& \ t_3 < t_2,$$

$$\mathfrak{M} \models [E]\,\varphi\,[\langle t_1, t_2 \rangle] \qquad \text{iff} \qquad \mathfrak{M} \models \varphi\,[\langle t_3, t_2 \rangle] \text{ holds for every } t_3 \in T \text{ such that } t_1 < t_3 \ \& \ t_3 \leq t_2,$$

$$\mathfrak{M} \models [\bar{A}]\,\varphi\,[\langle t_1, t_2 \rangle] \qquad \text{iff} \qquad \mathfrak{M} \models \varphi\,[\langle t_3, t_1 \rangle] \text{ holds for every } t_3 \in T \text{ such that } t_3 < t_1,$$

$$\mathfrak{M} \models [\bar{B}]\,\varphi\,[\langle t_1, t_2 \rangle] \qquad \text{iff} \qquad \mathfrak{M} \models \varphi\,[\langle t_1, t_3 \rangle] \text{ holds for every } t_3 \in T \text{ such that } t_2 < t_3,$$

$$\mathfrak{M} \models [\bar{E}]\,\varphi\,[\langle t_1, t_2 \rangle] \qquad \text{iff} \qquad \mathfrak{M} \models \varphi\,[\langle t_3, t_2 \rangle] \text{ holds for every } t_3 \in T \text{ such that } t_3 < t_1.$$

The above definition of satisfiability of a formula is based on the assumption that in a structure intervals of the form $\langle t, t \rangle$ exist. Otherwise both occurrences of the relation of nonstrict precedence $\leq$ should be replaced by its strict counterpart $<$.

It would undoubtedly be advisable to have a semantics for the logic of interval time based on relations between intervals, and not on relations between points. Clearly, one can base a semantics of Halpern & Shoham's logic on the classic structure $\mathfrak{I}$ or even on the structure $\mathfrak{G}$, but the best choice is to base it on the structure $\mathfrak{J} = \langle J, \|, \sqsubset_B, \sqsubset_E \rangle$ presented in section 2.2.4, where J is a set of intervals, $\|$ is a relation of meet of intervals over J, and $\sqsubset_B$ and $\sqsubset_E$ are relations of initial (terminal) inclusion over J. There are two reasons for this. Firstly, we have stated in section 2.1.4 that the structure PAIR($\mathfrak{T}$) of intervals viewed as pairs of points is itself a particular case of this very structure. Secondly, the modal operators of the considered logic correspond directly to the relations between intervals in this structure.

DEFINITIONS

The definition of a valuation remains the same as before—we have to do with the same set of intervals J. Instead, a model is now an ordered tuple $\mathfrak{M} = \langle J, \|, \sqsubset_B, \sqsubset_E, U \rangle$.

We define satisfaction of a formula φ in a model $\mathfrak{M}$ in an interval i (notation: $\mathfrak{M} \models \varphi\,[i]$) in the following way:

$\mathfrak{M} \models p\,[i]$	iff	$i \in U(p)$,
$\mathfrak{M} \models \neg\varphi\,[i]$	iff	$\mathfrak{M} \not\models \varphi\,[i]$,
$\mathfrak{M} \models (\varphi \rightarrow \psi)\,[i]$	iff	if $\mathfrak{M} \models \varphi\,[i]$, to $\mathfrak{M} \models \psi\,[i]$,
$\mathfrak{M} \models [A]\,\varphi\,[i]$	iff	$\mathfrak{M} \models \varphi\,[j]$ holds for every j such that $i \parallel j$,
$\mathfrak{M} \models [B]\,\varphi\,[i]$	iff	$\mathfrak{M} \models \varphi\,[j]$ holds for every j such that $i \sqsubset_B j$,
$\mathfrak{M} \models [E]\,\varphi\,[i]$	iff	$\mathfrak{M} \models \varphi\,[j]$ holds for every j such that $i \sqsubset_E j$,
$\mathfrak{M} \models [\bar{A}]\,\varphi\,[i]$	iff	$\mathfrak{M} \models \varphi\,[j]$ holds for every j such that $j \parallel i$,
$\mathfrak{M} \models [\bar{B}]\,\varphi\,[i]$	iff	$\mathfrak{M} \models \varphi\,[j]$ holds for every j such that $j \sqsubset_B i$,
$\mathfrak{M} \models [\bar{E}]\,\varphi\,[i]$	iff	$\mathfrak{M} \models \varphi\,[j]$ holds for every j such that $j \sqsubset_E i$.

Let φ be any formula in $\mathcal{H}$ and let $\mathfrak{M} = \langle \mathfrak{J}, U \rangle$ be any model. We say that $\mathfrak{M} \models \varphi$, if $\mathfrak{M} \models \varphi\,[i]$ holds for every $i \in J$. We say that $\mathfrak{J} \models \varphi$, if $\mathfrak{M} \models \varphi$ holds for every valuation U.

Let S be any set of formulas. We say that $S \models \varphi$ if $\mathfrak{J} \models \varphi$ holds for any structure $\mathfrak{J}$ such that $\mathfrak{J} \models S$.

We have stated in section 2.1.4 that in the linear case the interval structure PAIR($\mathfrak{T}$) satisfies all the axioms of the theory T_A from section 2.2.2. We can obtain a definition of satisfiability of formulas based on Allen & Hayes's structure $\mathfrak{J} = \langle J, \| \rangle$ applying definitions of the relations $\sqsubset_B$ and $\sqsubset_E$ presented in section 2.2.4. Then e.g. the definition of satisfiability for the operator $[B]$ would be the following:

$$\mathfrak{M} \models [B]\,\varphi\,[i] \quad \text{iff} \quad \mathfrak{M} \models \varphi\,[j] \text{ holds for every } j \text{ such that there exist } k,l,m$$
$$\text{such that } (k \parallel i \,\&\, i \parallel m) \,\&\, (k \parallel j \,\&\, j \parallel l \,\&\, l \parallel m).$$

Note, that in this case only the operators $[A]$ and $[\bar{A}]$ are directly connected with the considered structure—the remaining ones require auxiliary variables. On the other hand, a logic composed only of the operators $[A]$ and $[\bar{A}]$ is not expressive enough, and it would be impossible to distinguish its basic axiomatization from that of point time in section 3.1.1 (with G as $[A]$ and H as $[\bar{A}]$). Evidently this axiomatization could not be complete for any of the above semantics.

It should be noted that the semantics based on the structures $\mathfrak{S}$ and $\mathfrak{J}$ concerns only structure of "normal" convex intervals, because their theories are the only first order theories we have.

The logic under discussion has been formulated for structures satisfying the condition of atomicity. The atoms are intervals that have no initial nor terminal subintervals. Thus the formulas $[B]\,false$ and $[E]\,false$ are satisfied in atoms. We can therefore define the following additional operators:

$$[\![BP]\!]\varphi \equiv_{def} (\varphi \;\&\; [B]\,false) \vee \langle B\rangle\,(\varphi \;\&\; [B]\,false),$$

$$[\![EP]\!]\varphi \equiv_{def} (\varphi \;\&\; [E]\,false) \vee \langle E\rangle\,(\varphi \;\&\; [E]\,false).$$

meaning, that a formula φ is satisfied in the atom initiating (terminating) a particular interval. Note, that these operators are their own duals: $[\![BP]\!]\,\varphi \leftrightarrow \neg[\![BP]\!]\,\neg\varphi$, since there always exists exactly one relevant atom. In this case, also the operators $[A]$ and $[\bar{A}]$ can be defined by means of the remaining operators, similarly as the relation $\|$ was defined by means of the relations C_B and C_E in section 2.2.4. Venema (1988; 1990) presents the following definition of these operators:

$$\langle A\rangle\,\varphi \equiv_{def} [\![EP]\!]\,\langle \bar{B}\rangle\,\varphi,$$
$$\langle \bar{A}\rangle\,\varphi \equiv_{def} [\![BP]\!]\,\langle \bar{E}\rangle\,\varphi.$$

We have detected a kind of asymmetry in this definition, as shown in fig. 3.6. Under such a definition theorem 3.2.2.2 would not hold. Actually, this asymmetry is contained already in the original Halpern & Shoham's semantics. Note, that this asymmetry is caused by the same phenomenon that makes impossible in section 4.3.6 to represent points as atomic intervals. Since, in fact, genuine pointwise intervals cannot meet and be met by any other interval, the above definition of the operators can be simply modified to:

$$[A]\,\varphi \equiv_{def} [E]\,([\bar{B}]\,\varphi \vee \langle E\rangle\,true),$$
$$[\bar{A}]\,\varphi \equiv_{def} [B]\,([\bar{E}]\,\varphi \vee \langle B\rangle\,true).$$

Fig. 3.6. Asymmetry in the old definition of operators $\langle A\rangle$ and $\langle \bar{A}\rangle$

Axiomatization

Halpern & Shoham have not presented any axiomatization for their logic. The only axiomatization we know was proposed by Venema (1988; 1990) for the case of atomic interval time. We will present it here. This axiomatization, too, can be treated as a variation of the deductive system **K** for modal logic, nevertheless it has nothing in common with K_i. In what follows we will use the denotation K_S (the author uses L_{itv}).

The basic set of axioms is the same as for any multimodal logic.

Axioms

- S1 $\varphi \rightarrow (\psi \rightarrow \varphi)$,
- S2 $(\varphi \rightarrow (\psi \rightarrow \chi)) \rightarrow ((\varphi \rightarrow \psi) \rightarrow (\varphi \rightarrow \chi))$,
- S3 $(\neg\varphi \rightarrow \neg\psi) \rightarrow (\psi \rightarrow \varphi)$,
- S4 $[R](\varphi \rightarrow \psi) \rightarrow ([R]\varphi \rightarrow [R]\psi)$,
- S5 $[\bar{R}](\varphi \rightarrow \psi) \rightarrow ([\bar{R}]\varphi \rightarrow [\bar{R}]\psi)$,
- S6 $\varphi \rightarrow [R]\langle\bar{R}\rangle\varphi$,
- S7 $\varphi \rightarrow [\bar{R}]\langle R\rangle\varphi$.

Rules of inference

- $$\frac{\varphi,\ \varphi \rightarrow \psi}{\psi},$$

- $$\frac{\varphi}{[R]\varphi},$$ $$\frac{\varphi}{[\bar{R}]\varphi},$$

where $R = A,\ B,\ E$ and $\bar{R} = \bar{A},\ \bar{B},\ \bar{E}$ (or $R = B,\ E$ and $\bar{R} = \bar{B},\ \bar{E}$ only).

The above axiomatization can be treated as a minimal axiomatization for the structure $\mathfrak{J} = \langle J,\ \|,\ C_B,\ C_E \rangle$. Then the relations $\|$, C_B and C_E should be considered completely independent. In this case the axiomatization is certainly sound and complete. However, the above axiomatization is evidently not sufficient for the structure $\mathfrak{S}$. The axiomatization appropriate for this case was suggested by Venema (1988; 1990).

- S8 $[B]\varphi \rightarrow [B][B]\varphi$,
- S9 $[E]\varphi \rightarrow [E][E]\varphi$,
- S10 $\langle B\rangle[B]false \vee [B]false$,

- S11 $\langle E \rangle [E] \, false \ \vee \ [E] \, false$,

- S12 $[B] \, false \ \leftrightarrow \ [E] \, false$,

- S13 $[B][E] \varphi \ \leftrightarrow \ [E][B] \varphi$,

- S14 $[\bar{E}][B] \varphi \ \rightarrow \ [B][\bar{E}] \varphi$,

- S15 $\langle B \rangle \varphi \ \& \ \langle B \rangle \psi \ \rightarrow$
  $$(\langle B \rangle (\varphi \ \& \ \langle B \rangle \psi) \ \vee \ \langle B \rangle (\varphi \ \& \ \psi) \ \vee \ \langle B \rangle (\langle B \rangle \varphi \ \& \ \psi)),$$

- S16 $\langle E \rangle \varphi \ \& \ \langle E \rangle \psi \ \rightarrow$
  $$(\langle E \rangle (\varphi \ \& \ \langle E \rangle \psi) \ \vee \ \langle E \rangle (\varphi \ \& \ \psi) \ \vee \ \langle E \rangle (\langle E \rangle \varphi \ \& \ \psi)).$$

Venema stated that two additional rules of inference are needed:

$$\bullet \ \frac{(p \ \& \ \langle \bar{E} \rangle p \ \& \ \langle \bar{E} \rangle \langle B \rangle \neg p \ \& \ \langle \bar{B} \rangle (\neg p \ \& \ \langle E \rangle \neg p \ \& \ \langle \bar{E} \rangle \neg p)) \ \rightarrow \ \varphi}{\varphi},$$

$$\bullet \ \frac{(p \ \& \ \langle \bar{B} \rangle p \ \& \ \langle \bar{B} \rangle \langle E \rangle \neg p \ \& \ \langle \bar{E} \rangle (\neg p \ \& \ \langle B \rangle \neg p \ \& \ \langle \bar{B} \rangle \neg p)) \ \rightarrow \ \varphi}{\varphi},$$

provided p does not occur in φ.

DEFINITION

A formula φ is K_S-*derivable* (notation: $\vdash_{K_S} \varphi$), if there exists a finite sequence of formulas ending with φ such that each formula in the sequence either is an axiom in K_S, or is derived from the preceding formulas by an application of some rule of inference.

Theorem 3.2.2.1. For any formula φ we have $\vdash_{K_S} \varphi$ iff for every model $\mathfrak{M} = \langle T, \ J, \ <, \ U \rangle$ (or $\mathfrak{M} = \langle \ J, \ \|, \ \mathsf{C}_B, \ \mathsf{C}_E, \ U \ \rangle$ satisfying axioms V1–V8 presented in section 2.2.4) $\mathfrak{M} \models \varphi$ holds.

The proof of the theorem can be found in Venema (1988; 1990).

Perhaps the difference between axioms S13 and S14 is worth attention. The reason why the implication has only one direction in the latter is shown in fig. 3.7.

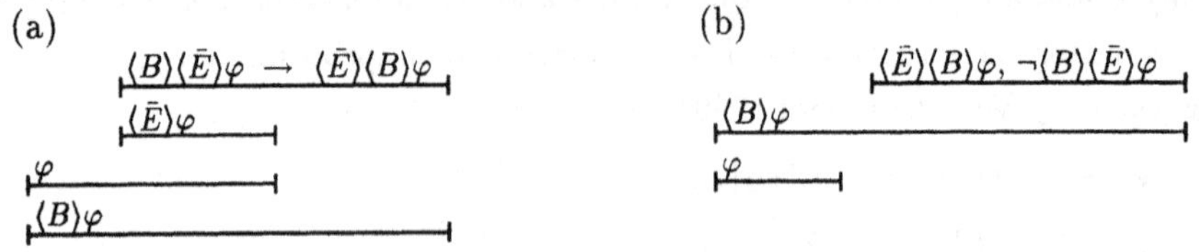

(a)   (b)

$\langle B \rangle \langle \bar{E} \rangle \varphi \ \rightarrow \ \langle \bar{E} \rangle \langle B \rangle \varphi$ $\langle \bar{E} \rangle \langle B \rangle \varphi, \ \neg \langle B \rangle \langle \bar{E} \rangle \varphi$

$\langle \bar{E} \rangle \varphi$ $\langle B \rangle \varphi$

φ φ

$\langle B \rangle \varphi$

Fig. 3.7. Graphical interpretation of axiom S14

Note also that some axioms only refer to structures of "normal" intervals. This is the case of axiom S16 (see fig. 3.8) and, for structures with partial order, also axiom S15 (the case is symmetrical to that presented in the figure). The consideration of these two axioms is justified, as both semantics of the logic are based on structures of "normal" intervals.

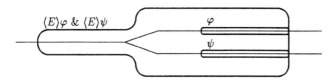

Fig. 3.8. An example of position of intervals which do not satisfy axiom S16

The operators $[A]$ and $[\bar{A}]$ not being primitive symbols of the logic, we want to show that axioms S4–S7 and the generalization rule are valid for them.

Theorem 3.2.2.2. Axioms S4–S7 and the generalization rule used for the operators $[A]$ and $[\bar{A}]$ are theorems (is a rule of inference) of the system K_S.

Proof

- S4 $[E]([\bar{B}](\varphi \to \psi) \vee \langle E\rangle true) \to$
  $([E]([\bar{B}]\varphi \vee \langle E\rangle true) \to [E]([\bar{B}]\psi \vee \langle E\rangle true))$

  Suppose that $\mathfrak{M} \models [E]([\bar{B}](\varphi \to \psi) \vee \langle E\rangle true)[\langle t,t'\rangle]$. Thus for every t_1 such that $t < t_1 \le t'$ we have $\mathfrak{M} \models ([\bar{B}](\varphi \to \psi) \vee \langle E\rangle true)[\langle t_1,t'\rangle]$. If $\mathfrak{M} \models \langle E\rangle true [\langle t_1,t'\rangle]$, then $\mathfrak{M} \models [E]\langle E\rangle true [\langle t_1,t'\rangle]$, and the implication is satisfied in a trivial way. Otherwise $\mathfrak{M} \models [\bar{B}](\varphi \to \psi)[\langle t_1,t'\rangle]$. Therefore by S5 $\mathfrak{M} \models ([\bar{B}]\varphi \to [\bar{B}\psi)[\langle t_1,t'\rangle]$. This means that if $\mathfrak{M} \models ([\bar{B}]\varphi \vee \langle E\rangle true)[\langle t_1,t'\rangle]$, then $\mathfrak{M} \models ([\bar{B}]\psi \vee \langle E\rangle true)[\langle t_1,t'\rangle]$. Therefore if $\mathfrak{M} \models [E]([\bar{B}]\varphi \vee \langle E\rangle true)[\langle t_1,t'\rangle]$, then $\mathfrak{M} \models [E]([\bar{B}]\psi \vee \langle E\rangle true)[\langle t_1,t'\rangle]$.

- S5 $[B]([\bar{E}](\varphi \to \psi) \vee \langle B\rangle true) \to$
  $([B]([\bar{E}]\varphi \vee \langle B\rangle true) \to [B]([\bar{E}]\psi \vee \langle B\rangle true))$

  The reasoning is analogous.

- S6 $\varphi \to [E]([\bar{B}]\langle B\rangle(\langle\bar{E}\rangle\varphi \,\&\, [B]false) \vee \langle E\rangle true)$
  Suppose that $\mathfrak{M} \models \varphi[\langle t,t'\rangle]$. Then by S6 $\mathfrak{M} \models [E]\langle\bar{E}\rangle\varphi[\langle t,t'\rangle]$. This means that for every t_1 such that $t < t_1 \le t'$ we have $\mathfrak{M} \models \langle\bar{E}\rangle\varphi[\langle t_1,t'\rangle]$. Since $\mathfrak{M} \models true [\langle t',t'\rangle]$, then if $t_1 < t' \le t'$ then $\mathfrak{M} \models \langle E\rangle true [\langle t_1,t'\rangle]$, and consequently $\mathfrak{M} \models [E]\langle E\rangle true [\langle t,t'\rangle]$. Otherwise $t_1 = t'$ and $\mathfrak{M} \models [E]false [\langle t',t'\rangle]$. Thus by S12 $\mathfrak{M} \models [B]false [\langle t',t'\rangle]$. We have

$\mathfrak{M} \models \langle \bar{E} \rangle \varphi \, [\langle t', t' \rangle]$. Therefore by S7 $\mathfrak{M} \models [\bar{B}] \langle B \rangle \langle \bar{E} \rangle \varphi \, [\langle t', t' \rangle]$. Thus for every t_2 such that $t' < t_2$, $\mathfrak{M} \models \langle B \rangle \langle \bar{E} \rangle \varphi [\langle t', t_2 \rangle]$ holds. On the other hand $\mathfrak{M} \models \langle \bar{E} \rangle \varphi \, [\langle t', t' \rangle]$ and $\mathfrak{M} \models [B] \, false \, [\langle t', t' \rangle]$ hold, hence $\mathfrak{M} \models \langle B \rangle (\langle \bar{E} \rangle \varphi \ \& \ [B] \, false) \, [\langle t', t_2 \rangle]$. Thus $\mathfrak{M} \models [\bar{B}] \langle B \rangle (\langle \bar{E} \rangle \varphi \ \& \ [B] \, false) \, [\langle t', t' \rangle]$, so $\mathfrak{M} \models ([\bar{B}] \langle B \rangle (\langle \bar{E} \rangle \varphi \ \& \ [B] \, false) \vee \langle E \rangle true) [\langle t_1, t' \rangle]$. Eventually we have $\mathfrak{M} \models [E]([\bar{B}] \langle B \rangle (\langle \bar{E} \rangle \varphi \ \& \ [B] \, false) \vee \langle E \rangle true) \, [\langle t_1, t' \rangle]$.

- S7 $\varphi \ \rightarrow \ [B] ([\bar{E}] \langle E \rangle (\langle \bar{B} \rangle \varphi \ \& \ [E] \, false) \vee \langle B \rangle true)$

  The reasoning is analogous.

- $$\frac{\varphi}{[E]([\bar{B}] \varphi \vee \langle E \rangle true)}$$

  Assume that $\mathfrak{M} \models \varphi$. Then by the generalization rule $\mathfrak{M} \models [\bar{B}] \varphi$, and hence obviously $\mathfrak{M} \models ([\bar{B}] \varphi \vee \langle E \rangle true)$. Therefore by the generalization rule we have $\mathfrak{M} \models [E] ([\bar{B}] \varphi \vee \langle E \rangle true)$.

- $$\frac{\varphi}{[B]([\bar{E}] \varphi \vee \langle B \rangle true)}$$

  The reasoning is analogous.   ∎

Axioms S8 and S9 can be interpreted as the property of transitivity for the relations of initial and terminal inclusion. The property of transitivity of the precedence relation is satisfied in a similar way, even though this relation is not directly represented in any of the considered semantics.

Theorem 3.2.2.3. The condition $[A] [A] \varphi \ \rightarrow \ [A] [A] [A] \varphi$ holds in every model $\mathfrak{M}$ of Halpern & Shoham's logic.

Proof

Suppose that for a particular $\langle t, t' \rangle$ we have $\mathfrak{M} \models (\langle A \rangle \langle A \rangle \langle A \rangle \neg \varphi) \, [\langle t, t' \rangle]$. This means that $\mathfrak{M} \models \langle E \rangle (\langle \bar{B} \rangle \langle E \rangle (\langle \bar{B} \rangle \langle E \rangle (\langle \bar{B} \rangle \neg \varphi \ \& \ [E] \, false) \ \& \ [E] \, false) \ \& \ [E] \, false) \, [\langle t, t' \rangle]$. Thus there exists t_1 such that $t < t_1 \leq t'$ and $\mathfrak{M} \models (\langle \bar{B} \rangle \langle E \rangle (\langle \bar{B} \rangle \langle E \rangle (\langle \bar{B} \rangle \neg \varphi \ \& \ [E] \, false) \ \& \ [E] \, false) \ \& \ [E] \, false) \, [\langle t_1, t' \rangle]$ holds. Then there exists t_2 such that $t' < t_2$ and $\mathfrak{M} \models \langle E \rangle (\langle \bar{B} \rangle \langle E \rangle (\langle \bar{B} \rangle \neg \varphi \ \& \ [E] \, false) \ \& \ [E] \, false) \, [\langle t_1, t_2 \rangle]$ holds. Thus by S14 and fact 2.3.2.1 we have $\mathfrak{M} \models \langle \bar{B} \rangle \langle E \rangle \langle E \rangle (\langle \bar{B} \rangle \neg \varphi \ \& \ [E] \, false) \, [\langle t_1, t_2 \rangle]$. Then there exists t_3 such that $t_2 < t_3$ and $\mathfrak{M} \models \langle E \rangle \langle E \rangle (\langle \bar{B} \rangle \neg \varphi \ \& \ [E] \, false) \, [\langle t_1, t_3 \rangle]$. Therefore by S9 we have $\mathfrak{M} \models \langle E \rangle (\langle \bar{B} \rangle \neg \varphi \ \& \ [E] \, false) \, [\langle t_1, t_3 \rangle]$, hence $\mathfrak{M} \models \langle \bar{B} \rangle \langle E \rangle (\langle \bar{B} \rangle \neg \varphi \ \& \ [E] \, false) \, [\langle t_1, t_2 \rangle]$ and $\mathfrak{M} \models \langle \bar{B} \rangle \langle \bar{B} \rangle \langle E \rangle (\langle \bar{B} \rangle \neg \varphi \ \& \ [E] \, false) \, [\langle t_1, t' \rangle]$ hold. Then by S8 and fact 2.3.2.1 $\mathfrak{M} \models \langle \bar{B} \rangle \langle E \rangle (\langle \bar{B} \rangle \neg \varphi \ \& \ [E] \, false) \, [\langle t_1, t' \rangle]$. Since furthermore $\mathfrak{M} \models [E] \, false \, [\langle t, t' \rangle]$, so $\mathfrak{M} \models \langle E \rangle (\langle \bar{B} \rangle \langle E \rangle (\langle \bar{B} \rangle \neg \varphi \ \& \ [E] \, false) \ \& \ [E] \, false) \, [\langle t, t' \rangle]$, and hence $\mathfrak{M} \models \langle A \rangle \langle A \rangle \neg \varphi \, [\langle t, t' \rangle]$ holds.   ∎

Moreover, for our further reasoning, we need a fact that holds for any (K_t-like) multimodal temporal logics, independently from its semantics.

Fact 3.2.2.1. For any sequence of pairs of mutually inverse operators $[R_1]$ and $[\bar{R}_1]$, $[R_2]$ and $[\bar{R}_2]$, ... $[R_1]\{[R_2]\}\varphi \rightarrow [R_3]\{[R_4]\}\varphi$ is a theorem of the corresponding deductive system if and only if $\{[\bar{R}_2]\}[\bar{R}_1]\varphi \rightarrow \{[\bar{R}_4]\}[\bar{R}_3]\varphi$ is a theorem of this system.

Finally, we want to consider two important properties of time structures that are not consequences of the above axiomatization. The first is infinity of time, and it can be imposed by the following axioms:

- $SSUCC$ $[A]\varphi \rightarrow \langle A \rangle \varphi$

  $[\bar{A}]\varphi \rightarrow \langle \bar{A} \rangle \varphi$.

The second is linearity of time. In fact, as in the case of extended tense logic, this condition cannot be formulated. Nevertheless, we can formulate the conditions of left and right linearity. They are defined in a natural way by: $\langle A \rangle \langle \bar{A} \rangle \varphi \rightarrow (\varphi \lor \langle E \rangle \varphi \lor \langle \bar{E} \rangle \varphi)$ and $\langle \bar{A} \rangle \langle A \rangle \varphi \rightarrow (\varphi \lor \langle B \rangle \varphi \lor \langle \bar{B} \rangle \varphi)$. Since, however, the operators $\langle A \rangle$ and $\langle \bar{A} \rangle$ are derived operators in the considered system, Venema considers linearity axioms based on the operators $\langle \bar{B} \rangle$ and $\langle \bar{E} \rangle$, (dual to "normality" axioms S15 and S16). It turns out that this property can be expressed by means of these operators in a way very close to the previous one (see fig. 3.9).

- SL_LIN $\langle E \rangle \langle \bar{E} \rangle \varphi \rightarrow (\varphi \lor \langle E \rangle \varphi \lor \langle \bar{E} \rangle \varphi)$,

- SR_LIN $\langle B \rangle \langle \bar{B} \rangle \varphi \rightarrow (\varphi \lor \langle B \rangle \varphi \lor \langle \bar{B} \rangle \varphi)$.

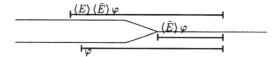

Fig. 3.9. A structure that does not satisfy the axiom SL_LIN

Theorem 3.2.2.4. The axioms SL_LIN, SR_LIN entail formulas $\langle A \rangle \langle \bar{A} \rangle \varphi \rightarrow (\varphi \lor \langle E \rangle \varphi \lor \langle \bar{E} \rangle \varphi)$ and $\langle \bar{A} \rangle \langle A \rangle \varphi \rightarrow (\varphi \lor \langle B \rangle \varphi \lor \langle \bar{B} \rangle \varphi)$, respectively.

Proof

Suppose that $\mathfrak{M} \models \langle A \rangle \langle \bar{A} \rangle \varphi [\langle t, t' \rangle]$. This means that by definition of $\langle A \rangle$ and $\langle \bar{A} \rangle$ we have $\mathfrak{M} \models \langle E \rangle (\langle \bar{B} \rangle \langle B \rangle (\langle \bar{E} \rangle \varphi \,\&\, [B]\,false) \,\&\, [E]\,false) [\langle t, t' \rangle]$. Thus there exists t_1 such that $t < t_1 \le t'$ and $\mathfrak{M} \models (\langle \bar{B} \rangle \langle B \rangle (\langle \bar{E} \rangle \varphi \,\&\, [B]\,false) \,\&\, [E]\,false)$ $[\langle t_1, t' \rangle]$. Suppose that $t_1 < t'$. Then $t_1 < t' \le t'$ and $\mathfrak{M} \models true\,[\langle t', t' \rangle]$, hence $\mathfrak{M} \models \langle E \rangle\,true\,[\langle t', t' \rangle]$. Contradiction. Therefore $t_1 = t'$. Then there exists t_2 such that $t' < t_2$ and $\mathfrak{M} \models \langle B \rangle (\langle \bar{E} \rangle \varphi \,\&\, [B]\,false) [\langle t', t_2 \rangle]$. Moreover, there exists t_3 such that $t' \le t_3 < t_2$ and $\mathfrak{M} \models (\langle \bar{E} \rangle \varphi \,\&\, [B]\,false) [\langle t', t_3 \rangle]$. Similarly, we can show that $t' = t_3$. Hence we have $\mathfrak{M} \models \langle E \rangle \langle \bar{E} \rangle \varphi [\langle t, t' \rangle]$. Therefore by SL_LIN we have $\mathfrak{M} \models (\varphi \lor \langle E \rangle \varphi \lor \langle \bar{E} \rangle \varphi) [\langle t, t' \rangle]$.

For the second case the reasoning is analogous. ∎

3.2.3 Comparison of extended tense logic and Halpern & Shoham's logic

As in the case of description of time structures by means of first order theories, a comparison of different modal temporal logics of interval time seems to be important and interesting, too. We are now interested in the extended tense logic and Halpern & Shoham's logic, The more so as the semantics of both logics are based on two different time structures presented in section 2.2, and the first order theories describing them turned to be equivalent for linear structures of convex intervals.

Analogously as for first order theories, such a comparison can be performed by translating one logic into the other. Unfortunately, it is not possible to formulate such a translation of Halpern & Shoham's logic into extended tense logic. This can be shown on an example. Consider the following formula:

$$\langle A \rangle true \ \lor \ \langle A \rangle \langle A \rangle true \ \rightarrow \ \langle A \rangle true.$$

Its semantic counterpart in Allen & Hayes's (and Venema's) theory is:

$$\forall i \ [(\exists j \ (i \parallel j) \ \lor \ \exists j, k \ (i \parallel j \ \& \ j \parallel k)) \ \rightarrow \ \exists j \ (i \parallel j)].$$

In [Hajnicz, 1991c; 1994a] translations of the axioms of Allen & Hayes's theory into the classic theory are presented and it is shown that the above formula is equivalent to the classic axiom *NEIGH*. On the other hand, van Benthem (1982) shows that this axiom cannot be expressed in extended tense logic (the axiom *NEIGH** presented in section 3.2.1 is another, stronger formula).

Therefore, we are not able to perform this translation, since otherwise we would be able to express the above formula (and hence the axiom *NEIGH*) in extended tense logic.

Also other conditions, which cannot be expressed in extended tense logic, can be formulated in Halpern & Shoham's logic. For instant, we are able to formulate the conditions *CONJ* and *DISJ* for linear structures.

$$\langle B \rangle \langle E \rangle \langle \bar{E} \rangle \langle \bar{B} \rangle \varphi \ \rightarrow \ \varphi \ \lor \ \langle B \rangle \varphi \ \lor \ \langle \bar{B} \rangle \varphi \ \lor \ \langle E \rangle \varphi \ \lor \ \langle \bar{E} \rangle \varphi \ \lor$$
$$\langle B \rangle \langle E \rangle \varphi \ \lor \ \langle \bar{B} \rangle \langle \bar{E} \rangle \varphi \ \lor \ \langle B \rangle \langle \bar{E} \rangle \varphi \ \lor \ \langle E \rangle \langle \bar{B} \rangle \varphi$$

$$\langle \bar{B} \rangle \langle \bar{E} \rangle \langle E \rangle \langle B \rangle \varphi \ \rightarrow \ \varphi \ \lor \ \langle B \rangle \varphi \ \lor \ \langle \bar{B} \rangle \varphi \ \lor \ \langle E \rangle \varphi \ \lor \ \langle \bar{E} \rangle \varphi \ \lor$$
$$\langle B \rangle \langle E \rangle \varphi \ \lor \ \langle \bar{B} \rangle \langle \bar{E} \rangle \varphi \ \lor \ \langle \bar{B} \rangle \langle E \rangle \varphi \ \lor \ \langle \bar{E} \rangle \langle B \rangle \varphi$$

These formulas (as a matter of fact their antecedents) are presented in figs. 3.10 and 3.11. It is quite easy to choose a relevant component of the consequent for each case, and we do not want to complicate the picture. These antecedents do not impose linearity of a structure (as figures seem to suggest) by any means, but for non-linear time consequents are not definable (see fig. 3.12). Note the essential symmetry between these formulas. Their consequents differ very insignificantly.

But in the case of formulas of the form $\langle B \rangle\, \varphi$, $\langle \bar{B} \rangle\, \varphi$, $\langle E \rangle\, \varphi$, $\langle \bar{E} \rangle\, \varphi$, $\langle B \rangle\, \langle E \rangle\, \varphi$, $\langle \bar{B} \rangle\, \langle \bar{E} \rangle\, \varphi$ one of the intervals i, j is their intersection, and the second is their union, hence these formulas are relevant for both cases. The essential difference lies in the remaining two cases, which follows from the asymmetry of axiom S14.

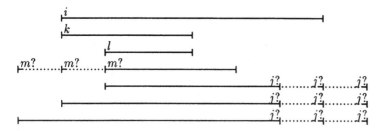

Fig. 3.10. Graphical interpretation of the property *CONJ*

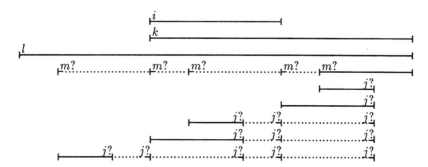

Fig. 3.11. Graphical interpretation of the property *DISJ*

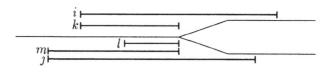

Fig. 3.12. An example of antecedent of *CONJ* for non-linear time

Now we ought to show that the above formulas are valid in Halpern & Shoham's logic.

Theorem 3.2.3.1. The conditions *NEIGH*, *CONJ* and *DISJ* presented above are valid in every model $\mathfrak{M}$ of Halpern & Shoham's logic (for linear time).
Proof

- *NEIGH*

  Consider any interval $\langle t, t' \rangle$. The case, when $\mathfrak{M} \models \langle A \rangle\, true\, [\langle t, t' \rangle]$ is trivial. Otherwise $\mathfrak{M} \models (\langle A \rangle\, \langle A \rangle\, true)[\langle t, t' \rangle]$. This means that there exists t'' such that $t' < t''$ and $\mathfrak{M} \models \langle A \rangle\, true\, [\langle t', t'' \rangle]$. Evidently $\mathfrak{M} \models true[\langle t', t'' \rangle]$, so by definition of $\langle A \rangle$ we have $\mathfrak{M} \models \langle A \rangle\, true\, [\langle t, t' \rangle]$.

- *CONJ*

  Let $\mathfrak{M} \models \langle B \rangle \langle E \rangle \langle \bar{E} \rangle \langle \bar{B} \rangle\, \varphi[\langle t, t' \rangle]$. This means that there exists t_1 such that $t < t_1 < t'$ and $\mathfrak{M} \models \langle E \rangle \langle \bar{E} \rangle \langle \bar{B} \rangle\, \varphi[\langle t, t_1 \rangle]$. Thus by *SL_LIN* we have $\mathfrak{M} \models (\langle \bar{B} \rangle\, \varphi \ \vee \ \langle E \rangle \langle \bar{B} \rangle\, \varphi \ \vee \ \langle \bar{E} \rangle \langle \bar{B} \rangle\, \varphi)[\langle t, t_1 \rangle]$, hence $\mathfrak{M} \models \langle B \rangle (\langle \bar{B} \rangle\, \varphi \ \vee \ \langle E \rangle \langle \bar{B} \rangle\, \varphi \ \vee \ \langle \bar{E} \rangle \langle \bar{B} \rangle\, \varphi) [\langle t, t' \rangle]$. This means that we have $\mathfrak{M} \models (\langle B \rangle \langle \bar{B} \rangle\, \varphi \ \vee \ \langle B \rangle \langle E \rangle \langle \bar{B} \rangle\, \varphi \ \vee \ \langle B \rangle \langle \bar{E} \rangle \langle \bar{B} \rangle\, \varphi) [\langle t, t' \rangle]$.

  If $\mathfrak{M} \models \langle B \rangle \langle \bar{B} \rangle\, \varphi\, [\langle t, t' \rangle]$, then by *SR_LIN* we have $\mathfrak{M} \models (\varphi \ \vee \ \langle B \rangle\, \varphi \ \vee \ \langle \bar{B} \rangle\, \varphi)\, [\langle t, t' \rangle]$, so the thesis is satisfied. If $\mathfrak{M} \models \langle B \rangle \langle E \rangle \langle \bar{B} \rangle\, \varphi[\langle t, t' \rangle]$, then by S13 we have $\mathfrak{M} \models \langle E \rangle \langle B \rangle \langle \bar{B} \rangle\, \varphi[\langle t, t' \rangle]$. Thus there exists t_2 such that $t < t_2 < t'$ and $\mathfrak{M} \models \langle B \rangle \langle \bar{B} \rangle\, \varphi[\langle t_2, t' \rangle]$. Therefore by *SR_LIN* we have $\mathfrak{M} \models (\varphi \ \vee \ \langle B \rangle\, \varphi \ \vee \ \langle \bar{B} \rangle\, \varphi)[\langle t_2, t' \rangle]$, hence $\mathfrak{M} \models (\langle E \rangle\, \varphi \ \vee \ \langle E \rangle \langle B \rangle\, \varphi \ \vee \ \langle E \rangle \langle \bar{B} \rangle\, \varphi)[\langle t, t' \rangle]$, so the thesis is satisfied. Otherwise $\mathfrak{M} \models \langle B \rangle \langle \bar{E} \rangle \langle \bar{B} \rangle\, \varphi\, [\langle t, t' \rangle]$ holds. This means that there exists t_3 such that $t < t_3 < t'$ and $\mathfrak{M} \models (\langle \bar{E} \rangle \langle \bar{B} \rangle\, \varphi)[\langle t, t' \rangle]$. Then by S13 and fact 3.2.2.1 we have $\mathfrak{M} \models (\langle \bar{B} \rangle \langle \bar{E} \rangle\, \varphi)[\langle t, t' \rangle]$, hence $\mathfrak{M} \models (\langle B \rangle \langle \bar{B} \rangle \langle \bar{E} \rangle\, \varphi)[\langle t, t' \rangle]$. This means by *SR_LIN* that $\mathfrak{M} \models (\langle \bar{E} \rangle\, \varphi \ \vee \ \langle B \rangle \langle \bar{E} \rangle\, \varphi \ \vee \ \langle \bar{B} \rangle \langle \bar{E} \rangle\, \varphi)[\langle t, t' \rangle]$, hence the thesis is satisfied.

- *DISJ*

  The reasoning is analogous.   ∎

Eventually, we only present a translation of extended tense logic into Halpern & Shoham's logic. A method of constructing the translation will be similar as for the first order theories in section 2.2.4.

Let $\varrho \colon X \longrightarrow Y$ be a function mapping the set of variables of extended tense logic onto the set of variables of Halpern & Shoham's logic. We define a function $\xi \colon \mathcal{G} \longrightarrow \mathcal{H}$ in the following way:

$$\xi(p) \quad = \quad \varrho(p) \qquad \text{for } p \in X,$$

$$\xi(\neg\varphi) \quad = \quad \neg\xi(\varphi),$$

$$\xi(\varphi \rightarrow \psi) \quad = \quad \xi(\varphi) \rightarrow \xi(\psi),$$

$$\xi(\mathrm{G}\varphi) \quad = \quad [A]\,\xi(\varphi) \ \& \ [A]\,[A]\,\xi(\varphi),$$

$$\xi(\mathrm{H}\varphi) \quad = \quad [\bar{A}]\,\xi(\varphi) \ \& \ [\bar{A}]\,[\bar{A}]\,\xi(\varphi),$$

$$\xi(\Box\varphi) \quad = \quad \xi(\varphi) \ \& \ [B]\,\xi(\varphi) \ \& \ [E]\,\xi(\varphi) \ \& \ [B]\,[E]\,\xi(\varphi),$$

$$\xi(\boxtimes\varphi) \quad = \quad \xi(\varphi) \ \& \ [\bar{B}]\,\xi(\varphi) \ \& \ [\bar{E}]\,\xi(\varphi) \ \& \ [\bar{E}]\,[\bar{B}]\,\xi(\varphi).$$

It is easy to show that:

$$\xi(\mathsf{F}\varphi) \;=\; \xi(\neg\mathsf{G}\neg\varphi) \;=\; \langle A\rangle\,\xi(\varphi) \;\vee\; \langle A\rangle\,\langle A\rangle\,\xi(\varphi),$$

$$\xi(\mathsf{P}\varphi) \;=\; \xi(\neg\mathsf{H}\neg\varphi) \;=\; \langle \bar{A}\rangle\,\xi(\varphi) \;\vee\; \langle \bar{A}\rangle\,\langle \bar{A}\rangle\,\xi(\varphi),$$

$$\xi(\Diamond\varphi) \;=\; \xi(\neg\Box\neg\varphi) \;=\; \xi(\varphi) \;\vee\; \langle B\rangle\,\xi(\varphi) \;\vee\; \langle E\rangle\,\xi(\varphi) \;\vee\; \langle E\rangle\,\langle B\rangle\,\xi(\varphi),$$

$$\xi(\spadesuit\varphi) \;=\; \xi(\neg\boxtimes\neg\varphi) \;=\; \xi(\varphi) \;\vee\; \langle \bar{B}\rangle\,\xi(\varphi) \;\vee\; \langle \bar{E}\rangle\,\xi(\varphi) \;\vee\; \langle \bar{E}\rangle\,\langle \bar{B}\rangle\,\xi(\varphi).$$

The remaining formulas are translated in an obvious way. Similarly as in the case of first order theories, we will not distinguish the standard logical symbols in both logics, their meaning being the same.

Expressing symbols of one logic in the other is not sufficient in itself—the validity of axioms and rules of inference is just as important. Therefore we need the following theorems.

Theorem 3.2.3.2. Translations of the basic axioms and rules of inference of extended tense logic K_i are theorems (rules of inference) of Halpern & Shoham's logic K_S.

Proof

Since propositional variables of Halpern & Shoham's logic do not occur in definitions of translations, we take the liberty to omit the symbol ϱ in what follows.

- The axioms of the classic propositional calculus remain unchanged.
- $\xi(\mathsf{G}(\varphi \to \psi) \to (\mathsf{G}\varphi \to \mathsf{G}\psi)) =$
  $[A]\,(\varphi \to \psi)\;\&\;[A]\,[A]\,(\varphi \to \psi) \to ([A]\,\varphi\,\&\,[A]\,[A]\,\varphi \to [A]\,\psi\,\&\,[A]\,[A]\,\psi)$
  Suppose that $\mathfrak{M} \models ([A](\varphi \to \psi)\;\&\;[A][A](\varphi \to \psi))\,[\langle t,t'\rangle]$. Then
  $\mathfrak{M} \models [A](\varphi \to \psi)\,[\langle t,t'\rangle]$ and $\mathfrak{M} \models [A]\,[A]\,(\varphi \to \psi)\,[\langle t,t'\rangle]$ hold. Therefore
  by theorem 3.2.2.2 (S4), if $\mathfrak{M} \models [A]\,\varphi\,[\langle t,t'\rangle]$, then $\mathfrak{M} \models [A]\,\psi\,[\langle t,t'\rangle]$.
  Moreover for every t'' such that $t' < t''$ we have $\mathfrak{M} \models [A]\,(\varphi \to \psi)\,[\langle t',t''\rangle]$.
  Thus by theorem 3.2.2.2 (S4) if $\mathfrak{M} \models [A]\,\varphi\,[\langle t',t''\rangle]$, then $\mathfrak{M} \models [A]\,\psi\,[\langle t,t''\rangle]$.
  Thus if $\mathfrak{M} \models [A]\,[A]\,\varphi\,[\langle t,t'\rangle]$, then $\mathfrak{M} \models [A]\,[A]\,\psi\,[\langle t,t'\rangle]$. Eventually if
  $\mathfrak{M} \models ([A]\,\varphi\;\&\;[A]\,[A]\,\varphi)\,[\langle t,t'\rangle]$, then $\mathfrak{M} \models ([A]\,\varphi\;\&\;[A]\,[A]\,\varphi)\,[\langle t,t'\rangle]$.
- $\xi(\mathsf{H}(\varphi \to \psi) \to (\mathsf{H}\varphi \to \mathsf{H}\psi)) =$
  $[\bar{A}](\varphi \to \psi)\;\&\;[\bar{A}][\bar{A}](\varphi \to \psi) \to ([\bar{A}]\varphi\,\&\,[\bar{A}][\bar{A}]\varphi \to [\bar{A}]\psi\,\&\,[\bar{A}][\bar{A}]\psi)$
  The reasoning is analogous (with S5 applied instead of S4).
- $\xi(\Box(\varphi \to \psi) \to (\Box\varphi \to \Box\psi)) =$
  $(\varphi \to \psi)\;\&\;[B](\varphi \to \psi)\;\&\;[E](\varphi \to \psi)\;\&\;[B][E](\varphi \to \psi) \to$
  $((\varphi\,\&\,[B]\varphi\,\&\,[E]\varphi\,\&\,[B][E]\varphi) \to (\psi\,\&\,[B]\psi\,\&\,[E]\psi\,\&\,[B][E]\psi))$
  The reasoning is somehow longer, but still analogous: for $[B]$ and $[E]$ as for $[A]$, and for $[B]\,[E]$ as for $[A]\,[A]$.
- $\xi(\boxtimes(\varphi \to \psi) \to (\boxtimes\varphi \to \boxtimes\psi)) =$
  $(\varphi \to \psi)\;\&\;[\bar{B}](\varphi \to \psi)\;\&\;[\bar{E}](\varphi \to \psi)\;\&\;[\bar{B}][\bar{E}](\varphi \to \psi) \to$
  $((\varphi\,\&\,[\bar{B}]\varphi\,\&\,[\bar{E}]\varphi\,\&\,[\bar{B}][\bar{E}]\varphi) \to (\psi\,\&\,[\bar{B}]\psi\,\&\,[\bar{E}]\psi\,\&\,[\bar{B}][\bar{E}]\psi))$
  The reasoning is analogous.

- $\xi(\varphi \to \mathtt{GP}\varphi) = \varphi \to ([A]\,(\langle\bar{A}\rangle\varphi \vee \langle\bar{A}\rangle\langle\bar{A}\rangle\varphi) \,\&\, [A]\,[A]\,(\langle\bar{A}\rangle\varphi \vee \langle\bar{A}\rangle\langle\bar{A}\rangle\varphi))$
  Suppose that $\mathfrak{M} \models \varphi\,[\langle t,t'\rangle]$. Then by theorem 3.2.2.2 (S6) $\mathfrak{M} \models [A]\,\langle\bar{A}\rangle\,\varphi$ $[\langle t,t'\rangle]$. Thus for every t'' such that $t' < t''$, $\mathfrak{M} \models \langle\bar{A}\rangle\,\varphi\,[\langle t',t''\rangle]$. Then $\mathfrak{M} \models (\langle\bar{A}\rangle\,\varphi \vee \langle\bar{A}\rangle\,\langle\bar{A}\rangle\,\varphi)\,[\langle t',t''\rangle]$. Moreover, by theorem 3.2.2.2 (S6) $\mathfrak{M} \models [A]\,\langle\bar{A}\rangle\,\langle\bar{A}\rangle\,\varphi\,[\langle t',t''\rangle]$, hence for every t''' such that $t'' < t'''$ we have $\mathfrak{M} \models \langle\bar{A}\rangle\,\langle\bar{A}\rangle\,\varphi\,[\langle t'',t'''\rangle]$, so $\mathfrak{M} \models (\langle\bar{A}\rangle\,\varphi \vee \langle\bar{A}\rangle\,\langle\bar{A}\rangle\,\varphi)\,[\langle t'',t'''\rangle]$. Therefore $\mathfrak{M} \models [A]\,(\langle\bar{A}\rangle\,\varphi \vee \langle\bar{A}\rangle\,\langle\bar{A}\rangle\,\varphi)\,[\langle t',t''\rangle]$. Eventually $\mathfrak{M} \models ([A]\,(\langle\bar{A}\rangle\varphi \vee \langle\bar{A}\rangle\langle\bar{A}\rangle\varphi) \,\&\, [A]\,[A]\,(\langle\bar{A}\rangle\varphi \vee \langle\bar{A}\rangle\langle\bar{A}\rangle\varphi))\,[\langle t,t'\rangle]$.

- $\xi(\varphi \to \mathtt{HF}\varphi) = \varphi \to [\bar{A}](\langle A\rangle\varphi \vee \langle A\rangle\langle A\rangle\varphi) \,\&\, [\bar{A}][\bar{A}](\langle A\rangle\varphi \vee \langle A\rangle\langle A\rangle\varphi)$
  The reasoning is analogous.

- $\xi(\varphi \to \Box\diamondsuit\varphi) = \varphi \to (\alpha \,\&\, [B]\,\alpha \,\&\, [E]\,\alpha \,\&\, [B]\,[E]\,\alpha)$,
  where $\alpha = \varphi \vee \langle\bar{B}\rangle\varphi \vee \langle\bar{E}\rangle\varphi \vee \langle\bar{B}\rangle\langle\bar{E}\rangle\varphi$
  The reasoning is somehow longer, but analogous.

- $\xi(\varphi \to \boxtimes\diamondsuit\varphi) = \varphi \to (\alpha \,\&\, [\bar{B}]\,\alpha \,\&\, [\bar{E}]\,\alpha \,\&\, [\bar{B}]\,[\bar{E}]\,\alpha)$,
  where $\alpha = \varphi \vee \langle B\rangle\varphi \vee \langle E\rangle\varphi \vee \langle B\rangle\langle E\rangle\varphi$
  The reasoning is analogous.

We have already considered all the basic axioms of the logic, now we ought to consider the rules of inference, too.

- The modus ponens rule is valid.

- $\xi(\dfrac{\varphi}{\mathtt{G}\varphi}) = \dfrac{\varphi}{[A]\,\varphi \,\&\, [A]\,[A]\,\varphi}$

  Suppose that $\mathfrak{M} \models \varphi$. Then by the generalization rule $\mathfrak{M} \models [A]\,\varphi$ and $\mathfrak{M} \models [A]\,[A]\,\varphi$ hold. Therefore $\mathfrak{M} \models [A]\,\varphi \,\&\, [A]\,[A]\,\varphi$.

- $\xi(\dfrac{\varphi}{\mathtt{H}\varphi}) = \dfrac{\varphi}{[\bar{A}]\,\varphi \,\&\, [\bar{A}]\,[\bar{A}]\,\varphi}$

  The reasoning is analogous.

- $\xi(\dfrac{\varphi}{\Box\varphi}) = \dfrac{\varphi}{\varphi \,\&\, [B]\,\varphi \,\&\, [E]\,\varphi \,\&\, [B]\,[E]\,\varphi}$

  The reasoning is analogous.

- $\xi(\dfrac{\varphi}{\boxtimes\varphi}) = \dfrac{\varphi}{\varphi \,\&\, [\bar{B}]\,\varphi \,\&\, [\bar{E}]\,\varphi \,\&\, [\bar{B}]\,[\bar{E}]\,\varphi}$

  The reasoning is analogous.   ■

Theorem 3.2.3.3. Translations of the remaining axioms (characterizing properties of structures) of extended tense logic are satisfied in every model of Halpern & Shoham's logic (which satisfies relevant axioms).
Proof
Let $\mathfrak{M}$ be any model of Halpern & Shoham's logic.

- $\xi(P\_TRANS) =$
  $[A]\,p\,\&\,[A]\,[A]\,p \;\rightarrow\; [A]\,([A]\,p\,\&\,[A]\,[A]\,p)\,\&\,[A]\,[A]\,([A]\,p\,\&\,[A]\,[A]\,p)$
  The consequent of the implication is equivalent to the formula: $[A]\,[A]\,p\,\&$
  $[A]\,[A]\,[A]\,p\,\&\,[A]\,[A]\,[A]\,[A]\,p$. Suppose that $\mathfrak{M} \models [A]\,p\,\&\,[A]\,[A]\,p$. This
  means that $\mathfrak{M} \models [A]\,[A]\,p$ holds. Then by theorem 3.2.2.3 we have
  $\mathfrak{M} \models [A]\,[A]\,[A]\,p$ and $\mathfrak{M} \models [A]\,[A]\,[A]\,[A]\,p$. Therefore the consequent
  of the implication is satisfied.

- $\xi(I\_TRANS) =$
  $p\,\&\,[B]\,p\,\&\,[E]\,p\,\&\,[B]\,[E]\,p \;\rightarrow\; p\,\&\,[B]\,p\,\&\,[E]\,p\,\&\,[B]\,[E]\,p\,\&$
  $[B]\,(p\,\&\,[B]\,p\,\&\,[E]\,p\,\&\,[B]\,[E]\,p)\,\&\,[E]\,(p\,\&\,[B]\,p\,\&\,[E]\,p\,\&\,[B]\,[E]\,p)\,\&$
  $[B]\,[E]\,(p\,\&\,[B]\,p\,\&\,[E]\,p\,\&\,[B]\,[E]\,p)$
  Suppose that there exist t, t' such that the thesis is not satisfied, i.e.
  $\mathfrak{M} \models (\neg p \vee \langle B\rangle\neg p \vee \langle E\rangle\neg p \vee \langle B\rangle\langle E\rangle\neg p \vee \langle B\rangle\langle B\rangle\neg p \vee \langle E\rangle\langle E\rangle\neg p \vee$
  $\langle E\rangle\langle B\rangle\neg p \vee \langle B\rangle\langle B\rangle\langle E\rangle\neg p \vee \langle B\rangle\langle E\rangle\langle B\rangle\neg p \vee \langle E\rangle\langle B\rangle\langle E\rangle\neg p \vee$
  $\langle B\rangle\langle E\rangle\langle E\rangle\neg p \vee \langle B\rangle\langle E\rangle\langle B\rangle\langle E\rangle\neg p)\,[\langle t,t'\rangle]$. If $\mathfrak{M} \models (\neg p \vee \langle B\rangle\neg p \vee$
  $\langle E\rangle\neg p \vee \langle B\rangle\langle E\rangle\neg p)\,[\langle t,t'\rangle]$, then the antecedent of the implication is
  not satisfied in an obvious way. If $\mathfrak{M} \models \langle B\rangle\langle B\rangle\neg p\,[\langle t,t'\rangle]$, then by
  S8 we have $\mathfrak{M} \models \langle B\rangle\neg p\,[\langle t,t'\rangle]$, hence the antecedent of the implication is not satisfied. If $\mathfrak{M} \models \langle E\rangle\langle E\rangle\neg p\,[\langle t,t'\rangle]$, then by S9 we have
  $\mathfrak{M} \models \langle E\rangle\neg p\,[\langle t,t'\rangle]$, hence the antecedent of the implication is not satisfied.
  If $\mathfrak{M} \models \langle E\rangle\langle B\rangle\neg p\,[\langle t,t'\rangle]$, then by S13 we have $\mathfrak{M} \models \langle B\rangle\langle E\rangle\neg p\,[\langle t,t'\rangle]$, so
  the antecedent of the implication is not satisfied. If $\mathfrak{M} \models \langle B\rangle\langle B\rangle\langle E\rangle\neg p$
  $[\langle t,t'\rangle]$, then by S8 $\mathfrak{M} \models \langle B\rangle\langle E\rangle\neg p\,[\langle t,t'\rangle]$, hence the antecedent of the
  implication is not satisfied. If $\mathfrak{M} \models \langle B\rangle\langle E\rangle\langle B\rangle\neg p\,[\langle t,t'\rangle]$, then by S13 we
  have $\mathfrak{M} \models \langle E\rangle\langle B\rangle\langle B\rangle\neg p\,[\langle t,t'\rangle]$. Thus there exists t_1 such that $t < t_1 \le t'$
  and $\mathfrak{M} \models \langle B\rangle\langle B\rangle\neg p\,[\langle t_1,t'\rangle]$. Then by S8 $\mathfrak{M} \models \langle B\rangle\neg p\,[\langle t_1,t'\rangle]$, hence
  $\mathfrak{M} \models \langle E\rangle\langle B\rangle\neg p\,[\langle t,t'\rangle]$. Thus by S13 we have $\mathfrak{M} \models \langle B\rangle\langle E\rangle\neg p\,[\langle t,t'\rangle]$, so
  the antecedent of the implication is not satisfied. If $\mathfrak{M} \models \langle E\rangle\langle B\rangle\langle E\rangle\neg p$
  $[\langle t,t'\rangle]$, then the reasoning is analogous. If $\mathfrak{M} \models \langle B\rangle\langle E\rangle\langle E\rangle\neg p\,[\langle t,t'\rangle]$,
  then there exists t_2 such that $t \le t_2 < t'$ and $\mathfrak{M} \models \langle E\rangle\langle E\rangle\neg p\,[\langle t,t_2\rangle]$.
  Then by S9 we have $\mathfrak{M} \models \langle E\rangle\neg p\,[\langle t,t_2\rangle]$, hence $\mathfrak{M} \models \langle B\rangle\langle E\rangle\neg p\,[\langle t,t'\rangle]$,
  so the antecedent of the implication is not satisfied. Otherwise we have
  $\mathfrak{M} \models (\langle B\rangle\langle E\rangle\langle B\rangle\langle E\rangle\neg p)\,[\langle t,t'\rangle]$, so by S13 $\mathfrak{M} \models (\langle E\rangle\langle B\rangle\langle B\rangle\langle E\rangle\neg p)$
  $[\langle t,t'\rangle]$ holds. This means that there exists t_3 such that $t < t_3 \le t'$ and
  $\mathfrak{M} \models (\langle B\rangle\langle B\rangle\langle E\rangle\neg p)\,[\langle t_3,t'\rangle]$. Then by S8 $\mathfrak{M} \models \langle B\rangle\langle E\rangle\neg p\,[\langle t_3,t'\rangle]$, so by
  S13 $\mathfrak{M} \models \langle E\rangle\langle B\rangle\neg p\,[\langle t_3,t'\rangle]$. Thus $\mathfrak{M} \models (\langle E\rangle\langle E\rangle\langle B\rangle\neg p)\,[\langle t,t'\rangle]$, hence
  by S9 $\mathfrak{M} \models \langle E\rangle\langle B\rangle\neg p\,[\langle t,t'\rangle]$. Eventually $\mathfrak{M} \models \langle B\rangle\langle E\rangle\neg p\,[\langle t,t'\rangle]$, so the
  antecedent of the implication is not satisfied.

- $\xi(I\_REF) =$
  $p\,\&\,[B]\,p\,\&\,[E]\,p\,\&\,[B]\,[E]\,p \;\rightarrow\; p$
  This is obvious.

- $\xi(MON^1) =$
  $\langle A\rangle\, p \vee \langle A\rangle\,\langle A\rangle\, p \;\rightarrow\; (\langle A\rangle\, p \vee \langle A\rangle\,\langle A\rangle\, p)\;\&\;[B]\,(\langle A\rangle\, p \vee \langle A\rangle\,\langle A\rangle\, p)\;\&$
  $[E]\,(\langle A\rangle\, p \vee \langle A\rangle\,\langle A\rangle\, p)\;\&\;[B]\,[E]\,(\langle A\rangle\, p \vee \langle A\rangle\,\langle A\rangle\, p)$

Suppose that $\mathfrak{M} \models \langle A\rangle\, p\,[\langle t,t'\rangle]$. Then evidently $\mathfrak{M} \models (\langle A\rangle\, p \vee \langle A\rangle\,\langle A\rangle\, p)$ $[\langle t,t'\rangle]$. By definition of $\langle A\rangle$ this means moreover that $\mathfrak{M} \models \langle E\rangle\,(\langle \bar{B}\rangle\, p\;\&$ $[E]\,false)\,[\langle t,t'\rangle]$. Thus there exists t'' such that $t < t'' \le t'$ and $\mathfrak{M} \models (\langle \bar{B}\rangle\, p\;\&\;[E]\,false)\,[\langle t'',t'\rangle]$ holds. Suppose that $t'' < t'$. Since $\mathfrak{M} \models true\,[\langle t',t'\rangle]$, we have $\mathfrak{M} \models \langle E\rangle\,true\,[\langle t'',t'\rangle]$. Contradiction. Therefore $t'' = t'$ and $\mathfrak{M} \models \langle \bar{B}\rangle\, p\,[\langle t',t'\rangle]$.

Suppose that $\mathfrak{M} \models \langle B\rangle\,([A]\,\neg p\;\&\;[A]\,[A]\,\neg p)\,[\langle t,t'\rangle]$. Then there exists t_1 such that $t \le t_1 < t'$ and $\mathfrak{M} \models ([A]\,\neg p\;\&\;[A]\,[A]\,\neg p)\,[\langle t,t_1\rangle]$. Consequently, for every t_2 such that $t_1 < t_2$ $\mathfrak{M} \models \neg p\,[\langle t_1,t_2\rangle]$ and $\mathfrak{M} \models [A]\,\neg p\,[\langle t_1,t_2\rangle]$ hold. Since $t_1 < t'$, the above conditions hold in particular for the interval $\langle t_1,t'\rangle$. By definition of $[A]$ this means that $\mathfrak{M} \models [E]\,([\bar{B}]\,\neg p \vee \langle E\rangle\,true)\,[\langle t_1,t'\rangle]$. Therefore for every t_3 such that $t_1 < t_3 \le t'$ we have $\mathfrak{M} \models ([\bar{B}]\,\neg p \vee \langle E\rangle\,true)\,[\langle t_3,t'\rangle]$. As $t_1 < t' \le t'$, this also means $t_3 = t'$. Since, moreover, $\mathfrak{M} \models [E]\,false\,[\langle t',t'\rangle]$, we have $\mathfrak{M} \models [E]\,([\bar{B}]\,\neg p \vee \langle E\rangle\,true)\,[\langle t,t'\rangle]$, so $\mathfrak{M} \models ([A]\,\neg p)\,[\langle t,t'\rangle]$. Contradiction. Suppose that $\mathfrak{M} \models \langle E\rangle\,([A]\,\neg p\;\&\;[A]\,[A]\,\neg p)\,[\langle t,t'\rangle]$. Then there exists t_1 such that $t < t_1 \le t'$ and $\mathfrak{M} \models [A]\,\neg p\,[\langle t_1,t'\rangle]$ and $\mathfrak{M} \models [A]\,[A]\,\neg p\,[\langle t_1,t'\rangle]$, and we can get a contradiction in an analogous way. Finally suppose that $\mathfrak{M} \models \langle B\rangle\,\langle E\rangle\,([A]\,\neg p\;\&\;[A]\,[A]\,\neg p)\,[\langle t,t'\rangle]$. Then there exists t_1 such that $t \le t_1 < t'$ and $\mathfrak{M} \models \langle E\rangle\,([A]\,\neg p\;\&\;[A]\,[A]\,\neg p)\,[\langle t_1,t'\rangle]$ and there exists t_2 such that $t < t_2 \le t_1$, $\mathfrak{M} \models [A]\,\neg p\,[\langle t_2,t_1\rangle]$ and $\mathfrak{M} \models [A]\,[A]\,\neg p\,[\langle t_2,t_1\rangle]$. Further reasoning proceeds as before.

Otherwise, $\mathfrak{M} \models \langle A\rangle\,\langle A\rangle\, p\,[\langle t,t'\rangle]$. Then evidently we have $\mathfrak{M} \models (\langle A\rangle\, p \vee \langle A\rangle\,\langle A\rangle\, p)\,[\langle t,t'\rangle]$. Moreover, the above means that there exists t'' such that $t' < t''$ and we have $\mathfrak{M} \models \langle A\rangle\, p\,[\langle t',t''\rangle]$. As before, we can prove from the definition of $\langle A\rangle$ that $\mathfrak{M} \models \langle \bar{B}\rangle\, p\,[\langle t'',t''\rangle]$.

Suppose that $\mathfrak{M} \models \langle B\rangle\,([A]\,\neg p\;\&\;[A]\,[A]\,\neg p)\,[\langle t,t'\rangle]$. Then there exists t_1 such that $t \le t_1 < t'$, $\mathfrak{M} \models [A]\,\neg p\,[\langle t_1,t'\rangle]$ and $\mathfrak{M} \models [A]\,[A]\,\neg p\,[\langle t_1,t'\rangle]$. Then by theorem 3.2.2.3 we have $\mathfrak{M} \models [A]\,[A]\,[A]\,\neg p\,[\langle t_1,t'\rangle]$. Then for every t_2 such that $t_1 < t_2$ we have $\mathfrak{M} \models [A]\,[A]\,\neg p\,[\langle t_1,t_2\rangle]$. Since $t_1 < t'$, the above condition holds in particular for the interval $\langle t_1,t'\rangle$. Therefore for every t_3 such that $t' < t_3$ we have $\mathfrak{M} \models [A]\,\neg p\,[\langle t,t_3\rangle]$. Since $t' < t''$, the above condition also concerns the interval $\langle t',t''\rangle$. By definition of $[A]$ this means that $\mathfrak{M} \models [E]\,([\bar{B}]\,\neg p \vee \langle E\rangle\,true)\,[\langle t',t''\rangle]$. Thus for every t_4 such that $t' < t_4 \le t''$ we have $\mathfrak{M} \models ([\bar{B}]\,\neg p \vee \langle E\rangle\,true)\,[\langle t_4,t''\rangle]$. Since $t' < t'' \le t''$, this also concerns $t_3 = t''$. Since moreover $\mathfrak{M} \models [E]\,false\,[\langle t'',t''\rangle]$, we have $\mathfrak{M} \models [E]\,([\bar{B}]\,\neg p \vee \langle E\rangle\,true)\,[\langle t',t''\rangle]$, so $\mathfrak{M} \models [A]\,\neg p\,[\langle t',t''\rangle]$. Contradiction.

The remaining cases can be proved in a similar way.

- $\xi(MON^2) =$
  $\langle \bar{A} \rangle p \vee \langle \bar{A} \rangle \langle \bar{A} \rangle p \rightarrow (\langle \bar{A} \rangle p \vee \langle \bar{A} \rangle \langle \bar{A} \rangle p)$ &
  $[B](\langle \bar{A} \rangle p \vee \langle \bar{A} \rangle \langle \bar{A} \rangle p)$ & $[E](\langle \bar{A} \rangle p \vee \langle \bar{A} \rangle \langle \bar{A} \rangle p)$ & $[B][E](\langle \bar{A} \rangle p \vee \langle \bar{A} \rangle \langle \bar{A} \rangle p)$

  The reasoning is analogous to the case of $\xi(MON^1)$.

- $\xi(CONV^1) =$
  $\langle A \rangle \alpha \vee \langle A \rangle \langle A \rangle \alpha \vee \langle B \rangle (\langle A \rangle \alpha \vee \langle A \rangle \langle A \rangle \alpha) \vee \langle E \rangle (\langle A \rangle \alpha \vee \langle A \rangle \langle A \rangle \alpha) \vee$
  $\langle B \rangle \langle E \rangle (\langle A \rangle \alpha \vee \langle A \rangle \langle A \rangle \alpha) \rightarrow (\langle A \rangle p \vee \langle A \rangle \langle A \rangle p \vee q \vee \langle B \rangle q \vee$
  $\langle E \rangle q \vee \langle B \rangle \langle E \rangle q)$

  where $\alpha = (p$ & $[B] p$ & $[E] p$ & $[B][E] p$ & $q)$.

  If $\mathfrak{M} \models \langle A \rangle \alpha [\langle t, t' \rangle]$, then $\mathfrak{M} \models \langle A \rangle p [\langle t, t' \rangle]$, so the thesis is satisfied. If $\mathfrak{M} \models \langle A \rangle \langle A \rangle \alpha [\langle t, t' \rangle]$, then $\mathfrak{M} \models \langle A \rangle \langle A \rangle p [\langle t, t' \rangle]$, so the thesis is satisfied. If $\mathfrak{M} \models \langle B \rangle \langle A \rangle \alpha [\langle t, t' \rangle]$, then there exists t_1 such that $t \leq t_1 < t'$ and we have $\mathfrak{M} \models \langle A \rangle \alpha [\langle t, t_1 \rangle]$. By definition of $\langle A \rangle$ this means that $\mathfrak{M} \models \langle E \rangle (\langle \bar{B} \rangle \alpha$ & $[E] false) [\langle t, t_1 \rangle]$, hence $\mathfrak{M} \models \langle \bar{B} \rangle \alpha [\langle t_1, t_1 \rangle]$, so we have $\mathfrak{M} \models \langle B \rangle \langle \bar{B} \rangle \alpha [\langle t_1, t' \rangle]$. Thus by SR_LIN we have $\mathfrak{M} \models (\alpha \vee \langle B \rangle \alpha \vee \langle \bar{B} \rangle \alpha) [\langle t_1, t' \rangle]$, hence $\mathfrak{M} \models (\langle E \rangle \alpha \vee \langle E \rangle \langle B \rangle \alpha \vee \langle E \rangle \langle \bar{B} \rangle \alpha) [\langle t, t' \rangle]$. If $\mathfrak{M} \models \langle E \rangle \alpha [\langle t, t' \rangle]$, then in particular $\mathfrak{M} \models \langle E \rangle q [\langle t, t' \rangle]$, so the thesis is satisfied. If $\mathfrak{M} \models \langle B \rangle \langle E \rangle \alpha [\langle t, t' \rangle]$, then in particular $\mathfrak{M} \models \langle B \rangle \langle E \rangle q [\langle t, t' \rangle]$, so the thesis is satisfied. Otherwise, $\mathfrak{M} \models \langle E \rangle \langle \bar{B} \rangle \alpha [\langle t, t' \rangle]$. This means that there exists t_2 such that $t < t_2 \leq t'$ and there exists t_3 such that $t' < t_3$ and $\mathfrak{M} \models \alpha [\langle t_2, t_3 \rangle]$. In particular $\mathfrak{M} \models [E] p [\langle t_2, t_3 \rangle]$, hence for every t_4 such that $t_2 < t_4 \leq t_3$ we have $\mathfrak{M} \models p [\langle t_4, t_3 \rangle]$. As $t_2 < t' < t_3$, we have $\mathfrak{M} \models p [\langle t', t_3 \rangle]$ and $\mathfrak{M} \models \langle A \rangle p [\langle t, t' \rangle]$, so the thesis is satisfied. If $\mathfrak{M} \models \langle B \rangle \langle A \rangle \langle A \rangle \alpha [\langle t, t' \rangle]$, then we can prove in a similar way that $\mathfrak{M} \models \langle B \rangle \langle \bar{B} \rangle \langle A \rangle \alpha [\langle t_1, t' \rangle]$. Then by SR_LIN $\mathfrak{M} \models (\langle A \rangle \alpha \vee \langle B \rangle \langle A \rangle \alpha \vee \langle \bar{B} \rangle \langle A \rangle \alpha) [\langle t_1, t' \rangle]$, so $\mathfrak{M} \models (\langle E \rangle \langle A \rangle \alpha \vee \langle E \rangle \langle B \rangle \langle A \rangle \alpha \vee \langle E \rangle \langle \bar{B} \rangle \langle A \rangle \alpha) [\langle t, t' \rangle]$. If $\mathfrak{M} \models \langle E \rangle \langle A \rangle \alpha [\langle t, t' \rangle]$, then in particular $\mathfrak{M} \models \langle E \rangle \langle A \rangle p [\langle t, t' \rangle]$. Then there exists t_2 such that $t < t_2 \leq t'$ and $\mathfrak{M} \models \langle A \rangle p [\langle t_2, t' \rangle]$. By definition of $\langle A \rangle$ this means that $\mathfrak{M} \models (\langle \bar{B} \rangle p$ & $[E] false) [\langle t', t' \rangle]$, and then $\mathfrak{M} \models \langle E \rangle (\langle \bar{B} \rangle p$ & $[E] false) [\langle t, t' \rangle]$. Thus $\mathfrak{M} \models \langle A \rangle p [\langle t, t' \rangle]$, so the thesis is satisfied. If $\mathfrak{M} \models \langle B \rangle \langle E \rangle \langle A \rangle \alpha [\langle t, t' \rangle]$, then there exists t_1 such that $t \leq t_1 < t'$ and $\mathfrak{M} \models \langle E \rangle \langle A \rangle \alpha [\langle t, t_1 \rangle]$, hence as before we can prove that $\mathfrak{M} \models \langle A \rangle \alpha [\langle t, t_1 \rangle]$, so $\mathfrak{M} \models \langle B \rangle \langle A \rangle \alpha [\langle t, t' \rangle]$, and such a case has already been considered. Otherwise we have $\mathfrak{M} \models \langle E \rangle \langle \bar{B} \rangle \langle A \rangle \alpha [\langle t, t' \rangle]$. This means that there exists t_2 such that $t < t_2 \leq t'$ and $\mathfrak{M} \models \langle \bar{B} \rangle \langle A \rangle \alpha [\langle t_2, t' \rangle]$. Thus there exists t_3 such that $t' < t_3$ and $\mathfrak{M} \models \langle A \rangle \alpha [\langle t_2, t_3 \rangle]$ and there exists t_4 such that $t_3 < t_4$ and $\mathfrak{M} \models \alpha [\langle t_3, t_4 \rangle]$. Hence $\mathfrak{M} \models \langle A \rangle \alpha [\langle t', t_3 \rangle]$ and $\mathfrak{M} \models \langle A \rangle \langle A \rangle \alpha [\langle t, t' \rangle]$. In particular $\mathfrak{M} \models \langle A \rangle \langle A \rangle p [\langle t, t' \rangle]$, so the thesis is satisfied. If $\mathfrak{M} \models \langle E \rangle \langle A \rangle \alpha [\langle t, t' \rangle]$, then there exists t_1 such that

$t < t_1 \leq t'$ and $\mathfrak{M} \models \langle A \rangle \alpha [\langle t_1, t' \rangle]$. This means that there exists t_2 such that $t' < t_2$ and $\mathfrak{M} \models \alpha [\langle t', t_2 \rangle]$. Thus $\mathfrak{M} \models \langle A \rangle \alpha [\langle t, t' \rangle]$, hence in particular $\mathfrak{M} \models \langle A \rangle p [\langle t, t' \rangle]$, so the thesis is satisfied. If $\mathfrak{M} \models \langle E \rangle \langle A \rangle \langle A \rangle \alpha [\langle t, t' \rangle]$, then we can show in a similar way that $\mathfrak{M} \models \langle A \rangle \langle A \rangle p [\langle t, t' \rangle]$, so the thesis is satisfied. If $\mathfrak{M} \models \langle B \rangle \langle E \rangle \langle A \rangle \alpha [\langle t, t' \rangle]$, then there exists t_1 such that $t \leq t_1 < t'$ and $\mathfrak{M} \models \langle E \rangle \langle A \rangle \alpha [\langle t, t_1 \rangle]$. We can prove analogously that $\mathfrak{M} \models \langle A \rangle \alpha [\langle t, t_1 \rangle]$, hence $\mathfrak{M} \models \langle B \rangle \langle A \rangle \alpha [\langle t, t' \rangle]$, and such a case has already been considered. The situation for $\langle B \rangle \langle E \rangle \langle A \rangle \langle A \rangle \alpha$ is analogous, but in this case we should use the reasoning for $\langle B \rangle \langle A \rangle \langle A \rangle \alpha$.

COMMENT: In fact, the above condition can be expressed in Halpern & Shoham's logic in a simpler way by the formula: $\langle B \rangle \langle A \rangle ([E] p \,\&\, q) \rightarrow (\langle A \rangle p \lor \langle E \rangle q \lor \langle B \rangle \langle E \rangle q)$. On the other hand, we have shown in section 3.2.4 that $CONV^1$ holds only in right linear structures. This concerns the above formula, too, hence the application of SR_LIN is justified.

- $\xi(CONV^2) =$
  $\langle \bar{A} \rangle \alpha \lor \langle \bar{A} \rangle \langle \bar{A} \rangle \alpha \lor \langle B \rangle (\langle \bar{A} \rangle \alpha \lor \langle \bar{A} \rangle \langle \bar{A} \rangle \alpha) \lor \langle E \rangle (\langle \bar{A} \rangle \alpha \lor \langle \bar{A} \rangle \langle \bar{A} \rangle \alpha) \lor \langle B \rangle \langle E \rangle (\langle \bar{A} \rangle \alpha \lor \langle \bar{A} \rangle \langle \bar{A} \rangle \alpha) \rightarrow (\langle \bar{A} \rangle p \lor \langle \bar{A} \rangle \langle \bar{A} \rangle p \lor q \lor \langle B \rangle q \lor \langle E \rangle q \lor \langle B \rangle \langle E \rangle q)$
  where $\alpha = (p \,\&\, [B] p \,\&\, [E] p \,\&\, [B][E] p \,\&\, q)$
  The reasoning is analogous to the case of $\xi(CONV^1)$.

- $\xi(NEIGH^{*1}) =$
  $p \,\&\, q \,\&\, [B] q \,\&\, [E] q \,\&\, [B][E] q \rightarrow (\langle A \rangle ([\bar{A}] \alpha \,\&\, [\bar{A}][\bar{A}] \alpha) \lor \langle A \rangle \langle A \rangle ([\bar{A}] \alpha \,\&\, [\bar{A}][\bar{A}] \alpha))$
  where $\alpha = \langle A \rangle p \lor \langle A \rangle \langle A \rangle p \lor q \lor \langle B \rangle q \lor \langle E \rangle q \lor \langle B \rangle \langle E \rangle q$
  Evidently $\xi(NEIGH^{*1})$ is not satisfied at the end of a finite structure. However, this case is not interesting, as it also concerns $NEIGH^*$. Therefore we assume $SSUCC$.
  Suppose that $\mathfrak{M} \models [A] \langle \bar{A} \rangle ([A] \neg p \,\&\, [A][A] \neg p \,\&\, \neg q \,\&\, [B] \neg q \,\&\, [E] \neg q \,\&\, [B][E] \neg q) [\langle t, t' \rangle]$. In particular, this means that for every t_1 such that $t' < t_1$ we have $\mathfrak{M} \models \langle \bar{A} \rangle (\neg q \,\&\, [E] \neg q) [\langle t', t_1 \rangle]$. Therefore (under our assumption) we have $\mathfrak{M} \models \langle A \rangle \langle \bar{A} \rangle (\neg q \,\&\, [E] \neg q) [\langle t, t' \rangle]$. Thus by theorem 3.2.2.4 $\mathfrak{M} \models ((\neg q \,\&\, [E] \neg q) \lor \langle E \rangle (\neg q \,\&\, [E] \neg q) \lor \langle \bar{E} \rangle (\neg q \,\&\, [E] \neg q)) [\langle t, t' \rangle]$. If $\mathfrak{M} \models \neg q [\langle t, t' \rangle]$, then the antecedent of the implication is not satisfied. If $\mathfrak{M} \models \langle E \rangle \neg q [\langle t, t' \rangle]$, then the antecedent of the implication is not satisfied. Otherwise, $\mathfrak{M} \models \langle \bar{E} \rangle [E] \neg q [\langle t, t' \rangle]$, so by S7 $\mathfrak{M} \models \neg q [\langle t, t' \rangle]$, hence the antecedent of the implication is also not satisfied.
  Suppose that $\mathfrak{M} \models ([A] \langle \bar{A} \rangle \langle \bar{A} \rangle ([A] \neg p \,\&\, [A][A] \neg p \,\&\, \neg q \,\&\, [B] \neg q \,\&\, [E] \neg q \,\&\, [B][E] \neg q) [\langle t, t' \rangle]$ holds. Under our assumption this means in particular that $\mathfrak{M} \models \langle A \rangle \langle \bar{A} \rangle \langle \bar{A} \rangle ([A] \neg p \,\&\, [A][A] \neg p \,\&\, \neg q \,\&\, [E] \neg q) [\langle t, t' \rangle]$,

hence by theorem 3.2.2.4 we have $\mathfrak{M} \models (\langle\bar{A}\rangle([A]\neg p \ \& \ [A][A]\neg p \ \& \ \neg q \ \& \ [E]\neg q) \lor \langle E\rangle\langle\bar{A}\rangle([A]\neg p \ \& \ [A][A]\neg p \ \& \ \neg q \ \& \ [E]\neg q) \lor \langle\bar{E}\rangle\langle\bar{A}\rangle([A]\neg p \ \& \ [A][A]\neg p \ \& \ \neg q \ \& \ [E]\neg q))[\langle t,t'\rangle]$. If $\mathfrak{M} \models \langle\bar{A}\rangle[A]\neg p)[\langle t,t'\rangle]$, then by S7 $\mathfrak{M} \models \neg p[\langle t,t'\rangle]$, so the antecedent of the implication is not satisfied. If $\mathfrak{M} \models \langle E\rangle\langle\bar{A}\rangle(\neg q \ \& \ [E]\neg q)[\langle t,t'\rangle]$, then there exists t_1 such that $t < t_1 \leq t'$ and $\mathfrak{M} \models \langle\bar{A}\rangle(\neg q \ \& \ [E]\neg q)[\langle t_1,t'\rangle]$. By definition of $\langle\bar{A}\rangle$ this means that $\mathfrak{M} \models \langle B\rangle(\langle\bar{E}\rangle(\neg q \ \& \ [E]\neg q))[\langle t_1,t'\rangle]$, so we have $\mathfrak{M} \models \langle E\rangle\langle B\rangle\langle\bar{E}\rangle(\neg q \ \& \ [E]\neg q)[\langle t,t'\rangle]$. Then by S13 $\mathfrak{M} \models \langle B\rangle\langle E\rangle\langle\bar{E}\rangle(\neg q \ \& \ [E]\neg q)[\langle t,t'\rangle]$, hence there exists t_2 such that $t \leq t_2 < t'$ and $\mathfrak{M} \models \langle E\rangle\langle\bar{E}\rangle(\neg q \ \& \ [E]\neg q)[\langle t,t_2\rangle]$. Thus by SL_LIN $\mathfrak{M} \models ((\neg q \ \& \ [E]\neg q) \lor \langle E\rangle(\neg q \ \& \ [E]\neg q) \lor \langle\bar{E}\rangle(\neg q \ \& \ [E]\neg q))[\langle t,t_2\rangle]$. If $\mathfrak{M} \models \neg q[\langle t,t_2\rangle]$, then $\mathfrak{M} \models \langle B\rangle\neg q[\langle t,t'\rangle]$, so the antecedent of the implication is not satisfied. If $\mathfrak{M} \models \langle E\rangle\neg q[\langle t,t_2\rangle]$, then $\mathfrak{M} \models \langle B\rangle\langle E\rangle\neg q[\langle t,t'\rangle]$, so the antecedent of the implication is not satisfied. Otherwise, $\mathfrak{M} \models \langle\bar{E}\rangle[E]\neg q[\langle t,t_2\rangle]$, so by S7 $\mathfrak{M} \models \neg q[\langle t,t_1\rangle]$. Thus $\mathfrak{M} \models \langle B\rangle\neg q[\langle t,t'\rangle]$, so the antecedent of the implication is not satisfied. Otherwise, $\mathfrak{M} \models \langle\bar{E}\rangle\langle\bar{A}\rangle[A]\neg p[\langle t,t'\rangle]$. Then there exists t_1 such that $t' < t_1$ and $\mathfrak{M} \models \langle\bar{A}\rangle[A]\neg p[\langle t,t_1\rangle]$. Thus there exists t_2 such that $t_2 < t$ and $\mathfrak{M} \models [A]\neg p[\langle t_2,t\rangle]$. This means that $\mathfrak{M} \models \langle\bar{A}\rangle[A]\neg p[\langle t,t'\rangle]$, so by S7 we have $\mathfrak{M} \models \neg p[\langle t,t'\rangle]$. Thus the antecedent of the implication is not satisfied.

But this is the end of our proof, due to the rule: $(\neg\beta \ \rightarrow \ \neg\alpha) \ \rightarrow \ (\alpha \ \rightarrow \ \beta \lor \gamma)$.

COMMENT: In Halpern & Shoham's logic $NEIGH^{*1}$ can be reduced to the formula $(q \ \& \ [E]q) \ \rightarrow \ \langle A\rangle[\bar{A}](q \lor \langle E\rangle q)$. However, such a formulation of the condition of neighbourhood in a logic, in which it is extremely natural would be pure folly. The more so as this formula is only satisfied in right linear structures (similarly as $NEIGH^{*1}$ itself, see section 3.2.4).

- $\xi(NEIGH^{*2}) =$
  $p \ \& \ q \ \& \ [B]q \ \& \ [E]q \ \& \ [B][E]q \ \rightarrow$
  $(\langle\bar{A}\rangle([A]\alpha \ \& \ [A][A]\alpha) \lor \langle\bar{A}\rangle\langle\bar{A}\rangle([A]\alpha \ \& \ [A][A]\alpha))$
  where $\alpha = \langle\bar{A}\rangle p \lor \langle\bar{A}\rangle\langle\bar{A}\rangle p \lor q \lor \langle B\rangle q \lor \langle E\rangle q \lor \langle B\rangle\langle E\rangle q$
  The reasoning is analogous to the case of $\xi(NEIGH^{*1})$.

- $\xi(DIR^1) =$
  $(\langle A\rangle p \lor \langle A\rangle\langle A\rangle p) \ \& \ (\langle A\rangle q \lor \langle A\rangle\langle A\rangle q) \ \rightarrow \ (\langle A\rangle\alpha \lor \langle A\rangle\langle A\rangle\alpha)$
  where $\alpha = (p \lor \langle B\rangle p \lor \langle E\rangle p \lor \langle B\rangle\langle E\rangle p) \ \& \ (q \lor \langle B\rangle q \lor \langle E\rangle q \lor \langle B\rangle\langle E\rangle q)$
  Suppose that $\mathfrak{M} \models (\langle A\rangle p \lor \langle A\rangle q)[\langle t,t'\rangle]$. This means that there exists t_1 such that $t' < t_1$ and $\mathfrak{M} \models p[\langle t',t_1\rangle]$. Then $\mathfrak{M} \models \langle\bar{A}\rangle\langle A\rangle q[\langle t',t_1\rangle]$. Thus by theorem 3.2.2.4 we have $\mathfrak{M} \models (q \lor \langle B\rangle q \lor \langle\bar{B}\rangle q)[\langle t',t_1\rangle]$. If $\mathfrak{M} \models q[\langle t',t_1\rangle]$, then $\mathfrak{M} \models \langle A\rangle(p \ \& \ q)[\langle t,t'\rangle]$, so the thesis is satisfied.

If $\mathfrak{M} \models \langle B \rangle\, q\, [\langle t', t_1 \rangle]$, then $\mathfrak{M} \models \langle A \rangle\, (p\, \&\, \langle B \rangle\, q)\, [\langle t, t' \rangle]$, so the thesis is satisfied. Otherwise, $\mathfrak{M} \models \langle \bar{B} \rangle\, q\, [\langle t', t_1 \rangle]$. This means that there exists t_2 such that $t_1 < t_2$ and $\mathfrak{M} \models q\, [\langle t', t_2 \rangle]$. But then $\mathfrak{M} \models \langle B \rangle\, p\, [\langle t', t_2 \rangle]$, so $\mathfrak{M} \models \langle A \rangle\, (\langle B \rangle\, p\, \&\, q)\, [\langle t, t' \rangle]$, and the thesis is satisfied.

Suppose that $\mathfrak{M} \models (\langle A \rangle\, p\, \&\, \langle A \rangle\, \langle A \rangle\, q)\, [\langle t, t' \rangle]$. This means that there exists t_1 such that $t' < t_1$ and $\mathfrak{M} \models p\, [\langle t', t_1 \rangle]$. Then $\mathfrak{M} \models (\langle \bar{A} \rangle\, \langle A \rangle\, \langle A \rangle\, q)\, [\langle t', t_1 \rangle]$. Thus by theorem 3.2.2.4 $\mathfrak{M} \models (\langle A \rangle\, q\, \vee\, \langle B \rangle\, \langle A \rangle\, q\, \vee\, \langle \bar{B} \rangle\, \langle A \rangle\, q)\, [\langle t', t_1 \rangle]$. If $\mathfrak{M} \models \langle A \rangle\, q\, [\langle t', t_1 \rangle]$, then by definition of $\langle A \rangle$ $\mathfrak{M} \models \langle E \rangle\, \langle \bar{B} \rangle\, q\, [\langle t', t_1 \rangle]$, and then by S14 and fact 3.2.2.1 we have $\mathfrak{M} \models \langle \bar{B} \rangle\, \langle E \rangle\, q\, [\langle t', t_1 \rangle]$. Thus there exists t_2 such that $t_1 < t_2$ and $\mathfrak{M} \models \langle E \rangle\, q\, [\langle t', t_2 \rangle]$. On the other hand, $\mathfrak{M} \models \langle B \rangle\, p\, [\langle t', t_2 \rangle]$. Therefore $\mathfrak{M} \models \langle A \rangle\, (\langle B \rangle\, p\, \&\, \langle E \rangle\, q)\, [\langle t, t' \rangle]$, so the thesis is satisfied. If $\mathfrak{M} \models \langle B \rangle\, \langle A \rangle\, q\, [\langle t', t_1 \rangle]$, then there exists t_2 such that $t' \leq t_2 < t_1$ and $\mathfrak{M} \models \langle A \rangle\, q\, [\langle t', t_2 \rangle]$. Thus by definition of $\langle A \rangle$ we have $\mathfrak{M} \models \langle \bar{B} \rangle\, q\, [\langle t_2, t_2 \rangle]$, hence $\mathfrak{M} \models \langle B \rangle\, \langle \bar{B} \rangle\, q\, [\langle t_2, t_1 \rangle]$. Then by SR_LIN $\mathfrak{M} \models (q\, \vee\, \langle B \rangle\, q\, \vee\, \langle \bar{B} \rangle\, q)\, [\langle t_2, t_1 \rangle]$. If $\mathfrak{M} \models q\, [\langle t_2, t_1 \rangle]$, then $\mathfrak{M} \models \langle E \rangle\, q\, [\langle t', t_1 \rangle]$, hence $\mathfrak{M} \models \langle A \rangle\, (p\, \&\, \langle E \rangle\, q)\, [\langle t, t' \rangle]$, so the thesis is satisfied. If $\mathfrak{M} \models \langle B \rangle\, q\, [\langle t_2, t_1 \rangle]$, then $\mathfrak{M} \models \langle E \rangle\, \langle B \rangle\, q\, [\langle t', t_1 \rangle]$, so by S14 $\mathfrak{M} \models \langle B \rangle\, \langle E \rangle\, q\, [\langle t', t_1 \rangle]$. Thus $\mathfrak{M} \models \langle A \rangle\, (p\, \&\, \langle B \rangle\, \langle E \rangle\, q)\, [\langle t, t' \rangle]$, so the thesis is satisfied. Otherwise, $\mathfrak{M} \models \langle \bar{B} \rangle\, q\, [\langle t_2, t_1 \rangle]$. Then $\mathfrak{M} \models \langle E \rangle\, \langle \bar{B} \rangle\, q\, [\langle t', t_1 \rangle]$, hence by S14 and fact 3.2.2.1 $\mathfrak{M} \models \langle \bar{B} \rangle\, \langle E \rangle\, q\, [\langle t', t_1 \rangle]$. This means that there exists t_3 such that $t_1 < t_3$ and $\mathfrak{M} \models \langle E \rangle\, q\, [\langle t', t_3 \rangle]$. On the other hand, $\mathfrak{M} \models \langle B \rangle\, p\, [\langle t', t_3 \rangle]$, hence $\mathfrak{M} \models \langle A \rangle\, (\langle B \rangle\, p\, \&\, \langle E \rangle\, q)\, [\langle t, t' \rangle]$, so the thesis is satisfied.

For the remaining cases the reasoning proceeds in a similar way.

COMMENT: The need for the condition of linearity stems from the fact that normal structures the axiom DIR is not valid in non-linear structures.

- $\xi(DIR^2) =$
  $(\langle \bar{A} \rangle\, p\, \vee\, \langle \bar{A} \rangle\, \langle \bar{A} \rangle\, p)\, \&\, (\langle \bar{A} \rangle\, q\, \vee\, \langle \bar{A} \rangle\, \langle \bar{A} \rangle\, q)\, \rightarrow\, (\langle \bar{A} \rangle\, \alpha\, \vee\, \langle \bar{A} \rangle\, \langle \bar{A} \rangle\, \alpha)$
  where $\alpha = (p\, \vee\, \langle B \rangle\, p\, \vee\, \langle E \rangle\, p\, \vee\, \langle B \rangle\, \langle E \rangle\, p)\, \&\, (q\, \vee\, \langle B \rangle\, q\, \vee\, \langle E \rangle\, q\, \vee\, \langle B \rangle\, \langle E \rangle\, q)$ The reasoning is analogous to the case of $\xi(DIR^1)$.

- $\xi(SUCC^1) =$
  $([A]\, p\, \&\, [A]\, [A]\, p)\, \rightarrow\, (\langle A \rangle\, p\, \vee\, \langle A \rangle\, \langle A \rangle\, p)$
  Let $\mathfrak{M} \models [A]\, p\, [\langle t, t' \rangle]$. Then by $SSUCC$ $\mathfrak{M} \models \langle A \rangle\, p\, [\langle t, t' \rangle]$, so the thesis is satisfied.

- $\xi(SUCC^2) =$
  $([\bar{A}]\, p\, \&\, [\bar{A}]\, [\bar{A}]\, p)\, \rightarrow\, (\langle \bar{A} \rangle\, p\, \vee\, \langle \bar{A} \rangle\, \langle \bar{A} \rangle\, p)$
  The reasoning is analogous to the case of $\xi(SUCC^1)$.

- $\xi(L\_LIN)$ =

$\langle \bar{A}\rangle((p \ \& \ [B]p \ \& \ [E]p \ \& \ [B][E]p) \vee \langle \bar{A}\rangle\langle \bar{A}\rangle(p \ \& \ [B]p \ \& \ [E]p \ \& \ [B][E]p)) \rightarrow$
$[\bar{A}](\langle A\rangle\,p \vee \langle A\rangle\langle A\rangle\,p \vee p \vee \langle B\rangle\,p \vee \langle E\rangle\,p \vee \langle B\rangle\langle E\rangle\,p \vee \langle \bar{A}\rangle\,p \vee$
$\langle \bar{A}\rangle\langle \bar{A}\rangle\,p) \ \& \ [\bar{A}][\bar{A}](\langle A\rangle\,p \vee \langle A\rangle\langle A\rangle\,p \vee p \vee \langle B\rangle\,p \vee \langle E\rangle\,p \vee \langle B\rangle\langle E\rangle\,p \vee$
$\langle \bar{A}\rangle\,p \vee \langle \bar{A}\rangle\langle \bar{A}\rangle\,p)$

Suppose that $\mathfrak{M} \models \langle \bar{A}\rangle\,([A]\neg p \ \& \ [A][A]\neg p \ \& \ \neg p \ \& \ [B]\neg p \ \& \ [E]\neg p \ \&$ $[B][E]\neg p \ \& \ [\bar{A}]\neg p \ \& \ [\bar{A}][\bar{A}]\neg p)\,[\langle t,t'\rangle]$ holds. Then there exists t_1 such that $t_1 < t$ and $\mathfrak{M} \models (\neg p \ \& \ [B]\neg p \ \& \ [E]\neg p \ \& \ [B][E]\neg p \ \& \ [\bar{A}]\neg p \ \&$ $[\bar{A}][\bar{A}]\neg p)\,[\langle t_1,t\rangle]$. If $\mathfrak{M} \models \langle \bar{A}\rangle\,(p \ \& \ [E]p)\,[\langle t,t'\rangle]$, then $\mathfrak{M} \models \langle A\rangle\langle \bar{A}\rangle\,(p \ \&$ $[E]p)\,[\langle t_1,t\rangle]$, hence by theorem 3.2.2.4 $\mathfrak{M} \models ((p \ \& \ [E]p) \vee \langle E\rangle(p \ \& \ [E]p) \vee$ $\langle \bar{E}\rangle\,(p \ \& \ [E]p))\,[\langle t_1,t\rangle]$. Clearly, $\mathfrak{M} \not\models (p \vee \langle \ E\rangle p)\,[\langle t_1,t\rangle]$. Thus $\mathfrak{M} \models ((\langle \bar{E}\rangle\,[E]\,p)\,[\langle t_1,t\rangle]$, hence by S7 $\mathfrak{M} \models p\,[\langle t_1,t\rangle]$. Contradiction.

Otherwise, $\mathfrak{M} \models \langle \bar{A}\rangle\langle \bar{A}\rangle\,(p \ \& \ [E]p)\,[\langle t,t'\rangle]$, so $\mathfrak{M} \models \langle A\rangle\langle \bar{A}\rangle\langle \bar{A}\rangle\,(p \ \&$ $[E]p)\,[\langle t_1,t\rangle]$, hence by theorem 3.2.2.4 $\mathfrak{M} \models ((\langle \bar{A}\rangle\,(p \ \& \ [E]p) \vee \langle E\rangle\langle \bar{A}\rangle$ $(p \ \& \ [E]p) \vee \langle \bar{E}\rangle\langle \bar{A}\rangle\,(p \ \& \ [E]p))\,[\langle t_1,t\rangle]$. Evidently $\mathfrak{M} \not\models \langle \bar{A}\rangle\,p\,[\langle t_1,t\rangle]$. Suppose that $\mathfrak{M} \models \langle E\rangle\langle \bar{A}\rangle\,(p \ \& \ [E]p)\,[\langle t_1,t\rangle]$. Then there exists t_2 such that $t_1 < t_2 \le t$ and $\mathfrak{M} \models \langle \bar{A}\rangle\,(p \ \& \ [E]p)\,[\langle t_2,t'\rangle]$. Thus by definition of $\langle \bar{A}\rangle$ we have $\mathfrak{M} \models \langle \bar{E}\rangle\,(p \ \& \ [E]p)\,[\langle t_2,t_2\rangle]$, hence $\mathfrak{M} \models \langle E\rangle\langle \bar{E}\rangle\,(p \ \& \ [E]p)$ $[\langle t_1,t_2\rangle]$, so by SL_LIN $\mathfrak{M} \models ((p \ \& \ [E]p) \vee \langle E\rangle\,(p \ \& \ [E]p) \vee \langle \bar{E}\rangle\,(p \ \&$ $[E]p))\,[\langle t_1,t_2\rangle]$. If $\mathfrak{M} \models p\,[\langle t_1,t_2\rangle]$, then $\mathfrak{M} \models \langle B\rangle\,p\,[\langle t_1,t\rangle]$, which contradicts the fact that $\mathfrak{M} \models [B]\neg p\,[\langle t_1,t\rangle]$. If $\mathfrak{M} \models \langle E\rangle\,p\,[\langle t_1,t_2\rangle]$, then $\mathfrak{M} \models \langle B\rangle\langle E\rangle\,p\,[\langle t_1,t\rangle]$, which is contradictory to $\mathfrak{M} \models [B][E]\neg p\,[\langle t_1,t\rangle]$. Otherwise, $\mathfrak{M} \models \langle \bar{E}\rangle\,[E]\,p\,[\langle t_1,t_2\rangle]$, hence by S7 $\mathfrak{M} \models p\,[\langle t_1,t_2\rangle]$, so we obtain contradiction analogously. Otherwise $\mathfrak{M} \models \langle \bar{E}\rangle\langle \bar{A}\rangle\,(p \ \& \ [E]p)\,[\langle t_1,t\rangle]$. Then there exists t_2 such that $t_2 < t_1$ and $\mathfrak{M} \models \langle \bar{A}\rangle\,p\,[\langle t_2,t\rangle]$ and there exists t_3 such that $t_3 < t_2$ and $\mathfrak{M} \models p\,[\langle t_3,t_2\rangle]$. This means that $\mathfrak{M} \models \langle \bar{A}\rangle\,p\,[\langle t_2,t_1\rangle]$ and $\mathfrak{M} \models \langle \bar{A}\rangle\langle \bar{A}\rangle\,p\,[\langle t_1,t\rangle]$, which is contradictory to $\mathfrak{M} \models [\bar{A}][\bar{A}]\neg p\,[\langle t_1,t\rangle]$.

So suppose that $\mathfrak{M} \models \langle \bar{A}\rangle\langle \bar{A}\rangle\,([A]\neg p \ \& \ [A][A]\neg p \ \& \ \neg p \ \& \ [B]\neg p \ \&$ $[E]\neg p \ \& \ [B][E]\neg p \ \& \ [\bar{A}]\neg p \ \& \ [\bar{A}][\bar{A}]\neg p)\,[\langle t,t'\rangle]$. Then there exists t_1 such that $t_1 < t$ and $\mathfrak{M} \models \langle \bar{A}\rangle\,([A]\neg p \ \& \ [A][A]\neg p \ \& \ \neg p \ \& \ [B]\neg p \ \& \ [E]\neg p \ \&$ $[B][E]\neg p)\,[\langle t_1,t\rangle]$. If $\mathfrak{M} \models \langle \bar{A}\rangle\,(p \ \& \ [E]p)\,[\langle t,t'\rangle]$, then $\mathfrak{M} \models \langle A\rangle\langle \bar{A}\rangle\,(p \ \&$ $[E]p)\,[\langle t_1,t\rangle]$, so by theorem 3.2.2.4 $\mathfrak{M} \models ((p \ \& \ [E]p) \vee \langle E\rangle\,(p \ \& \ [E]p) \vee$ $\langle \bar{E}\rangle\,(p \ \& \ [E]p))\,[\langle t_1,t\rangle]$. The case when $\mathfrak{M} \models p\,[\langle t_1,t\rangle]$ is contradictory to $\mathfrak{M} \models \langle \bar{A}\rangle\,[A]\neg p\,[\langle t_1,t\rangle]$, as it means by S7 that $\mathfrak{M} \models \neg p\,[\langle t_1,t\rangle]$. If $\mathfrak{M} \models \langle E\rangle\,p\,[\langle t_1,t\rangle]$, then there exists t_2 such that $t_1 < t_2 \le t$ and $\mathfrak{M} \models p\,[\langle t_2,t\rangle]$. This means that $\mathfrak{M} \models \langle A\rangle\,p\,[\langle t_1,t_2\rangle]$. Then by S7 $\mathfrak{M} \models [\bar{A}]\langle A\rangle\langle A\rangle\,p\,[\langle t_1,t_2\rangle]$. Thus for every t_3 such that $t_3 < t_1$ we have $\mathfrak{M} \models \langle A\rangle\langle A\rangle\,p\,[\langle t_3,t_1\rangle]$, hence $\mathfrak{M} \models [\bar{A}]\langle A\rangle\langle A\rangle\,p\,[\langle t_1,t\rangle]$. This contradicts the fact that $\mathfrak{M} \models \langle \bar{A}\rangle[A][A]\neg p\,[\langle t_1,t\rangle]$. Otherwise, $\mathfrak{M} \models \langle \bar{E}\rangle[E]\,p\,[\langle t_1,t\rangle]$, so by S7 $\mathfrak{M} \models p\,[\langle t_1,t\rangle]$, and this case has already been considered.

Otherwise, $\mathfrak{M} \models \langle \bar{A} \rangle \langle \bar{A} \rangle (p \ \& \ [E]p)[\langle t, t' \rangle]$. There exists t_2 such that $t_2 < t_1$ and $\mathfrak{M} \models ([A] \neg p \ \& \ [A][A] \neg p \ \& \ \neg p \ \& \ [B] \neg p \ \& \ [E] \neg p \ \& \ [B][E] \neg p \ \&[\bar{A}] \neg p \ \& \ [\bar{A}][\bar{A}] \neg p)[\langle t_2, t_1 \rangle]$. Thus $\mathfrak{M} \models \langle A \rangle \langle A \rangle \langle \bar{A} \rangle \langle \bar{A} \rangle (p \ \& \ [E]p)[\langle t_2, t_1 \rangle]$. This means that there exists t_3 such that $t_1 < t_3$ and $\mathfrak{M} \models \langle A \rangle \langle \bar{A} \rangle \langle \bar{A} \rangle (p \ \& \ [E]p)[\langle t_1, t_3 \rangle]$. Then by theorem 3.2.2.4 we have $\mathfrak{M} \models (\langle \bar{A} \rangle (p \ \& \ [E]p) \ \vee \ \langle E \rangle \langle \bar{A} \rangle (p \ \& \ [E]p) \ \vee \ \langle \bar{E} \rangle \langle \bar{A} \rangle (p \ \& \ [E]p))$ $[\langle t_1, t_3 \rangle]$. If $\mathfrak{M} \models \langle \bar{A} \rangle (p \ \& \ [E]p)[\langle t_1, t_3 \rangle]$, then $\mathfrak{M} \models \langle A \rangle \langle \bar{A} \rangle (p \ \& \ [E]p)$ $[\langle t_2, t_1 \rangle]$. An analogous situation was considered (for the interval $\langle t_1, t \rangle$) at the beginning of the proof. If $\mathfrak{M} \models \langle E \rangle \langle \bar{A} \rangle (p \ \& \ [E]p)[\langle t_1, t_3 \rangle]$, then there exists t_4 such that $t_1 < t_4 \leq t_3$ and $\mathfrak{M} \models \langle \bar{A} \rangle (p \ \& \ [E]p)[\langle t_4, t_3 \rangle]$. By definition of $\langle \bar{A} \rangle$ this means that $\mathfrak{M} \models \langle \bar{E} \rangle (p \ \& \ [E]p)[\langle t_4, t_4 \rangle]$, so $\mathfrak{M} \models \langle E \rangle \langle \bar{E} \rangle (p \ \& \ [E]p)[\langle t_1, t_4 \rangle]$. Thus by SL_LIN $\mathfrak{M} \models ((p \ \& \ [E]p) \ \vee \langle E \rangle (p \ \& \ [E]p) \ \vee \ \langle \bar{E} \rangle (p \ \& \ [E]p))[\langle t_1, t_4 \rangle]$. If $\mathfrak{M} \models p[\langle t_1, t_4 \rangle]$, then $\mathfrak{M} \models \langle A \rangle p[\langle t_2, t_1 \rangle]$ holds, which contradicts $\mathfrak{M} \models [A] \neg p[\langle t_2, t_1 \rangle]$. If $\mathfrak{M} \models \langle E \rangle p[\langle t_1, t_4 \rangle]$, then there exists t_5 such that $t_1 < t_5 \leq t_4$ and $\mathfrak{M} \models p[\langle t_5, t_4 \rangle]$. Then $\mathfrak{M} \models \langle A \rangle p[\langle t_1, t_5 \rangle]$ and $\mathfrak{M} \models \langle A \rangle \langle A \rangle p[\langle t_2, t_1 \rangle]$, which is contradictory to $\mathfrak{M} \models [A][A] \neg p[\langle t_2, t_1 \rangle]$. Otherwise, we have $\mathfrak{M} \models \langle \bar{E} \rangle [E]p[\langle t_1, t_4 \rangle]$, so by S7 $\mathfrak{M} \models p[\langle t_1, t_4 \rangle]$, and further reasoning is analogous to this case. Otherwise, we have $\mathfrak{M} \models \langle \bar{E} \rangle \langle \bar{A} \rangle (p \ \& \ [E]p)[\langle t_1, t_3 \rangle]$. Then there exists t_4 such that $t_4 < t_1$ and $\mathfrak{M} \models \langle \bar{A} \rangle p[\langle t_4, t_3 \rangle]$ and there exists t_5 such that $t_5 < t_4$ and $\mathfrak{M} \models p[\langle t_5, t_4 \rangle]$. Thus $\mathfrak{M} \models \langle \bar{A} \rangle p[\langle t_4, t_1 \rangle]$, $\mathfrak{M} \models \langle \bar{A} \rangle \langle \bar{A} \rangle p[\langle t_1, t \rangle]$ and $\mathfrak{M} \models \langle A \rangle \langle \bar{A} \rangle \langle \bar{A} \rangle p[\langle t_2, t_1 \rangle]$. An analogous situation (for the interval $\langle t_1, t \rangle$) have already been considered.

- $\xi(R\_LIN) =$
$\langle A \rangle ((p \ \& \ [B]p \ \& \ [E]p \ \& \ [B][E]p) \ \vee \ \langle \bar{A} \rangle \langle \bar{A} \rangle (p \ \& \ [B]p \ \& \ [E]p \ \& \ [B][E]p)) \ \rightarrow$
$[A] (\langle A \rangle p \ \vee \ \langle A \rangle \langle A \rangle p \ \vee \ p \ \vee \ \langle B \rangle p \ \vee \ \langle E \rangle p \ \vee \ \langle B \rangle \langle E \rangle p \ \vee \ \langle \bar{A} \rangle p \ \vee$
$\langle \bar{A} \rangle \langle \bar{A} \rangle p) \ \& \ [A][A] (\langle A \rangle p \ \vee \ \langle A \rangle \langle A \rangle p \ \vee \ p \ \vee \ \langle B \rangle p \ \vee \ \langle E \rangle p \ \vee \ \langle B \rangle \langle E \rangle p \ \vee$
$\langle \bar{A} \rangle p \ \vee \ \langle \bar{A} \rangle \langle \bar{A} \rangle p)$
The reasoning is analogous to the case of $\xi(L\_LIN)$.   ∎

3.2.4 Non-linear time in extended tense logic

While discussing time structures in the first order predicate calculus, we have spent much time on non-linear interval structures. This results from the specific character of such structures—namely, from the fact that the absence of the linearity axiom is not sufficient for their complete characterization. In this section we shall try to reformulate in the extended tense logic described in section 3.2.1 the axioms which have been introduced then. Our choice of the logic is a consequence of the choice made before—it describes time structures with relations $<$ and $\subseteq$. We intend to use all the operators, including ⊠ and ⊕.

In formulas described in section 2.2.5 we have often used the auxiliary relation !, which indicates that two intervals do not lie on the same branch. Therefore, it would be useful to define an operator corresponding to this relation, i.e. having the following semantics:

$$M \models \clubsuit\varphi[i] \quad \text{iff} \quad \text{for every } j \text{ such that } i \, ! \, j \text{ we have } M \models \varphi[j].$$

and its existential counterpart $\spadesuit \equiv_{def} \neg\clubsuit\neg$. Unfortunately, we are not able to define such operators in the language we have in our disposal. However, we are able to define a similar operator:

$$\bowtie \varphi \quad \equiv_{def} \quad \neg(P\varphi \vee \Diamond\spadesuit\varphi \vee F\varphi).$$

The semantics of this operator is rather surprising:

$$M \models \bowtie \varphi[i] \quad \text{iff} \quad \text{for every } j \text{ such that } M \models \varphi[j] \text{ we have } i \, ! \, j.$$

It is indeed a very peculiar operator, in particular $M \models \bowtie false$ holds for every M. Actually, it says that a certain formula does not hold on the current branch, i.e. it holds on other branches or nowhere. However, it turns out that even this odd operator can be useful. On the other hand, adding a completely new operator would make it impossible to determine what can be expressed in the language we have at our disposal.

It turns out that the basic properties suggested in section 2.2.5, namely *NORMAL* and *SOLID*, can be expressed in our language:

- *NORMAL* $(Pp \vee \Diamond p \vee Fp) \rightarrow \Box(Pp \vee \Diamond\spadesuit p \vee Fp)$,

- *SOLID* $\Diamond Fp \rightarrow Fp \vee \Diamond\spadesuit p$

  $\Diamond Pp \rightarrow Pp \vee \Diamond\spadesuit p$.

The main consequence of solidity is that subintervals of intervals lying on different branches cannot be collinear. Now we express this in the following way.

Theorem 3.2.4.1. The axioms *SOLID* and *I_TRANS* imply $\bowtie \varphi \rightarrow \Box \bowtie \varphi$.
Proof
Consider any model M in which *SOLID* and *I_TRANS* are satisfied. Suppose that $M \models \Diamond\neg \bowtie \varphi$, so $M \models \Diamond(P\varphi \vee \Diamond\spadesuit\varphi \vee F\varphi)$. Consider any $i \in I$ such that $M \models \Diamond P\varphi[i]$. Then by *SOLID* $M \models P\varphi \vee \Diamond\spadesuit\varphi[i]$, and this means that $M \not\models\bowtie \varphi[i]$. Suppose that $M \models \Diamond\Diamond\spadesuit\varphi[i]$. Then by *I_TRANS* $M \models \Diamond\spadesuit\varphi[i]$, which means that $M \not\models\bowtie \varphi[i]$. Otherwise, $M \models \Diamond F\varphi[i]$. Then by *SOLID* $M \models (F\varphi \vee \Diamond\spadesuit\varphi)[i]$. This means that $M \not\models \bowtie \varphi[i]$. ∎

The next important property of abnormal structures of interval time is their *ordinariness*. It follows from the analysis in section 2.2.5 that this property is somehow connected with *convexity*. Van Benthem also presents another version of this property (besides the one presented before): simpler, but less adequate with respect to the denotation of convexity in the first order predicate calculus:

$$\Diamond P\Box p \rightarrow (Pp \vee \Diamond p)$$
$$\Diamond F\Box p \rightarrow (Fp \vee \Diamond p).$$

The following formulation of the condition of ordinariness shows some similarity to the above formulas:

- *ORDINAR* $\Diamond P \Diamond \Box p$ & $(Pp \lor \Diamond p \lor Fp) \rightarrow (Pp \lor \Diamond p)$

  $\Diamond F \Diamond \Box p$ & $(Pp \lor \Diamond p \lor Fp) \rightarrow (Fp \lor \Diamond p)$.

Unfortunately, an attempt to define a property of *embedment* of intervals in the extended tense logic is only partially successful. We have only manage to formulate the following formula:

- *embed* $\Diamond(p \ \& \ \bowtie q) \rightarrow (\Diamond q \rightarrow (\Diamond(Fp \ \& \ Fq) \lor \Diamond(Pp \ \& \ Pq))$ &

  $Fq \rightarrow \Diamond(Fp \ \& \ Fq)$ &

  $Pq \rightarrow \Diamond(Pp \ \& \ Pq)$.

It means:

$\forall x, u, v \ (u \subseteq x \ \& \ u \ ! \ v \rightarrow$

$(v \subseteq x \rightarrow \exists y \ (y \subseteq x \ \& \ (y < u \ \& \ y < v \lor u < y \ \& \ v < y)))$ &

$(x < v \rightarrow \exists y \ (y \subseteq x \ \& \ y < u \ \& \ y < v))$

$(v < x \rightarrow \exists y \ (y \subseteq x \ \& \ u < y \ \& \ v < y)))$,

which is weaker than the formula proposed in section 2.2.5, where we demand the existence of an interval y embedding an interval x, i.e. of a single interval satisfying all the above conditions.

The next issue consists of two "classic" properties that need not be satisfied in abnormal structures. These properties are *monotonicity* and *conjunction*. We have presented their weaker counterparts in section 2.2.5. Unfortunately, even though *monotonicity* was defined in section 3.2.1 without problems, *weak monotonicity* is not definable. This follows from the weakness of the operator $\bowtie$—it can be used with difficulty in an antecedent of an implication, but not in a consequent of an implication, as we cannot "forbid" satisfaction of a formula (propositional variable) in some interval. Nevertheless, in this situation we can use the operator $\clubsuit$ (in fact, its existential counterpart $\spadesuit$), and then we obtain the following axioms:

- *WMON* $Pp \rightarrow (\Box(Pp \lor \spadesuit p)$

  $Fp \rightarrow (\Box(Fp \lor \spadesuit p)$.

On the other hand, the property of *intersection* was not tense-logically definable in the normal case, and the property of *branch conjunction* is not tense-logically definable, either.

Now only the properties of filling intervals remain to be discussed. Unfortunately, we have managed to formulate none of these formulas. This follows precisely from the peculiarity of the operator $\bowtie$, which "forbids" satisfaction of formulas in some intervals. Let us consider this by taking *FILL*

as an example. The antecedent of the first implication can be formulated as
$F(p \\& \\bowtie q) \\& \\Diamond(q \\& \\bowtie p)$. Unfortunately, the condition:

$$F(p \\& \\bowtie q) \\& \\Diamond(q \\& \\bowtie p) \\rightarrow \\Diamond Fp \\& FPq$$

is too weak, as it is satisfied in a/the structure presented in fig. 3.13, and the
condition:

$$F(p \\& \\bowtie q) \\& \\Diamond(q \\& \\bowtie p) \\rightarrow \\Diamond(Fp \\& \\bowtie q) \\& F(Pq \\& \\bowtie p)$$

is too strong, as it excludes the structure presented in fig. 3.14.

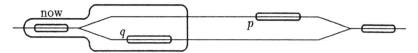

Fig. 3.13. A structure satisfying too weak filling

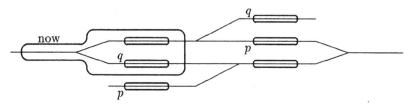

Fig. 3.14. A structure not satisfying too strong filling

Nevertheless, most of the filling properties can be formulated when the operators ♣ and ♠ are allowed. However, obtained formulas are not direct of
the axioms presented in section 2.2.5 (as it was the case with) formulas already
considered). We shall therefore discuss them in detail.

The basic filling axiom is *FILL*. It would seem that this axiom can be formulated as:

$$F(p \\& \\spadesuit q) \\& \\Diamond(q \\& \\spadesuit p) \\rightarrow \\Diamond(Fp \\& \\spadesuit q) \\& F(Pq \\& \\spadesuit p)$$
$$P(p \\& \\spadesuit q) \\& \\Diamond(q \\& \\spadesuit p) \\rightarrow \\Diamond(Pp \\& \\spadesuit q) \\& P(Fq \\& \\spadesuit p).$$

Unfortunately, the first formula, for instance, is not satisfied in the structure
presented in fig. 3.15, so we have to strengthen the premises.

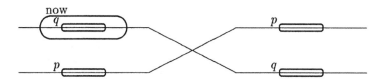

Fig. 3.15. Justification for additional premises for the property *FILL*

- *FILL*   F(p & ♠q & H¬p) & ◇(q & ♠p & G¬q)   →
  ◇(Fp & ♠q) & F(Pq & ♠p)
  P(p & ♠q & G¬p) & ◇(q & ♠p & H¬q)   →
  ◇(Pp & ♠q) & P(Fq & ♠p)

The next filling axiom is *OFILL*. We can formulate it in a natural way as:

◇(p & Fq) & ◇(♦q & ♠p)   →   ◇(Pp & ♦q).

Unfortunately, also in this case, there exist correct structures excluded by this condition. An example of such a structure is presented in fig. 3.16. Thus we have to use a weaker formulation:

- *OFILL*   ◇(p & Fq) & G¬q & ◇(♦q & ♠p)   →   ◇(Pp & ♦q)
  ◇(p & Pq) & H¬q & ◇(♦q & ♠p)   →   ◇(Fp & ♦q).

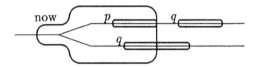

Fig. 3.16. Justification for additional premises for the property *OFILL*

Unfortunately, we have not managed to formulate *BFILL*. Nevertheless, we are able to formulate *EFILL*. The first approximation of it is the following:

◇(p & ♦q) & ◇(Pq & ♠p)   →   ◇(Pp & Pq).

This condition is also too strong, as shown in fig. 3.17. The final formulation is:

- *EFILL*   ◇(p & ♦q♣¬q & □H¬q) & ◇(Pq & ♠p)   →   ◇(Pp & Pq)
  ◇(p & ♦q♣¬q & □G¬q) & ◇(Fq & ♠p)   →   ◇(Fp & Fq).

(a)   (b)

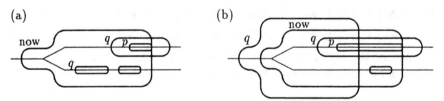

Fig. 3.17. Justification for additional premises for the property *EFILL*

Now only the counterpart of *BEFILL* remains to be defined. Let us analyse the axiom with the premise $y < x$ & ¬(x ! z) & ∃u ($u \subseteq y$ & $z < u$). Then the only possible dependency between z and y is $z < y$ ∨ ∃w ($w \subseteq z$ & $w \subseteq y$). If $z < y$, then y itself satisfies the consequent of the implication, while the condition $z \subseteq y$ covers most of the situations corresponding to the second case.

Since $y < x$ & $z \subseteq y$ and $\neg(x\,!\,z)$, by *WMON* we have $z < x$. Thus in a natural way we would formulate our axiom as:

$$\Diamond(p\,\&\,Fq)\,\&\,\Diamond Pp\,\&\,Fq\;\rightarrow\;\Diamond(Pp\,\&\,Fq).$$

Unfortunately, this axiom is not satisfied in correct structures presented in fig. 3.18. The final formulation of the axiom is the following (taking into account that by *SOLID* we have $\Diamond Fq\,\&\,\Box\boxtimes\neg q\;\rightarrow\;Fq$, which justifies its omission):

- *BEFILL* $\Diamond(p\,\&\,Fq\clubsuit\neg p)\,\&\,\Box\boxtimes\neg q\,\&\,\Diamond Pp\;\rightarrow\;\Diamond(Pp\,\&\,Fq)$
  $\Diamond(p\,\&\,Pq\clubsuit\neg p)\,\&\,\Box\boxtimes\neg q\,\&\,\Diamond Fp\;\rightarrow\;\Diamond(Fp\,\&\,Pq)$.

(a)   (b)

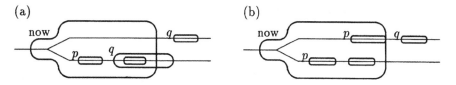

Fig. 3.18. Structures not satisfying too strong *BEFILL*

Finally, we present two properties formulated in extended tense logic, which in the case of non-linear time turn out to be stronger (in an unfavourable way!) than their counterparts formulated in the first order predicate calculus.

The first such property is *CONV*. We have shown in section 2.2.5 that it is not satisfied in non-solid partially ordered structures. However, in the modal case, $CONV^1$ does not hold for left linear order (see fig. 3.19), and $CONV^2$ does not hold for right linear order.

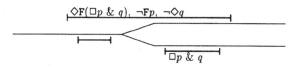

Fig. 3.19. A structure not satisfying $CONV^1$

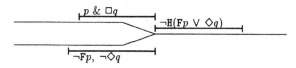

Fig. 3.20. A structure not satisfying $NEIGH^{*1}$

The second such property is *NEIGH*—a property, which has caused no problems in the first order predicate calculus case. And now $NEIGH^{*1}$ does not hold in *normal, solid* structures with right linear order (see fig. 3.20), and $NEIGH^{*2}$— with left linear order.

4. Temporal reasoning algorithms

The main goal of artificial intelligence is, in fact, designing techniques of knowledge representation and reasoning from this knowledge, rather than creation of formal models for some aspects of human reasoning (in this case concerning time related issues). In this chapter we want to present several well-known systems intended entirely for representation of time-dependent knowledge.

In practical solutions it is essential to take into account two criteria that are not necessarily consistent with each other. The first one is the easiness of data transformation from the form in which they are introduced by and returned to the user (so-called *external form of data*) to the form assumed in the representation (so-called *internal form of data*) and vice versa. The second one is the easiness of data manipulating—of introducing, removing and inferencing from them. Usually these criteria are not satisfied by formal solutions, e.g. by temporal logics based on the first order predicate calculus (see chapter 2) or modal temporal logics (see chapter 3).

4.1 Kahn & Gorry's time specialist

One of the first practical solutions concerning representation of time-dependent knowledge is the *time specialist* of Kahn & Gorry (1977). In this system time is viewed as composed of points, non-punctual events are represented as pairs of points—the initial and terminal moments of the event. Besides events, dates are represented, too, and the present is represented by a special point. The second main information is constituted by distances between points, called *time intervals* by the authors.

Kahn & Gorry have noticed that in natural language texts information concerning time is given in one of the following three ways:

- by locating an occurrence of an event in relation to calendar dating,

- by presenting a sequence of subsequent events,

- by locating an occurrence of an event in relation to some "material" event (someone's day of birth or the first day on a job; a special reference point of this kind is "now").

Accordingly to such a classification, the authors create three methods of data representation:

- the date line

  Events introduced in relation to a certain date are placed in this structure. There exists one date line in the system.

- in relation to a special reference event

  A special event, called *reference event* is distinguished, other events are related with it by a time interval between a given event and the reference event.

  There may be several reference events in the system and hence several such structures.

- before/after chains

  A chain consists of subsequent events, connected by intervals of time that have passed between them. No event in a chain is distinguished.

  There may be several such chains in the system.

Certainly, an event may occur n several data structures.

Kahn & Gorry pay much attention to imprecision, fuzziness of time-dependent information. This fuzziness can concern references to dates (e.g. *about December 12th, in June*) as well as distances between events (e.g. *2–3 days before, several months after*). For this reason events can be placed on the date line "between" some dates, rather than "pinned" to the date line. Thus time intervals between events do not have a precisely determined length, only some constraints on this length are known.

In order to obtain answer to questions, an inference is necessary. The main information needed is the position of an event on the date line (the date of the event), and the time interval between two events.

If an event is placed on the date line, determining the date of its occurrence is trivial. If an event is represented in relation to some reference event, then often the date of occurrence of the reference event is known. Thus we can determine the date of occurrence of the event by means of the date of occurrence of the reference event and the time interval between them. A situation in which the date of occurrence of the reference event is unknown, whereas we know the date of occurrence of another event in the structure, is unusual (as it is natural to assume that our knowledge about the reference event is the greatest). But also in such a situation determination of the date of occurrence of a considered event is not difficult.

If an event is placed in a before/after chain, we have to find a nearest event in the chain for which the date of occurrence is known, calculate the time interval between these two events and thus determine the date of occurrence of the required event. Certainly, it is possible that the date of occurrence of a certain event is unknown.

When looking for a time interval between two events, it is crucial to know whether both events occur in the same structure. If this is the date line, then the time interval between the events can be calculated from the dates of their occurrence. If it is a structure based on a reference event, then appropriate compositions of time intervals between the required events and their reference event yields the required time interval. If it is a before/after chain, then we must compose time intervals placed between these two events. On the other hand, if these events are not in the same structure, then actually they are not related to each other, and the authors put in doubt the sensibleness of any calculations.

Since an event can occur in several structures, the choice of a method of inference, i.e. the choice of a structure to extract information from, is crucial. It should be observed that imprecision of represented information causes some loss of information at every step of calculations, hence it is crucial to minimize the number of steps. Certainly, the system has at its disposal procedures for composition of two time intervals, or of a time interval with a date and for calculating the time interval between two dates.

At the moment of introducing a new fact to the system, it is checked whether this fact is consistent with those already existing. In the case of detection of inconsistency the user should renounce the new fact or indicate another incorrect fact to be deleted. The authors claim that the user can force the system to store inconsistent data, and then this inconsistency is only marked.

Kahn & Gorry's time specialist is an interesting proposal of a universal time-dependent knowledge representation system. However, this solution has a hybrid character, as information is represented in different ways. This reduces the readability of the representation and hinders a formal description. It is evident that this representation is better adapted to the external form of information than to the convenience of reasoning. Moreover, note that the present is represented as a temporally fixed, unchangeable reference event, which is contrary to the character of this phenomenon [Hajnicz, 1990].

4.2 Allen's constraint propagation algorithm for relations between intervals

One of the most famous, most frequently cited, developed and modified solutions is Allen's (1983) constraint propagation algorithm. In contrast to the solution presented above, Allen assumed time intervals as basic time individuals—points do not appear in his conception at all. Events, facts etc. can occur in these intervals. He does not consider dates and distances between intervals, but only their mutual position on the time axis, i.e. a purely qualitative information.

Even though Allen presents his algorithm for intervals placed on a linear time axis only, the algorithm can be applied to different individuals (e.g. intervals, points) forming different structures. Therefore we present in this section its foundations independently of the kind of individuals involved. It is only important that we have at our disposal a set **P** of all so-called *primitive relations* representing all possible mutual positions of individuals in time.

Allen's basic assumption is that we are able to represent in the system information in which the exact mutual position of individuals is not known, and we know only some constraints on this information. Therefore a relation between intervals (also called *a compound relation*) is any subset of the set of all primitive relations. If we have no information about the mutual position of two particular intervals, then the relation between them consists of all primitive relations (and it is called *no information* relation).

Example

If we know that an event occurring in an interval A has started before an event occurring in interval an B has, then we represent this by the following relation (names of primitive relations for intervals are presented in section 4.3.4):
A { *before, meets, overlaps, contains, finished by* } B.

For each primitive relation there exists a relation inverse to it. This means that if a relation r holds between individuals A and B, then its inverse relation INV(r) holds between individuals B and A. A relation inverse to a compound relation R is the set of primitive relations inverse to all the members of R. For every set of primitive relations the operation INV has the property that INV(INV(R)) = R holds for every relation R.

For each pair of primitive relations r_1 and r_2 there exists a relation which is their composition. It is a relation COMP$_P(r_1, r_2)$ such that if A r_1 B and B r_2 C hold for some individuals A, B and C in some structure, then A COMP$_P(r_1, r_2)$ C holds in it. Note, that a composition of two primitive relations need not be a primitive relation.

Example

The composition of the relations *starts* and *finished by* is the following relation:
                { *before, meets, overlaps* }
(see fig. 4.1).

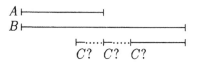

Fig. 4.1. The composition of the primitive relations *starts* and *finished by*

A value of relation COMP$_P$ depends on the choice of individuals and time structures, which they form. Eventually, it depends also on a chosen set of primitive relations.

The above statements serve as a basis for a constraint propagation algorithm used to derive inferences concerning mutual positions of individuals in time. The version of the algorithm presented here is somewhat different from that of Allen, in particular relations are stored in an array, and not in a network. This means that all represented individuals are enumerated. The algorithm is written in a language that does not correspond fully to any specific programming language; in particular it contains settheoretical operations. This is intended to make the algorithm more readable.

First we present an operation COMP which composes compound relations by means of the composition operation for primitive relations COMP$_P$. Let r_1, r_2 be primitive relations and let R, R_1, R_2 be compound relations.

```
COMP ( R₁, R₂ )
begin
    R := ∅;
    for each r₁ ∈ R₁ do
        for each r₂ ∈ R₂ do
            R := R ∪ COMPₚ ( r₁, r₂ );
    return R
end.
```

This function represents the following property of relations COMP($R_1 \cup R_2$, $R_3 \cup R_4$) = COMP(R_1, R_3) $\cup$ COMP(R_1, R_4) $\cup$ COMP(R_2, R_3) $\cup$ COMP(R_2, R_4). In practice, relations can be represented as bit maps (vectors) of primitive relations, and COMP$_P$ can be represented as a table with positions of particular primitive relations in vectors as indices, and corresponding vectors of compositions as values. For any set of primitive relations the relation *no information* has the property that nothing can be derived from it, i.e. COMP (*noinformation, R*) = COMP (*R, noinformation*) = *noinformation* (see [Hajnicz, 1987]). An important property connecting operations INV and COMP that should hold for every set of relations is INV (COMP (R$_1$, R$_2$)) = COMP (INV (R$_2$), INV (R$_1$)).

Now we can present the main algorithm. INFO is an array containing relations between individuals—at the beginning its entries are either axioms (data introduced by the user) or the *no information* relation. The diagonal is an exception—the value of INFO[i,i] is a relation determining equality (simultaneousness) of individuals; which belongs to every set of primitive relations. The numbers of individuals become indices of the array INFO. QUEUE is a queue of pairs of numbers of individuals. At the beginning, pairs from the axioms and pairs inverse to them (connected with relations inverse to relations from the axioms) are stored in the queue. These are all the elements different from the

relation *no information*, except for the entries on the diagonal of the array, since
nothing can be derived from them. Generally, the queue contains pairs of indices
of those elements of the array INFO which can be used to derive new inferences
(i.e. elements which have only just been modified). N is the total number of
individuals in the system.

ALGORITHM
begin
    while Queue is not empty do
    begin
      get <i,j> from Queue;
      for k := 1 to N do
      begin
        R := INFO[i,k] ∩ COMP (INFO[i,j], INFO[j,k]);
        if R ⊆ INFO[i,k] then
        begin
          INFO[i,k] := R;
          put <i,k> to Queue
        end;
        R := INFO[k,j] ∩ COMP (INFO[k,i], INFO[i,j]);
        if R ⊆ INFO[k,j] then
        begin
          INFO[k,j] := R;
          put <k,j> to Queue
        end
      end
    end
end.

Thus only these relations that have just undergone change are considered as a
source of information for inference. The space complexity of the algorithm is
$\mathcal{O}(N^2)$, whereas its time complexity is $\mathcal{O}(N^3)$. It follows from the above that
every element of the array INFO can undergo change (and hence be placed in the
queue) finitely many times (maximally as many as there are primitive relations
in a particular set). Thus the algorithm is decidable, at least for finite sets of
primitive relations.

    It may happen that a set of data introduced by a user is inconsistent. Then
inference yields a relation which is empty set of primitive relations. It is called

an *inconsistent relation*, since there is always some relationship between any two points on the time axis, so the empty set of primitive relations is equivalent to impossible, inconsistent information.

Example
For relations between intervals (or points) to be presented later, the set of data { *A before B, B before C, A after C* } is inconsistent, since we infer that *A before C*, which contradicts the fact that *A after C*. Evidently { *before* } ∩ { *after* } = ∅.

In the above algorithm inconsistency is not detected in any way. An occurrence of inconsistency results only in an appearance of the inconsistent relation in all elements of the array INFO. An extension of the algorithm to control the occurrence of inconsistency (with a corresponding message and an interruption of the algorithm) is certainly no problem at all.

4.3 Application of the constraint propagation algorithm to different sets of relations

In the previous section we have presented a general scheme of the constraint propagation algorithm, whereas in this section we want to present particular sets of relations with their corresponding operations INV and COMP. Even though Allen presents his algorithm for intervals, we start with a simpler case—from points.

4.3.1 Linear point time

Vilain & Kautz (1986) applied the constraint propagation algorithm to linear point time. Primitive relations between points are the following:

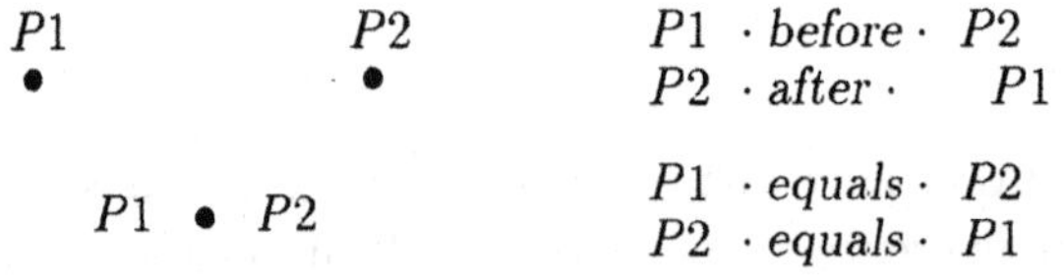

$P1$	$P2$	$P1$ · before · $P2$
•	· •	$P2$ · after · $P1$
$P1$ • $P2$		$P1$ · equals · $P2$
		$P2$ · equals · $P1$

Fig. 4.2. Primitive relations between points

Mutually inverse primitive relations are presented in the figure jointly. Such a set of primitive relations corresponds to a typical linear order of points. In fig. 4.3 we present a composition table for primitive relations between points (representing the operation COMP$_P$ for linear time and presented by Vilain & Kautz (1986)). As these authors, we will denote the relation ·*before*· by <, the relation ·*equals*·

by = and the relation ·after· by >. Since the number of compound relations is 8 in this case (including the inconsistent relation), it is possible to present a composition table for compound relations (as bit maps constitute subsequent natural numbers) and to do without the operation COMP at all.

$y\ r_2\ z$ $x\ r_1\ y$	before	equals	after
before	<	<	<=>
equals	<	=	>
after	<=>	>	>

Fig. 4.3. Composing primitive relations between points

Among points, dates can be distinguished. However, in the case of linear time they do not cause any special problems. Their only characteristic feature is that a relation between any two dates is always composed of exactly one primitive relation. Since it is known *a priori* (it depends only on the choice of dates), the system should be extended by a function calculating the relation for any two particular dates [Vilain, 1982; Hajnicz, 1989a].

4.3.2 Non-linear point time

In many papers authors assume non-linear order of time. In the previous chapters we have presented a logical description of non-linear time. Also among the requirements imposed on time representation by concrete applications presented in the introduction, the assumption of non-linearity of time structure is essential.

Allen's conception has been formulated for linear time. But Allen himself in [Allen & Koomen, 1983] points out the shortcomings of this solution. It turns out, however, that the set of primitive relations between points as well as the set of primitive relations between intervals can be enlarged so as to allow for non-linear time.

As is well-known, when we treat point time in the usual way as a structure with a particular order, then if we want to give up linearity of the order, we must remove the linearity condition. And in Allen's representation this condition can be denoted as A { *before, equals, after* } B, for any points A and B. Unfortunately, such elimination is not possible in the relational approach, since the relation which is the set of all primitive relations must hold for every pair of points. Therefore a new primitive relation for representing exactly such a situation is indispensable. We have decided to call it *excludes*, as it means that an occurrence of one point in a course of events **excludes** an occurrence of the second point in the same course of events.

Relations inverse to the relations *before*, *equals* and *after* remain the same as in the linear case, and the relation inverse to the relation *excludes* is *excludes*. Thus we now have two relations being their own inverses—*equals* and *excludes*. Thus, we have defined the operation INV. The main task consists now in defining the operation COMP$_P$ for the set of primitive relations *before*, *equals*, *after* and *excludes*.

It would seem that composition rules for these relations should remain the same as for points lying on the single axis. However, this is not the case—in some situations our inferences will be weaker, i.e. the relation *excludes* may be added. We discuss precisely these situations more in detail, as well as composition rules for relations such that one of them is the relation *excludes*.

Certainly, the relations *before* and *after* remain transitive—this is a fundamental property of any order, not necessarily linear. The basic property of the relation *equals* is "transparency", i.e. it preserves satisfaction of the relation it is composed with. There are no exceptions to this rule, so it concerns also the relation *excludes*. Thus composing x *equals* y & y *excludes* z results in x *excludes* z.

In contrast, the relation *excludes* is not transitive. It is not obvious at first glance what a composition of x *excludes* y & y *excludes* z is. Looking at fig. 4.4 it is easy to state that the relation between x and z is the set of all primitive relations.

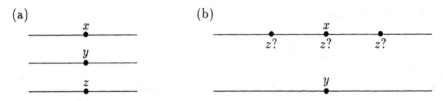

Fig. 4.4. Possible positions of points x, y and z when
x *excludes* y and y *excludes* z

In order to be able to analyse the remaining pairs of composed relations we have to make some additional assumptions on the characteristics of time structures our set of relations is to represent. After giving up the linearity axiom and preserving transitivity of the relations *before* and *after* and the property of "transparency" of the relation *equals* we have as a result a partial order. On the other hand, however, as it was mentioned in chapter 2, we can restrict our considerations to left linear orders (branching structures).

Composition rules for our current set of primitive relations can be arranged so as to satisfy each of the above assumptions. In the sequel we shall take into account both these possibilities. As a result we obtain two solutions describing two kinds of time structures—two different relation composition tables. It is worth emphasizing that in both cases the set of primitive relations is the same. We will see an analogous phenomenon in the case of intervals.

First we consider cases of the composition of the relations *before* and *after*. Under both assumptions, the composition x *after* y & y *before* z gives a disjunction of all primitive relations—see fig. 4.5.

(a)   (b)

Fig. 4.5. Possible positions of points x, y and z when x *after* y and y *before* z

In contrast, the composition x *before* y & y *after* z depends clearly on the assumed choice of solution. For a partial order we obtain, similarly as for relations inverse to those considered above, a disjunction of all primitive relations, whereas for branching time a case symmetrical to the one presented in fig. 4.5 (b) is not possible. Therefore we obtain x { *before, equals, after* } y, which after all denotes exactly the condition of left linearity in our approach.

The above two cases of relation composition show clearly that for structures with partial order symmetry between the relations *before* and *after* holds (similarly as for linear time), whereas for branching time we do not have such symmetry. This is also true of our subsequent composition rules.

Composing relations x *before* y & y *excludes* z gives x { *before, excludes* } z (fig. 4.6).

(a)   (b)

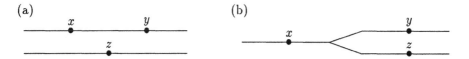

Fig. 4.6. Possible positions of points x, y and z when
x *before* y and y *excludes* z

On the other hand, composing x *after* y & y *excludes* z we obtain different results again. For partially ordered structures we obtain x { *after, excludes* } z, while for branching time structures a situation symmetrical to the one presented in fig. 4.6 (b) is not possible, so we obtain x *excludes* z.

In the above considerations we omit these cases of relation composition that follow from rules for inverse relations. Thus we now have composition rules for all primitive relations. We present them in the tables below—fig. 4.7 (a) contains dependencies for partial order, whereas fig. 4.7 (b) contains dependencies for left linear order. In the tables we use the same denotations as before and we denote the relation *excludes* by e. We omit the relation *equals* in the tables, since it is treated in an obvious way.

(a)

$y\ r_2\ z$ $x\ r_1\ y$	before	after	excludes
before	$<$	$<=>e$	$<\ e$
after	$<=>e$	$>$	$>\ e$
excludes	$<\ e$	$>\ e$	$<=>e$

(b)

$y\ r_2\ z$ $x\ r_1\ y$	before	after	excludes
before	$<$	$<=>$	$<\ e$
after	$<=>e$	$>$	e
excludes	e	$>\ e$	$<=>e$

Fig. 4.7. Relation composition tables for non-linear point time —
(a) partial order,   (b) left linear order

When point time is taken into consideration, we cannot neglect dates. In the previous section dates were treated as any other points; they were distinguished only by the property that their mutual position is always univocally known. As it was for formal logical description, also in the case of introducing dates to a representation of points by means of the constraint propagation algorithm it is much harder to do, when the time is non-linear. We have shown in section 2.1.1 that dates cannot lie on different branches. Thus in the present situation dates should be treated as a distinct kind of individuals.

Mutual position of a date and an "ordinary" point need not be univocally determined. Nevertheless there is no possibility for a date and a point to be connected by the relation *excludes*. Thus a relation between a date and a point must be a subset of the set of "linear" relations *before, equals* and *after*.

So, we ought to discuss now composition rules for relations between dates and points. Composition of relations between a point and a date and between this date and another date (and *vice versa*) proceeds analogously as in the linear case. Composing relations between two points and between the second point and a date proceeds as in the linear case, too, if these points lie on the same branch, otherwise we have no knowledge about the mutual position of the first point and the date (see fig. 4.8).

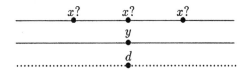

Fig. 4.8. Composing relations between two points and a date, when
x excludes y i y equals d

Composing relations between a point and a date and between this date and another points proceeds as in the linear case, but we always add the relation *excludes*. The above rules does not depend on whether we deal with partial order or with left linear order.

The fact that we have to do with two different kinds of individuals evidently complicates the algorithm. We will discuss this in a more precise way for intervals and points (section 4.3.6).

4.3.3 Relativistic point time

In section 2.1.1 a special case of partial order, concerning relativistic time structures was distinguished. It is completely different from the one presented above. Thus, it cannot be represented by means of the above relations. However, since this structure is 2-dimensional, Rodriguez (1993) defines 6 primitive relations by means of the set of primitive relations for the linear case (see fig. 4.9). A composition table for this set of primitive relations is presented in fig. 4.10. The relation consisting of all primitive relations will be denoted by *no info*.

Rodriguez (1993) considers also relativistic interval time. She treats an interval as a pair of points related by the relation *reaches* and states that there are 82 primitive relations in this case. However, the presentation of these relations is rather complicated and we shall not discuss them here.

Relation	Symbol	Name
$(<,<)$	$\prec$	*reaches*
$\{(<,=),(=,<)\}$	$\ll$	*projects to*
$\{(<,>),(>,<)\}$	$\updownarrow$	*incomparable*
$\{(>,=),(=,>)\}$	$\gg$	*projected to*
$(>,>)$	$\succ$	*reached by*
$(=,=)$	$=$	*equal*

Fig. 4.9. The set of primitive relations for relativistic time

$y\ r_2\ z$ / $x\ r_1\ y$	reaches	projects to	incompar.	projected to	reached by
reaches	$\prec$	$\prec$	$\prec, \ll, \updownarrow$	$\prec, \ll, \updownarrow$	no info
projects to	$\prec$	$\prec, \ll$	$\prec, \ll, \updownarrow$	$\ll, \updownarrow, \gg, =$	$\updownarrow, \succ, \gg$
incompar.	$\prec, \ll, \updownarrow$	$\prec, \ll, \updownarrow$	no info	$\updownarrow, \succ, \gg$	$\updownarrow, \succ, \gg$
projected to	$\prec, \ll, \updownarrow$	$\ll, \updownarrow, \gg, =$	$\updownarrow, \succ, \gg$	$\succ, \gg$	$\succ$
reached by	no info	$\updownarrow, \succ, \gg$	$\updownarrow, \succ, \gg$	$\succ$	$\succ$

Fig. 4.10. Composition rules for primitive relations for relativistic time points

4.3.4 Metric point time

As we have mentioned before, the possibility of representing metric information is as important as the possibility of representing non-linear time. In natural language texts formulations such as *3 days after* or *in 2 hours* are frequently met. In medicine we often use expressions like *2–3 days after administration of the medicine the patient should recover.* Also expressions like *I will visit you tomorrow or in three days* are possible. Therefore representing constraints as well as disjunctions of metric data is useful. It turns out that the constraint propagation algorithm offers a possibility of manipulating such information.

The idea has been suggested by Dechter et al. (1989, 1991). However, they do not use the term *relation* and start by representing metric dependencies as binary inequalities. In contrast, we have decided to show similarities between the qualitative and the quantitative approaches and to start with the concept of *primitive relation.* We will discuss this issue more precisely now.

Time distances and relations between points

The notion of distance between two points is a basis for the notion of relation between points. Since we may have an arbitrary sequence of units, which actually depends on a concrete application, we will consider an arbitrary set of distances **O**, without going into its structure for the moment.

DEFINITION

A *primitive relation* between two points is a vector, i.e. a time distance between them together with a designation of their mutual position in time by the sign "+" (*before*) or "−" (*after*).

<u>Example</u>

For the sequence of units *hour, minute, second* and some points A and B, the following sample primitive relations between these points can be defined:

A +2 hours +15 minutes B.

B −2 hours −15 minutes A.

It is an implementational question whether the sign appears before the whole distance or before each of its components. The second variant is necessary when operations on distances can lead to a loss of consistency between different distance components, which may unfortunately happen in some cases.

Evidently a set of primitive relations P can be created out of a set of time distances O by preceding each distance by "+ or "−" (obviously $+0 = -0 = 0$). Then, from sets isomorphic to Z^+ or Q^+ we may get sets isomorphic to Z or Q, respectively. Thus we have at our disposal two closely related sets: besides the set of time distances O also the set of primitive relations P. Note, that contrary to other cases, the set of primitive relations is countably infinite.

The definition of a compound relation remains unchanged—it is an arbitrary subset (finite or not) of the set of primitive relations P. We will represent a relation R as a list of succeeding intervals (open or closed), i.e. of maximal convex subsets of P. Now the set of relations R is a set of cardinality continuum.

In an implementation we shall represent only finite lists of intervals. This means that in practice we will allow only for a small (countable) part of subsets of P. It should be noted, however, that all the remaining subsets (e.g. the set of all primitive relations such that the time distance between points (in days) is divisible by 3) are not typical of commonsense reasoning, and are simply not useful from the point of view of time-dependent knowledge representation (at least in AI). On the other hand, the concept of representing repeated events in a framework of metric temporal constraint representation is presented by Poesio & Brachman (1991).

A representation of relations by lists of intervals is possible only if the set of time distances O and the set of primitive relations P are linearly ordered (of course, the orders in both these sets are mutually related).

If O is a set of time distances with a singleton unit sequence, then imposing such an order is trivial—this is the order on the corresponding numerical values. In the case of longer sequences the order is evidently more complicated. If any unit of a higher level consists of a fixed number of units of a lower level (e.g. *1 hour = 60 minutes*, hence *1 hour 30 minutes = 90 minutes*), then any two distances (vectors) can be compared. Unfortunately this is not always the case. For instance *1 month* is composed of *28–31 days*. Therefore, we cannot compare such distances as *1 month 10 days* and *40 days*, hence the order on the set of distances is not linear. Thus, it may happen that we are not able to establish the beginning or the ending of an interval. Certainly, we can assume that relations are introduced already in the form of intervals. In what follows all operations on relations will be realized as actions on lists of intervals.

From now on an interval will be denoted by $\{r_1, r_2\}$, where $r_1, r_2 \in \mathbf{P}$, $r_1 < r_2$, "$\{$" = "(" or "[" and "$\}$" = ")" or "]".

Example

Here are some examples of relations between points A and B:

$A\ [-7, -4] \cup (+5, +8)\ B$,

$A\ [+2, +2]\ B$,

$A\ [-6, +4) \cup [+8, +12)\ B$,

$A\ (-\infty, +3) \cup (+3, +\infty)\ B$,

$A\ [0, 0]\ B$.

The name of a unit (e.g. days) has been omitted in order to improve the readability of the notation.

Besides primitive relations, we want to distinguish two additional relations. The empty set of relations will be called an *inconsistent relation*, and the set of all primitive relations will be called *no-information relation*.

The above definitions are identical as for other sets of relations. Our present set of relations can be viewed as an extension of qualitative relations between points, i.e. these relations can be represented in the following way:

A before B : $A\ (-\infty, 0)\ B$

A equals B : $A\ [0, 0]\ B$

A after B : $A\ (0, +\infty)\ B$

The method of representing compound relations is evident. For example, the qualitative *no information* relation $\{before, equals, after\}$ is expressed by the metric *no information* relation $(-\infty, +\infty)$.

We also want to point out that in the presented case relations express our imprecise (incomplete) knowledge about mutual time positions of points in two ways: as a disjunction of several possible time distances (*3 days or 5 days before*) or as bounds on time distances (*from 3 days to 5 days before*). The second possibility was considered by Kahn & Gorry (1977). They represent fuzziness of time distances between points as well as of absolute positions of events, and lower and upper bounds on such information is always known. However, in our solution only time distances can be *fuzzy*.

Reasoning

In order to enable an application of the constraint propagation algorithm, a definition of the operations INV and COMP for this set of relations is necessary. In the algorithm, the settheoretical intersection operation ∩ is also used. The implementation of this operation for lists of intervals should not lead to any serious troubles.

However, since this operation is based on the comparison of endpoints of intervals, incomparability of some distances for sequences of units such that a unit of higher level may be composed of a varying number of units of lower level is a real problem now.

Example

Let us consider two single-interval relations for the sequence of units *month* and *day*.

[+10 days, +1 month +10 days]
[+5 days, +40 days]

Evidently these intervals are not disjoint—the left endpoint of the intersection is *+10 days*. But we cannot determine the right endpoint, distances *1 month 10 days* and *40 days* being incomparable.

In contrast to the previous case, it is now a real implementational problem and we have to make a decision on it. There seem to exist two simple solutions—either to make a random choice of one of possible bounds (which means that we assume that they are equal), or to treat an occurrence of such a situation as an error and to alert the user (e.g. to let him make a choice).

Certainly, none of these solutions is good. There exists another, probably better, though somewhat more complicated. We present it for the sequence *year*, *month* and *day*, but in general it can be used for any sequence of units. The idea consists in choosing one unit (e.g. *day*) and converting a primitive relation to an interval in the following way: *1 month = [28 days, 31 days], 2 months = [59 days, 62 days], 3 months = [89 days, 92 days]* etc. The complete table of these conversions can be found in [Hajnicz, 1988]. Such a table is necessary, because applying only the rule concerning one month entails a serious reduction of information, e.g. *3 months = [84 days, 93 days]*.

An inverse operation is also possible—to "extract" the number of months from a given number of days, obtaining distances in terms of months and days. The same table can be applied for this purpose (in reverse direction). Thus, for instance, *59 days = [1 month 28 days, 2 months]* and *62 days = [2 months, 2 months 3 days]*.

If two primitive relations are endpoints of intervals, then they are replaced by the respective (left or right) endpoints of their conversions.

Although such a conversion can be done in both directions, it is not an entirely invertible operation. For instance, using the above calculations we can infer that *2 months = [1 month 28 days, 2 months 3 days]*. In practice, if such calculations are necessary, they should be performed only once for each relation, and always in the same direction (without deleting the source formulations). For instance, all data could be converted into days, and the inverse operation would be used only when answering user's questions (to avoid distances such as *3582 days*).

Example
With this technique, the intersection of the relations in the previous example is the following:

[+10 days, +1 month +10 days] ∩ [+5 days, +40 days] =
[+10 days, +41 days] ∩ [+5 days, +40 days]) = [+10 days, +40 days]

This solution is certainly not perfect, as it causes loss of information (expansion of intervals). In some particular cases this can lead to "hidden" inconsistency. Nevertheless, we have not managed to find a better solution.

Now we shall discuss the inversion operation INV. We start with primitive relations. A relation inverse to a primitive relation is a vector with the opposite sign.

Example
Examples of application of the operation INV to primitive relations:

INV (+3 days) = −3 days,
INV (0 days) = 0 days.

Of course, a relation inverse to a certain compound relation is still the set of all primitive relations inverse to the primitive relations in the source relation. An implementation of this operation for lists of intervals consists in inverting the whole list (i.e. inverting all intervals as well as their order). The inversion of an interval is defined as follows:

$$\text{INV} (\{r_1, r_2\}) = \{ \text{INV} (r_2), \text{INV} (r_1) \},$$

and the brackets "[" and "(" are mapped onto the brackets "]" and ")" respectively and *vice versa*. In effect a mirror reflection of a relation is obtained.

The operation INV is obviously invertible, i.e. it satisfies the condition $r = \text{INV}(\text{INV}(r))$ for any relation r.

What remains to be discussed is the relation composition operation COMP. We start with the primitive relation composition operation COMP$_P$. Since we now have an infinite set of primitive relations, we cannot produce a pattern (table) representing COMP$_P$, but instead we need a method for computing it. This method consists in adding (unit by unit) both primitive relations.

The best way to present this operation is an example.

Example
Here are some examples of compositions of primitive relations:

$$\mathtt{COMP}_P(+2,+4) \;=\; +6,$$
$$\mathtt{COMP}_P(-3,+2) \;=\; -1,$$
$$\mathtt{COMP}_P(-4,+7) \;=\; +3,$$
$$\mathtt{COMP}_P(+2,-2) \;=\; 0.$$

Evidently the operation of composing primitive relations for multi-element sequences of units is more complicated, especially if their vectors have different signs.

Example
Let us consider examples of compositions of primitive relations:

$\mathtt{COMP}_P$ (+4 hours +30 minutes, −2 hours −50 minutes) =

$\quad$ +2 hours −20 minutes = +1 hour +40 minutes = +100 minutes,

$\mathtt{COMP}_P$ (+1 month +20 days, −3 months −10 days) = −2 months +10 days,

$\mathtt{COMP}_P$ (−1 month −10 days, +40 days) = −1 month +30 days.

As can be seen in the above example, for sequences of units such that a unit of higher level is composed of a varying number of units of lower one, addition of distances is rather complicated. In particular, it may happen that individual units have different signs. Then the only possible solution is the conversion of distances into intervals suggested above.

The definition of the operation $\mathtt{COMP}$ via the above-defined operation $\mathtt{COMP}_P$, suggested in section 4.2, is rather not constructive, as a relation may be composed of an infinite number of primitive relations. We are interested in an algorithm for composing relations which are represented as lists of intervals. The operation $\mathtt{COMP}$ can be defined, however, as a union of the operation $\mathtt{COMP}_I$ of composing all pairs of intervals from both relations. And the definition of the operation $\mathtt{COMP}_I$ by means of the operation $\mathtt{COMP}_P$ is rather simple:

$$\mathtt{COMP}_I \left(\{_1\, r_{11},\; r_{12}\,\}_1,\; \{_2\, r_{21}, r_{22}\,\}_2 \right) \;=\; \{\, \mathtt{COMP}_P\left(r_{11},\, r_{21} \right), \mathtt{COMP}_P\left(r_{12},\, r_{22} \right) \,\},$$

where "$\{$" $=$ "$[$" iff "$\{_1$" $=$ "$[$" and "$\{_2$" $=$ "$[$", and "$\}$" $=$ "$]$" iff "$\}_1$" $=$ "$]$" and "$\}_2$" $=$ "$]$".

Example
Example of the operation of interval composition:

$$\mathtt{COMP}_I \left([-3,\; +2],\; (+7,\; +10] \right) \;=\; (+4, +12],$$
$$\mathtt{COMP}_I \left([-9,\; +1],\; [+3,\; +\infty) \right) \;=\; [-6,\; +\infty),$$
$$\mathtt{COMP}_I \left((-\infty,\; -6),\; [+8,\; +\infty) \right) \;=\; (-\infty, +\infty).$$

Certainly, primitive relations $-\infty$ or $+\infty$ do not exist, but infinity has the property of "absorbing" of other values.

Moreover, it should be noticed that the primitive relation composition operation $\mathtt{COMP}_P$ is commutative and associative, hence the relation composition operation $\mathtt{COMP}$ is commutative and associative, too.

Thus, all the operations required for inferring with the constraint propagation algorithm have been defined. Finally, it is worth mentioning that when the operations $\mathtt{COMP}$ and $\mathtt{INV}$ are applied to relations representing qualitative relations between points, the same result is obtained as for the original solution.

In spite of the fact that our set of primitive relations makes possible the representation of relatively precise information, a reduction of information occurs when a path of inference grows longer. Such a reduction of information does not occur only in the case of precise information, i.e. information represented by primitive relations.

Example

Let us consider points A, B and C:

$$A\ [+2,\ +6]\ B\ \&\ B\ [+3,\ +5]\ C\ \implies\ A\ [+5,\ +11]\ C,$$
$$A\ [+5,\ +11]\ C\ \&\ C\ [-5,\ -3]\ B\ \implies\ A\ [0,\ +12]\ B.$$

Evidently the interval $[+2,\ +6]$ is contained in the interval $[0,\ +12]$, so the obtained inference is weaker. On the other hand:

$$A\ [+2,\ +2]\ B\ \&\ B\ [+3,\ +3]\ C\ \implies\ A\ [+5,\ +5]\ C,$$
$$A\ [+5,\ +5]\ C\ \&\ C\ [-3,\ -3]\ B\ \implies\ A\ [+2,\ +2]\ B.$$

The property of reduction of information in the case of incomplete information has already been noticed by Kahn & Gorry (1977). This means that in this sense even primitive relations of the original, qualitative point case do not represent precise, complete information.

Dates

As we have mentioned several times, not only mutual time positions of points, but also their absolute positions (i.e. positions in relation to calendar dates) are often discussed in the literature.

As it has been already mentioned, Kahn & Gorry (1977) consider the fuzziness of absolute positions of events on the time axis. Dechter et al. (1991), Poesio & Brachman (1991) and Koubarakis (1992) consider dates in a framework of constraint propagation. They treat constraints on absolute positions of points as unary inequalities, hence they make no difference between absolute and relative dates (distances), which is valid only in an idealistic case, when the hierarchy of time units is a singleton (see section 2.1.3). Thus we present a slighty different approach, in which such information is represented as an appropriate relation between an event and a date.

Example

The information:

A occurred between the 3rd and 10th of May, 1989.

may be represented as:

A [0 days, +7 days] 1989.05.03

or as:

A [+2 days, +9 days] 1989.05.01.

A specific feature of dates is that their mutual position on the time axis is univocally determined. Also in this case we can define a function computing relations between dates, and these will always be primitive relations.

Example

Sample dependencies between dates are:

1987.07.15 −35 days 1987.06.10
1987.12.09 +5 days 1988.01.03
12:30:10 −3 hours −40 minutes 8:50:10

Given a function computing distances between dates, we can draw inferences concerning dates which we have no explicit information about.

Example

When the information:

A −5 days 1987.07.15

is stored in the system, then the information:

A −40 days 1987.06.10

can be inferred from it.

As it was mentioned in chapter 2, the algorithm requires $\mathcal{O}(N^3)$ executions of the operations COMP and INV, apart from the fact that the time of execution of these operations depends on the length of the list of intervals. It is therefore evident that a minimization of the number of points significantly cuts down the time of inference. Complete comparability of absolute dates allows a realization of the following idea, suggested by Poesio & Brachman (1991). Namely, a unique base date (e.g. *1980.01.01*) would be represented in the system. Information concerning a relation between a point and an arbitrary date would be transformed into a relation between this point and the base date (one COMP operation); the inverse operation would be performed only for a question concerning a relation between a point and a date. Relations between dates being primitive the above operation reduces to shifting a relation by some vector, so it is an invertible operation.

In the case of a large number of stored dates the solution is really economical, especially if dates occurring in questions differ often from dates introduced in the data. Nevertheless, in practice, this idea can be implemented only when operations performed on stored data are very limited, e.g. information once entered cannot be deleted. It should be realized, after all, that a relation between some point and the base date can be an intersection of relations obtained from other data. On the other hand, this problem can be partially solved by storing axioms (informations given directly by the user) and inferences separately.

Koubarakis (1992) suggests to represent inequations (negations of equations) in addition to inequalities. He claims that the above solution is not powerful enough to represent disjunctions of inequations. However, in my opinion a disjunction of at least two inequations provides no new information, as if $x \neq \alpha \lor x \neq \beta$, then x is actually arbitrary.

4.3.5 Linear interval time

Now we present the original system of Allen's primitive relations representing all possible mutual positions of two intervals on the time-axis (see fig. 4.11). Also in this case pairs of mutually inverse primitive relations are presented in fig. 4.11 together, which constitutes a basis for defining the operation INV for this set of relations.

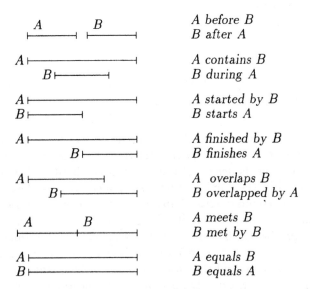

Fig. 4.11. Primitive relations between intervals in linear time

Allen (1983) introduces a table containing compositions of all pairs of primitive relations, as shown in fig. 4.12. In the table we use the denotations for primitive relations similar to those suggested by Allen (1983): *before* – *b*, *meets* – *m*, *overlaps* – *o*, *finished by* – *fi*, *contains* – *di*, *starts* – *s*, *equals* – *eq*, *started by* – *si*, *during* – *d*, *finishes* – *f*, *overlapped by* – *oi*, *met by* – *mi*, *after* – *bi*. In addition, the relation {*b*, *m*, *o*, *fi*, *di*, *s*, *eq*, *si*, *d*, *f*, *oi*, *mi*, *bi*} is denoted as *no information* (*no info*), the relation {*s*, *d*, *f*} — by *DUR* and the relation {*fi*, *di*, *si*} — by *CON*.

4. Temporal reasoning algorithms

r_1 \ r_2	b	m	o	fi	di	si	s	d	f	oi	mi	bi
b	b	b	b	b	b	b	b	b	b,s m,d o	b,s m,d o	b,s m,d o	no info
m	b	b	b	b	b	m	m	o s d	o s d	o s d	f fi eq	di,si oi,mi bi
o	b	b	b m o	b m o	b,fi m,di o	o fi di	o	o s d	o s d	o,oi eq DUR CON	di si oi	di,si oi,mi bi
fi	b	m	o	fi	di	di	o	o s d	f fi eq	di si oi	di si oi	di,si oi,mi bi
di	b,fi m,di o	o fi di	o fi di	di	di	di	fi di oi	o,oi eq DUR CON	di si oi	di si oi	di si oi	di,si oi,mi bi
si	b,fi m,di o	o fi di	o fi di	di	di	si	s eq si	d f oi	oi	oi	mi	bi
s	b	b	b m o	b m o	b,fi m,di o	s eq si	s	d	d	d f oi	mi	bi
d	b	b	b,s m,d o	b,s m,d o	no info	oi,d mi,f bi	d	d	d	oi,d mi,f bi	bi	bi
f	b	m	o s d	fi eq f	di,si oi,mi bi	oi mi bi	d	d	f	oi mi bi	bi	bi
oi	b,fi m,di o	o fi di	o,oi eq DUR CON	di si oi	di,si oi,mi bi	oi mi bi	d f oi	d f oi	oi	oi mi bi	bi	bi
mi	b,fi m,di o	s eq si	d f oi	mi	bi	bi	d f oi	d f oi	mi	bi	bi	bi
bi	no info	oi,d mi,f bi	oi,d mi,f bi	bi	bi	bi	oi,d mi,f bi	oi,d mi,f bi	bi	bi	bi	bi

Fig. 4.12. Composition rules for primitive relations between intervals
in linear time

As we have mentioned, the constraint propagation algorithm is decidable. Unfortunately, for the set of relations between intervals the algorithm is not complete (see section 5.7), i.e. derived conclusions can be weaker than the actual constraints. Thus we can say that the algorithm approximates the real solution, which is an **NP**-complete problem (see Vilain & Kautz, 1986). Nevertheless Allen's algorithm is complete for every set of relations between three intervals.

The algorithm is not complete for points, either. Unfortunately, for intervals the incompleteness of the algorithm is so strong that real inconsistency is may not be detected. Allen (1983) gives an example of such a set of data.

The representation and algorithm suggested by Allen were intended, similarly as Kahn & Gorry's solution, to conveniently denote information coming from natural language. Allen's representation is weaker inasmuch as it does not contain metric information. Nevertheless it is uniform and has elegant notation. Due to these features it is easy to formalize. Allen & Hayes's logic contains the above mechanism (i.e. all primitive relations are defined in it). Another formalization was suggested in [Hajnicz, 1991a]. This subject will be further developed in chapter 5.

4.3.6 Non-linear interval time

As we have already mentioned, from the artificial intelligence point of view, a time interval is the time of occurrence of some individuals from the metalevel relative to pure temporal logic, namely events, facts, processes etc. [McDermott, 1982; Allen, 1984]. This should be kept in mind while determining primitive relations between intervals. Evidently it is possible that no event occurs in a particular interval, nevertheless the mutual position of intervals cannot be such that an occurrence of an event in a particular interval makes no sense. The subject of representation of intervals in non-linear time has been already discussed in [Hajnicz, 1991c, 1995c].

It is evident that, as in the case of points, the set of primitive relations has to be extended. Following considerations of section 2.2.5, we shall not represent relations between intervals corresponding to positions of intervals from fig. 2.12 (b) and (c). Actually, a whole class of such positions is presented in fig. 4.13.

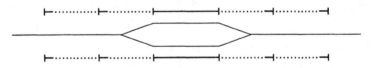

Fig. 4.13. A whole class of "non-solid" positions of two intervals

Nevertheless, this does not mean that no interval can lie in an area of branch fork—in section 2.2.5 we have argued in favour of intervals containing several mutually excluding subintervals. This requires considering new possible positions of two intervals, the sensibleness of which (or its lack) is not as evident as before. In [Hajnicz, 1995c] we have enumerated 34 new primitive relations corresponding for locations for intervals viewed in this way (see figs. 2.16, 2.20, 2.21, 2.22).

The worst, however, is the fact that composition rules for this kind of primitive relations would be very weak.

Example

Consider a situation presented in fig. 4.14. Here the relations x before/meets y and z finishes x hold. Evidently, it follows from the figure that z meets y holds. But we do not know on which branch z is (on both, perhaps?)—actually, we are not able to identify branches at all. Thus we are only able to deduce z {before, meets, before/meets} y.

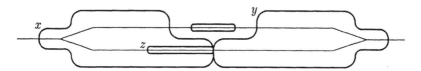

Fig. 4.14. An example of composing "strange" relations between intervals

In section 2.2.5 such positions of time intervals as presented above were questioned (though they were not definitely rejected). See also more technical argumentation against them in [Hajnicz, 1995c]. Eventually, we decided to add only one more relation to the thirteen primitive relations representing the mutual positions of intervals in linear time (on a single branch). This new relation represents the position of two intervals on two branches (as presented in fig. 2.12 (a)). It is called (as in the case of points) excludes.

Now, we propose composition tables for this new set of primitive relations, enriched by the relation excludes. Seemingly, the rules for composing "linear" relations should not be changed, so the only thing to do is to consider the rules for composing the relation excludes with the other relations. This is exactly what Tsang [1986] had in mind, when he introduced an analogous relation (called undefined) representing the fact that particular time intervals do not lie on the same branch. In his solution, Tsang assumed that the composition rules for relations remain unchanged, and that we can deduce nothing using the relation undefined, i.e. we always deduce the relation no information. It turned out that both these assumptions were not correct. First, in some cases inferences are weaker, i.e. the relation excludes is added to the "linear" composition, because sometimes one interval can be collinear with two other intervals lying on different branches. Second, the composition of the relation excludes with other relations is usually significantly stronger than the relation no information. Moreover, Tsang's representation does not distinguish different time structures.

In further considerations we will consider structures with partial and left linear order simultaneously, whereas structures allowing mutually excluding subintervals or not will be discussed separately. We will use the same abbreviations for denotations of primitive relations as those introduced in section 4.3.4. The relation *excludes* will be denoted by e, as it was for points. Like in the linear case, the relation { b, m, o, fi, di, s, eq, si, d, f, oi, mi, bi, e } will be denoted by *no information* (*no info*). In [Hajnicz, 1995c] we analyse to which primitive relations compositions a relation *excludes* should be added in detail. Here we give only some representative examples.

Let us first consider relation composition rules for the case when no interval can include mutually exclusive subintervals. This is reasonable for the applications in which there is no uncertainty concerning the occurrence of some events during other events. Then, we can formulate a general rule: Let two intervals be not disjoint (i.e. the relation between them is o, fi, di, s, eq, si, d, f or oi). If the second interval is in any relation except *excludes* with a third one, then the composition of these two relations does not contain the relation *excludes*. On the other hand, if the second relation is *excludes*, then the composition is *excludes*.

Now, consider the information: x *after* y & y *meets* z. The mutual position of intervals presented in fig. 4.15 is possible, so we get x { d, f, oi, mi, bi, e } z. However, for the pair of relations x *before* y & y *met by* z, the situation symmetrical with respect to time arrow to the one presented in fig. 4.15 is possible only for partial order, so it should be considered only in that case. For the pairs of relations x *after* y & y *before* z, x *met by* y & y *meets* z, x *before* y & y *after* z and x *meets* y & y *met by* z, we can reason similarly.

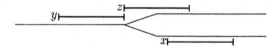

Fig. 4.15. The case of mutual exclusion of the intervals x and z
x $for the in formation$ *after* y & y *meets* z

(a)   (b)

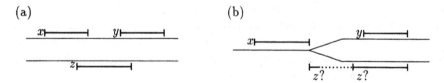

Fig. 4.16. Possible positions of intervals satisfying: x *before* y & y *excludes* z

Consider the pair of relations x *before* y & y *excludes* z. In this case we obtain x { b, m, e } z irrespectively of the considered order (see fig. 4.16). On the other hand, for the relations x *after* y & y *excludes* z, the situation symmetrical to that presented in fig. 4.16 (b) is possible only for partial order. Exactly the same situation occurs for the pairs of relations x *meets* y & y *excludes* z and x *met by* y & y *excludes* z.

The table of composition of primitive relations for partial order is presented in fig. 4.17, and the table of composition of primitive relations for left linear order is presented in fig. 4.18. In both cases we have assumed that no interval can contain mutually exclusive subintervals. For most relations we have only shown whether the relation *excludes* has been added or not. The complete composition rule is presented only in the case when one of composed relations is *excludes*, as these rules are completely new ones. Additional frames point out differences between tables.

r_1\\r_2	b	m	o	fi	di	si	s	d	f	oi	mi	bi	e
b											+e	+e	b m e
m											+e	+e	b m e
o													e
fi													e
di													e
si													e
s													e
d													e
f													e
oi													e
mi	+e	+e											mi bi e
bi	+e	+e											mi bi e
e	b m e	b m e	e	e	e	e	e	e	e	e	mi bi e	mi bi e	no info

Fig. 4.17. Primitive relation composition rules for partial order
without containment of mutually excluding intervals

r_1\\r_2	b	m	o	fi	di	si	s	d	f	oi	mi	bi	e
b													b m e
m													b m e
o													e
fi													e
di													e
si													e
s													e
d													e
f													e
oi													e
mi	+e	+e											e
bi	+e	+e											e
e	e	e	e	e	e	e	e	e	e	e	mi bi e	mi bi e	no in-fo

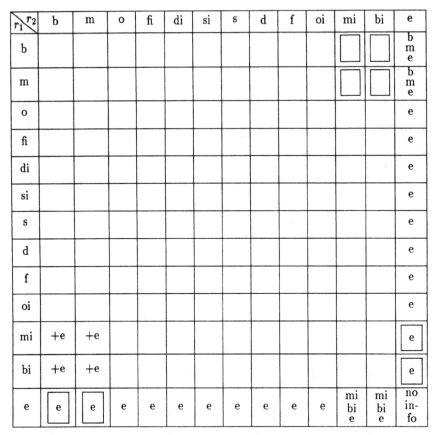

Fig. 4.18. Primitive relation composition rules for left linear order
without containment of mutually excluding intervals

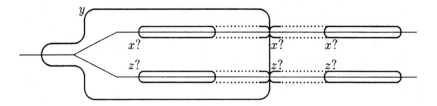

Fig. 4.19. The case of excluding intervals x and z for composing relations
$x\ r_1\ y$ (r_1 = during, finishes, overlapped by, met by, after)   and
$y\ r_2\ z$ (r_2 = before, meets, overlaps, finished by, contains)

Now, suppose that intervals can contain some mutually exclusive subintervals. We decided to exclude intervals as one form fig. 2.9 (cf. [Hajnicz, 1995c]).

Thus we make an assumption that even though an interval need not lie on a single branch, at least one its fragment should (see fig. 2.10). In fig. 4.19, cases of relation composition are presented such that the result of composing $x \; r_1 \; y$ and $y \; r_2 \; z$ is the relation x excludes z. For instance, in the linear case the composition of x during y and y before z is x during z, whereas now we obtain $x \; \{during, \; excludes\} \; z$. These cases hold for both partial and left-linear orders. For partial order cases symmetrical to those presented in the figure hold, too.

r_1 \ r_2	b	m	o	fi	di	si	s	d	f	oi	mi	bi	e
b					+e	+e				+e	+e	+e	b di m fi o e
m					+e	+e				+e	+e	+e	b di m fi o e
o					+e	+e				+e	+e	+e	b di m fi o e
fi													b di m fi o e
di													−(eq DUR)
si													di si oi bi mi e
s				+e	+e					+e	+e	+e	e
d	+e	+e	+e	+e	+e	+e				+e	+e	+e	e
f	+e	+e	+e	+e	+e								e
oi	+e	+e	+e	+e	+e								di si oi bi mi e
mi	+e	+e	+e	+e	+e								di si oi bi mi e
bi	+e	+e	+e	+e	+e								di si oi bi mi e
e	b d m s o e	b d m s o e	b d m s o e	e	e	e	b d m s o e	−(eq CON)	d oi f mi bi e	d oi f mi bi e	d oi f mi bi e	d oi f mi bi e	no info

Fig. 4.20. Primitive relation composition rules for partial order allowing containment of mutually excluding intervals

r_1\\r_2	b	m	o	fi	di	si	s	d	f	oi	mi	bi	e
b					□	□				□	□	□	b di m fi o e
m					□	□				□	□	□	b di m fi o e
o					□	□				□	□	□	b di m fi o e
fi													b di m fi o e
di													b di m fi o e
si													e
s				□	□					□	□	□	e
d	+e	+e	+e	+e	+e	□				□	□	□	e
f	+e	+e	+e	+e	+e								e
oi	+e	+e	+e	+e	+e								e
mi	+e	+e	+e	+e	+e								e
bi	+e	+e	+e	+e	+e								e
e	e	e	e	e	e	e	e	e	d oi f mi bi e	d oi f mi bi e	d oi f mi bi e	d oi f mi bi e	no in-fo

Fig. 4.21. Primitive relation composition rules for left linear order
allowing containment of mutually excluding intervals

If we performed deduction for y *rel* x & x *excludes* z according to fig. 4.19
(*rel* = *before, meets, overlaps, finished by, contains*), we would obtain y { b, m,
o, fi, di, e } z as a result (after enclosing the relation *excludes*). As before,
this dependence concerns both partial and left-linear orders. In the case of
partial order, situations symmetrical with respect to time arrow to the presented ones should also be considered. So, for x *rel* y & y *excludes* z we
have x { di, si, oi, mi, bi, e } z. The relation *contains* is worth special at-

tention, as both cases should be considered for it. Thus, the composition of
x contains y & *y excludes z* is *x* { *b, m, o, fi, di, si, oi, mi, bi, e* } *z*.

The table of compositions of primitive relations for partial order is presented
in fig. 4.20, and the table of compositions of primitive relations for left linear order
is presented in fig. 4.21. In both cases we have assumed that intervals can contain
mutually exclusive subintervals. As before, frames (rectangular) point out that
there exist differences between these two cases. Certainly, derived conclusions
are weaker than under the assumption forbidding intervals containing mutually
exclusive subintervals. Differences following from this fact (for the same orders)
are marked in the tables by oval frames.

It should be mentioned that in most cases derived conclusions have not undergone any changes in relation to the original Allen's table, which means that
the power of derived conclusions has not decreased too much. In the most "lib-
eral" case presented in fig.4.20 the relation *excludes* has been added to 50 from
among 169 entries, i.e. to about 1/3 of them. Nevertheless, note that precisely in
this case conclusions derived with the relation *excludes* are rather weak, which
in turn makes further inferences weaker, too. Certainly, the choice of a table
(and hence time positions of intervals that are allowed) depends on a particular
application and its specific needs.

4.3.7 Linear interval/point time

Besides structures composed of one kind of individuals, also heterogeneous structures can be considered, e.g. structures in which intervals as well as points occur.
Vilain (1982) suggests a solution based on the constraint propagation algorithms,
taking into account both intervals and points.

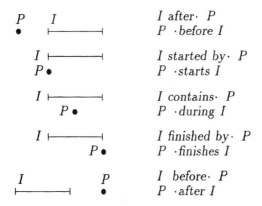

Fig. 4.22. Primitive relations between intervals and points

Since we have two different kinds of individuals, we also have different sets of primitive relations that should be differently denoted. Therefore relations between points (see fig. 4.2) will be denoted by ·before·, ·equals· and ·after·, whereas relations between intervals preserve their denotations. Sets of relations between intervals and points and between points and intervals (fig. 4.22) are added to the above sets.

As it follows from the figure, the sets of relations between intervals and points and between points and intervals are not closed under the operation INV, but they are complementary—primitive relations inverse to relations from one set belong to the other. Accordingly to our rule we present mutually inverse relations in the figure together.

(a)

r_1\\r_2	·b	·s	·d	·f	·bi
b·	b	b	b,m,o s,d	b,m,o s,d	no info
fi·	b	m	o,s,d	f,fi eq	di,si,oi mi,bi
di·	b,m,o fi,di	fi,di oi	−(b,bi m,mi)	di,si oi	di,si,oi mi,bi
si·	b,m,o fi,di	s,si eq	d,f oi	mi	bi
bi·	no info	d,f,oi mi,bi	d,f,oi mi,bi	bi	bi

(b)

r_1\\r_2	b·	fi·	di·	si·	bi·
·b	b	b	b	b	b,bi eq
·s	b	b	b	eq	bi
·d	b	b	b,bi eq	bi	bi
·f	b	eq	bi	bi	bi
·bi	b,bi eq	bi	bi	bi	bi

(c)

r_1\\r_2	b	m	o	fi	di	s	si	d	f	oi	mi	bi
·b	b	b	b	b	b	b	b	b,s d	b,s d	b,s d	b,s d	no in.
·s	b	b	b	b	b	s	s	d	d	d	f	bi
·d	b	b	b,s d	b,s d	no in.	d	d,f bi	d	d	d,f bi	bi	bi
·f	b	s	d	f	di	d	bi	d	f	bi	bi	bi
·bi	no in.	d,f bi	d,f bi	bi	bi	d,f bi	bi	d,f bi	bi	bi	bi	bi

(d)

r_1\\r_2	·b·	·bi·
b·	b	no in.
fi·	b	di,si bi
di·	b,f di	di,si bi
si·	b,fi di	bi
bi·	no in.	bi

Fig. 4.23. Additional tables for composing relations between individuals
(a) interval–point–interval   (b) point–interval–point
(c) point–interval–interval   (d) interval–point–point

Since in this system different individuals and various sets of relations exist, there should exist several arrays containing data (relations between individuals). Actually four such arrays are needed—two square and two rectangular (as the number of intervals and the number of points need not be equal). If a triangular array were considered (see section 4.4.1), it would be replaced by two triangular and one rectangular arrays. Also the main algorithm becomes more complicated. There exist eight ways of composing relations, since three individuals take part in the composition operation, and each of them can be an interval or a point. Thus eight operations COMP$_P$ are needed. Therefore in order to make the algorithm executable, we have to present six more tables defining compositions between individuals. In fact, it is enough to present four of them, accordingly to the rule for composing inverse relations introduced in section 4.2. These tables are presented in fig. 4.23.

Furthermore, four queues Queue corresponding to four data arrays INFO are needed. The above changes do not influence space and time computational complexity of the algorithm, nevertheless they impair its readability.

Vilain suggests to distinguish some points as absolute dates. The characteristic of dates is the same as presented before.

We would also like to consider whether differentiation of intervals and points is indeed necessary, or perhaps a special group of *atomic* intervals (see section 2.2.6) could be distinguished in the set of intervals, such that only some specific relations between them and other intervals (actually those presented in figs. 4.2 and 4.22) would be satisfiable. Then it would not be necessary to define additional arrays and queues, but it would be enough to select an adequate *no information* relation for each pair of intervals (only while creating an array or adding new intervals) depending only on the type of intervals.

Unfortunately, it turns out that a situation, when an atomic interval is placed in the endpoint of a "normal" interval causes some trouble. Namely, an atomic interval, even though indivisible, can be located either "inside" the "normal" interval (i.e. *starts* or *finishes* it) or "outside" the "normal" interval (i.e. *meets* it). In the case of points these situations are not differentiated, and consequently the derived conclusions are different.

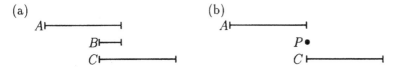

Fig. 4.24. Differences in positions of different individuals on the time axis
(a) three intervals   (b) two intervals and a point

Example

Let us consider an inference for the following three intervals (see fig. 4.24 (a)):

    A finished by B   &   B starts C.

Then we will infer:

    A overlaps C,

whereas an analogous inference for two intervals and a point (fig. 4.23 (b)):

   A finished by · P & P · starts C

leads to the conclusion:

   A meets C.

This is not the only case, when an inference for different individuals proceeds in a different way than it does for intervals only. Therefore an implementation of points as atomic intervals is impossible.

4.4 Extensions and modifications of Allen's constraint propagation algorithm

Allen's constraint propagation algorithm has raised broad interest. It is not exaggerated to say that it is one of most frequently discussed and applied algorithms. Moreover, many modifications of the algorithm have been created, extending its power in various ways.

4.4.1 Direct extensions of the algorithm

First we discuss basic extensions that do not change the main idea of the algorithm. Vilain (1982) suggests the incorporation of some truth maintenance system (TMS, see Doyle, 1978) in order to show which axioms lead to inconsistency. However, Vilain does not specify how the mechanism is to be used. In the system which we have implemented [Hajnicz, 1987; 1988] we realize Vilain's postulate in the simplest way—by relating to each element of the array INFO a list of axioms which have lead to the particular inference. At the beginning, lists are either empty or singletons (for axioms). Whenever an element of the array INFO is modified, the list connected with this element is modified, too, by adding lists related to the premises of the inference, and if a new inference is completely included in the old one, the previous content of the list is deleted. When inconsistency appears, the user has to delete one of the axioms occurring on the corresponding list. We have shown in [Hajnicz, 1987] that sometimes one axiom can be inconsistent with several sets of axioms.

Example
Consider the following set of data { *A overlaps B, A before D, B meets C, C finishes D*} (see fig. 4.25).
We can infer *A before C* either from *A overlaps B & B meets C*, or from *A before D & D finished by C*. Depending on which formula is applied first, the corresponding list contains different axioms. Adding the information *C before A* leads to inconsistency. Evidently deleting any axiom from the list (except the

new one) would not restore consistency—the second rule would be unblocked and a second list of inconsistent axioms would appear.

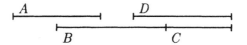

Fig. 4.25. Four examples of intervals in linear time

Another extension suggested by us consists in representing only one relation in each pair of mutually inverse ones, i.e. representing data in a triangular array. This follows from the already mentioned property of relation composition, stating that:

$$\text{COMP}(\text{INV}(R_1), \text{INV}(R_2)) = \text{INV}(\text{COMP}(R_2, R_1))$$

The above idea complicates somehow the notation of the algorithm, but does not increase its time complexity.

Allen himself suggests an improvement of this algorithm by introducing so-called *reference intervals*. Namely, intervals are grouped into classes with common reference intervals (these are not equivalence classes, in particular no interval is a reference interval for itself). Such a class contains semantically related intervals (in fact, events occurring in these intervals). An interval can have several reference intervals, and as a result we obtain a hierarchy forming a directed graph. It is typical for intervals to be included in their reference intervals.

The idea depends on the fact that only relations between intervals having a common reference interval are computed and stored. If the system is asked a question about a relation concerning intervals from different classes, paths concerning these intervals are found in the hierarchy graph and additional reasoning is performed along these paths. But if reference intervals are well designed, such a necessity should appear rather seldom, so we avoid computing relations between intervals that have nothing in common. Such an approach significantly decreases the time of reasoning. Unfortunately, it also decreases its power, i.e. derived inferences can sometimes be weaker than those derived by the original algorithm [Koomen, 1987, 1989]. In the latter paper Koomen suggests an algorithm of automatic references for intervals that overcomes these shortcomings.

Song & Cohen (1991) and Song (1994) analyse such hierarchy based on the relation *CON*. They demand a decomposition of an interval into subintervals to be complete, i.e. the subinterval(s) starting first should start the whole interval etc. This approach is entirely different from the other presented in this book. It can be treated as a case of the *closed world assumption*, hence it is non-monotonic; new data can negate previous conclusions (e.g. when an earlier subinterval is added). On the other hand, data consistent from the constraint-satisfaction point of view can turn to be inconsistent (e.g. when none of subintervals of a given interval is supposed to start it).

Poesio & Brachman (1991) observe that dates (viewed as intervals) constitute an excellent reference hierarchy (e.g. day, week, month, day). The *reference date* of an interval is the smallest date that properly contains it.

Keretho & Loganantharaj (1993) suggest other improvements to speed-up the algorithm. First, they create an auxiliary boolean array showing whether a pair of individuals is in the queue or not. This enables avoiding a redundant consideration of the pair. Second, they apply the so-called *Most-Constrained First Principle*, by ordering the queue regarding to how many elements the relation between individuals from a pair contains.

Another constraint propagation algorithm faster than the original one is presented by [Ladkin & Reinefeld, 1992]. They analyse on random networks how much time they use, but they do not present any symbolic time complexity.

4.4.2 Metric information for interval/point time

In section 4.3.3 we have presented a set of primitive relations for metric point time. One can imagine a set of primitive relations for interval/point time, in which relations between points have metric character, whereas relations between intervals have the usual, qualitative character. Unfortunately, in such a situation it is difficult to determine relations between intervals and points and between points and intervals.

In [Hajnicz, 1987; 1988; 1989a] we take another approach that is also a continuation of Vilain's idea. We have introduced there the concept of a *relative date*. A relative date is composed of a *reference point* and an *offset* (determining a distance in time), so this concept is somewhat similar to Kahn & Gorry's *reference event*. The name *relative date* originates from the fact that this concept describes position in time <u>relative</u> to a *reference point*. A similar notion was introduced by Rescher & Urquhardt (1977). All points in the system are absolute or relative dates (a reference point is a relative date being a reference point for itself and having offset zero). Every relative date has exactly one reference point.

The introduction of metric information (offsets of relative dates, i.e. distances between points) makes the system assume a hybrid character, not to such an extent, however, as Kahn & Gorry's solution. Relations between individuals are stored in data arrays as before (if a distance between points is known, then a relation between them should be composed of one primitive relation). Additionally there is an array containing reference points and offsets with respect to these points for all relative dates. The original algorithm is extended only for the case when equality of two points is detected. Then the classes the two points belong to are merged, and a single reference point is determined. If one of the two dates is an absolute date, all the dates from the other class become absolute, too.

The solution can be formalized—an attempt to formalize it has been presented in [Hajnicz, 1991a].

Kautz & Ladkin (1991) suggest another solution to this problem. They represent qualitative relations between intervals and metric dependencies between their endpoints (which are the only points). They allow only for single-interval metric dependencies. The two representations are kept mutually consistent by transferring information back and forth between them by means of algorithms translating one representation into the other.

The most powerful solution is presented by Dechter et al. (1991). They represent qualitative relations between two intervals, an interval and a point and a point and an interval as presented in section 4.3.7. Furthermore they represent quantitative relations between points. They combine the information by transforming qualitative and quantitative relations between points (back and forth) in an obvious way (see section 4.3.4).

4.4.3 Representing the present in the constraint propagation algorithm

As Kahn & Gorry, Allen (1983) also considers the possibility of representing the present in his system. However, in contrast to that solution, Allen represents the present by means of intervals and it is not constant, but is regularly moving towards the future. His method consists in using a variable pointing at the current interval. A certain hierarchy of reference intervals (see section 4.4.1), determining the current day, week etc., and of intervals connected with concrete events—lunch, conference, being in work etc., is built over the present. Each subsequent reference to the present implies moving the variable to a later interval (without changing the reference interval). The change of the reference interval should be caused explicitly by the user, (i.e. it should follow from his statements). Such a representation minimizes the number of modifications imposed on a database by the passing of time, i.e. by the movement of the present towards the future.

However, the present can be viewed not only as an interval, but also as a point—a specific date. A system can acquire knowledge of the current moment in many different ways. First, it can use a clock [Ladkin, 1986b; Lâasri et al., 1988], e.g. a computer clock, and receive therefrom the current date. But then *now* is just a keyword, and we use only absolute dates in the system. Unfortunately this solution has several weak points. First of all, date formats used in some applications need not be consistent with the information available from the computer clock. Besides, the system time need not coincide with the real time, hence also the system *now* can differ from the real *now*. Analogously, the present in a novel is different from the present of its reader.

Second, *now* can be changed by the user. It turns out that in such a situation it is possible to represent the present by means of metric relations between points in a satisfactory way, i.e. enabling changes of *now*. The present interpreted in such a way is a discrete process (all references to *now* between successive changes concern the same value of *now*). Evidently the real *now* changes continuously. But still some doubts remain. Since we distinguish two times—the time of the represented knowledge and the real (user) time, and since these times have different *now* moments and they pass with different speed, they are entirely independent from each other and their *time arrows* (see Denbigh, 1975) can also be different. In other words, can we allow *now* to go backward? There is no good answer to this question, the problem depends on a particular application. In modern novels one can often find retrospections, rapid changes of time backward and forward. Also in a knowledge representation system an arbitrary focus of attention (what setting *now* actually is) could be allowed, similarly as introducing and deleting data independently of their chronology is often allowed. Therefore we suggest the following three operations for *now*:

(i) Setting *now* to a particular *absolute date*.

(ii) Shifting *now* by a particular *offset* (forward or backward).

(iii) Indefinite change of *now*.

Note, that while all other represented time points are <u>constants</u>, *now* with such properties has to be a <u>variable</u>, not a <u>constant</u>. This variable points at different time points (in practice, at their indices). Setting *now* to a particular date means "pinning" it up on the time axis. This operation does not change the value of the *variable now*. Evidently this command should not be inconsistent with the previous knowledge concerning *now*, e.g. setting *now* again to a different date leads to inconsistency. Certainly, it is also possible to determine that *now* is located between two particular dates, and to make this information more precise at a later stage.

Shifting *now* by an offset forward or backward reduces to assigning it to a date being in an appropriate relation with the "old" *now*. Actually, the offset need not necessarily be a primitive relation, one can imagine "fuzzy" shifting *now* by a certain interval (in our opinion, shifting *now* by an arbitrary relation makes no sense). This can involve the necessity of adding a new point to the set of points, if a correctly placed point has not been represented yet. On the other hand, a point indicated by the "old" *now* can be deleted—the whole essential information is transferred to the "new" *now*. Eventually, the operation of shifting *now* reduces to composing an appropriate primitive relation with all relations connecting points with *now*.

An indefinite change of *now* means that the "new" *now* loses any relationship with the "old" one. This implies adding a new point to the set of points and *now* points at it since that moment. If the "old" *now* has not been set to any particular date, then we lose knowledge <u>when</u> the points connected with it occur—this is not *tomorrow* or *3 hours before* any longer. Certainly, relative dependencies between these points remain, but in such a case why have they been introduced in relation to *now*? For this reason it seems justified to forbid an indefinite change of *now* we know nothing about.

<u>Example</u>

We have information:

   Dinner finished 2 hours ago.

If we perform the operation:

   It is 20:20:00 now.

   Indefinite change of now.

then we can infer:

   Dinner finished at 18:20:00.

whereas if we perform the operation:

   Shifting now by 3 hours 10 minutes forward.

then we can infer:

   Dinner finished 5 hours 10 minutes ago.

But if we perform only the operation:

   Indefinite change of now.

then we do not know, when has the dinner actually finished.

4.4.4 Absolute duration of events

Allen (1983, 1984) rejected categorically to consider points in his discussion of the constraint propagation algorithm for intervals. On the other hand, considerations on metric information presented in the previous sections were based precisely on the notion of point. In this section we want to discuss metric information for intervals without reference to the notion of point.

Kautz (1987) extends Allen's algorithm to the case encompassing *fuzzy interval constraints*, denoted as $(start_{min}, start_{max}, end_{min}, end_{max})$. They describe (approximately, of course) absolute time positions of intervals, so they are useless when no such information is available.

The duration of an interval being equivalent to the time distance between its endpoints, we will use the concepts introduced in section 4.3.3. The concept of relation (restricted to its "positive part") will be now called a *duration constraint* (denoted as $d(A)$ for an interval A). Now, we define two auxiliary unary operations on the duration constraint of an interval $d(A)$: $MAX(d(A))$ is its supremum and $MIN(d(A))$ is its infimum. Moreover, we need four binary partial functions on intervals, returning the appropriate intervals if they exist, i.e. if they are to exist under Allen's (1984) axiomatization. The function CONV returns an interval such that A *starts* CONV (A, B) and B *finishes* CONV (A, B). The function INTERSEC returns the longest interval such that A *contains* INTERSEC (A, B) and B *contains* INTERSEC (A, B). For overlapping intervals A and B the functions DIFF_L and DIFF_R return intervals such that A *started by* DIFF_L (A, B), B *met by* DIFF_L (A, B), A *finished by* DIFF_R (A, B) and B *meets* DIFF_R (A, B).

By means of these concepts we can describe rules connecting relations between intervals A and B and their absolute durations in the following way:

A *before* B $\implies$ $d(\text{CONV}(A, B)) = (\text{MIN}(\text{COMP}(d(A), d(B))), \infty)$

A *meets* B $\implies$ $d(\text{CONV}(A, B)) = \text{COMP}(d(A), d(B))$

A *overlaps* B $\implies$ $d(\text{CONV}(A, B)) = \cap((\text{MIN}(d(A)), \infty), (\text{MIN}(d(B)), \infty),$
$$(0, \text{MAX}(\text{COMP}(d(A), d(B))))) \qquad \&$$
$$d(\text{DIFF\_L}(A, B)) = (0, \text{MAX}(d(A))) \qquad \&$$
$$d(\text{DIFF\_R}(B, A)) = (0, \text{MAX}(d(B))) \qquad \&$$
$$d(\text{INTERSEC}(A, B)) = \cap((0, \text{MAX}(d(A))), (0, \text{MAX}(d(B))))$$

A *starts* B $\implies$ $d(\text{DIFF\_R}(B, A)) = \text{COMP}(d(B), \text{INV}(d(A)))$

A *contains* B $\implies$ $d(\text{DIFF\_L}(A, B)) = (0, \text{MAX}(\text{COMP}(d(A), \text{INV}(d(B))))) \ \&$
$$d(\text{DIFF\_R}(A, B)) = (0, \text{MAX}(\text{COMP}(d(A), \text{INV}(d(B)))))$$

A *finishes* B $\implies$ $d(\text{DIFF\_L}(B, A)) = \text{COMP}(d(B), \text{INV}(d(A)))$

A *equals* B $\implies$ $d(A) = d(B) = \cap(d(A), d(B))$

For the remaining primitive relations such dependencies can be inferred by means of inverse relations.

If in addition to simple intervals we allow interval dates, such as Ladkin (1986b) suggests, then we are also able to express in our language information corresponding to Kautz's (1987) concepts.

4.4.5 Relative duration of events

Besides determining the absolute duration of events (intervals these events occur in), we can also determine the duration of an event by means of durations of other events. Such an idea was suggested by Koomen (1987). Even though his solution can be treated as an application of the constraint propagation algorithm for some set of relations, we decided to see it as a modification of the algorithm, since in this case we do not operate on time positions of individuals (at least not directly).

The idea is founded upon the observation that even though we sometimes do not know how long a certain interval lasts, we know how many times it is longer (shorter) than another interval. Denoting, as before, the duration of an interval A by $d(A)$ we can state that $d(A)$ 3 times $d(B)$ and $d(B)$ 1/3 time $d(A)$.

Koomen suggests to represent also constraints and disjunctions of relative durations of time intervals, apart from the exact dependencies.

Example

Examples of relative duration of time intervals together with inverse relationships:

$d(A)$ 1 time $d(B)$, $d(B)$ 1 time $d(A)$,

$d(A)$ $(1, \infty)$ times $d(B)$, $d(B)$ $(0, 1)$ times $d(A)$,

$d(A)$ $\{(3, 6], [8, 12)\}$ times $d(B)$, $d(B)$ $\{(1/12, 1/8], [1/6, 1/3)\}$ times $d(B)$.

The first example represents equal duration of both time intervals, in the second A lasts longer than B. Koomen, similarly to Allen (1983) does not allow null duration of intervals (moments), hence 0 cannot be a closed bound of an interval.

There is a striking similarity of this construction not only to absolute durations of events, but also to usual metric relations between points. Therefore essential differences should be stress. Now we do not deal here with any metric— first of all there are no units, but purely qualitative dependencies. Therefore values listed above are "ordinary" numbers. The fact that these numbers can only be non-negative is obvious, and it follows directly from the fact that the duration of events is positive. This is just the same as for absolute duration of events.

The possibility of applying the constraint propagation algorithm to such data is obvious. However, since we do not want to abuse the term *relation*, we will speak of *dependencies* between durations of intervals.

DEFINITION

A *primitive dependency* between durations of two intervals is a number determining how many times one interval is longer than the other. The set of all primitive dependencies is the set of all positive rational numbers $\mathbf{Q}^+$. A *compound dependency (a dependency)* is any subset of the set of all primitive dependencies.

As for metric relations between points, we will take into consideration only these dependencies, which can be written as a finite sequence of intervals (convex subsets of $\mathbf{Q}^+$).

If we want to apply the constraint propagation algorithm to the above dependencies, we must define the operations INV and COMP for them. A dependency inverse to a certain primitive dependency is its numerical inverse. It should be mentioned here that for metric relations between points we have to do with opposite numbers (vectors). Obviously, a dependency inverse to a certain compound dependency is the set of all primitive dependencies inverse to the ones belonging to the dependency under consideration.

For dependencies treated as sequences of rational intervals the operation INV is denoted just in the same way as in the case of inverting metric relations between points:

$$\text{INV} (\{r_1, r_2\}) = \{ \text{ INV} (r_2), \text{INV} (r_1) \},$$

with brackets interpreted as before.

Now we shall discuss the composition operation for dependencies. As for metric relations between points, we are not able to produce a table representing the composition operation for primitive dependencies between durations of intervals, but an appropriate formula only. In contrast to the previous case, it is now based on multiplication, not on addition:

$$\text{COMP}_P (p, q) = p * q.$$

The definition of the operation COMP_I also remains analogous to the one defined for metric relations between points as presented in section 4.3.3.

$$\text{COMP}_I (\{_1 r_{11}, r_{12} \}_1, \{_2 r_{21}, r_{22} \}_2) = \{ \text{COMP}_P (r_{11}, r_{21}), \text{COMP}_P (r_{12}, r_{22}) \}$$

with brackets interpreted as before, too—round brackets "beat" square brackets. The operation COMP presented in section 4.2 should evidently be applied to COMP_I and not to COMP_P.

We can finally state that operating on dependencies between durations of intervals is based on the multiplicative group $\langle \mathbf{Q}^+, * \rangle$, in contrast to operations on metric relations between points, based on the additive group $\langle \mathbf{Z}, + \rangle$.

(a)   (b)

REL	DEPENDENCIES
b	$(0, \infty)$
m	$(0, \infty)$
o	$(0, \infty)$
fi	$(1, \infty)$
di	$(1, \infty)$
s	$(0, 1)$
eq	1
si	$(1, \infty)$
d	$(0, 1)$
f	$(0, 1)$
oi	$(0, \infty)$
mi	$(0, \infty)$
bi	$(0, \infty)$

DEP	RELATIONS
1	b,m ,o, eq, oi, mi, bi
$(0, 1)$	b, m, o, s, d, f, oi, mi, bi
$(0, 1]$	b, m, o, s, eq, d, f, oi, mi, bi
$(1, \infty)$	b, m, o, fi, di, si, oi, mi, bi
$[1, \infty)$	b, m, o, fi, di, eq, si, oi, mi, bi
$(0, \infty)$	no info

Fig. 4.26. (a) Determination of admissible durations of intervals from their mutual positions
(b) Determination of admissible positions of intervals from their mutual durations

Koomen (1987) treats the use of relative durations of time intervals as complementary to usual Allenean relations between time intervals. It is therefore necessary to take into account the limitations imposed by one type of information onto the other. If one interval precedes (is *before*), *meets* or *overlaps* another, then this has no influence on their relative duration and is itself independent of this second information. The relation *equals* imposes equal durations and *vice versa* (with respect to the remaining relations). An interval contained in another lasts a shorter time and an interval containing another lasts longer. All the appropriate interdependencies can be found in the table presented in fig. 4.26.

Evidently calculations for compound relations and compound dependencies requires auxiliary procedures—for a relation we must compute the union of rational intervals corresponding to primitive relations belonging to the source relation, while for a dependency we must find in a table its minimal superset, which determines an admissible compound relation.

The main algorithm also becomes somewhat more complicated. Apart from the array INFO we have an array DINFO, containing dependencies between durations of two time intervals. We also have two operations COMP$_P$ (the second may be called DCOMP$_P$), and for durations (dependencies) the procedure COMP is based on DCOMP$_I$ and not on DCOMP$_P$. Thus we also need two queues Queue and DQueue. Furthermore, for every pair of time intervals from Queue we must check whether new information about the mutual position of time intervals influences data concerning their duration. If so, we must modify the appropriate entry in the array DINFO, and then put the considered pair of intervals into DQueue. For every pair of intervals from DQueue the procedure is similar.

When we deal with two types of data for one kind of individuals, the situation is evidently completely different from the case, when we deal with two kinds of individuals. Thus, the modification of the algorithm presented above is different from the one presented in section 4.3.6.

4.4.6 Interval relation network with distinguished transition chains

Hrycej (1986) criticizes Allen's network representation of relations between intervals for its non-transparency. What he means is that in a network (the more so in an array) containing relations between all intervals, time passing is not visible, i.e. dependencies *before/after* are not distinguished in any way. He also criticizes big time and space complexity of the solution. This has become an important objection, considering that the number of represented individuals grows dramatically. Nevertheless, Hrycej emphasizes the power of Allen's solution in relation to Kahn & Gorry's data line and before/after chains, which represent time passing remarkably well.

Therefore he decides to unite these two approaches. Among Allen's relations he distinguishes the transitive ones, i.e. relations which composed with themselves give the same relation. Primitive relations *before, starts, during, finishes* and their inverses are transitive relations, and in a trivial way also the relation *equals* is. Additionally the relation {*before, meets*} (and its inverse) can be admitted, since composed with itself it gives the relation *before*, which is a subrelation of the considered relation. A similar situation occurs with the relations {*starts, during*}, {*during, finishes*} and {*starts, during, finishes*}. Hrycej introduces the concept of a *transitivity chain*; successive elements of such a chain are intervals connected by a certain transitive relation. Then we can avoid representing connections between non-neighbouring elements of a chain. In the resulting network also direct connections exist (between intervals that do not belong to the same chain).

Transitive relations have been chosen in such a way that relations from a chain cannot be further constrained (as they are primitive), and the information derived is the same as in the original Allen's algorithm, by inferring conclusions only from relations between intervals that are directly represented in the network. We present below the algorithm suggested by Hrycej, based on the above properties. We only change somewhat the notation in order to adjust it to the one used before. Clearly, now an array representation makes no sense, so the use of INFO[i,j] only means that the relation between intervals i and j is represented directly. In the algorithm a queue Queue of pairs of intervals occurs, as before. CR is a relation characterizing direct connections in a chain (i.e. {*before, meets*}). N is obviously the number of represented intervals. At the beginning Queue contains all pairs of intervals for which information has been modified since the last call of the algorithm (at the first call all the data are introduced by the user, i.e. relations other than *no information* for different intervals), as it was in the original algorithm. It is essential that when a new relation is introduced into a chain, "old" connections must be deleted. The procedure Chaining is designed for this purpose:

```
Chaining ( i, j )
begin
    for k := 1 to N do
      if before (k, i) then    delete_connection (k, j);
    for l := 1 to N do
      if before (j, l) then    delete_connection (i, l);
    for k := 1 to N do
      for l := 1 to N do
        if before (k, i) & before (j, l) then
          delete_connection (k, l);
end;
```

```
ALGORITHM
begin
   while Queue is not empty do
   begin
     get <i,j> from Queue;
     for k := 1 to N do    if triangle(i,j,k) then
     begin
       R := INFO[i,k] ∩ COMP(INFO[i,j], INFO[j,k]);
       if R ⊆ INFO[i,k] then
       begin
         put <i,k> to Queue;
         if (R ⊆ CR & ¬(INFO[i,k] ⊆ CR)) then  Chaining(i,k);
         INFO[i,k] := R
       end;
       R := INFO[k,j] ∩ COMP(INFO[k,i], INFO[i,j]);
       if R ⊆ INFO[k,j] then
       begin
         put <k,j> to Queue;
         if (R ⊆ CR & ¬(INFO[k,j] ⊆ CR)) then  Chaining(k,j);
         INFO[k,j] := R
       end
     end
   end
end.
```

The function triangle(i, j, k) informs whether all three pairs of considered intervals are directly connected. The use of this function decreases the complexity of the "pure" constraint propagation algorithm. The function before(i, j) informs whether an element i precedes an element j in a chain. The above algorithm applies to chains of one kind, but an extension to several kinds of chains does not seem to be difficult.

Hrycej lays special stress to chains in which relations connecting directly elements of chains can be *before* or *meets*, whereas the relation connecting non-neighbouring elements is *before*. He remarks in [Hrycej, 1988] that in practical applications events and facts occur "one by one", and only in rare situations they can occur more or less simultaneously. Comparing time complexity of the original Allen's algorithm and of the above one, Hrycej states that the number of direct connections of an interval with other ones can be bounded by a constant, and then space complexity can be reduced to $\mathcal{O}(N)$, whereas time complexity can be reduced to $\mathcal{O}(N^2)$.

Note, that in contrast to Allen's hierarchy of reference intervals, the above representation contains the same information as the original Allen's network containing all connections between nodes (without necessity of additional inference). Certainly, this solution inherits the property of incompleteness.

4.4.7 A more precise constraint propagation algorithm

As we have already mentioned, Allen's constraint propagation algorithm ensures completeness only for three-element subsets of the set of intervals. Van Beek (1989) suggests an improvement of the algorithm, i.e. obtaining constraints closer to real, *minimal* constraints on relations between intervals. His algorithm ensures completeness for four-element subsets of the set of intervals.

Van Beek bases his reasoning on the following observation: when one wants to compute a relation between intervals i and j from relations between intervals i,k; k,1 and 1,j, he first computes COMP (INFO[i,k], INFO[k,1]) and COMP (INFO[k,1], INFO[1,j]), and then he intersects compositions COMP (INFO[i,1], INFO[1,j]) and COMP (INFO[i,k], INFO[k,j]) neglecting the fact that the same primitive relation obtained in both cases can be derived from different primitive relations from among INFO[i,k], INFO[k,1] and INFO[1,j]. Hence the author decides to perform the above computations for every such triple of primitive relations separately. This results in a new operation COMP:

```
COMP ( i, k, l, j )
begin
    R := ∅;
    for each r₁ ∈ INFO[i,k] do
      for each r₂ ∈ INFO[k,l] do
        for each r₃ ∈ INFO[l,j] do
        begin
            R₁ := COMPₚ(r₁, r₂) ∩ INFO[i,l];
            R₂ := COMPₚ(r₂, r₃) ∩ INFO[k,j];
            for each r₄ ∈ R₁ do
              for each r₅ ∈ R₂ do
                R := R ∪ COMPₚ (r₁, r₅) ∩ COMPₚ (r₂, r₄);
        end;
    return R
end;
```

Since the operation COMP is based on four intervals, and not on three, the main algorithm has to change, too. We present it in a form somewhat different from the one van Beek uses, and more similar to the notation we have used before. The meaning of INFO, Queue and N does not change.

ALGORITHM
begin
```
    while Queue is not empty do
    begin
      get <i,j> from Queue;
      for k := 1 to N do
        for l := 1 to N do
        begin
          R := INFO[k,l] ∩ COMP (k, i, j, l);
          if R ⊆ INFO[k,l] then
          begin
            INFO[k,l] := R;
            put <k,l> to Queue
          end;
          R := INFO[i,l] ∩ COMP (i, j, k, l);
          if R ⊆ INFO[i,l] then
          begin
            INFO[i,l] := R;
            put <i,l> to Queue
          end;
          R := INFO[k,j] ∩ COMP (k, l, i, j);
          if R ⊆ INFO[k,j] then
          begin
            INFO[k,j] := R;
            put <k,j> to Queue
          end
        end
    end
end.
```

Since, as before, each pair of intervals can land in a queue finitely many times (at most 13), the computational complexity of the above algorithm is $\mathcal{O}(N^4)$. Looking at the above algorithm one can easily imagine algorithms with complexity $\mathcal{O}(N^k)$, ensuring completeness for k-element subsets of the set of intervals.

In section 5.3 we cite van Beek & Cohen's (1990) statement that the above algorithm is complete for points and that the only source of incompleteness for the original Allen's algorithm in this case is the situation presented in the example on page 178. Therefore van Beek (1990) concludes that in the case of points we can forget the above algorithm and use the original Allen's algorithm enriched by the following procedure, which finds "forbidden" subsets of data.

```
FIND_SUBGRAPHS
begin
    for i := 1 to N do
        for j := 1 to N do    if INFO[i,j] = { <, > } then
            for k := 1 to N do
                if INFO[k,i] = { <, = } and INFO[k,j] = { <, = } then
                    for l := 1 to N do
                        if INFO[i,l] = { <, = } and INFO[j,l] = { <, = }
                        then
                            begin
                            INFO[k,i] := { < };    INFO[i,k] := { > };
                            INFO[k,j] := { < };    INFO[j,k] := { > };
                            INFO[i,l] := { < };    INFO[l,i] := { > };
                            INFO[j,l] := { < };    INFO[l,j] := { > }
                            end
end.
```

The procedure is applied after the constraint propagation algorithm is finished. A question may arise whether changes introduced to array INFO do not have further consequences (which would require repeating the constraint propagation algorithm). The author shows that there is no such possibility.

The worst-case complexity of the above procedure is, in fact, $\mathcal{O}(N^4)$ again, but in practice we reach the deepest nesting of the loop very rarely (the more so that $\neq$ is a relation very rarely met!), hence the average complexity is in this case much better than before. Van Beek claims that for a set of random problems, a program implementing this solution spends only 2% of time, on the average, on the procedure FIND_SUBGRAPHS.

Furthermore, van Beek (1990) points out that, in the case of intervals, a subset of the set of interval relations exists that can be represented as point relations between endpoints of intervals. Unfortunately, it is composed only of

188 relations (from among 2^{13}). Since the cost of transforming a set of interval relations into point relations (and *vice versa*) is $\mathcal{O}(N^2)$, the above algorithm can be applied also to this case. However, van Beek speaks nothing about complexity of the ordinary (precise) algorithm applied for relations from this set without transformation into point relations.

Nebel & Bürkert (1993) extend the above class of interval relations, allowing disjunctions of endpoints relations of the form $t_1 \{<, >\} t_2$.

Example
The information $\langle x_1, x_2 \rangle \{o, s, fi\} \langle y_1, y_2 \rangle$ can be represented by means of conjunction of relations:

$$x_1 \{<\} x_2, \qquad\qquad y_1 \{<\} y_2,$$
$$x_1 \{<, =\} y_1, \qquad\qquad x_2 \{<, =\} y_2,$$
$$x_1 \{<\} y_2, \qquad\qquad y_1 \{<\} x_2,$$
$$x_1 \{<, >\} y_1 \ \vee \ x_2 \{<, >\} y_2.$$

Without the last constraint we obtain the relation $\langle x_1, x_2 \rangle \{o, s, eq, fi\}$ $\langle y_1, y_2 \rangle$. This constraint actually determines that we cannot have $x_1 = y_1$ and $x_2 = y_2$ at the same time, which exactly excludes the relation *equals*.

There are 868 interval relations that can be represented in this way. The authors represent relations by means of Horn clauses. They claim that for their class of interval relations the consistency (satisfiability) of a set of data can be checked in $\mathcal{O}(N^3)$, and a complete solution can be found in $\mathcal{O}(N^5)$. They also prove that their class is the maximal class of interval relations for which checking consistency is not NP-hard. Actually, they claim that this is the unique greatest subclass (closed under composition, inversion and intersection) of interval relations, which contradicts Freksa's (1992) claim (see below).

Freksa (1992) organizes Allen's primitive relations by their conceptual neighbourhood. By his definition, two intervals are *(conceptual) neighbours*, if they can be directly transformed into one another by a continuous deformation of intervals (i.e. moving their endpoints). Thus, *before* and *meets* are conceptual neighbours, whereas *before* and *overlaps* are not. Primitive relations in tables presented in this book (see eg. fig. 4.12) are ordered in a way that subsequent relations are conceptual neighbours. A set of primitive relations between intervals forms a *coarse relation* if its elements form a path of conceptual neighbours. The author claims that other compound relations are less natural, as their components have drastically different perceptual appearance.

It is easy to check that the composition of every pair of coarse relations is a coarse relation. The author claims that there are 1255 such relations. It would be interesting to compare this class with the class of interval relations defined by means of point relations between their endpoints. It turns out that there are pointwise-representable relations (even van Beek's relations) that are not coarse (e.g. $\{b, o\}$). On the other hand, there are coarse relations that cannot be represented by means of relations between endpoints, even Nebel & Bürkert's relations. For instance, to represent $\{b, m, o, s, d, f, oi, mi, bi\}$ we should exclude the relations fi, di, eq, si from $no\ info$. To do this we need a forbidden clause $y_1 < x_1 \ \lor \ x_2 < y_2$.

Freksa chooses some sets of basic coarse relations and analyses Allen's algorithm from this perspective. He claims that it is possible to obtain a global consistency for this set of relations in polynomial time, but he does not give the concrete time complexity.

4.5 Constraint propagation for a distinguished interval

Allen's constraint propagation algorithm and all its modifications considered before compute dependencies between all the represented individuals (intervals and points). However, in practice situations may appear, when an individual causes a particular attention and all dependencies we need concern just this interval. Van Beek & Cohen (1990) present an algorithm concerning exactly this situation.

Similarly to most of the authors, they present their algorithm in a network notation, whereas our intention is to use consequently array notation. The algorithm uses the same operation COMP as the original Allen's algorithm presented in section 4.2. The same array INFO, indices i, j, k and the number of individuals in the system N are used. The fundamental difference is the occurrence of a list of individuals List instead of a queue of pairs of individuals Queue. At the beginning, List contains all the individuals except the distinguished one (with index i). The algorithm computes relations between the individual with index i and the remaining individuals.

```
ALGORITHM
begin
    while List is not empty do
    begin
        get j from List such that INFO[i,j] is minimal;
        for k := 1 to N do
        begin
            R := INFO[i,k] ∩ COMP ( INFO[i,j], INFO[j,k] );
            if R ⊆ INFO[i,k] then
            begin
                INFO[i,k] := R;
```

```
        put k to List;
    end;
  end
end
```
end.

The time complexity of the above algorithm is $\mathcal{O}(N^2)$. Unfortunately, it is obvious that conclusions obtained by means of this algorithm are weaker than those obtained by means of the original Allen's algorithm, since the only computed (hence modified) relations are relations of the form INFO[i,j] for some individual j, whereas a modification of the relation INFO[j,k] used in the algorithm (for some individual k) could influence the further course of the algorithm. Nevertheless the authors show that in the case of points, if the relation $\{<, >\}$ does not occur in a set of data, then the obtained relations are "minimal" (which corresponds to completeness). This concerns also these sets of relations between intervals, in which all relations can be denoted by means of the above point relations.

4.6 Consistent Labeling Problem for interval relations

Because of lack of completeness, Allen's constraint propagation algorithm can be unable to detect inconsistency for some particularly nasty sets of data. Moreover, in some applications, it is necessary to attach intervals to the time-axis, i.e. to determine exactly one primitive relation between every two intervals (determining their univocal mutual position). This task is a case of the *Consistent Labeling Problem* (CLP), also called the *Constraint Satisfaction Problem*. One of the first who associated Allen's algorithm with CLP was Tsang (1987b). CLP is defined in the following way: We have a finite set of variables $Z = \{x_1, ..., x_n\}$. Each variable has a finite set of values. Furthermore, constraints on different subsets of Z are defined. An assignment of a value to a variable is called a *label*. The problem consists in finding one or all the labels for the whole set of variables Z.

Temporal reasoning is represented by CLP as follows: relations between intervals constitute variables (a number of intervals is known to the system at any moment, and it is used to define a set of variables). The value of a variable can be any primitive relation. The rules for composing primitive relations ($COMP_P$) constitute a set of permanent constraints concerning all triples of variables. Data typical for Allen's system constitute constraints on the values of single variables. However, in Tsang's system more complicated data are also allowed: e.g. a requirement that intervals A, B and C cannot have any common subinterval (even though every pair of them can) is a constraint on the value of three variables.

The algorithm proposed to solve the problem under discussion consists in assigning values to successive variables with *backtracking*. Its computational complexity is exponential. Two assumptions may be helpful in reducing the search tree. On the one hand, first to assign values to those variables that have stricter constraints (i.e. less possibilities for assigning a value). On the other hand, to choose those primitive relations that are less restrictive, the author presents a corresponding ordering of primitive relations. In some applications, a different preferred choice of primitive relations may be suggested, e.g. in order to limit the time occupied by all the intervals together.

Another algorithm for checking consistency of an arbitrary set of data for Allen's algorithm has been introduced by Valdés-Péres (1987). It is also based on *backtracking*, and its worst-case complexity is exponential. However, in contrast to the algorithm described above, in this case relation composition rules are not treated analogously to typical data (relations between two intervals), and the only admissible data are the same as for the original Allen's algorithm. Moreover, its input consists of a network (array) which is an output of Allen's algorithm (called a *closed network*). What is interesting is that after assigning a concrete primitive relation to a certain pair of intervals, an on-line checking is performed to check whether this does not cause any immediate inconsistency following from composing this relation with a relation connecting one of the considered intervals with any other interval. This is an important way of reducing the search tree.

In the case of point time, the problem can be solved with a much better complexity. Van Beek (1990) suggests an algorithm for finding a consistent labeling (he calls it a *consistent scenario*) in time $\mathcal{O}(N^2)$. Let us recall that we deal with a set of relations $\{\emptyset, <, =>, \leq, \geq, \neq, ?\}$. Van Beek suggests first to go over the network to find all loops with edges labeled by $=$, $\leq$ or $<$. When the relation $<$ occurs in such a loop, then the whole network is inconsistent. Otherwise all elements of the loop can be replaced by a single node. As a result a new network arises, and its edges are labeled by intersections of the labels of edges composing the new ones. If it is $\emptyset$, then certainly the whole network is inconsistent. Identification of loops as well as the compression of the graph costs $\mathcal{O}(N^2)$. Next, all labels $\leq$ are replaced by $<$ (and at the same time their "counterparts" $\geq$ are replaced by $>$). Therefore the graph should be searched through (in time $\mathcal{O}(N^2)$). A network transformed in such a way can be an input for the algorithm of topological sort, which in time $\mathcal{O}(N^2)$ assigns a number to each point (assigns to it a point on the time-axis). Such an assignment allows to ascribe a single-element label to each node. Time complexity of the whole algorithm is $\mathcal{O}(N^2)$. Note, that the above algorithm prefers the relation $<$ to the relation $\leq$, e.g. for data $a \leq b \leq c$ we obtain $a < b < c$. In other words, for every set of data we obtain one concrete labeling. But remember, then in the example from page 178 the unacceptable relation between c and d is exactly *equals*.

The above algorithm can be applied for the interval case, if the relation between intervals can be expressed in terms of point relations.

Keretho & Loganantharaj (1993) present a further improved algorithm for the general CLP for temporal information, with best-case complexity $\mathcal{O}(N^3)$ and worst-case complexity $\mathcal{O}(N13^e)$ (where e is the number of edges), while other known algorithms have best-case complexity $\mathcal{O}(N^4)$ and worst-case complexity at least $\mathcal{O}(N^2 6^e)$.

A *backtracking* algorithm for CLP in the case of metric time is presented by Dechter et al. (1991).

4.7 Efficient algorithms for representation of relations between points

When designing a representation for a certain class of information, the cost of two operations should be taken into account—data manipulation (inserting and deleting) and extraction of information. In the original Allen's solution all the conclusions are represented, so extraction of information has a constant cost, whereas deleting any information actually requires performing the whole reasoning from the beginning (in the case of reference intervals this concerns an appropriate group of intervals). On the other hand, if only axioms were stored, then for each extraction of information the whole reasoning must be performed, which is even more expensive. Ghalab & Alaoui (1989) suggest a representation which balances both these costs. The representation is based on point time, and relations connecting points are $\leq$ and $\neq$. As a result, the representation consists of a directed graph with two types of edges corresponding to the above relations, which enables representing all the 8 relations between points (see section 4.3.1) by means of 0, 1 or 2 edges. If there exists a loop composed of edges $\leq$ in the graph, then this means that all nodes belonging to it are equal and represent one time moment, so they can be replaced by one node. If moreover between these points (in the loop) there exists any connection by an edge $\neq$, inconsistency occurs in the graph. Edges $\neq$ are used only to detect inconsistency, as no other conclusions can be derived from them. If inconsistency is not detected, the graph (viewed with edges $\leq$ exclusively) becomes a partial order. We add a point t_0 preceding all the other points.

Point u precedes point v (notation: $u \ll v$), if there exists a path in the graph from u to v.

A maximum spanning tree is defined in a graph in the following way: To each node u a range $r(u)$ is assigned—the length of the longest path in a graph from t_0 to u. Next, a tree path is constructed by finding a node u of the graph with a maximal range (one that is still not in the tree), and its predecessor with range $r(u) - 1$ is added to the path. The procedure is repeated as long as there are nodes with suitable range that are outside the tree. The first path is finished when t_0 is added to it. Such a path is attached to a predecessor of its head u with range $r(u) - 1$ which has a minimal number of sons. The operation is repeated as long as there are nodes outside the tree.

Let us assume the following denotations: the set of sons of a node u in the tree will be denoted by $s(u)$, the set of its descendants will be denoted by $\hat{s}(u)$ and its father will be denoted by $p(u)$.

Indices of nodes are used to decide whether $v \in \hat{s}(u)$. The index of a node is a sequence of integers $I(u) = [i_1, ..., i_n]$. $I(t_0) = [0]$. The index of the first son of u is $[i_1, ..., i_n - 1, i_n + 1]$, the index of the second son is $[i_1, ..., i_n, 1]$, and the index of the subsequent son is $[i_1, ..., i_n, 3 - nr, 1]$, where nr is the a number of the son. The range of a node is the sum of all the positive elements of its index. The tree is designed in such a way that the index is the shortest possible.

The most important feature of such an index is the fact that $v \in \hat{s}(u)$ holds for $I(u) = [i_1, ..., i_n]$ and $I(v) = [j_1, ..., j_m]$ if and only if $n \leq m$ & $[i_1, ..., i_{n-1}] = [j_1, ..., j_{n-1}]$ & $i_n < j_n$. Two nodes with the same range are incomparable.

There exist some connections in the original graph that do not belong to the paths of the tree. They are considered as an auxiliary kind of branches. We will denote the set of such auxiliary successors of u by $a(u)$.

Now we present the algorithms for the basic operations on this structure. A function comparing two points u and v is:

```
COMPARE ( u, v )
begin
    if r(u) = r(v) then    return (nil)
    else
        if r(u) ≥ r(v) then    Relate ( v, u )
        else    Relate ( u, v )
end;
```

This function uses a recursive function:

```
Relate ( u, v )
begin
    if v ∈ ŝ(u) then    return ( u ≪ v );
    if v ∈ a(u) then    return ( u ≪ v );
    for each w ∈ a(u) do
```

```
    begin
      if r(w) < r(v) and Relate (w, v)  =  (w ≪ v) then
        return (u ≪ v)
      else    return (nil);
    end
end;
```

A procedure designed for adding a new relation between points $(w \leq v)$ is:

```
ADDRELATION (w, v)
begin
if v ≪ w then
    if no pair of nodes in a path from v to w are distinct then
      Collapse (v, w)
    else    return (inconsistency)
else
    if w ≪ v then    return (already true)
    else
      if r(w) ≥ r(v) then
      begin
        x := p(v);
        add v to a(x) and remove v from s(x);
        add v to s(w) and Reindex (v);
        Propagate (x, v);
        p(v) := w;
      end
      else    add v to a(w) and Propagate (w, v)
end;
```

A procedure adding a point w after the point u is:

```
ADDPOINT (w, u)
begin
    add w to s(u);
    calculate index of w (from that of p(w));
    p(w) := u;
end;
```

The recursive function `Reindex` (v) reindexes the whole subtree with root v in a way leading to a proper index. Furthermore the function `Propagate` (u, v) is applied when an auxiliary edge exists between u and v ($v \in a(u)$). It adds such an auxiliary edge between all predecessors of u and v whenever the function `Relate` does not state such a dependency.

It only remains to discussed the operations related to deleting. Deletion of a point u consists in setting $p(u)$ as a father for all the sons of u, and reindexing a tree with root $p(u)$. Deleting a relation between u and v, which is a branch in the tree consists in finding a predecessor of v with maximal range and treating it as a father for v. Evidently the tree with root v must be reindexed. If the deleted relation is *auxiliary*, then v should be deleted from $a(u)$ together with other *auxiliary connections* between v and predecessors of u resulting from this information.

The empirically stated average complexity of the algorithm presented here is linear in relation to the number of nodes in a tree (a graph).

Another interesting concept of an efficient representation of relations between points is described by Miller & Schubert (1990). This representation is based on a graph with distinguished chains of points consecutive in time. Each point belongs to exactly one chain. Relations between subsequent points in a chain are called *in-chain links*, whereas relations between points from different chains are called *cross-chain links*. An integer number called *pseudotime* is connected with every element of a chain—these numbers grow within every chain.

Such a representation can be used to describe either the relation of strict precedence $<$ or that of unstrict precedence $\leq$, but not both at once. In order to enable this third possibility, the authors assign two new numbers to each point: *minimum-pseudo* and *maximum-pseudo*. Minimum-pseudo is the pseudotime of the last point which precedes the one considered (and maximum-pseudo analogously). A precedence relation between points is unstrict, if the pseudotime of one of them (and actually of <u>both</u> of them) lies between the minimum-pseudo and the maximum-pseudo of the second. After changing the minimum-pseudo or maximum-pseudo of a certain point, it is necessary to propagate this constraint: The first one forward (until a greater one is found), the second backward. On cross-chain links the relation $<$ or $\leq$ is represented explicitly.

We are deeply convinced that this representation is redundant—only one of these numbers is sufficient, e.g. the maximum-pseudo. Under such an assumption a precedence relation would be unstrict, if the pseudotime of <u>each</u> point is smaller than maximum-pseudo of the other. In both methods we have to perform two comparisons, but in the modified one propagation time and space are smaller. Both methods can be compared on the following example (taken from the discussed paper):

Example

Consider points a, b, c, d, e such that $a \leq b \leq c \leq d \leq e$ and $a < d$ and $c < e$. The corresponding chain is represented as follows:

points	a	b	c	d	e
pseudotime	1	1000	2000	3000	4000
minimum-psuedo	$-\infty$	$-\infty$	$-\infty$	1	2000
maximum-pseudo	3000	4000	4000	$+\infty$	$+\infty$

Furthermore, both a maximal and a minimal date of occurrence (possibly ∞) is connected with every point, and a maximal and a minimal distance between points is associated with every link. The format of dates is year, month, day, hour, minute, second; distances are presented in seconds. Also minimal and maximal dates are propagated in a graph (distances between points being taken into account), but this time also via cross-chain links.

Apart from the main graph, there exists a metagraph, in which chains become nodes, whereas edges are constituted by cross-chain links of the original graph.

A comparison of two points proceeds in the following way: If they occur in the same chain, then their pseudotimes are compared (and strictness of the precedence relation is decided). Otherwise their absolute dates are compared (to check whether they form disjoint sets). If this fails, a metagraph is searched through, and paths found in it are then "realized" in the source graph until a relation is found. Failure means that the relation between points is undetermined. Finding a distance between points can be performed only by means of the last two methods. Unfortunately, when searching through the graph is needed, all paths must be considered (in order to find the strictest constraint), which in practice means full search in a source graph.

Introduction of new information about already existing points is realized by creating new cross-chain links or propagating new constraints. On the other hand, when adding a new point, it should be stated whether it can be added to any existing chain. Otherwise a new chain should be created.

The authors claim that their algorithm is complete, which probably is a consequence of the fact that the relation $\neq$ cannot be represented. This representation is especially advantageous in the case of long chains with a small amount of cross-chain links (then the searching time is almost constant). This is the case, for instance, in natural language processing. In cases when at the beginning points are not ordered, and next the number of links between them gradually increases (e.g. in planning), it is advisable to reorganize structures from time to time by joining chains so that their elements be totally ordered.

Miller & Schubert do not speak about a possibility of deleting data from a graph. Nevertheless it seems that this should not be too expensive, even though distinguishing axiomatic data that are not represented by direct links in a graph would be indispensable. In sum, even though this representation is weaker than those based on Allen's algorithm (impossibility of representing the relation $\neq$ and more complex constraints on dates and distances), and resembles more Kahn & Gorry's (1977) *time specialist*, it is interesting because of a much lower computational complexity.

4.8 Representation of collections of intervals

In some situations, a need to use certain sets of intervals instead of individual intervals may arise. For instance, some natural language statements (e.g. a first Thursday in a month) refer by assumption to a whole series of these units. The approaches considered before do not offer a possibility of dealing with such situations.

Leban et al. (1986) suggest a solution to this problem. They define the notion of a *collection of intervals*. A collection of intervals is a structured set of intervals. A collection of order **0** is a convex interval; a collection of order **1** is an ordered list of intervals; a collection of order **n** is an ordered list of collections of order **n-1**. An interval is represented as $\langle \alpha, \beta \rangle$ or $\langle \alpha, \delta \rangle$, where α, β, $\alpha + \delta$ are real numbers denoting moments in time and δ is a duration of an interval.

Collections are often denoted in form of sets; then their order is treated as "natural".

<u>Example</u>
Let $t_0 = 1904.12.31$, Saturday. Then:

$$\text{Thursdays} \quad = \quad \{\, \langle \alpha; 1 \text{ day} \rangle \mid \alpha = (t_0 + 5 \text{ days}) + n * 7 \text{ days} \,\},$$

$$\text{Januarie} \quad = \quad \{\, \langle \alpha; 31 \text{ days} \rangle \mid (\alpha + t_0) \bmod 1461 \in \{0, 365, 730, 1095\} \,\}.$$

The representation of a collection is founded on a set of primitive collections called *calendars*. A calendar is a collection of an infinite sequence of meeting unit intervals. Thus calendars cover the time-axis. Examples of calendars are collections of days, months or years.

A calendar need not be composed of identical units. Thus it is formally defined as:

$$\langle \langle \alpha; \delta_1; \delta_2; ...; \delta_n \rangle \rangle,$$

which means an infinite set:

$$\{\, \langle \alpha; \delta_1 \rangle, \langle \alpha + \delta_1; \delta_2 \rangle, ..., \langle \alpha + \sum_{i=1}^{n-1} \delta_i; \delta_n \rangle, \langle \alpha + \sum_{i=1}^{n} \delta_i; \delta_1 \rangle, ... \,\}$$

(the list of δ-values is treated as if it were a circular list).

A calendar can also be defined by specifying how it is to be constructed from another calendar—then subsequent elements of the new calendar are created from the appropriate number of elements of the old calendar.

<u>Example</u>

Let *second* be our basic unit. Then we can define:

$$\text{Days} \quad = \quad \langle\langle t_0 \qquad 86400 \rangle\rangle$$

$$\begin{aligned}
\text{Months} \ = \ \langle\langle\, \text{Days}; \ \ &31;\,28;\,31;\,30;\,31;\,30;\,31;\,31;\,30;\,31;\,30;\,31;\\
&31;\,28;\,31;\,30;\,31;\,30;\,31;\,31;\,30;\,31;\,30;\,31;\\
&31;\,28;\,31;\,30;\,31;\,30;\,31;\,31;\,30;\,31;\,30;\,31;\\
&31;\,29;\,31;\,30;\,31;\,30;\,31;\,31;\,30;\,31;\,30;\,31 \,\rangle\rangle
\end{aligned}$$

We can represent in the system as long an initial part of a calendar as needed.

The main operations on collections of intervals are *slicing* and *dicing*. *Slicing* operations are denoted as f/C and $[f]/C$, where C is a collection and f is a certain characteristic function. When operating on a collection of order **1**, the operation f/C returns the first interval satisfying the condition f, whereas the operation $[f]/C$ returns a collection containing all such intervals. Therefore the operation f/C applied to a collection of order **n** returns a collection of order **n-1**, whereas $[f]/C$ returns a collection with the same order. If the collection C is a collection of order **1** such that no intervals satisfying the condition F belong to it, then the result of both operations is the empty collection ε.

The authors present the following examples of a function f:

- n/C selects the nth interval in C and $-n/C$ selects the nth interval from the end,

- any/C selects a single, random interval of C, $[any\ n]/C$ selects randomly n intervals of C, and $[any\ -n]/C$ selects randomly all but n intervals of C,

- the/C "extracts" an interval from a singleton collection, and it returns ε for a multi-element collection.

Dicing operations are based on relations between intervals. These relations are defined by means of an order on endpoints of intervals and they are counterparts of all Allenean primitive relations and of some compound relations (e.g. *starting earlier*). Dicing operations are denoted as $C : R : t$ and $C.R.t$, where C is a collection, R is a relation between intervals, and t is a time interval. These operations do not change the order of a collection. As before, they can be defined for collections of order **1**, since on higher levels nothing is changed. A formal definition of these operations is the following:

$$C:R:t \quad = \quad \{\, c \cap t \mid c \in C \ \& \ cRt \,\} - \{\varepsilon\},$$
$$C.R.t \quad = \quad \{\, c \mid c \in C \ \& \ cRt \,\} - \{\varepsilon\}.$$

The authors call the operation $C:R:t$ *strict dicing*. It is designed to split an interval t into parts accordingly to the corresponding conditions. In contrast, the operation $C.R.t$, called *relaxed dicing*, is designed to select all intervals from the collection C which are in relation R with the interval t.

<u>Example</u>

Let us consider an interval **January-1986** and the calendar **Weeks**. The operation **Weeks:***overlaps***:January-1986** will split the month into weeks, and the first and the last week of the month will be "cut off". On the other hand, the operation **Weeks.***overlaps***.January-1986** select the collection of all weeks overlapping January.

The authors do not present any implementational details of their solution.

5. Formalization of the constraint propagation algorithm

In the previous sections, we have presented first a formal description of time structures (using the first order predicate calculus as well as modal temporal logics), and next a set of algorithms for representing time-dependent knowledge and reasoning about it in different time structures. As we have mentioned in the introduction, formal description of time and practical algorithmical solutions should not exist independently, especially as they concern the same time structures. In this section, we intend to connect these two approaches by formalizing the algorithmical solutions.

Unfortunately, some algorithmical solutions are hard to formalize. For instance, Kahn & Gorry's (1977) *time specialist* is hard to formalize because of its hybrid character—it has several different, alternative representation structures. Moreover, the description of the solution is underspecified and it needs some complementary details. In contrast to it, Allen's (1983) constraint propagation algorithm has a very regular character and therefore is easy to formalize. In this section we want to focus on the formalization of this very popular algorithm.

When we formalize some algorithmical solution by means of a chosen logic, we have two approaches to choose—to define the algorithmical solution in this logic or to create a new logic with semantics based on the chosen logic. The formalizations presented below are based on both these approaches.

5.1 Allen & Hayes's formalization

When Allen & Hayes (1985) formulated a theory based on the relation of meeting intervals $\|$ (see section 2.2.2), they already had in mind a formalization of Allen's (1983) interval relations constraint propagation algorithm. They applied the first of the methods mentioned above. First of all, they defined all the primitive relations between intervals (for linear time) in the following way:

- A *before* B (B *after* A) $\equiv_{def}$
  $\exists k\ (A \| k\ \&\ k \| B)$
- A *meets* B (B *met by* A) $\equiv_{def}$ $A \| B$
- A *overlaps* B (B *overlapped by* A) $\equiv_{def}$
  $\exists i, j, k, l, m\ ((i \| A\ \&\ A \| l\ \&\ l \| m)\ \&\ (i \| j\ \&$
  $\qquad\qquad j \| B\ \&\ B \| m)\ \&(j \| k\ \&\ k \| l))$

- A starts B (B started by A) $\equiv_{def}$

  $\exists i, j, k \, ((i \parallel A \& A \parallel j \& j \parallel k) \& (i \parallel B \& B \parallel k))$

- A equal B (B equal A) $\equiv_{def}$

  $\exists i, j \, ((i \parallel A \& A \parallel j) \& (i \parallel B \& B \parallel j))$

- A during B (B contains A) $\equiv_{def}$

  $\exists i, j, k, l \, ((i \parallel j \& j \parallel A \& A \parallel k \& k \parallel l) \& (i \parallel B \& B \parallel l))$

- A finishes B (B finished by A) $\equiv_{def}$

  $\exists i, j, k \, ((i \parallel j \& j \parallel A \& A \parallel k) \& (i \parallel B \& B \parallel k))$

Moreover, they showed that all the composition rules for primitive relations (the COMP_P operation) are theorems of their theory. Then certainly also composition rules for compound relations (the COMP operation) are theorems of this theory—this follows directly from the properties of disjunction. Therefore all the conclusions drawn by means of the algorithm can be proved in this theory.

The above does not mean that Allen's & Hayes's theory is equivalent to Allen's constraint propagation algorithm. First, this theory contains in an obvious way all the properties of the first order predicate calculus, hence its deductive apparatus is by definition stronger than the algorithm itself—theorems can be proved in it that cannot be derived by means of the algorithm. Also the theory itself is stronger than the requirements set by the algorithm. For instance, axiom M4 requires a predecessor and successor of every interval to exist. And the algorithm evidently does not set such requirements—in practice it is certainly used only for finite sets of intervals. Therefore this formalization, event though showing some important properties of the algorithm (e.g. its logical soundness), is not able to show all its properties (e.g. lack of its logical completeness). In the next section we will show a direct formalization of this algorithm by presenting a logic being its direct counterpart. Moreover, this solution can be used for various sets of relations and various (point and interval) time structures.

5.2 The basis of direct formalization of constraint propagation algorithm

Even though we have actually to do with different formalizations, when we consider different sets of relations for different individuals, these formalizations have many common features, since in all the cases we use the same algorithm. This algorithm, in spite of some implementational features optimizing its complexity, realizes the transitive closure of the operation of relation composition, which is not a particularly original operation. Ladkin & Maddux (1987) notice that such a representation always (independently of the set of relations) corresponds to some relation algebra. For this reason the formalization presented below is similar to relation algebras. Only similar, though. In the considered algorithm, if $A \ R_1 \ B$ & $B \ R_2 \ C$ holds, then $A \ R_1 \circ R_2 \ C$ holds, whereas in relation algebras we have to do with equivalence, not with implication. This has its far-reaching consequences. First of all, Ladkin & Maddux (1987) show that the only countable model (up to isomorphism) of the *Point Algebra* corresponding to linear point time from section 4.3.1 is the set of rationals $\mathbf{Q}$, and the only countable model of *Interval Algebra* corresponding to linear interval time from section 4.3.5 is the set of intervals with rational endpoints $INT(\mathbf{Q})$. In contrast, in the algorithm, by the nature of things we operate on finite sets of individuals. Thus it is recommendable that the considered formalization have finite models. On the other hand, as a result of weakening the inferential power in comparison with relation algebras, we loose the property of logical completeness. As we will show in the subsequent sections, it is satisfied in none) of the cases considered by us.

There are also essential notational differences making the notation used below difficult for people used to relation algebra notation. In the algebras, relations are denoted as subsets of the cartesian product of a set of individuals, for which this relation may hold. This concerns primitive relations, too. In contrast, in the algorithm any primitive relation is just a certain symbol, code, constant, whereas any compound relation is a set of primitive relations (e.g. represented as a bit map), and it is not actually their union, as it is in the case of relation algebras. This notation is proper only if primitive relations are disjoint, i.e. two different primitive relation cannot hold simultaneously between two individuals. This condition is satisfied in all the cases considered in section 4 (whereas it is not satisfied e.g. for the set of "primitive" relations $\leq$, $=$ and $\geq$). Certainly, the semantics of both notations is the same and we can obtain one of them from the other.

In this section we want to present the syntax of the considered formalization, which is the same for all the cases (up to the set of primitive relations), since the same algorithm is used. Unfortunately, we can hardly speak of axiomatizations, since the algorithm is not logically complete. However, we present axioms and rules of inference corresponding to the algorithm which is formalized.

Syntax

Alphabet

- A nonempty, countable set of variables Z,
- a set of primitive relation operators $\mathbf{P}$,
- set-theoretical symbols.

Evidently the set $\mathbf{P}$ depends on the choice of individuals and primitive relations between them. Moreover, we define a set of relations (compound relations)

$\mathbf{R} = 2^{\mathbf{P}}$, a set of atomic formulas $\mathcal{A} = \{\, x\, r\, y \mid x, y \in Z,\ r \in \mathbf{P} \,\}$ and a set of formulas $\mathcal{F} = \{\, x\, \alpha\, y \mid x, y \in Z,\ \alpha \in \mathbf{R} \,\}$. Since the set of variables Z is countable, hence when the set of primitive relations is finite, the set of relations $\mathbf{R}$ is also finite and the set of formulas $\mathcal{F}$ is countable. Elements of the set Z will be denoted by x, y, z; elements of the set $\mathbf{P}$ will be denoted by r, r_1; elements of the set $\mathbf{R}$ will be denoted by α, β, δ; and elements of the set $\mathcal{F}$ will be denoted by f, g.

DEFINITIONS

The relation $\emptyset$ is called the *empty* relation, and a formula $x\, \emptyset\, y$ is called an *inconsistent* formula.

A relation $-\alpha$ is called a relation *opposite* to α. The following conditions: $-(-\alpha) = \alpha$, $\alpha \cup -\alpha = \mathbf{R}$, $\alpha \cap -\alpha = \emptyset$ suggest that this is a notion corresponding to negation in classic propositional calculus. We will therefore denote $x\, -\alpha\, y$ by $\neg f$ for $f = x\, \alpha\, y$. Moreover, for simplicity we will write $f \subseteq g$, when $f = x\, \alpha\, y$, $g = x\, \beta\, y$ and $\alpha \subseteq \beta$.

The relation *inverse* to a primitive relation r (notation: r^{-1}) is a corresponding primitive relation. Inverse relations for every set of primitive relations were shown in section 4.3. The relation inverse to a relation α (notation: α^{-1}) is such a relation $\delta \in \mathbf{R}$ that for every $r \in \mathbf{P}$ we have $r \in \alpha$ if and only if $r^{-1} \in \delta$.

The *composition* of primitive relations r_1 and r_2 (notation: $r_1 \circ r_2$) is a relation $\delta \in \mathbf{R}$ defined in the corresponding primitive relation composition table (depending on the set of primitive relations). The composition of relations α and β (notation: $\alpha \circ \beta$) is the smallest relation $\delta \in \mathbf{R}$ such that for every $r_1 \in \alpha$, $r_2 \in \beta$ we have $r_1 \circ r_2 \subseteq \delta$.

   Since what we have presented are not general, algebraic definitions of operations of composition and inversion of relations, but specific ones, corresponding to the way these operations are treated in the algorithm, we ought to show that operations defined in such a way satisfy conditions imposed by algebra.

Theorem 5.2.1. Let $\alpha, \beta \in \mathbf{R}$. The following properties of relations are satisfied:

   (i) $(\alpha^{-1})^{-1} = \alpha$,

   (ii) $(\alpha \cup \beta)^{-1} = \alpha^{-1} \cup \beta^{-1}$,

   (iii) $(\alpha \cap \beta)^{-1} = \alpha^{-1} \cap \beta^{-1}$,

   (iv) If $\alpha \subseteq \beta$, then $\alpha^{-1} \subseteq \beta^{-1}$,

   (v) $(\alpha \circ \beta)^{-1} = \beta^{-1} \circ \alpha^{-1}$,

   (vi) $(\alpha \cup \beta) \circ (\gamma \cup \delta) = \alpha \circ \gamma \cup \alpha \circ \delta \cup \beta \circ \gamma \cup \beta \circ \delta$.

Proof

(i) The validity of the property for primitive relations follows directly from the definition of inverse relation and should by "manually" checked for every set of relations.

Consider any relation $\alpha \in \mathbf{R}$ and any $r \in \alpha$. Then $r^{-1} \in \alpha^{-1}$ and $(r^{-1})^{-1} \in (\alpha^{-1})^{-1}$. But $(r^{-1})^{-1} = r$, hence $r \in (\alpha^{-1})^{-1}$.

Consider any $r \in (\alpha^{-1})^{-1}$. Then there exist $r' \in \alpha^{-1}$ such that $r = (r')^{-1}$ and $r'' \in \alpha$ such that $r' = (r'')^{-1}$. Then $r = ((r'')^{-1})^{-1} = r''$, hence $r \in \alpha$.

(ii) Consider any $r \in \alpha^{-1} \cup \beta^{-1}$. If $r \in \alpha^{-1}$, then there exists $r' \in \alpha$ such that $r = (r')^{-1}$. Evidently $r' \in \alpha \cup \beta$. And then $r = (r')^{-1} \in (\alpha \cup \beta)^{-1}$. Analogously if $r \in \beta^{-1}$, then $r \in (\alpha \cup \beta)^{-1}$.

Consider any $r \in (\alpha \cup \beta)^{-1}$. Then there exists $r' \in \alpha \cup \beta$ such that $(r')^{-1} = r$. If $r' \in \alpha$, then $r = (r')^{-1} \in \alpha^{-1}$, and consequently $r \in \alpha^{-1} \cup \beta^{-1}$. Analogously if $r' \in \beta$, then $r \in \alpha^{-1} \cup \beta^{-1}$.

(iii) Consider any $r \in \alpha^{-1} \cap \beta^{-1}$. This means that $r \in \alpha^{-1}$ and $r \in \beta^{-1}$. Thus there exists $r' \in \mathbf{P}$ such that $r = (r')^{-1}$, so $r' \in \alpha$ and $r' \in \beta$. Thus $r' \in \alpha \cap \beta$, hence $r = (r')^{-1} \in (\alpha \cap \beta)^{-1}$.

Consider any $r \in (\alpha \cap \beta)^{-1}$. Then there exists $r' \in \alpha \cap \beta$ such that $(r')^{-1} = r$. Thus $r' \in \alpha$ and $r' \in \beta$, hence $r = (r')^{-1} \in \alpha^{-1} \cap \beta^{-1}$.

(iv) Consider any $r \in \alpha$. Then $r^{-1} \in \alpha^{-1}$. But $\alpha \subseteq \beta$ implies $r \in \beta$, and hence $r^{-1} \in \beta^{-1}$, which proves $\alpha^{-1} \subseteq \beta^{-1}$.

(v) The validity of the property for primitive relations follows directly from the definitions of inverse relation and composition of relations and should by "manually" checked for every set of relations.

Consider any $\alpha, \beta \in \mathbf{R}$ and any $r_1 \in \alpha$, $r_2 \in \beta$. Then by definition of $\circ$ we have $r_1 \circ r_2 \subseteq \alpha \circ \beta$, and, since $r_1^{-1} \in \alpha^{-1}$ and $r_2^{-1} \in \beta^{-1}$, we have $r_2^{-1} \circ r_1^{-1} \subseteq \beta^{-1} \circ \alpha^{-1}$. Therefore $(r_1 \circ r_2)^{-1} = r_2^{-1} \circ r_1^{-1}$ and by (iv) $(r_1 \circ r_2)^{-1} \subseteq (\alpha \circ \beta)^{-1}$. Thus finally $(\alpha \circ \beta)^{-1} = \beta^{-1} \circ \alpha^{-1}$.

(vi) Consider any $r_1 \in \alpha \cup \beta$ and $r_2 \in \gamma \cup \delta$. Then by definition of $\circ$ we have $r_1 \circ r_2 \subseteq (\alpha \cup \beta) \circ (\gamma \cup \delta)$. If $r_1 \in \alpha$ and $r_2 \in \gamma$, then by definition of $\circ$ we have $r_1 \circ r_2 \subseteq \alpha \circ \gamma$, so $r_1 \circ r_2 \subseteq \alpha \circ \gamma \cup \alpha \circ \delta \cup \beta \circ \gamma \cup \beta \circ \delta$. For the remaining cases the reasoning is analogous.

Consider any $r \in \alpha \circ \gamma \cup \alpha \circ \delta \cup \beta \circ \gamma \cup \beta \circ \delta$. If $r \in \alpha \circ \gamma$, then there exist $r_1 \in \alpha$, $r_2 \in \gamma$ such that $r \in r_1 \circ r_2$. But then $r_1 \in \alpha \cup \beta$ and $r_2 \in \gamma \cup \delta$, so $r_1 \circ r_2 \in (\alpha \cup \beta) \circ (\gamma \cup \delta)$. For the remaining cases the reasoning is analogous. ∎

Axioms

1. x equals x for $x \in Z$
2. $x \mathbf{P} y$ for $x, y \in Z$

Rules of inference

Let $x, y, z \in Z$, $\alpha, \beta \in \mathbf{R}$.

1. $\dfrac{x \; \alpha \; y, \; y \; \beta \; z}{x \; \alpha \circ \beta \; z}$

2. $\dfrac{x \; \alpha \; y, \; x \; \beta \; y}{x \; \alpha \cap \beta \; y}$

3. $\dfrac{x \; \alpha \; y}{y \; \alpha^{-1} \; x}$

4. $\dfrac{x \; \alpha \; y}{x \; \delta \; y}$ for every $\delta \in \mathbf{R}$ such that $\alpha \in \delta$.

Certainly the relation *equals* or its counterpart exists in every set of relations.

DEFINITION

Let Th $= \{ f_j \}_{j \in J}$ be a theory, $f_j \in \mathcal{F}$. A *formal proof* of a formula $f \in \mathcal{F}$ based on the theory Th is a sequence of formulas $f_1, f_2, ..., f_n$ such that:

(i) f_1 is an axiom of the calculus or $f_1 \in$ Th,

(ii) f_2 is an axiom of the calculus or $f_2 \in$ Th or f_2 follows from f_1 by application of inference rule 3 or 4,

(iii) for every i, where $3 \leq i \leq n$, f_i is an axiom of the calculus or $f_i \in$ Th or f_i follows from formulas f_j, f_k, where $1 \leq j \leq k < i$ by application of inference rule 1 or 2, or f_i follows from a formula f_j, where $1 \leq j < i$ by application of inference rule 3 or 4,

(iv) $f = f_n$.

We will write Th $\vdash f$ if a formula f has a proof from theory Th. Theory Th is *consistent* if Th $\nvdash x \; \emptyset \; y$ for every $x, y \in Z$. Theory Th is *maximal* if Th $\vdash f$ or Th $\vdash \neg f$ for every $f \in \mathcal{F}$.

We have presented above a common foundation for the described formalization. In the following sections we discuss in turn formalizations of the constraint propagation algorithm for particular sets of relations. In particular, the semantics can be introduced only for concrete calculi, as it depends on the choice of individuals and of a set of primitive relations together with corresponding composition tables as well as on the choice of a time structure forming a model for the calculus. We will present particular calculi in the same order as we have presented algorithmical solutions in section 4.3 and time structures in chapter 2.

5.3 Point calculus for linear time

In this section we discuss the point calculus for linear time. It was presented in [Hajnicz, 1989b; 1991a] with a slightly different notation.

Now we extend the alphabet of the calculus presented in the previous section by establishing the set of primitive relations $\mathbf{P} = \{$ before, equals, after $\}$. Now we can present the semantics of this calculus.

Semantics

DEFINITIONS

Let $\mathfrak{T} = \langle T, < \rangle$ be a point time structure which satisfies the theory $\mathcal{T}_L$ (see section 2.1). A *valuation* is a function $W : Z \longrightarrow T$. A *model* is an ordered triple $\mathcal{M} = \langle T, <, W \rangle$.

Let $x, y \in Z$. We define *satisfiability* of a formula f in a model $\mathcal{M}$ (notation: $\mathcal{M} \models f$) in the following way:

$\mathcal{M} \models x$ before y iff $W(x) < W(y)$,

$\mathcal{M} \models x$ equals y iff $W(x) = W(y)$,

$\mathcal{M} \models x$ after y iff $W(y) < W(x)$,

$\mathcal{M} \models x \; \alpha \; y$ iff $\mathcal{M} \models x \; r_1 \; y$ or $\mathcal{M} \models x \; r_2 \; y$ or ... or

                      $\mathcal{M} \models x \; r_n \; y$ for $\alpha = \{r_1, r_2, ..., r_n\}$.

No formula of the form $x \; \emptyset \; y$ is satisfied in a model.

Let Th $= \{ f_j \}_{j \in J}$ be a theory, $f_j \in \mathcal{F}$. A model $\mathcal{M} = \langle T, <, W \rangle$ is a *model of the theory* Th if and only if $\mathcal{M} \models f$ holds for every $f \in$ Th.

Lemma 5.3.1. Only one of the three formulas x before y, x equals y and x after y can be satisfied in a model.

A proof of this lemma can be found in [Hajnicz, 1989b].

Theorem 5.3.1. (soundness) For any formula $f \in \mathcal{F}$ and theory Th $= \{ f_j \}_{j \in J}$, if Th $\vdash f$, then $\mathcal{M} \models f$ holds for every model $\mathcal{M}$ of the theory Th.

Sketch of proof

Th $\vdash f$, i.e. there exists a formal proof of the formula f. We will show that all the formulas in this proof (hence also f) are valid in every model of the theory Th.

First, we show that the axioms of the calculus are valid in every model.

       x equals x

$\mathcal{M} \models x$ equals x iff $W(x) = W(x)$, which is a property of "$=$".

       $x \; \{$before, equals, after$\} \; y$

$\mathcal{M} \models x \; \{$before, equals, after$\} \; y$ iff

$\mathcal{M} \models x$ before y or $\mathcal{M} \models x$ equals y or $\mathcal{M} \models x$after y iff

$W(x) < W(y)$ or $W(x) = W(y)$ or $W(y) < W(x)$.

This is valid for every $x, y \in Z$, since this is the linearity axiom.

The axioms of the theory Th are satisfied in every model of this theory by definition. We will show that inference rules yield valid conclusions for valid premises. A proof of the fact that rules 1 and 3 are valid when their premises are primitive relations can be found in [Hajnicz, 1989b]. Therefore, we consider inference rules 1–4 for arbitrary $\alpha, \beta \in \mathbf{R}$. However, we only consider $\alpha, \beta \neq \emptyset$, as $\mathcal{M} \not\models x \alpha y$ holds for every $\alpha = \emptyset$ and every $\mathcal{M}$.

$$\frac{x \; \alpha \; y, \; y \; \beta \; z}{x \; \alpha \circ \beta \; z}$$

$\mathcal{M} \models x \alpha y$ iff $\mathcal{M} \models x r_1 y$ or $\mathcal{M} \models x r_2 y$ or ... or

$\mathcal{M} \models x r_n y$, where $\alpha = \{r_1, r_2, ..., r_n\}$

$\mathcal{M} \models y \beta z$ iff $\mathcal{M} \models y r'_1 z$ or $\mathcal{M} \models y r'_2 z$ or ... or

$\mathcal{M} \models y r'_m z$, where $\beta = \{r'_1, r'_2, ..., r'_m\}$

Consider $r \in \alpha$, $r' \in \beta$ such that $\mathcal{M} \models x r y$ and $\mathcal{M} \models y r' z$. Then $\mathcal{M} \models x r \circ r' z$. Consider $s \in r \circ r'$ such that $\mathcal{M} \models x s z$. Evidently $s \in \alpha \circ \beta$, hence $\mathcal{M} \models x \alpha \circ \beta z$.

$$\frac{x \; \alpha \; y, \; x \; \beta \; y}{x \; \alpha \cap \beta \; y}$$

$\mathcal{M} \models x \alpha y$ iff $\mathcal{M} \models x r_1 y$ or $\mathcal{M} \models x r_2 y$ or ... or

$\mathcal{M} \models x r_n y$, where $\alpha = \{r_1, r_2, ..., r_n\}$

$\mathcal{M} \models x \beta y$ iff $\mathcal{M} \models x r'_1 y$ or $\mathcal{M} \models x r'_2 y$ or ... or

$\mathcal{M} \models x r'_m y$, where $\beta = \{r'_1, r'_2, ..., r'_m\}$

Consider $r \in \alpha$, $r' \in \beta$ such that $\mathcal{M} \models x r y$ and $\mathcal{M} \models x r' y$. Then $r = r'$ holds by lemma 5.3.1, so we can infer that $r \in \alpha$ and $r \in \beta$. This means that $r \in \alpha \cap \beta$, hence $\mathcal{M} \models x \alpha \cap \beta y$.

$$\frac{x \; \alpha \; y}{y \; \alpha^{-1} \; x}$$

$\mathcal{M} \models x \alpha y$ iff $\mathcal{M} \models x r_1 y$ or $\mathcal{M} \models x r_2 y$ or ... or

$\mathcal{M} \models x r_n y$, where $\alpha = \{r_1, r_2, ..., r_n\}$

Consider $r \in \alpha$ such that $\mathcal{M} \models x r y$. Then $\mathcal{M} \models y r^{-1} x$. Since $r^{-1} \in \alpha^{-1}$ holds by definition of α^{-1}, we get $\mathcal{M} \models y \alpha^{-1} x$.

$$\frac{x \; \alpha \; y}{x \; \delta \; y}$$

$\mathcal{M} \models x \alpha y$ iff $\mathcal{M} \models x r_1 y$ or $\mathcal{M} \models x r_2 y$ or ... or

$\mathcal{M} \models x r_n y$, where $\alpha = \{r_1, r_2, ..., r_n\}$

Consider $r \in \alpha$. Since $\alpha \subseteq \delta$, hence $r \in \delta$, so $\mathcal{M} \models x \delta y$.

We have shown that for all the inference rules, if we start from valid premises, then we obtain valid conclusions. As Th $\vdash f$, we can consider a sequence of formulas $f_1, f_2, ..., f_n$ which is a formal proof of the formula f. We know that f_1 is an axiom of the calculus or $f_1 \in$ Th. Consider a formula f_i, where $2 \leq i \leq n$.

Assume that for every $k < i$ we have shown that $\mathcal{M} \models f_k$. If f_i is an axiom of the calculus or $f_i \in$ Th, then $\mathcal{M} \models f_k$. Otherwise there exist two (or one— e.g. for f_2) formulas occurring earlier in the proof such that f_i is derived from them by an application of one of the inference rules. These formulas are satisfied in any model $\mathcal{M}$ (by inductive assumption). We have already shown that all the inference rules lead from formulas satisfied in a model $\mathcal{M}$ to formulas satisfied in this model. Therefore $\mathcal{M} \models f_i$. Thus $\mathcal{M} \models f_n$, so $\mathcal{M} \models f$.   ∎

Unfortunately, the inverse theorem is not true, i.e. the calculus is not complete. In [Hajnicz, 1989b] we show that in spite of lack of completeness, a weaker basic property of formal systems holds, i.e. every consistent theory has a model. We present below a sketch of the argument for the formalism considered there. It is based on the proof of the completeness of the classic propositional calculus presented in [Rasiowa, 1968].

Lemma 5.3.2. A theory Th is maximal and consistent if and only if for any two variables $x, y \in Z$ there exists exactly one primitive relation $r \in \mathbf{P}$ such that Th $\vdash x\, r\, y$.

Lemma 5.3.3. Every inconsistent theory Th contains a finite inconsistent subtheory $\text{Th}_0 \subseteq$ Th.

Lemma 5.3.4. For every theory Th and every formula $f \in \mathcal{F}$, if Th $\nvdash f$ and Th $\nvdash \neg f$, then the theory Th $\cup \{f\}$ is consistent or the theory Th $\cup \neg\{f\}$ is consistent.

Sketch of proof

"Essential" inferences (i.e. minimal with respect to set-theoretical inclusion) can be derived only by means of inference rules 1 and 2. The idea of the proof consists in observing that reasoning can be conducted step by step, i.e. if we derive all the "essential" inferences from new data (together with their inverses), then further reasoning can be based on these inferences only. These assumptions constitute, actually, the basis of Allen's constraint propagation algorithm—it only computes "essential" inferences.

Let $f = x\, \varphi\, y$.

Let $\text{Th}_0 = \{\, w\, \beta\, z \mid \text{Th} \vdash w\, \beta\, z \,\}$, and $\text{Th}_1 = \text{Th}_0 \cup \{\, x\, \varphi\, y,\ y\, \varphi^{-1}\, x \,\}$.

Consider $\varphi = before$, $-\varphi = \{equals, after\}$. It turns out that new inferences can be derived only from data of the following form:

$$t_1\, \alpha_1\, x,\quad x\ before\ y,\quad y\, \alpha_2\, t_2$$

where $\alpha_1, \alpha_2 \subseteq \{before,\ equals\}$, $t_1, t_2 \in Z$. Thus we obtain the following inferences:

$$t_1\ before\ y,\quad x\ before\ t_2,\quad t_1\ before\ t_2.$$

In [Hajnicz, 1989b] we show that these inferences are not inconsistent with the theory Th_0 (i.e. *before* $\in \beta_1$ and *before* $\in \beta_2$ hold for $t_1\ \beta_1\ y$, $x\ \beta_2\ t_2 \in Th_0$). No further inferences can be derived. For instance, for $t_3\ \alpha_3\ t_1 \in Th_0$, $\alpha_3 \subseteq \{before,\ equals\}$ should hold, if a new conclusion were derivable by means of the above inference. But then we have $\alpha_3 \circ \alpha_1' = \{before,\ equals\}$ and $t_3\ \alpha_3 \circ \alpha_1\ x \in Th_0$, hence now we do not obtain a new inference. Therefore $Th \cup \{\,x\ before\ y\,\}$ is consistent.

For $\varphi = after$ and $-\varphi = \{before,\ equals\}$ the reasoning is analogous.

Consider $\varphi = \{before,\ after\}$, $-\varphi = equals$. We have $Th \nvdash x\ before\ y$ and $Th \nvdash x\ after\ y$ by assumption (since otherwise $Th \vdash x\ \{before,\ after\}\ y$ would hold by rule 4).

Suppose that $Th \vdash x\ \{before,\ equals\}\ y$ and $Th \vdash x\ \{equals,\ after\}\ y$. Then, by rule 2, we have $Th \vdash x\ equals\ y$, which contradicts the assumption. If $Th \nvdash x\ \{before,\ equals\}\ y$, then (as $Th \nvdash \neg\ x\ after\ y$) it has already been proved that $Th \cup \{\,x\ before\ y\,\}$ is consistent. If $Th \nvdash x\ \{equals,\ after\}\ y$, then (as $Th \nvdash \neg\ x\ before\ y$) it has already been proved that $Th \cup \{\,x\ after\ y\,\}$ is consistent. In both cases $Th \cup \{\,x\ \{before,\ after\}\ y\,\}$ is consistent.

Evidently $Th \cup \{x\ before,\ equals,\ after\ y\}$ is consistent. Thus for every relation $\varphi \in \mathbf{R}$ the theory $Th \cup \{\,x\ \varphi\ y\,\}$ is consistent or the theory $Th \cup \{\,x\ \varphi\ y\,\}$ is consistent. ∎

Lemma 5.3.5. A theory Th is maximal if and only if for every formula $f \in \mathcal{F}$, if $Th \nvdash f$, then $Th \cup \{f\}$ is inconsistent.

Lemma 5.3.6. Every consistent theory can be extended to a maximal consistent theory.

Proof

Suppose that there exists a consistent theory Th which cannot be extended to a maximal consistent theory.

The set of all the formulas $\mathcal{F}$ is countable, hence it can be arranged into an infinite sequence F such that every formula $f \in \mathcal{F}$ occurs in this sequence at least once.

We define a sequence of theories (Th_n) and a sequence of formulas (g_n) in the following way. Let $Th_1 = Th$. Since this theory is not maximal (by assumption), so (by lemma 5.3.5) there exists a formula $g \in \mathcal{F}$ such that $Th_1 \nvdash g$ and $Th_1 \cup \{g\}$ is still consistent. Let g_1 be the first such formula in the sequence F. We define $Th_2 = Th_1 \cup \{\,g_1\,\}$. Evidently $Th_1 \subseteq Th_2$ and by assumption it is not maximal. Continuing this reasoning we define by induction:

$$Th_{n+1} = Th_n \cup \{\,g_n\,\},$$

where g_n is the first formula in the sequence F such that $Th_n \nvdash g_n$ and $Th_n \cup \{g_n\}$ is consistent. It follows from the above definition and lemma 5.3.5 that $Th_n \subseteq Th_{n+1}$ and Th_{n+1} is consistent. Now we define a theory Th^*:

$$\text{Th}^* = \bigcup_{n=1}^{\infty} \text{Th}_n.$$

Evidently $\text{Th} \subseteq \text{Th}^*$. Suppose that Th^* is inconsistent. Then by lemma 5.3.3 there exists a finite inconsistent subtheory of Th^*. This subtheory should be included in some theory Th_n, what means that this Th_n is inconsistent. This contradicts the definition of Th_n. Suppose that Th^* is not maximal. Then by lemma 5.3.5 there exists a formula $g \in F$ such that $\text{Th}^* \nvdash g$ and $\text{Th}^* \cup \{g\}$ is still consistent. But by the definition of the sequence (g_n) there exists a j such that $g = g_j$. Thus $g \in \text{Th}_{j+1}$, hence $\text{Th}^* \vdash g$, which contradicts the assumption. Therefore Th^* is consistent and maximal.   ■

Theorem 5.3.2. A theory Th is consistent if and only if it has a model.

Proof

Consider any consistent theory Th. By lemma 5.3.6 it can be extended to a maximal consistent theory Th^*; $\text{Th} \subseteq \text{Th}^*$.

As Th^* is maximal, $\text{Th}^* \vdash g$ or $\text{Th}^* \vdash \neg g$ for every $g \in \mathcal{F}$. Since Th^* is consistent, $\text{Th}^* \nvdash g$ or $\text{Th}^* \nvdash \neg g$ for every $g \in \mathcal{F}$. Thus <u>exactly</u> one of the conditions: $\text{Th}^* \vdash g$ or $\text{Th}^* \vdash \neg g$ holds for every $g \in \mathcal{F}$. As Th^* is maximal and consistent, it follows from lemma 5.3.2 that for very $x, y \in Z$ exactly one of the conditions: $\text{Th}^* \vdash x$ before y, $\text{Th}^* \vdash x$ equals y and $\text{Th}^* \vdash x$ after y holds.

The set of variables Z being countable, we can arrange its elements in a sequence $x_1, x_2, \dots$. We define a model $\mathcal{M} = \langle T, <, W \rangle$ in the following way. First we set $W(x_1)$ and $W(x_2)$ such that:

if $\text{Th}^* \vdash x_1$ before x_2,   then $W(x_1) < W(x_2)$,

if $\text{Th}^* \vdash x_1$ equals x_2,   then $W(x_1) = W(x_2)$,

if $\text{Th}^* \vdash x_1$ after x_2,   then $W(x_2) < W(x_1)$.

We define a set $X_n = \{x_1, x_2, \dots, x_{n-1}\}$. For every $n \geq 3$ we set $W(x_n)$ in the following way. If there exists $x_i \in X_n$ such that $\text{Th}^* \vdash x_n$ equals x_i, then $W(x_n) = W(x_i)$. Otherwise we divide the set X_n into two subsets X_n^- and X_n^+ such that:

$$X_n^- = \{ x_i \in X_n \mid \text{Th}^* \vdash x_i \text{ before } x_n \},$$
$$X_n^+ = \{ x_i \in X_n \mid \text{Th}^* \vdash x_i \text{ after } x_n \}.$$

Let $W(X_n^-) = \{ W(x_i) \mid x_i \in X_n^- \}$, $W(X_n^+) = \{ W(x_i) \mid x_i \in X_n^+ \}$. At least one of these two sets is not empty. If $W(X_n^-)$ is not empty, then as it is a finite set and $<$ is a strict linear order, there exists a greatest element x_k in it. Let $W(x_k) < W(x_n)$. On the other hand, if $W(X_n^+)$ is not empty, then as it is a finite set and $<$ is a strict linear order, there exists a least element x_j in it. Let $W(x_n) < W(x_j)$.

If $W(X_n^-)$ and $W(X_n^+)$ are both non-empty, then we must show that $W(x_k) < W(x_j)$ in order to make this construction correct.   We have

$W(x_k) \in W(X_n^-)$, hence $\text{Th}^* \vdash x_k$ before x_n and $W(x_j) \in W(X_n^+)$, hence $\text{Th}^* \vdash x_j$ after x_n. Thus (by rule 3) $\text{Th}^* \vdash x_n$ before x_j. Then by rule 1 we obtain that $\text{Th}^* \vdash x_k$ before x_j. Let $k < j$. Then $W(x_k) \in W(X_j^-)$, so $W(x_k) < W(x_j)$. For $k > j$ the reasoning is analogous.

Now we will show that for $\mathcal{M}$ defined in such a way, for every $f \in \mathcal{A}$ such that $\text{Th}^* \vdash f$ also $\mathcal{M} \models f$ holds. Consider any $x_k, x_j \in Z$ (the numbering is the same as the numbering in the sequence used to construct $\mathcal{M}$). There exists exactly one relation $r \in \mathbf{P}$ such that $\text{Th}^* \vdash x_k \ r \ x_j$. Suppose that $k < j$ (the case for $k > j$ is symmetrical; for $k = j$ we have the axiom of the calculus x_k equals x_k that is satisfied in every model). If $r = $ before, then $x_k \in X_j^-$, hence $W(x_k) < W(x_j)$, so $\mathcal{M} \models x_k$ before x_j. If $r = $ equals, then there exists $x_i \in X_j$ such that $\text{Th}^* \vdash x_i$ equals x_j. This is an equivalence relation because of the calculus axiom 1 and because $equals^{-1} = equals$ and $equals \circ equals = equals$. Therefore $\text{Th}^* \vdash x_p$ equals x_q holds for $x_p, x_q \in X_j^= \subseteq X_j$, where $X_j^= = \{ x_i \in X_j \mid x_i \text{ equals } x_j \}$. For all the elements $x_l \in X_j^=$ (except the first element) the condition for the existence of $x_i \in X_l$ such that $\text{Th}^* \vdash x_i$ equals x_l is satisfied. We can show by a simple inductive proof that $W(x_p) = W(x_q)$ holds for all $x_p, x_q \in X_j^=$. Since $W(x_j) = W(x_i)$ for some $x_i \in X_j^=$ (by the construction of $\mathcal{M}$), $W(x_j) = W(x_l)$ for any $x_l \in X_j^=$. As $x_k \in X_j^=$, $W(x_k) = W(x_j)$. Thus $\mathcal{M} \models x_k \ r \ x_j$. Otherwise, if $r = $ after, then $x_k \in X_j^+$, so $W(x_j) < W(x_k)$, hence $\mathcal{M} \models x_k \ r \ x_j$.

Finally, we will show that $\mathcal{M} \models g$ holds for every $g \in \mathcal{F}$ such that $\text{Th}^* \vdash g$. Let $g = x \ \alpha \ y$, $\alpha \in \mathbf{R}$ ($\alpha \neq \emptyset$, since Th^* is consistent). By lemma 5.3.2 there exists exactly one $r \in \mathbf{P}$ such that $\text{Th}^* \vdash x \ r \ y$. It follows from the construction of the model that $\mathcal{M} \models x \ r \ y$. Evidently $r \in \alpha$ (since otherwise we would be able to derive $x \ \emptyset \ y$ by means of rule 2, whereas the theory Th^* is consistent). And from this it follows that $\mathcal{M} \models g$. Since $\text{Th} \subseteq \text{Th}^*$, $\mathcal{M}$ is evidently a model of the theory Th, too.   ■

We have mentioned above that the constraint propagation algorithm for points in linear time lacks logical completeness. It can be shown on the following example:

Example

$$\text{Th} = \{ \ a \ \{before, \ equals\} \ c, \ a \ \{equals, \ after\} \ d, \ b \ \{before, \ equals\} \ c,$$
$$b \ \{equals, \ after\} \ d, \ a \ \{before, \ after\} \ b \ \}$$

$$d \ \leq \ a \ \leq \ c$$
$$\cancel{\parallel}$$
$$d \ \leq \ b \ \leq \ c$$

$\text{Th} \nvdash c$ equals d and $\text{Th} \nvdash c$ after d and $\text{Th} \vdash c \ \{equals, \ after\} \ d$. However, $\mathcal{M} \models c$ after d for every model $\mathcal{M}$ of the theory Th.

This example was presented in [Hajnicz, 1991a; Valdés-Péres, 1987].

Lack of completeness is a direct consequence of the fact that a stronger version of lemma 5.3.4 reading as follows: *For any theory Th and formula $f \in \mathcal{F}$, if Th $\not\vdash \neg f$, then the theory $Th \cup \{f\}$ is consistent* does not hold. Consider the same example as before. We have Th $\not\vdash c$ equals d and Th $\not\vdash c$ {*before*, *after*} d, but the theory $Th \cup \{ c$ equals $d \}$ is inconsistent. If the above property were to hold, then with the assumption that Th $\not\vdash f$ we would have that $Th \cup \{\neg f\}$ is a consistent theory, and then by theorem 5.3.2 there would exist a model of this theory $\mathcal{M}$ and evidently $\mathcal{M} \not\models f$ would hold. In the classic propositional calculus such asymmetry between a formula and its negation is absurd, and for this precise reason the property of logical completeness and the property of existence of a model for every consistent theory are equivalent (see e.g. [Lyndon, 1966]).

The formalization of point relation constraint propagation algorithm presented in this section shows the fundamental properties of the algorithm for this set of relations. It shows that it is logically sound, but not logically complete. Nevertheless it possesses the important property of existence of a model for every consistent theory, which means from an algorithmical point of view that any occurrence of inconsistency in a set of data will be detected.

Observe that van Beek & Cohen (1990) show that the algorithm presented in section 4.4.7 is complete for linear point time. Moreover, they show that original Allen's algorithm is complete when we exclude the relation $\{ <, > \}$ (i.e. $\neq$) from the set of relations $\mathbf{R}$. In fact, they present still a stronger result—namely, they state that in the case of points the above example is the only source of inconsistency. Therefore, the algorithm finds a minimal solution ("is complete") for every set of data (axioms) such that no subset (subnetwork) of four points isomorphic to this example can be distinguished in it.

5.4 Dates in the point calculus

In the previous section we discussed time composed of a uniform set of points, time positions of which can be known with different precision. However, among points we can distinguish *dates*, the position in time of which is by definition univocally determined. In section 4.3.1 we have stated that in such a case the algorithm should be enriched with a function calculating primitive relations between dates. Now we present a formalization of this case. It is somewhat untypical, so we present its syntax first.

<u>Syntax</u>

<u>Alphabet</u>

- nonempty, countable sets of variables Z_P and Z_D,
- a set of primitive relation operators
  $\mathbf{P} = \{$ *before, equals, after* $\}$,

- set-theoretical symbols,
- a function $F: Z_D \times Z_D \longrightarrow \mathbf{P}$.

Definitions of the set of relations $\mathbf{R}$, the set of formulas $\mathcal{F}$, the empty relation, an inconsistent formula, an opposite relation, an inverse relation and of the composition of relations are the same as in section 5.2, with the only difference that in this case variables x, y come from the set $Z_P \cup Z_D$.

Axioms

1. x equals x for $x \in Z_P \cup Z_D$.

2. $x \mathbf{P} y$ for $x, y \in Z_P$.

3. $x F(x,y) y$ for $x, y \in Z_D$.

Moreover, the function F evidently cannot disturb the order, i.e. a theory in which it does not preserve the rules for composing relations is inconsistent. The rules of inference are the same as in section 5.2. Also definitions of a consistent theory and of a formal proof of a formula are the same.

Semantics

We have not presented a linear time structure with distinguished dates in section 2, because this is actually beside the purpose—from a formal point of view these individuals do not differ, as they can be compared by means of the same precedence relation $<$. Therefore, for a time structure $\mathfrak{T} = \langle T, < \rangle$ the definition of satisfiability of a formula is the same as in the previous section, again for variables coming from the set $Z_P \cup Z_D$. However, one can imagine a structure in which dates and "simple" points are distinguished—a structure $\mathfrak{T}_D = \langle T, D, < \rangle$, where T is a set of time points, D is a set of dates and $<$ is a precedence relation over $T \cup D$ which is a strict linear order. A valuation is a pair of functions $W = \langle W_P, W_D \rangle$, where $W_P: Z_P \longrightarrow T$ and $W_D: Z_D \longrightarrow D$. A model is an ordered quadruple $\mathcal{M} = \langle T, D, <, W \rangle$. The definition of satisfiability of a formula remains itself still unchanged, since in the above structure we have again one precedence relation $<$.

Theorem 5.4.1. (soundness) For any formula $f \in \mathcal{F}$ and theory $\text{Th} = \{ f_j \}_{j \in J}$, if $\text{Th} \vdash f$, then $\mathcal{M} \models f$ holds for every model $\mathcal{M}$ of the theory Th.

5.5 Point calculus for non-linear time

In this section point calculus for non-linear time will be discussed. It was presented in [Hajnicz, 1991c]. The main difference with regard to point calculus presented in section 5.3 is the addition of the relation *excludes*. Thus this time we consider a larger set of primitive relations $\mathbf{P} = \{ \text{ before, equals, after, excludes } \}$.

Semantics

DEFINITIONS

Let $\mathfrak{T} = \langle T, \, < \rangle$ be a point time structure (see section 2.1). A *valuation* is a function $W: Z \longrightarrow T$. A *model* is an ordered triple $\mathcal{M} = \langle T, \, <, \, W \rangle$.

Let $x, y \in Z$. We define *satisfiability* of a formula f in a model $\mathcal{M}$ (notation: $\mathcal{M} \models f$) in the following way:

$\mathcal{M} \models x$ before y iff $W(x) < W(y)$,

$\mathcal{M} \models x$ equals y iff $W(x) = W(y)$,

$\mathcal{M} \models x$ after y iff $W(y) < W(x)$,

$\mathcal{M} \models x$ excludes y iff $\neg(W(x) < W(y) \vee W(x) = W(y) \vee W(y) < W(x))$,

$\mathcal{M} \models x \, \alpha \, y$ iff $\mathcal{M} \models x \, r_1 \, y$ or $\mathcal{M} \models x \, r_2 \, y$ or ... or

$$\mathcal{M} \models x \, r_n \, y \quad \text{for } \alpha = \{r_1, r_2, ..., r_n\}.$$

No formula of the form $x \, \emptyset \, y$ is satisfied in a model.

The definition of a model of a theory is the same as in section 5.3.

The interpretation of the relations *before*, *equals* and *after* is the same as in the linear case. However, an interpretation of the relation *excludes* seems to be less intuitive. Unfortunately, it is not possible to formulate it in a more direct way; the above formulation means exactly that two points do not lie on the same branch, that they are incomparable with each other by means of the precedence relation $<$.

Since two relation composition tables were presented in section 4.3.2, we have to do with two theories. They correspond to two classes of point time structures presented in section 2.1.1—partially ordered structures (theory $\mathcal{T}_P$) and left linearly ordered structures (theory $\mathcal{T}_B$).

Clearly, the soundness theorem also holds in this case:

Theorem 5.5.1. (soundness) For any formula $f \in \mathcal{F}$ and theory $\text{Th} = \{ f_j \}_{j \in J}$, if $\text{Th} \vdash f$, then $\mathcal{M} \models f$ holds for every model $\mathcal{M}$ of the theory Th.

The proof follows analogously as for the linear case. Obviously two proofs are needed for the two theories. A complete proof can be found in [Hajnicz, 1991c].

The calculus not being complete for linear order, it is not complete for left linear or partial order, either. The counterexample presented in section 5.3 can be applied to these cases, too. Unfortunately, an attempt to prove a weaker theorem about the existence of a model for every consistent theory has failed—this case turned out to be much more complicated. First of all this concerns the proof of a lemma being counterpart of lemma 5.3.4. Let us try to perform a reasoning analogous to the one sketched in section 5.3:

For instance, consider $\varphi =$ *before*, $-\varphi = \{$*equals*, *after*, *excludes*$\}$. It turns out that new inferences can only be derived from data of the form:

$$t_1 \, \alpha_1 \, x, \quad x \text{ before } y, \quad y \, \alpha_2 \, t_2,$$

where $t_1, t_2 \in Z$ and $\alpha_1, \alpha_2 \subseteq$ {*before, equals, excludes*}, and not {*before, equals*} as before. This has its far reaching consequences. First, inferences that are obtained now are the following:

$$t_1 \text{ \{before, excludes\} } y, \quad x \text{ \{before, excludes\} } t_2,$$

and the relation between t_1 and t_2 also depends on the theory Th_0. Second, for $t_3 \, \alpha_3 \, t_1 \in Th_0$, where $\alpha_3 \subseteq$ {*before, equals, excludes*}, we have $\alpha_3 \circ \alpha_1$ = *no information*, hence no inference between t_3 and y has been derived yet. Nevertheless it can be derived later. Let us show this on an example.

Example

Consider the following theory:

Th = { t_3 {*before, equals, excludes*} t_1, t_1 {*before, equals, excludes*} x,

    y {*before, equals, excludes*} t_2, t_2 {*before, equals, excludes*} t_4,

    t_1 {*before, equals, after*} y, t_3 {*before, equals, after*} y, .

    x {*before, equals, after*} t_2, x {*before, equals, after*} t_4 }.

No new inferences except trivial ones can be derived from this theory. Now we add to this theory an axiom x *before* y. In the first step we derive (from the introductory data) t_1 *before* y and x *before* t_2. In the second step we derive (from these inferences) t_3 *before* y, x *before* t_4 and t_1 {*before, excludes*} t_2. In the third step we derive t_3 {*before, excludes*} t_2 and t_1 {*before, excludes*} t_4.

As we can see, the number of derivation steps depends on the size of a theory. Thus proving consistency of a theory in the general case becomes extremely complicated—it cannot be performed in a finite number of steps, hence an inductive proof is necessary. On the other hand, we have failed in finding a counterexample for this lemma. In our deepest conviction it is true. Then also a theorem about the existence of a model for every consistent theory would be true. In such a case logical properties of the algorithm for non-linear point time would not be worse than for linear point time.

We will not discuss a formalization for point calculus with dates in the case of non-linear time. In this case not only have we to do with two kinds of individuals, but also with several sets of primitive relations between them. Thus from the syntactic point of view this formalization would be similar to the formalization of the calculus of intervals and points from section 5.9, whereas from the semantic point of view it would add nothing new.

5.6 Calculus of distances between points

In this section we want to present a formalization for the next case of point time, i.e. for metric point time. This solution is called the calculus of distances between points. Since distances between points were to some extend taken into consideration in the formalization of dates suggested in [Hajnicz, 1991b], we will use here the concepts presented in that work.

We want to emphasize that this formalization concerns the general version of the calculus of distances between points, not its implementationally limited version, i.e. we will not consider relations written as finite sequences of intervals. Nevertheless we will be sometimes forced to reduce the set of formulas to its countable subset; an excellent example of such a subset is the set of all these relations that can be represented in the form of a finite sequence of intervals.

We restrict this formalization to countable, discrete sets of primitive relations. Moreover, we assume that the hierarchy of distance units contains only one element (or every unit of the higher level is composed of a fixed number of units of the lower level, hence we are able to transform every distance to a certain number of units of the lowest level). Thus we can assume that $\mathbf{P} = \{r_i\}_{i \in \mathbf{Z}}$, which means that the set of primitive relations is isomorphic to the set of integers $\mathbf{Z}$. As in [Hajnicz, 1991b], operations on primitive relations will be reduced to predefined operations on their indices, i.e. $r_i \circ r_j = r_i + r_j = r_{i+j}$ and $r_i^{-1} = -r_i = r_{-i}$.

With such an assumption, the set of relations $\mathbf{R}$ is evidently not countable, hence also the set of formulas $\mathcal{F}$ is not countable.

The axiomatization remains the same as it has been presented in section 5.2, but the axiom x equals x for $x \in Z$ will be now denoted as $x\ r_0\ x$ for $x \in Z$, since in this case r_0 is a counterpart of the relation equals from other sets of relations.

Semantics

The semantics of the calculus of distances between points is based on a metric point structure $\mathfrak{T} = \langle T,\ \mathcal{C},\ <,\ \delta \rangle$ (see section 2.1.2).

DEFINITIONS

Let $\mathcal{C} = \langle C,\ +,\ 0 \rangle$ be a set of distances between points. We have stated in section 2.1.2 that in typical cases it is a set isomorphic to the set of natural numbers $\mathbf{N}$. Therefore we can say that $C = \{o_i\}_{i \in \mathbf{N}}$, where $o_0 = 0$ and $o_i = i * o_1$ for $i \in \mathbf{N}$, $i \neq 0$. Then o_1 is called a *unit distance*, and the remaining distances are, in a natural way, its multiples.

An *interpretation* of a primitive relation is a function $S : \mathbf{P} \longrightarrow \mathcal{C}$ such that $S(r_i) = |i| * S(r_1) = |i| * o_1 = o_i$. A *valuation* is a function $W : Z \longrightarrow T$. A *model* is an ordered tuple $\mathcal{M} = \langle T,\ \mathcal{C},\ <,\ \delta,\ S,\ W \rangle$.

Let $x, y \in Z$. We define *satisfiability* of a formula f in a model $\mathcal{M}$ (notation: $\mathcal{M} \models f$) in the following way:

$$\mathcal{M} \models x\ r_i\ y \quad \text{iff} \quad \begin{aligned} &W(x) < W(y),\ \text{if}\ i > 0, \\ &W(x) = W(y),\ \text{if}\ i = 0, \\ &W(y) < W(x),\ \text{if}\ i < 0 \\ &\text{and}\ \ \delta(W(x), W(y)) = S(r_i) \end{aligned}$$

$$\mathcal{M} \models x\ \alpha\ y \quad \text{iff} \quad \text{there exists}\ r_i \in \alpha\ \text{such that}\ \mathcal{M} \models x\ r_i\ y$$

A formula of the form $x \: \emptyset \: y$ is not satisfied in any model.

In spite of the considered case being non-typical, the definitions of a proof of a formula, a consistent theory, a maximal theory and of a model of a theory are the same as in all the other cases.

Now we present properties of the considered calculus.

Lemma 5.6.1. For any pair of formulas $x \: r_i \: y$ and $x \: r_j \: y$ we have $\mathcal{M} \models x \: r_i \: y$ and $\mathcal{M} \models x \: r_j \: y$ if and only if $i = j$.

Sketch of proof

Consider any two variables $x, y \in Z$. We must consider three different cases.

1. $W(x) < W(y)$ and $\delta(W(x), W(y)) = o_k$.
   Evidently then $o_k = S(r_i) = S(r_j)$, hence $|i| = |j|$. Since by definition of $\models$ we have $i > 0, j > 0$, so $i = j$.

2. $W(x) = W(y)$.
   Then $i = j = 0$.

3. $W(y) < W(x)$ and $\delta(W(x), W(y)) = o_k$.
   Evidently then $o_k = S(r_i) = S(r_j)$, hence $|i| = |j|$. Since by definition of $\models$ we have $i < 0, j < 0$, so $i = j$.

Therefore for all the cases $i = j$ holds. ∎

Theorem 5.6.1. (soundness) For any formula $f \in \mathcal{F}$ and theory $\mathrm{Th} = \{ f_j \}_{j \in J}$, if $\mathrm{Th} \vdash f$, then $\mathcal{M} \models f$ holds for every model $\mathcal{M}$ of the theory Th.

Sketch of proof

Assume $\mathrm{Th} \vdash f$, i.e. there exists a formal proof of the formula f. We will show that all the formulas from this proof (thus also f) are valid in every model of the theory Th.

First we show that the axioms of the calculus are valid in every model.

$$x \: r_0 \: x \quad \text{for } x \in Z.$$

$\mathcal{M} \models x \: r_0 \: x$ iff $W(x) = W(x)$ and $\delta(W(x), W(x)) = S(r_0)$.

This is true by definition of precedence relation $<$ and of metric δ.

$$x \: \mathbf{P} \: y \quad \text{for } x, y \in Z.$$

$\mathcal{M} \models x \: \alpha \: y$ iff   there exists $r_i \in \alpha$ such that $\mathcal{M} \models x \: r_i \: y$.

Consider $o_i \in C$ such that $\delta(W(x), W(y)) = o_i, i \geq 0$. According to our notation $o_i = S(r_i) = S(r_{-i})$. If $W(x) = W(y)$, then $\mathcal{M} \models x \: r_0 \: y$, i.e. $i = 0$. Evidently $r_0 \in \mathbf{P}$. If $W(x) < W(y)$, then $\mathcal{M} \models x \: r_i \: y$, and obviously $r_i \in \mathbf{P}$, whereas if $W(y) < W(x)$, then $\mathcal{M} \models x \: r_{-i} \: y$, and evidently $r_{-i} \in \mathbf{P}$. Thus in all cases there exists $r_i \in \mathbf{P}$ such that $\mathcal{M} \models x \: r_i \: y$. Therefore finally $\mathcal{M} \models x \: \mathbf{P} \: y$.

Axioms of the theory Th are satisfied in every model of this theory by definition. We will show that starting from valid premises of inference rules we obtain valid conclusions. First we will show that rule 1 is valid when its premises are primitive relations.

$$\frac{x \; r_i \; y, \quad y \; r_j \; z}{x \; r_{i+j} \; z}$$

$\mathcal{M} \models x \; r_i \; y$ iff $W(x) < W(y)$, if $i > 0$, $W(x) = W(y)$, if $i = 0$,
$\qquad\qquad\qquad\qquad\quad W(y) < W(x)$, if $i < 0$ and $\delta(W(x), W(y)) = S(r_i)$

$\mathcal{M} \models y \; r_j \; z$ iff $W(y) < W(z)$, if $j > 0$, $W(y) = W(z)$, if $j = 0$,
$\qquad\qquad\qquad\qquad\quad W(z) < W(y)$, if $j < 0$ and $\delta(W(y), W(z)) = S(r_j)$

If $i > 0$ and $j > 0$, then $W(x) < W(y)$ & $W(y) < W(z)$, and then by definition of δ we have $\delta(W(x), W(z)) = \delta(W(x), W(y)) + \delta(W(y), W(z)) = S(r_i) + S(r_j) = o_i + o_j = o_{i+j} = S(r_{i+j})$. Moreover we have then $W(x) < W(z)$. As $i + j > 0$, we infer $\mathcal{M} \models x \; r_{i+j} \; z$.

If $i > 0$ and $j = 0$, then $W(x) < W(y)$ & $W(y) = W(z)$. Then $W(x) < W(z)$ and $\delta(W(x), W(y)) = \delta(W(x), W(z)) = S(r_i) = S(r_{i+0}) = S(r_{i+j})$. Therefore, since $i + j > 0$, we have $\mathcal{M} \models x \; r_{i+j} \; z$.

If $i > 0$ and $j < 0$, then $W(x) < W(y)$ and $W(z) < W(y)$. Then if $|i| = |j|$, i.e. $i = -j$, then $\delta(W(x), W(y)) = \delta(W(y), W(z)) = S(r_i) = S(r_j) = o_i$. Suppose that $W(x) < W(z)$ and $\delta(W(x), W(z)) = o_k$, $k > 0$. Then $W(x) < W(z)$ & $W(z) < W(y)$, so by definition of δ we have $\delta(W(x), W(y)) = \delta(W(x), W(z)) + \delta(W(z), W(y)) = o_k + o_i = o_{k+i} \neq o_i$. Contradiction. The reasoning is analogous, when we know that $W(z) < W(x)$. Therefore, from the axiom of linearity of structures, $W(x) = W(z)$ holds, i.e. $\delta(W(x), W(z)) = o_0 = S(r_0)$. But $r_{i+j} = r_{i-i} = r_0$, so $\mathcal{M} \models x \; r_{i+j} \; z$.

If $|i| > |j|$, then $\delta(W(x), W(y)) > \delta(W(y), W(z))$, as $S(r_i) = |i| * o_1 > |j| * o_1 = S(r_j)$. Then evidently $W(x) \neq W(z)$. Suppose that $W(z) < W(x)$ and $\delta(W(x), W(z)) = o_k$, $k > 0$. Then $W(z) < W(x)$ & $W(x) < W(y)$, hence by definition of δ we have $\delta(W(z), W(y)) = \delta(W(z), W(x)) + \delta(W(x), W(y)) = o_k + o_i = o_{k+i}$, i.e. $o_{|j|} = o_{k+i}$, what contradicts the assumption that $|i| > |j|$. Thus $W(x) < W(z)$. Therefore, by the axiom of linearity of structure, $W(x) < W(z)$ & $W(z) < W(y)$ holds, so $\delta(W(x), W(y)) = \delta(W(x), W(z)) + \delta(W(z), W(y))$, i.e. $\delta(W(x), W(z)) = \delta(W(x), W(y)) - \delta(W(z), W(y)) = o_{|i|} - o_{|j|} = o_{|i|-|j|} = o_{i+j} = S(r_{i+j})$, as $|j| = -j$ and $i+j > 0$. Thus $\mathcal{M} \models x \; r_{i+j} \; y$.

If $|i| < |j|$ then the reasoning proceeds in a similar way. We obtain that $W(z) < W(x)$ and $\delta(W(x), W(z)) = o_{|j|-|i|} = o_{-j-i} = o_{-(i+j)} = S(r_{i+j})$, as $i + j < 0$. Therefore $\mathcal{M} \models x \; r_{i+j} \; y$.

For the remaining values of i and j the reasoning proceeds in a similar way.

$$\frac{x \; r_i \; y}{y \; r_{-i} \; x}$$

$\mathcal{M} \models x \; r_i \; y$ iff $W(x) < W(y)$, if $i > 0$, $W(x) = W(y)$, if $i = 0$,

$\qquad\qquad W(y) < W(x)$, if $i < 0$ and $\delta(W(x), W(y)) = S(r_i)$

If $i > 0$, then $W(x) < W(y)$ and $\delta(W(x), W(y)) = \delta(W(y), W(x)) = s(r_i) = |i| * S(r_1) = S(r_{-i})$. Therefore $\mathcal{M} \models y \; r_{-i} \; x$.

For $i < 0$ the reasoning is analogous.

If $i = 0$, then $W(x) = W(y)$ and $\delta(W(x), W(y)) = \delta(W(y), W(x)) = S(r_0) = S(r_{-0})$, so $\mathcal{M} \models y \; r_{-i} \; x$.

Thus we have shown that rules 1 and 3 are valid when their premises are primitive relations. The proof of validity of rules 1–4 for arbitrary relations from **R** proceeds in the same way as for theorem 5.2.1, with slight notational differences.

∎

Unfortunately, the constraint propagation algorithm is not complete in the case of metric time. This is obvious inasmuch as the algorithm is not complete for "ordinary" point time, which has been shown in section 5.3. The example presented there can be translated into the language of distances between points in the following way:

Example

Let us consider the following theory Th, formulated in terms of intervals. The symbols $-\infty$, $+\infty$ were not used in the language of the calculus; their interpretation (obvious and consistent with the previous sections) is the following:

$$(-\infty, r_i] = \{\, r_j \mid r_j \in \mathbf{P}, \; j \le i \,\},$$
$$[r_i, +\infty) = \{\, r_j \mid r_j \in \mathbf{P}, \; j \ge i \,\}.$$

$$\text{Th} = \{\, a \; [r_0, +\infty) \; c, \; c \; [r_0, +\infty) \; b, \; a \; [r_0, +\infty) \; d, \; d \; [r_0, +\infty) \; b,$$
$$c \; (-\infty, r_1] \cup [r_1, +\infty) \; d \,\}$$

Th $\vdash$ $a \; [r_0, +\infty) \; b$ and Th $\nvdash$ $a \; (r_1, +\infty) \; b$. Nevertheless, $\mathcal{M} \models a \; r_0 \; b$ holds for no model of the theory Th.

In the calculus of distances between points an obvious generalization of this example is given by the following theory:

$$\text{Th}' = \{\, a \; [r_i, +\infty) \; c, \; c \; [r_j, +\infty) \; b, \; a \; [r_{i+k}, +\infty) \; d, \; d \; [r_{j-k}, +\infty) \; b,$$
$$c \; (-\infty, r_{k-l}] \cup [r_{k+l}, +\infty) \; d \,\} \qquad (l > 0)$$

Th' $\vdash$ $a \; [r_{i+j}, +\infty) \; b$ and Th' $\nvdash$ $a \; [r_{i+j+l}, +\infty) \; b$, or even Th' $\nvdash$ $a \; [r_{i+j+1}, +\infty) \; b$. Nevertheless, for no model of the theory Th, $\mathcal{M} \models a \; r_{i+j} \; b$, nor even $\mathcal{M} \models a \; [r_{i+j}, r_{i+j+l-1}] \; b$ holds.

Dechter et al. (1991) show that determining consistency of the metric constraint representation is in the general case **NP**-hard. Nevertheless, they also show that if we restrict ourselves to relations composed of one rational interval, then the resulting calculus is complete.

In [Hajnicz, 1989b] we show that every consistent theory of point calculus has a model (see section 5.3). Unfortunately, this is not true for the calculus of distances between points.

Example
Let us consider the following theory Th:

$$Th = \{ \, a \, -\{r_i\} \, b \mid r_i \in \mathbf{P} \, \}$$

Evidently this theory has no model, since for every $r_i \in \mathbf{P}$ there exists a formula $f \in Th$, $f = a \, -\{r_i\} \, b$ such that if $\mathcal{M} \models a \, r_i \, b$, then $\mathcal{M} \not\models f$. On the other hand $Th \not\vdash a \, \emptyset \, b$, as a proof of this formula (applying inference rule 4) should be infinite.

This property is not satisfied even when we restrict ourselves to a countable set of formulas (countability of a set of formulas was an important condition for a proof of this property for the point calculus). An excellent example of a countable set of formulas is, after all, the one in which relations are written in the form of finite sequences of intervals. Evidently a relation $-\{r_i\}$ can be written as $(-\infty, r_{i-1}] \cup [r_{i+1}, +\infty)$, so the theory presented in the above example is a theory of this limited language.

The next step is to limit our considerations, in a framework of a countable subset of the language, to finite theories (i.e. theories containing finite sets of axioms). This limitation is reasonable from an artificial intelligence point of view, since in inference systems we can represent only finite theories. Then it is also necessary to limit the set of variables Z to a finite set (otherwise we would not be able to obtain a maximal theory—a maximal theory must contain at least one axiom for each variable). Unfortunately, Dechter et al. (1991) present an example of a finite theory that has no model.

Also in this case we will not consider a formalization of the considered calculus with dates added. It is very similar to the "typical" linear case, though the relations are clearly different.

5.7 Interval calculus for linear time

Now we turn to interval time. As in the case of points, we start from linear order. This case was presented in [Hajnicz, 1989b; 1991a].

For linear interval time the set of primitive relation operators is $\mathbf{P} = \{$ *before, meets, overlaps, finished by, contains, starts, equals, started by, during, finishes, overlapped by, met by, after* $\}$. Now we present the semantics of this calculus.

Semantics

DEFINITIONS

Let $\Im = \langle I, <, \subseteq \rangle$ be an interval time structure, in which a theory $\mathcal{T}_C$ is satisfied (see section 2.2.1). A *valuation* is a function $W : Z \longrightarrow I$. A *model* is an ordered quadruple $\mathcal{M} = \langle T, <, \subseteq, W \rangle$.

Let $x, y \in Z$. We define *satisfiability* of a formula f in a model $\mathcal{M}$ (notation: $\mathcal{M} \models f$) in the following way:

$\mathcal{M} \models x \ b \ y$	iff	$\exists i \ (W(x) < i \ \& \ i < W(y))$
$\mathcal{M} \models x \ m \ y$	iff	$W(x) < W(y) \ \& \ \forall i \ \neg(W(x) < i \ \& \ i < W(y))$
$\mathcal{M} \models x \ o \ y$	iff	$\exists i \ (i \subseteq W(x) \ \& \ i < W(y)) \ \&$
		$\exists i \ (i \subseteq W(x) \ \& \ i \subseteq W(y)) \ \&$
		$\exists i \ (W(x) < i \ \& \ i \subseteq W(y))$
$\mathcal{M} \models x \ fi \ y$	iff	$\exists i \ (i \subseteq W(x) \ \& \ i < W(y)) \ \&$
		$\forall i \ (W(x) < i \ \leftrightarrow \ W(y) < i)$
$\mathcal{M} \models x \ di \ y$	iff	$\exists i \ (i \subseteq W(x) \ \& \ i < W(y)) \ \&$
		$\exists i \ (i \subseteq W(x) \ \& \ W(y) < i)$
$\mathcal{M} \models x \ s \ y$	iff	$\exists i \ (W(x) < i \ \& \ i \subseteq W(y)) \ \&$
		$\forall i \ (i < W(x) \ \leftrightarrow i < W(y))$
$\mathcal{M} \models x \ eq \ y$	iff	$W(x) = W(y)$
$\mathcal{M} \models x \ si \ y$	iff	$\mathcal{M} \models y \ s \ x$
$\mathcal{M} \models x \ d \ y$	iff	$\mathcal{M} \models y \ di \ x$
$\mathcal{M} \models x \ f \ y$	iff	$\mathcal{M} \models y \ fi \ x$
$\mathcal{M} \models x \ oi \ y$	iff	$\mathcal{M} \models y \ o \ x$
$\mathcal{M} \models x \ mi \ y$	iff	$\mathcal{M} \models y \ m \ x$
$\mathcal{M} \models x \ bi \ y$	iff	$\mathcal{M} \models y \ b \ x$
$\mathcal{M} \models x \ \alpha \ y$	iff	$\mathcal{M} \models x \ r_1 \ y$ or $\mathcal{M} \models x \ r_2 \ y$ or ... or
		$\mathcal{M} \models x \ r_n \ y$ for $\alpha = \{r_1, r_2, ..., r_n\}$

No formula of the form $x \ \emptyset \ y$ is satisfied in a model.
The definition of a model of a theory is the same as in section 5.3.

It is clear that sometimes individuals that are not images of any variable from the language can occur in a model. However, a specific feature of this semantics is the <u>necessity</u> of the occurrence of such individuals, i.e. they occur in all the models of a given theory.

Example

Let Th = $\{ x \ b \ y \}$. The simplest model of this theory is $\mathcal{M} = \langle T, <, \subseteq, W \rangle$ such that $I = \{i, j, k\}$, where $i < j < k$, $W(x) = i$ and $W(y) = k$. The individual j is not an image of any variable of the theory.

Such a situation never occurs in the point calculus, i.e. for every theory there exists a model such that all the individuals are images of variables of the theory.

Example

Let us consider an analogous theory of the point calculus Th $= \{ x \ before \ y \}$. The simplest model of this theory is $\mathcal{M} = \langle T, <, W \rangle$ such that $I = \{ t_1, t_2 \}$, where $t_1 < t_2$, $W(x) = t_1$ and $W(y) = t_2$. At the same time it should be noticed that in the case of interval calculus a model $\mathcal{M} = \langle T, <, \subseteq, W \rangle$ such that $I = \{ i, k \}$, where $i < k$, $W(x) = i$ and $W(y) = k$, is a model of the theory Th $= \{ x \ m \ y \}$, and it is not a model of the theory Th $= \{ x \ b \ y \}$.

Theorem 5.7.1. (soundness) For any formula $f \in \mathcal{F}$ and theory Th $= \{ f_j \}_{j \in J}$, if Th $\vdash f$, then $\mathcal{M} \models f$ holds for every model $\mathcal{M}$ of the theory Th.
The proof (presented in [Hajnicz, 1989b]) proceeds similarly as for points. Clearly a much greater number of composition rules for primitive relations than in the case of point time must be taken into account. Also the proof of each particular rule is not as trivial as it was in that case. We present therefore an example of proof for one such rule.

$\mathcal{M} \models x \ m \ y$ iff $W(x) < W(y) \ \& \ \forall i \ \neg(W(x) < i \ \& \ i < W(y))$

$\mathcal{M} \models y \ o \ z$ iff $\exists i \ (i \subseteq W(y) \ \& \ i < W(z)) \ \ \&$

                               $\exists i \ (i \subseteq W(y) \ \& \ i \subseteq W(z)) \ \ \&$

                               $\exists i \ (W(y) < i \ \& \ i \subseteq W(z))$

Consider j_0 such that $j_0 \subseteq W(y) \ \& \ j_0 < W(z)$. By *MON* we have $W(x) < j_0$. Therefore $\exists j \ (W(x) < j \ \& \ j < W(z))$, hence $\mathcal{M} \models x \ b \ z$.

Unfortunately, also in this case the inverse theorem is not true, i.e. the calculus is not complete. Moreover, also the weaker theorem about the existence of a model for every consistent theory is not true.

Example

This example is taken from [Allen, 1983].

$$Th \ = \ \{ \ a \ \{contains, \ during\} \ b, \ a \ \{finished \ by, \ finishes\} \ c,$$
$$b \ \{contains, \ during\} \ c, \ d \ \{meets, \ starts\} \ a,$$
$$d \ overlaps \ b, \ d \ \{meets, \ starts\} \ c \ \}$$

No new inferences (except trivial ones) can be derived from this theory. However, this theory has no model. Therefore we can say about any formula that it is satisfied in every model of this theory, whereas some formulas cannot be derived from it.

Therefore a greater complexity of the set of primitive relations implies that the constraint propagation algorithm for interval relations (even in linear time) has weaker logical properties than the same algorithm applied to relations between points.

The incompleteness of the algorithm for this set (and other sets) of primitive relations is an evident shortcoming. However, McDermott (1982) wrote that *it is relatively unimportant and in practice unattainable that the programs be logically complete—it is enough that they are sound with respect to underlying logic.* Nevertheless, it is useful to show other properties, certainly weaker than completeness, but revealing the strength of the algorithm. The property of the existence of a model for every consistent theory is such a property. Defining other properties of this kind reduces to a determination of those bounded subsets of formulas for which the algorithm is complete. In the case of points, we determine such a set of formulas (i.e. relations) in section 5.3. Valdés-Péres (1987) shows that the algorithm is complete if all the introduced data are primitive relations (i.e. $\mathbf{R} = \mathbf{P}$). Van Beek & Cohen (1990) extend the set of admissible relations. Their result is closely related to the above result for point time. Namely, they show that the original Allen's algorithm is complete for relations that can be represented by means of point relations (holding between endpoints of intervals) in which the relation $\{ <, > \}$ does not occur (there are 82 such relations). On the other hand, the algorithm from section 4.4.7 is complete for those interval relations that can be represented by any point relations (there are 188 such relations). The authors present tables containing corresponding sets of relations.

Moreover, van Beek & Cohen perform a statistical research showing that the results of running the algorithm are the worse (i.e. the more often the obtained relations are not "minimal" or even inconsistency is not detected), the larger part of represented relations are "bad" relations.

We have also an impression that Allen's constraint propagation algorithm is consistent (perhaps even complete) for relations from the class Freksa (1992) determines. However, the author does not says this explicitly.

5.8 Interval calculus for non-linear time

Now we discuss a formalization of the constraint propagation algorithm for non-linear interval time. It was presented in [Hajnicz, 1991c].

The set of primitive relation operators for non-linear interval time is $\mathbf{P} = \{$ before, meets, overlaps, finished by, contains, starts, equals, started by, during, finishes, overlapped by, met by, after, excludes $\}$, so it is enlarged with respect to the set of primitive relation operators for linear interval time by the relation *excludes*. As it was in the previous cases, now we present the semantics of the considered calculus.

Semantics

DEFINITIONS

Let $\mathfrak{I} = \langle I, <, \subseteq \rangle$ be an interval time structure. A *valuation* is a function $W: Z \longrightarrow I$. A *model* is an ordered quadruple $\mathcal{M} = \langle T, <, \subseteq, W \rangle$.

Let $x, y \in Z$. We define *satisfiability* of a formula f in a model $\mathcal{M}$ (notation: $\mathcal{M} \models f$) in the following way:

$\mathcal{M} \models x \, b \, y$ iff $\exists i \, (W(x) < i \ \& \ i < W(y))$

$\mathcal{M} \models x \, m \, y$ iff $W(x) < W(y) \ \& \ \forall i \, \neg(W(x) < i \ \& \ i < W(y))$

$\mathcal{M} \models x \, o \, y$ iff $\exists i \, (i \subseteq W(x) \ \& \ i < W(y)) \ \&$
$\qquad\qquad\qquad\qquad \exists i \, (i \subseteq W(x) \ \& \ i \subseteq W(y)) \ \&$
$\qquad\qquad\qquad\qquad \exists i \, (W(x) < i \ \& \ i \subseteq W(y))$

$\mathcal{M} \models x \, \text{fi} \, y$ iff $\exists i \, (i \subseteq W(x) \ \& \ i < W(y)) \ \&$
$\qquad\qquad\qquad\qquad \forall i \, ((W(x) < i \ \rightarrow \ W(y) < i \ \vee \ W(y) \, ! \, i) \ \&$
$\qquad\qquad\qquad\qquad\quad (W(y) < i \ \rightarrow \ W(x) < i))$

$\mathcal{M} \models x \, \text{di} \, y$ iff $\exists i \, (i \subseteq W(x) \ \& \ i < W(y)) \ \&$
$\qquad\qquad\qquad\qquad \exists i \, (i \subseteq W(x) \ \& \ W(y) < i)$

$\mathcal{M} \models x \, s \, y$ iff $\exists i \, (W(x) < i \ \& \ i \subseteq W(y)) \ \&$
$\qquad\qquad\qquad\qquad \forall i \, ((i < W(x) \ \rightarrow \ i < W(y)) \ \&$
$\qquad\qquad\qquad\qquad\quad (i < W(y) \ \rightarrow \ i < W(x) \ \vee \ W(x) \, ! \, i))$

$\mathcal{M} \models x \, \text{eq} \, y$ iff $W(x) = W(y)$

$\mathcal{M} \models x \, \text{si} \, y$ iff $\mathcal{M} \models y \, s \, x$

$\mathcal{M} \models x \, d \, y$ iff $\mathcal{M} \models y \, \text{di} \, x$

$\mathcal{M} \models x \, f \, y$ iff $\mathcal{M} \models y \, \text{fi} \, x$

$\mathcal{M} \models x \, \text{oi} \, y$ iff $\mathcal{M} \models y \, o \, x$

$\mathcal{M} \models x \, \text{mi} \, y$ iff $\mathcal{M} \models y \, m \, x$

$\mathcal{M} \models x \, \text{bi} \, y$ iff $\mathcal{M} \models y \, b \, x$

$\mathcal{M} \models x \, e \, y$ iff $W(x) \, ! \, W(y)$

$\mathcal{M} \models x \, \alpha \, y$ iff $\mathcal{M} \models x \, r_1 \, y$ or $\mathcal{M} \models x \, r_2 \, y$ or ... or
$\qquad\qquad\qquad\qquad \mathcal{M} \models x \, r_n \, y \quad$ for $\alpha = \{r_1, r_2, ..., r_n\}$

No formula of the form $x \, \emptyset \, y$ is satisfied in a model.

The definition of a model of a theory is the same as in section 5.3.

As it was in the case of point time, we describe the relation *excludes* by stating that no dependencies characterizing collinear positions of two intervals, i.e. those expressed by relations of precedence and inclusion, occur between these points.

The definition of satisfiability remains unchanged for most of primitive relations, as compared to the linear case. An exception to the rule are the relations *starts, started by, finishes, finished by*. This follows from the fact that the property of monotonicity of a structure is lost. The dependency between this property and the change in the definition of satisfiability for the considered relations can be observed in fig. 5.1. In the case of points no such differences occur—this follows from the simplicity of that case, in particular from the fact that we include all the axioms of a point structure except linearity.

(a) (b)

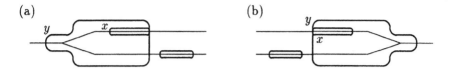

Fig. 5.1. Explanation for the change in the definitions of relations:

(a) x finishes y (b) x starts y

In our considerations we must take into account four different theories of the calculus corresponding to four relation composition tables from section 4.3.5 and the corresponding classes of models described by classic theories from section 2.2.5—i.e. classic theory $\mathcal{T}_P$ for the interval calculus theory based on the table presented in fig. 4.17, theory $\mathcal{T}_{PN}$ for the table from fig. 4.14, theory $\mathcal{T}_{LL}$ for the table from fig. 4.18, and theory $\mathcal{T}_{LN}$ for the table from fig 4.15.

Theorem 5.8.1. (soundness) For any formula $f \in \mathcal{F}$ and theory $\text{Th} = \{f_j\}_{j \in J}$, if $\text{Th} \vdash f$, then $\mathcal{M} \models f$ holds for every model $\mathcal{M}$ of the theory Th.

The proof (presented in [Hajnicz, 1991c]) proceeds analogously to the previous cases, obviously except for the problem of applying the rules 1 and 3 to primitive relations. A proof for each of the four theories is necessary, of course. This proof is much more complicated than it was in the case of linear time. As an example we present a proof of validity of rule 1 for one pair of primitive relations—for the sake of comparison it is the same pair that was chosen for linear time. For this pair of relations the proof proceeds identically for all four theories (the same inferences are derived in all the cases).

$\mathcal{M} \models x \, m \, y$ iff $W(x) < W(y) \ \& \ \forall i \ \neg(W(x) < i \ \& \ i < W(y))$

$\mathcal{M} \models y \, o \, z$ iff $\exists i \ (i \subseteq W(y) \ \& \ i < W(z)) \ \ \&$

                     $\exists i \ (i \subseteq W(y) \ \& \ i \subseteq W(z)) \ \ \&$

                     $\exists i \ (W(y) < i \ \& \ i \subseteq W(z))$

Consider j_0 such that $j_0 \subseteq W(y) \ \& \ j_0 < W(z)$ and j_1 such that $W(y) < j_1 \ \& \ j_1 \subseteq W(z)$. $W(x) < W(y) \ \& \ W(y) < j_1$ holds, so by P_TRANS we have $W(x) < j_1$. Then we have $W(x) < j_1 \ \& \ j_1 \subseteq W(z)$, so by $SOLID$ $W(x) < W(z) \ \lor \ \exists k \ (k \subseteq W(x) \ \& \ k \subseteq W(z))$. Therefore $\neg(W(x) \, ! \, W(z))$. Thus we have $W(x) < W(y) \ \& \ \neg(W(x) \, ! \, W(z)) \ \& \ j_0 \subseteq W(y) \ \& \ j_0 < W(z)$, so by $BEFILL \ \exists v \ (W(x) < v \ \& \ v < W(z))$. Therefore $\mathcal{M} \models x \, b \, z$.

Certainly, also in this case neither the considered calculus is complete, nor a model of each consistent theory has to exist. The counterexample for these properties presented in the previous section remains valid in the same form.

Certainly, there is a possibility to determine a subclass of relations between intervals representable by means of relations between their endpoints, as in the linear case. However, this gives us nothing unless we establish properties of the calculus for nonlinear point time.

5.9 Calculus of points and intervals

Finally, the calculus of points and intervals will be discussed. This is a special case, since we have to do with two kinds of individuals and with four sets of relations between them. Thus the language of the calculus will be somewhat different from those previously discussed.

Syntax
Alphabet

- Nonempty, countable sets of variables Z_P and Z_I,

- sets of primitive relation operators

  $\mathbf{P}_{PP} = \{$ ·before·, ·equals·, ·after· $\}$
  $\mathbf{P}_{PI} = \{$ ·before, ·starts, ·during, ·finishes, ·after $\}$
  $\mathbf{P}_{IP} = \{$ before·, finished by·, contains·, started by·, after· $\}$
  $\mathbf{P}_{II} = \{$ before, meets, overlaps, finished by, contains, starts, equals, started by, during, finishes, overlapped by, met by, after $\}$

- set-theoretical symbols.

DEFINITIONS

Sets of relations are $\mathbf{R}_{PP} = 2^{\mathbf{P}_{PP}}$, $\mathbf{R}_{PI} = 2^{\mathbf{P}_{PI}}$, $\mathbf{R}_{IP} = 2^{\mathbf{P}_{IP}}$ and $\mathbf{R}_{II} = 2^{\mathbf{P}_{II}}$, while the set of formulas is $\mathcal{F} = \{\, x \, \alpha \, y \mid x, y \in Z_P,\ \alpha \in \mathbf{R}_{PP}$ or $x \in Z_P$, $y \in Z_I,\ \alpha \in \mathbf{R}_{PI}$ or $x \in Z_I,\ y \in Z_P,\ \alpha \in \mathbf{R}_{IP}$ or $x, y \in Z_I,\ \alpha \in \mathbf{R}_{II} \,\}$.

The definitions of the empty relation, an inconsistent formula, an opposite relation, an inverse relation, a composition of relations and of their properties are the same as in section 5.2 (for every set of relations). Certainly, composition of relations can apply to relations from different sets, as it was shown in section 4.3.6.

Axioms

1. x ·equals· x for $x \in Z_P$
2. x equals x for $x \in Z_I$
3. $x \, \mathbf{P}_{PP} \, y$ for $x, y \in Z_P$
4. $x \, \mathbf{P}_{PI} \, y$ for $x \in Z_P$, $y \in Z_I$
5. $x \, \mathbf{P}_{IP} \, y$ for $x \in Z_I$, $y \in Z_P$
6. $x \, \mathbf{P}_{II} \, y$ for $x, y \in Z_I$

Rules of inference

Rules of inference are the same as those presented in section 5.2—the kinds of variables and relations are mutually univocally determined. Operations on primitive relations should obviously be consistent with the tables from section 4.3.6.

The definition of a formal proof is the same as in section 5.2.

Semantics

A choice of a structure is indispensable in order to define semantics. It is possible to define an interval-point structure in which intervals as well as points are primitive individuals. However, we have not discussed such a structure in section 2. Nevertheless we can use a point structure with intervals defined in it, as it was presented in section 2.1.4.

DEFINITIONS

Let $\mathfrak{T} = \langle T, < \rangle$ be a point time structure in which the theory $\mathcal{T}_L$ is satisfied (see section 2.1). An interval-point structure is $\mathfrak{T}_{\Im} = \langle T, <, J, L, R \rangle$, where T is a set of points, $<$ is a precedence relation over T and J is a set of time intervals $\langle x, y \rangle$, $x, y \in T$, $x < y$. Moreover, $L(X) = x$ and $R(X) = y$ holds for $X \in J$, $X = \langle x, y \rangle$. A *valuation* is a function $W = W_P \cup W_I$, $W_P : Z_P \longrightarrow T$ and $W_I : Z_I \longrightarrow J$. A *model* is an ordered tuple $\mathcal{M} = \langle T, <, J, L, R, W \rangle$. Let $x, y \in Z$. We define *satisfiability* of a formula f in a model $\mathcal{M}$ (notation: $\mathcal{M} \models f$) in the following way (we use the same abbreviations as in section 2.3.6):

Let $x, y \in Z_P$. We say that:

$$\mathcal{M} \models x \cdot b \cdot y \qquad \text{iff} \qquad W_P(x) < W_P(y)$$
$$\mathcal{M} \models x \cdot eq \cdot y \qquad \text{iff} \qquad W_P(x) = W_P(y)$$
$$\mathcal{M} \models x \cdot bi \cdot y \qquad \text{iff} \qquad \mathcal{M} \models y \cdot b \cdot x$$

Let $x \in Z_P$, $y \in Z_I$. We say that:

$$\mathcal{M} \models x \cdot b\, y \qquad \text{iff} \qquad W_P(x) < L(W_I(y))$$
$$\mathcal{M} \models x \cdot s\, y \qquad \text{iff} \qquad W_P(x) = L(W_I(y))$$
$$\mathcal{M} \models x \cdot d\, y \qquad \text{iff} \qquad L(W_I(y)) < W_P(x) \ \& \ W_P(x) < R(W_I(y))$$
$$\mathcal{M} \models x \cdot f\, y \qquad \text{iff} \qquad W_P(x) = R(W_I(y))$$
$$\mathcal{M} \models x \cdot bi\, y \qquad \text{iff} \qquad R(W_I(y)) < W_P(x)$$

Let $x \in Z_I$, $y \in Z_P$. We say that:

$$\mathcal{M} \models x\, b \cdot y \qquad \text{iff} \qquad \mathcal{M} \models y \cdot bi\, x$$
$$\mathcal{M} \models x\, f \cdot y \qquad \text{iff} \qquad \mathcal{M} \models y \cdot f\, x$$
$$\mathcal{M} \models x\, di \cdot y \qquad \text{iff} \qquad \mathcal{M} \models y \cdot d\, x$$
$$\mathcal{M} \models x\, si \cdot y \qquad \text{iff} \qquad \mathcal{M} \models y \cdot s\, x$$
$$\mathcal{M} \models x\, bi \cdot y \qquad \text{iff} \qquad \mathcal{M} \models y \cdot b\, x$$

Let $x, y \in Z_I$. We say that:

$\mathcal{M} \models x\ b\ y$	iff	$R(W_I(x)) < L(W_I(y))$
$\mathcal{M} \models x\ m\ y$	iff	$R(W_I(x)) = L(W_I(y))$
$\mathcal{M} \models x\ o\ y$	iff	$L(W_I(x)) < L(W_I(y))\ \&\ L(W_I(y)) < R(W_I(x))\ \&$
		$R(W_I(x)) < R(W_I(y))$
$\mathcal{M} \models x\ fi\ y$	iff	$L(W_I(x)) < L(W_I(y))\ \&\ R(W_I(x)) = R(W_I(y))$
$\mathcal{M} \models x\ di\ y$	iff	$L(W_I(x)) < L(W_I(y))\ \&\ R(W_I(y)) < R(W_I(x))$
$\mathcal{M} \models x\ s\ y$	iff	$L(W_I(x)) = L(W_I(y))\ \&\ R(W_I(x)) < R(W_I(y))$
$\mathcal{M} \models x\ eq\ y$	iff	$L(W_I(x)) = L(W_I(y))\ \&\ R(W_I(x)) = R(W_I(y))$
$\mathcal{M} \models x\ si\ y$	iff	$\mathcal{M} \models y\ s\ x$
$\mathcal{M} \models x\ d\ y$	iff	$\mathcal{M} \models y\ di\ x$
$\mathcal{M} \models x\ f\ y$	iff	$\mathcal{M} \models y\ fi\ x$
$\mathcal{M} \models x\ oi\ y$	iff	$\mathcal{M} \models y\ o\ x$
$\mathcal{M} \models x\ mi\ y$	iff	$\mathcal{M} \models y\ m\ x$
$\mathcal{M} \models x\ bi\ y$	iff	$\mathcal{M} \models y\ b\ x$
$\mathcal{M} \models x\ \alpha\ y$	iff	$\mathcal{M} \models x\ r_1\ y$ or $\mathcal{M} \models x\ r_2\ y$ or ... or
		$\mathcal{M} \models x\ r_n\ y$ for $\alpha = \{r_1, r_2, ..., r_n\}$,

$$\alpha \in \mathbf{R}_{PP},\ \alpha \in \mathbf{R}_{PI},\ \alpha \in \mathbf{R}_{IP} \text{ and } \alpha \in \mathbf{R}_{II}.$$

No formula of the form $x\ \emptyset\ y$ is satisfied in a model.

It should be noticed here that the definition of satisfiability of a formula in a model presented above can also be viewed as a definition of satisfiability of a formula of the interval calculus in a point structure. Moreover, in contrast to the original solution, this definition does not require the existence of any intervals or points in a structure that are not images of variables of the theory.

Theorem 5.9.1. (soundness) For any formula $f \in \mathcal{F}$ and theory $\text{Th} = \{f_j\}_{j \in J}$, if $\text{Th} \vdash f$, then $\mathcal{M} \models f$ holds for every model $\mathcal{M}$ of the theory Th.

5.10 A sketch of formalization of a more precise constraint propagation algorithm

In section 4.4.7 a more precise constraint propagation algorithm is presented. In this section we will sketch how to change the basic formalization presewnted in section 5.2 in order to obtain a formalization of this case. For this sake we need a stronger composition operation $\bullet$ of composing three relations instead of two. It is defined only for composed relations, and based on a usual compostion operation for primitive relations $\circ$. So, the *strong composition* of relations α, β, γ

(notation: $\bullet(\alpha, \beta, \gamma; \delta_1, \delta_2)$) is the smallest relation $\delta \in \mathbf{R}$ such that for every $r_1 \in \alpha$, $r_2 \in \beta$, $r_3 \in \gamma$, $r_4 \in (r_1 \circ r_2) \cap \delta_1$ and $r_5 \in (r_2 \circ r_3) \cap \delta_2$ we have $r_4 \circ r_3 \cap r_1 \circ r_5 \subseteq \delta$. δ_1, δ_2 are auxiliary relations.

We can also prove for $\bullet$ similar properties as for $\circ$.

Theorem 5.10.1. Let $\alpha, \beta, \gamma, \delta_1, \delta_2 \in \mathbf{R}$. The following properties of relations are satisfied:

(i) $(\bullet(\alpha, \beta, \gamma; \delta_1, \delta_2))^{-1} = \bullet(\gamma^{-1}, \beta^{-1}, \alpha^{-1}; \delta_2^{-1}, \delta_1^{-1})$,

(ii) $\bullet(\alpha_1 \cup \alpha_2, \beta_1 \cup \beta_2, \gamma_1 \cup \gamma_2; \delta_1, \delta_2) = \bullet(\alpha_1, \beta_1, \gamma_1; \delta_1, \delta_2) \cup \bullet(\alpha_1, \beta_1, \gamma_2; \delta_1, \delta_2) \cup$
$\bullet(\alpha_1, \beta_2, \gamma_1; \delta_1, \delta_2) \cup \bullet(\alpha_1, \beta_2, \gamma_2; \delta_1, \delta_2) \cup \bullet(\alpha_2, \beta_1, \gamma_1; \delta_1, \delta_2) \cup$
$\bullet(\alpha_2, \beta_1, \gamma_2; \delta_1, \delta_2) \cup \bullet(\alpha_2, \beta_2, \gamma_1; \delta_1, \delta_2) \cup \bullet(\alpha_2, \beta_2, \gamma_2; \delta_1, \delta_2)$.

Proof

(i) Consider any $\alpha, \beta, \gamma, \delta_1, \delta_2 \in \mathbf{R}$ and any $r_1 \in \alpha$, $r_2 \in \beta$, $r_3 \in \gamma$ and $r_4 \in r_1 \circ r_2 \cap \delta_1$, $r_5 \in r_2 \circ r_3 \cap \delta_2$. Then $r_1^{-1} \in \alpha^{-1}$, $r_2^{-1} \in \beta^{-1}$, $r_3^{-1} \in \gamma$ and $r_4^{-1} \in (r_2^{-1} \circ r_1^{-1}) \cap \delta_1^{-1}$, $r_5^{-1} \in (r_3^{-1} \circ r_2^{-1}) \cap \delta_2^{-1}$ by th. 5.2.1 (iii), (v). Then by definition of $\bullet$ we have $(\bullet(\alpha, \beta, \gamma; \delta_1, \delta_2))^{-1} \supseteq (r_4 \circ r_3 \cap r_1 \circ r_5)^{-1} = r_5^{-1} \circ r_1^{-1} \cap r_3^{-1} \circ r_4^{-1} \subseteq \bullet(\gamma^{-1}, \beta^{-1}, \alpha^{-1}; \delta_2^{-1}, \delta_1^{-1})$.

(ii) Consider any $r_1 \in \alpha_1 \cup \alpha_2$, $r_2 \in \beta_1 \cup \beta_2$ and $r_3 \in \gamma_1 \cup \gamma_2$. Then by definition of $\bullet$ for every $r_4 \in (r_1 \circ r_2) \cap \delta_1$ and $r_5 \in (r_2 \circ r_3) \cap \delta_2$ we have $r_4 \circ r_3 \cap r_1 \circ r_5 \subseteq \bullet(\alpha_1 \cup \alpha_2, \beta_1 \cup \beta_2, \gamma_1 \cup \gamma_2; \delta_1, \delta_2)$. Suppose that $r_1 \in \alpha_1$, $r_2 \in \beta_1$ and $r_3 \in \gamma_1$. Then $r_4 \circ r_3 \cap r_1 \circ r_5 \subseteq \bullet(\alpha_1, \beta_1, \gamma_1; \delta_1, \delta_2)$, which is one of the elements of the required union. The other cases are similar.
If $r \in \bullet(\alpha_1, \beta_1, \gamma_1; \delta_1, \delta_2)$, then by definition of $\bullet$ there exist $r_1 \in \alpha_1, r_2 \in \beta_1$, $r_3 \in \gamma_1$ and $r_4 \in r_1 \circ r_2 \cap \delta_1$, $r_5 \in r_2 \circ r_3 \cap \delta_2$ such that $r \in r_4 \circ r_3 \cap r_1 \circ r_5$. But $r_1 \in \alpha_1 \cup \alpha_2$, $r_2 \in \beta_1 \cup \beta_2$ and $r_3 \in \gamma_1 \cup \gamma_3$, hence $r \in \bullet(\alpha_1 \cup \alpha_2, \beta_1 \cup \beta_2, \gamma_1 \cup \gamma_2; \delta_1, \delta_2)$. The other cases are similar.   ∎

Now we should exchange the inference rule 1 with

$$\frac{x \; \alpha \; y, \; y \; \beta \; u, \; u \; \gamma \; z, \; x \; \delta_1 \; u, \; y \; \delta_2 \; z}{x \; \bullet (\alpha, \beta, \gamma; \delta_1, \delta_2) \; z}.$$

It is not so hard to show that if the logic with the inference rule is sound (i.e. composition rules for primitive relations are correct), then the logic with this new inference rule is sound, too. Nevertheless, it is important to show that the new rule entails the new one. For prove this, we need to distinguish a relation *equals* in $\mathbf{P}$, which is actually present in all the concrete calculi.

Theorem 5.10.2. The inference rule $\dfrac{x \; \alpha \; y, \; y \; \beta \; u, \; u \; \gamma \; z, \; x \; \delta_1 \; u, \; y \; \delta_2 \; z}{x \; \bullet (\alpha, \beta, \gamma; \delta_1, \delta_2) \; z}$ entails the rule $\dfrac{x \; \alpha \; y, \; y \; \beta \; z}{x \; \alpha \circ \beta \; z}$.

Proof

Consider any $x, y, z \in Z$ and any $\alpha, \beta \in \mathbf{P}$. Assume that $x \, \alpha \, y$, $y \, \beta \, z$ holds. Then we have $x \, \alpha \, y$, y *equalsy*, $y \, \beta \, z$, hence $x \, \bullet (\alpha, equals, \beta; \alpha, \beta) \, z$ holds. By definition of $\bullet$ we obtain that for every $r_1 \in \alpha$, $r_2 = equals$, $r_3 \in \beta$ and every $r_4 \in \alpha \circ equals \cap \alpha$, $r_5 \in \beta \circ equals \cap \beta$ we have $r_1 \circ r_5 \cap r_4 \circ r_3$. But this means that $r_4 \in \alpha$, $r_5 \in \beta$, so evidently this concern also $r_1 = r_4$ and $r_2 = r_5$. But $r_1 \circ r_2 \cap r_1 \circ r_2 \supseteq r_1 \circ r_5 \cap r_4 \circ r_3 \subseteq r_4 \circ r_5 \cap r_4 \circ r_5$. Thus all elements of $\alpha \circ \beta$ are contained in $\bullet(\alpha, equals, \beta; \alpha, \beta)$, and nothing but them. Therefore $x \, \alpha \circ \beta \, z$ holds.   ∎

However, it is not so evident that this new logic is realy stronger that the old one—this should be shown for every case separately (it is usfficient to show an example). For instance, in the linear point case we should obtain completeness of the logic now, as there exists a proof of completeness of the algorithm being represented by it [van Beek & Cohen, 1990]. The proof would be very similar to that presented in section 5.3, but the proof of a (stronger) version of lemma 5.3.4 would be much more complicated.

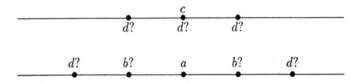

Fig. 5.2. Exemplary locations of points in a modified example

It is easy to check that the stronger rule "works" for the example from page 178 also in the cases of point partially or left linearly ordered time. However, this does not mean that the algorithm (or the calculus representing it) is complete in these cases. On the other hand, if we exchange all occurences of the relation {*before, equals*} with the relation {*before, equals, exludes*} in this example, both rules (both algorithms) provide the same result (i.e. the *no info* relation). But surprisingly this is proper result for this theory (see fig. 5.2).

6. Translations of Allen's calculi into modal temporal logic

As we have stated in the introduction, the main goal of this book is to organize knowledge concerning various time structures. Thus we have presented a formal description of these structures by means of the first order predicate calculus and of modal temporal logics. The modal logics presented here depend essentially on the first order description of time structures—their semantics is based on the corresponding structures.

On the other hand, we have presented various algorithms for reasoning about position of points and intervals in time. Most of them concern reasoning in concrete structures. Allen's (1983) constraint propagation algorithm is an exception, as it can be applied in principle to an arbitrary structure, clearly on condition that an appropriate set of primitive relations together with composition rules is determined. This approach is the more elegant as it is easy to formalize—we have presented some propositions for formalizations of this algorithm in the previous chapter. This allows to prove the soundness of this algorithm for time structures the semantics of presented calculi was based on.

Thus we now have at our disposal modal temporal logics and a formal presentation of Allen's constraint propagation algorithm for various sets of primitive relations. The semantics of both is based on the same structures, which shows the connections between them. In this chapter we want to compare these formalisms in a more direct way, in order to examine more carefully their similarities as well as differences. Evidently differences are very significant—there is no doubt that modal logics have bigger expressive power). For this reason we will only consider translations of Allen's calculi into modal temporal logics. A very important difference is e.g. the fact that in Allen's calculi a valuation assigns individual elements of a domain to variables, whereas in modal logics—subsets of elements of a domain (also empty ones). In order to make these approaches more similar, we will limit ourselves to single-element valuations also in the case of modal logics. This limitation is so substantial that one can ask whether we still have to do with modal logics. After all, we can hardly speak of satisfaction of axioms in a structure, since this involves <u>all</u> valuations. Evidently all the models with valuations from the limited class are not sufficient—in this case axioms would be satisfied in some structures, in which in general they are not. On the other hand, this makes possible formulation of axioms which in general do not hold in any structure.

Keeping in mind the above objections showing the extend of differences between the considered approaches, we have decided to enter into this risky comparison. After all, Allen's calculi are not complete, and modal temporal logics preserve their soundness even for the limited class of models. On the other hand, as we have mentioned in chapter 3, time-dependent knowledge representation systems based on modal temporal logics [Mays, 1983; Orłowska, 1982] use for their reasoning the knowledge stored in concrete models, as general axioms (satisfied in all the moments) cannot contain particular facts. Thus it should not be surprising that we proceed similarly here. In subsequent sections we will discuss translations of the calculi chosen from among those presented in the previous chapter into corresponding modal temporal logics. This subject has been already taken up in [Hajnicz, 1989b; 1991a; 1991c].

6.1 Translation of the point calculus for linear time into instant tense logic

As in previous chapters, we start from the simplest case, i.e. from linear point time structure. We will attempt to discuss this simplest case in a most precise way.

Recall that we have to do with a linear point structure $\mathfrak{T} = \langle T, < \rangle$. Moreover, we consider a point calculus with a set of propositional variables Z, a set of formulas $\mathcal{F}$ and a model $\mathcal{M} = \langle T, <, W \rangle$, and an instant tense logic with a set of propositional variables X, a set of formulas $\mathcal{G}$ and a model $\mathsf{M} = \langle T, <, V \rangle$.

DEFINITION
Let $\mathfrak{T} = \langle T, < \rangle$ be a point structure, and $\varrho : Z \longrightarrow X$ be a function transforming the set of variables of the point calculus to the set of variables of instant tense logic. The models $\mathcal{M} = \langle T, <, W \rangle$ and $\mathsf{M} = \langle T, <, V \rangle$ are *weakly compatible* if $W(x) \subseteq V(\varrho(x))$ holds for every $x \in Z$, and they are *compatible*, if $W(x) = V(\varrho(x))$ holds for every $x \in Z$.

Both the above definitions impose the limitation on the class of models we spoke about in the introduction to this chapter. A model *compatible* with any model $\mathcal{M}$ can only be such a model M that the valuation is a singleton set for all essential propositional variables. Thus in practice we can say that in this case $V : X \longrightarrow T$. A model *weakly compatible* with any model $\mathcal{M}$ can only be such a model M that the valuation of no essential propositional variable is the empty set. Thus *weak compatibility* limits the class of models in a less degree, nevertheless it still remains a limitation.

DEFINITION

Let $\varrho: Z \longrightarrow X$ be a function transforming the set of variables of the point calculus to the set of variables of instant tense logic. We define a function $\xi^\circ : \mathcal{F} \longrightarrow \mathcal{G}$ transforming formulas of the point calculus onto formulas of instant tense logic in the following way:

$$\xi^\circ(x \ before \ y) \quad = \quad \varrho(x) \ \rightarrow \ F\varrho(y)$$

$$\xi^\circ(x \ equals \ y) \quad = \quad \varrho(x) \ \rightarrow \ \varrho(y)$$

$$\xi^\circ(x \ after \ y) \quad = \quad \varrho(x) \ \rightarrow \ P\varrho(y)$$

$$\xi^\circ(x \ \alpha \ y) \quad = \quad \xi^\circ(x \ r_1 \ y) \ \vee \ ... \ \vee \ \xi^\circ(x \ r_n \ y), \quad \text{where } \alpha = \{\, r_1, \ ..., \ r_n \,\}$$

$$\xi^\circ(x \ \emptyset \ y) \quad = \quad p \ \& \ \neg p$$

where p is an arbitrary, chosen element of X.

Unfortunately, this definition is not sufficient unless we take into consideration that valuations are singletons. The differences caused by the dissimilarity of these valuations are so important that the translation of the axiom of the point calculus:

$$\xi^\circ(x \ \{before, \ equals, \ after\} \ y) \ = \ \varrho(x) \ \rightarrow \ (P\varrho(y) \ \vee \ \varrho(y) \ \vee \ F\varrho(y))$$

is not valid in instant tense logic. Moreover, rules of inference 2 and 3 do not hold.

Example

Consider $M \ = \ \langle T, \ <, \ V \rangle$ such that $T \ = \ \{t, \ t', \ t''\}$, $V(\varrho(x)) = \{t', \ t''\}$, $V(\varrho(y)) = \{t\}$ and $t' < t < t''$ (see fig. 6.1). Evidently $M \models \xi^\circ(\, \varrho(y) \ before \ \varrho(x)\,)$ and $M \not\models \xi^\circ(\, \varrho(x) \ after \ \varrho(y)\,)$, so inference rule 2 does not hold.

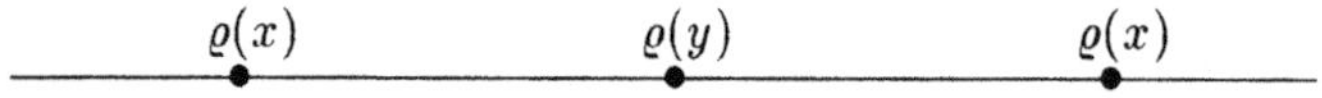

$$\varrho(x) \qquad\qquad \varrho(y) \qquad\qquad \varrho(x)$$

Fig. 6.1. Model M in which a relation inverse to a given one does not hold

In order to force rule 2 to hold, a small modification of the translation is sufficient.

DEFINITION

We define a function $\xi: \mathcal{F} \longrightarrow \mathcal{G}$ transforming formulas of the point calculus onto formulas of instant tense logic in the following way:

$$\xi(x \ before \ y) \quad = \quad (\varrho(x) \ \rightarrow \ F\varrho(y)) \ \& \ (\varrho(y) \ \rightarrow \ P\varrho(x))$$

$$\xi(x \ equals \ y) \quad = \quad \varrho(x) \ \leftrightarrow \ \varrho(y)$$

$$\xi(x \ after \ y) \quad = \quad (\varrho(x) \ \rightarrow \ P\varrho(y)) \ \& \ (\varrho(y) \ \rightarrow \ F\varrho(x))$$

$$\xi(x \ \alpha \ y) \quad = \quad \xi(x \ r_1 \ y) \ \vee \ ... \ \vee \ \xi(x \ r_n \ y), \quad \text{where } \alpha = \{\, r_1, \ ..., \ r_n \,\}$$

$$\xi(x \ \emptyset \ y) \quad = \quad p \ \& \ \neg p$$

where, as before, p is an arbitrary, fixed element of X.

For this translation the following basic basic theorem holds.

Theorem 6.1.1. For any compatible models $\mathcal{M} = \langle T, <, W \rangle$ and $\mathsf{M} = \langle T, <, V \rangle$, and for every formula $f \in \mathcal{F}$ we have $\mathcal{M} \models f$ iff $\mathsf{M} \models f$.

Proof

- $f = x$ *before* y

$$\mathcal{M} \models f \quad \text{iff} \quad W(x) < W(y)$$
$$\mathsf{M} \models \xi(f)[t] \quad \text{iff} \quad \mathsf{M} \models ((\varrho(x) \to F\varrho(y)) \,\&\, (\varrho(y) \to P\varrho(x)))[t]$$
$$\text{iff} \quad \text{if } \mathsf{M} \models \varrho(x)[t], \text{ then there exists } t' \text{ such that } t < t'$$
$$\text{and } \mathsf{M} \models \varrho(y)[t'] \text{ and if } \mathsf{M} \models \varrho(y)[t], \text{ then}$$
$$\text{there exists } t' \text{ such that } t' < t \text{ and } \mathsf{M} \models \varrho(x)[t']$$

If $t = V(\varrho(x))$, then $\mathsf{M} \models \varrho(x)[t]$. Hence there exists t' such that $t < t'$ and $t' = V(\varrho(y))$. Otherwise, if $t \neq V(\varrho(x))$, then $\mathsf{M} \not\models \varrho(x)[t]$ and $\mathsf{M} \models (\varrho(x) \to F\varrho(y))[t]$. If $t = V(\varrho(y))$, then $\mathsf{M} \models \varrho(y)[t]$, and then there exists t'' such that $t'' < t$ and $t'' = V(\varrho(x))$. Conversely, if $t \neq V(\varrho(y))$, then $\mathsf{M} \not\models \varrho(y)[t]$ and $\mathsf{M} \models (\varrho(y) \to F\varrho(x))[t]$. Thus $\mathsf{M} \models \xi(f)[t]$ iff $V(\varrho(x)) < V(\varrho(y))$. But $V(\varrho(x)) = W(x)$ and $V(\varrho(y)) = W(y)$.
Therefore $\mathcal{M} \models f$ iff $\mathsf{M} \models \xi(f)$.

- $f = x$ *after* y
An analogous reasoning is valid here.

- $f = x$ *equals* y

$$\mathcal{M} \models f \quad \text{iff} \quad W(x) = W(y)$$
$$\mathsf{M} \models \xi(f)[t] \quad \text{iff} \quad \mathsf{M} \models (\varrho(x) \leftrightarrow \varrho(y))[t]$$
$$\text{iff} \quad \text{if } \mathsf{M} \models \varrho(x)[t], \text{ then } \mathsf{M} \models \varrho(y)[t] \text{ and}$$
$$\text{if } \mathsf{M} \models \varrho(y)[t], \text{ then } \mathsf{M} \models \varrho(x)[t].$$

If $t = V(\varrho(x))$, then $\mathsf{M} \models \varrho(x)[t]$, hence $\mathsf{M} \models \varrho(y)[t]$, so $t = V(\varrho(y))$. Otherwise if $t \neq V(\varrho(x))$, then $\mathsf{M} \not\models \varrho(x)[t]$, hence $\mathsf{M} \models (\varrho(x) \to \varrho(y))[t]$. Analogously if $t = V(\varrho(y))$, then $\mathsf{M} \models \varrho(y)[t]$, hence $\mathsf{M} \models \varrho(x)[t]$, so $t = V(\varrho(x))$. Otherwise, if $t \neq V(\varrho(y))$, then $\mathsf{M} \not\models \varrho(y)[t]$, so $\mathsf{M} \models (\varrho(y) \to \varrho(x))[t]$.
Therefore $\mathsf{M} \models \xi(f)[t]$ holds for $V(\varrho(x)) = V(\varrho(y))$. But we have $V(\varrho(x)) = W(x)$ and $V(\varrho(y)) = W(y)$. Finally $\mathcal{M} \models f$ iff $\mathsf{M} \models \xi(f)$.

- $f = x \{r_1, ..., r_n\} y$

$$\mathcal{M} \models f \quad \text{iff} \quad \mathcal{M} \models x \, r_1 \, y \text{ or } ... \text{ or } \mathcal{M} \models x \, r_n \, y$$
$$\mathsf{M} \models \xi(f)[t] \quad \text{iff} \quad \mathsf{M} \models \xi(x \, r_1 \, y \lor ... \lor x \, r_n \, y)[t]$$
$$\text{iff } \mathsf{M} \models \xi(x \, r_1 \, y)[t] \text{ or } ... \text{ or } \mathsf{M} \models \xi(x \, r_n \, y)[t]$$

Evidently $\mathcal{M} \models x \, r_i \, y$ iff $\mathsf{M} \models \xi(x \, r_i \, y)[t]$. Therefore $\mathcal{M} \models f$ iff $\mathsf{M} \models \xi(f)$.

- For any models $\mathcal{M} = \langle T, <, W \rangle$ and $\mathtt{M} = \langle T, <, V \rangle$ and every $x, y \in Z$ and $p \in X$ we have $\mathcal{M} \not\models x \emptyset y$ and $\mathtt{M} \not\models p \,\&\, \neg p$. Thus also for $f = x \emptyset y$ we have $\mathcal{M} \models f$ iff $\mathtt{M} \models \xi(f)$.

Thus we have shown that for every $f \in \mathcal{F}$ we have $\mathcal{M} \models f$ iff $\dot{\mathtt{M}} \models \xi(f)$. ∎

Corollary For weakly compatible models $\mathcal{M} = \langle T, <, W \rangle$ and $\mathtt{M} = \langle T, <, V \rangle$, and for every formula $f \in \mathcal{F}$, if $\mathcal{M} \models f$, then $\mathtt{M} \models \xi(f)$.

It is easy to check that theorems analogous to the above ones can be also proved for the weaker translation ξ°. Unfortunately, even for this stronger translation ξ, the translation of the axiom x {*before, equals, after*} y is still not valid:

$\xi(x$ {*before, equals, after*} $y)$ $=$

$(\varrho(x) \rightarrow F\varrho(y)) \,\&\, (\varrho(y) \rightarrow P\varrho(x)) \lor (\varrho(x) \leftrightarrow \varrho(y)) \lor$

$(\varrho(x) \rightarrow P\varrho(y)) \,\&\, (\varrho(y) \rightarrow F\varrho(x))$ $=$

$\varrho(x) \rightarrow (P\varrho(y) \lor \varrho(y) \lor F\varrho(y))$ $\&$

$(\varrho(x) \rightarrow (P\varrho(y) \lor \varrho(y)) \lor \varrho(y) \rightarrow P\varrho(x))$ $\&$

$(\varrho(x) \rightarrow (P\varrho(y) \lor F\varrho(y)) \lor \varrho(y) \rightarrow \varrho(x))$ $\&$

$(\varrho(x) \rightarrow (\varrho(y) \lor F\varrho(y)) \lor \varrho(y) \rightarrow F\varrho(x))$ $\&$

$(\varrho(x) \rightarrow F\varrho(y) \lor \varrho(y) \rightarrow (F\varrho(x) \lor \varrho(x)))$ $\&$

$(\varrho(x) \rightarrow \varrho(y) \lor \varrho(y) \rightarrow (F\varrho(x) \lor P\varrho(x)))$ $\&$

$(\varrho(x) \rightarrow P\varrho(y) \lor \varrho(y) \rightarrow (\varrho(x) \lor P\varrho(x)))$ $\&$

$\varrho(y) \rightarrow (F\varrho(x) \lor \varrho(x) \lor P\varrho(x)),$

since there exist models in which $V(\varrho(x)) = \emptyset$ and $V(\varrho(y)) = \emptyset$. However, for models satisfying the condition of *weak compatibility*, i.e. those in which valuations of all the variables are non-empty, an adequate axiom can be formulated:

$$Pp \lor p \lor Fp.$$

We can say that this axiom imposes non-emptiness of valuation. Evidently it entails the above formula. The question remains whether it imposes linearity of structures, which property is not definable in general. In fact, this axiom is satisfied in all the models of linear structures with non-empty valuations, but it also holds in some models of non-linear structures, when valuations have more than one element (for all the variables!). So the problem is whether we can speak about all the models with non-empty (or single-element) valuations.

However, for models with single-element valuations we can add one axiom more:

$$p \rightarrow H\neg p \,\&\, G\neg p.$$

Unfortunately, this axiom only imposes single-element valuations for linear structures. In the case of non-linear structures (their left and right linearity ensure

that such a structure is composed of separate axes), there is exactly one time
point satisfying p on each axis, and then both the above axioms will hold.

Lemma 6.1.1. For every $x, y \in Z$, the translation of at most one of the three
formulas x *before* y, x *equals* y, x *after* y holds in every model $M = \langle T, <, V \rangle$
satisfying the above axioms.

Proof
Consider any model $M = \langle T, <, V \rangle$, any $t \in T$ and any $x, y \in Z$. Evidently,
if $t \notin V(\varrho(x))$ and $t \notin V(\varrho(y))$, then all three formulas are satisfied at this time
moment.

Consider any $t \in V(\varrho(x))$.

Let $M \models \xi(x \text{ before } y)[t]$, i.e. $M \models ((\varrho(x) \rightarrow F\varrho(y)) \& (\varrho(y) \rightarrow P\varrho(x)))[t]$. This
means that there exists $t' \in T$ such that $t < t'$ and $M \models \varrho(y)[t']$.

Suppose that $M \models \xi(x \text{ equals } y)[t]$. Then $M \models (\varrho(x) \leftrightarrow \varrho(y))[t]$. Under our
assumption this means that $M \models \varrho(y)[t]$. We have a contradiction with the axiom
$p \rightarrow H\neg p \& G\neg p$, since also $M \models \varrho(y)[t']$ for some $t' > t$.

Suppose that $M \models \xi(x \text{ after } y)[t]$. Then $M \models (\varrho(x) \rightarrow P\varrho(y)) \& (\varrho(y) \rightarrow$
$F\varrho(x))[t]$. This means that there exists $t'' \in T$ such that $t'' < t$ and $M \models \varrho(y)[t'']$.
We have $t'' < t \& t < t'$, hence $M \models FF\varrho(y)[t'']$, and by transitivity $M \models F\varrho(y)[t'']$.
We have contradiction with the axiom $p \rightarrow H\neg p \& G\neg p$.

Let $M \models \xi(x \text{ equals } y)[t]$, i.e. $M \models (\varrho(x) \leftrightarrow \varrho(y))[t]$. Suppose that we have
$M \models \xi(x \text{ after } y)[t]$. Then $M \models (\varrho(x) \rightarrow P\varrho(y)) \& (\varrho(y) \rightarrow F\varrho(x))[t]$. This
means that there exists $t'' \in T$ such that $t'' < t$ and $M \models \varrho(y)[t'']$. We have
contradiction with the axiom $p \rightarrow H\neg p \& G\neg p$.

For every $t \in V(\varrho(y))$ the reasoning proceeds analogously. The axiom $Pp \vee p \vee Fp$
ensures that valuations are non-empty, hence there exists at least one t such that
at most one of the considered formulas is satisfied in it. Thus also in the whole
model only one such a formula can be satisfied. Nevertheless it is possible that
no such a formula is satisfied in a model—when in some moments one of them is
satisfied, and in other moments another. The required axioms imply that these
moments lie on different time axes. Evidently such a situation cannot appear in
a model with single-element valuation nor in a linear structure. Certainly this
does not change the fact that their disjunction is satisfied in every model. ∎

Theorem 6.1.2. The translations of inference rules 1, 3 and 4 are tautologies of
instant tense logic. The translation of rule 2 holds in it only under the assumption
that both the additional axioms considered above hold.

Proof
First we will show that the translation of rule 1 holds when its premises are
atomic formulas.

x before y & y before $z \implies x$ before z.

$M \models \xi(x$ before $y)[t]$ iff

   if $M \models \varrho(x)[t]$, then there exists t' such that $t < t'$ and $M \models \varrho(y)[t']$

   and if $M \models \varrho(y)[t]$, then there exists t' such that $t' < t$ and $M \models \varrho(x)[t']$,

$M \models \xi(y$ before $z)[t]$ iff

   if $M \models \varrho(y)[t]$, then there exists t' such that $t < t'$ and $M \models \varrho(z)[t']$

   and if $M \models \varrho(z)[t]$, then there exists t' such that $t' < t$ and $M \models \varrho(y)[t']$.

Consider any t such that $M \models \varrho(x)[t]$, i.e. $t \in V(\varrho(x))$. Moreover, there exists t' such that $t < t'$ and $M \models \varrho(y)[t']$. Then there exists t'' such that $t' < t''$ and $M \models \varrho(z)[t'']$. But then $M \models FF\varrho(z)[t]$, so by transitivity $M \models F\varrho(z)[t]$, hence $M \models (\varrho(x) \to F\varrho(z))[t]$.

For any t such that $t \notin V(\varrho(x))$ we have $M \not\models \varrho(x)[t]$, hence $M \models (\varrho(x) \to F\varrho(z))[t]$.

Consider any t such that $M \models \varrho(z)[t]$, i.e. $t \in V(\varrho(z))$. Then there exists t' such that $t' < t$ and $M \models \varrho(y)[t']$. Then there exists t'' such that $t'' < t'$ and $M \models \varrho(x)[t'']$. But then $M \models PP\varrho(x)[t]$, so by transitivity $M \models P\varrho(x)[t]$, hence $M \models (\varrho(z) \to P\varrho(x))[t]$.

For every t such that $t \notin V(\varrho(z))$ we have $M \not\models \varrho(z)[t]$, so $M \models (\varrho(z) \to P\varrho(x))[t]$. Thus for every $t \in T$ we have $M \models ((\varrho(x) \to F\varrho(z))$ & $(\varrho(z) \to P\varrho(x)))[t]$, hence $M \models \xi(x$ before $z)$.

x before y & y equals $z \implies x$ before z.

$M \models \xi(x$ before $y)[t]$ iff

   if $M \models \varrho(x)[t]$, then there exists t' such that $t < t'$ and $M \models \varrho(y)[t']$

   and if $M \models \varrho(y)[t]$, then there exists t' such that $t' < t$ and $M \models \varrho(x)[t']$,

$M \models \xi(y$ equals $z)[t]$ iff

   if $M \models \varrho(y)[t]$, then $M \models \varrho(z)[t]$ and if $M \models \varrho(z)[t]$, then $M \models \varrho(y)[t]$.

Consider any t such that $M \models \varrho(x)[t]$, i.e. $t \in V(\varrho(x))$. Then there exists t' such that $t < t'$ and $M \models \varrho(y)[t']$. Then $M \models \varrho(z)[t']$, hence $M \models (\varrho(x) \to F\varrho(z))[t]$.

For every t such that $t \notin V(\varrho(x))$ we have $M \not\models \varrho(x)[t]$, so $M \models (\varrho(x) \to F\varrho(z))[t]$.

Consider any t such that $M \models \varrho(z)[t]$, i.e. $t \in V(\varrho(z))$. Then $M \models \varrho(y)[t]$. Thus there exists t' such that $t' < t$ and $M \models \varrho(x)[t']$. This means that $M \models (\varrho(z) \to P\varrho(x))[t]$.

For every t such that $t \notin V(\varrho(z))$ we have $M \not\models \varrho(z)[t]$, hence $M \models (\varrho(z) \to P\varrho(x))[t]$.

Therefore for every $t \in T$ we have $M \models ((\varrho(x) \to F\varrho(z))$ & $(\varrho(z) \to P\varrho(x)))[t]$, so $M \models \xi(x$ before $z)$.

x before y & y after z $\implies$ x {before, equals, after} z.

$\mathsf{M} \models \xi(x$ before $y)[t]$ iff

if $\mathsf{M} \models \varrho(x)[t]$, then there exists t' such that $t < t'$ and $\mathsf{M} \models \varrho(y)[t']$

and if $\mathsf{M} \models \varrho(y)[t]$, then there exists t' such that $t' < t$ and $\mathsf{M} \models \varrho(x)[t']$,

$\mathsf{M} \models \xi(y$ after $z)[t]$ iff

if $\mathsf{M} \models \varrho(x)[t]$, then there exists t' such that $t' < t$ and $\mathsf{M} \models \varrho(y)[t']$

and if $\mathsf{M} \models \varrho(y)[t]$, then there exists t' such that $t < t'$ and $\mathsf{M} \models \varrho(x)[t']$.

Consider any t such that $\mathsf{M} \models \varrho(x)[t]$, i.e. $t \in V(\varrho(x))$. Then there exists t' such that $t < t'$ and $\mathsf{M} \models \varrho(y)[t']$. Moreover, there exists t'' such that $t'' < t'$ and $\mathsf{M} \models \varrho(z)[t'']$. But then $\mathsf{M} \models \mathsf{P}\varrho(z)[t']$, so by left linearity $\mathsf{M} \models \mathsf{H}(\mathsf{P}\varrho(z) \lor \varrho(z) \lor \mathsf{F}\varrho(z))[t']$, hence $\mathsf{M} \models (\mathsf{P}\varrho(z) \lor \varrho(z) \lor \mathsf{F}\varrho(z))[t]$ (as $t < t'$).

Suppose that $\mathsf{M} \models \varrho(z)[t]$, i.e. $t \in V(\varrho(z))$. Then $\mathsf{M} \models (\varrho(x) \leftrightarrow \varrho(z))[t]$, hence $\mathsf{M} \models \xi(x$ {before, equals, after} $z)[t]$. Otherwise $t \notin V(\varrho(z))$. We have two possibilities: either $\mathsf{M} \models \mathsf{P}\varrho(z)[t]$, and then $\mathsf{M} \models ((\varrho(x) \to \mathsf{P}\varrho(z))$ & $(\varrho(z) \to \mathsf{F}\varrho(x)))[t]$ (the second part follows from the fact that $\mathsf{M} \not\models \varrho(z)[t]$), hence $\mathsf{M} \models \xi(x$ {before, equals, after} $z)[t]$, or $\mathsf{M} \models \mathsf{F}\varrho(z)[t]$—and the reasoning is analogous.

Consider any t such that $\mathsf{M} \models \varrho(z)[t]$, i.e. $t \in V(\varrho(z))$. The reasoning is analogous as before, but this time for right linearity.

It is easy to check that for every t such that $t \notin V(\varrho(x))$ and $t \notin V(\varrho(z))$ we have $\mathsf{M} \models \xi(x$ {before, equals, after} $z)[t]$.

Thus for every $t \in T$ we have $\mathsf{M} \models \xi(x$ {before, equals, after} $z)[t]$.

x equals y & y before z $\implies$ x before z.

The reasoning is analogous as for x before y & y equals z $\implies$ x before z.

x equals y & y equals z $\implies$ x equals z.

The reasoning is straightforward.

x equals y & y after z $\implies$ x after z.

The reasoning is analogous as for x before y & y equals z $\implies$ x before z.

x after y & y before z $\implies$ x {before, equals, after} z.

The reasoning is analogous as for x before y & y after z $\implies$ x {before, equals, after} z.

x after y & y equals z $\implies$ x after z.

The reasoning is analogous as for x before y & y equals z $\implies$ x before z.

x after y & y after z $\implies$ x after z.

The reasoning is analogous as for x before y & y before z $\implies$ x before z.

We have shown that rule 1 is valid when its premises are atomic formulas. Now we will show that it is valid for arbitrary formulas, i.e. for $x \; \alpha \; y \; \& \; y \; \beta \; z \implies x \; \alpha{\circ}\beta \; z$, where $\alpha = \{r_1, ,..., r_n\}$, $\beta = \{r'_1, ,..., r'_m\}$.

$\mathsf{M} \models \xi(x \; \alpha \; y)[t]$ iff

   $\mathsf{M} \models \xi(x \; r_1 \; y) \vee ... \vee \xi(x \; r_n \; y)[t]$,

$\mathsf{M} \models \xi(y \; \beta \; z)[t]$ iff

   $\mathsf{M} \models \xi(y \; r'_1 \; z) \vee ... \vee \xi(y \; r'_m \; z)[t]$.

By definition of $\models$ there exist i, j such that $\mathsf{M} \models \xi(x \; r_i \; y)[t]$ and $\mathsf{M} \models \xi(y \; r'_j \; z)[t]$. It follows from the above proof that $\mathsf{M} \models \xi(x \; r_i \circ r'_j \; z)[t]$. On the other hand, it follows from the definition of $\circ$ that $r_i \circ r'_j \subseteq \alpha \circ \beta$. And this already means that $\mathsf{M} \models \xi(x \; \alpha \circ \beta \; z)[t]$.

Now we must show that rule 2 is valid, i.e. $\xi(x \; \alpha \; y \; \& \; x\beta \; y) \implies \xi(x \; \alpha \cap \beta \; y)$, where $\alpha = \{r_1, ,..., r_n\}$, $\beta = \{r'_1, ,..., r'_m\}$.

$\mathsf{M} \models \xi(x \; \alpha \; y)[t]$ iff

   $\mathsf{M} \models \xi(x \; r_1 \; y) \vee ... \vee \xi(x \; r_n \; y)[t]$,

$\mathsf{M} \models \xi(x \; \beta \; y)[t]$ iff

   $\mathsf{M} \models \xi(x \; r'_1 \; y) \vee ... \vee \xi(x \; r'_m \; y)[t]$.

By definition of $\models$ there exist i, j such that $\mathsf{M} \models \xi(x \; r_i \; y)[t]$ and $\mathsf{M} \models \xi(x \; r'_j \; y)[t]$. On the other hand, it follows from lemma 6.1.1 that only one such formula can be satisfied at any moment t, i.e. $r_i = r'_j$. And this means that $r_i \in \alpha \cap \beta$, hence $\mathsf{M} \models \xi(x \; \alpha \cap \beta \; y)[t]$.

The fact that the translation of rule 3 is valid when its premises are atomic formulas is straightforward—the translations of the formulas $x \; r \; y$ and $y \; r^{-1} \; x$ are identical. So we must show that this rule is valid in the general case, i.e. that $\xi(x \; \alpha \; y) \implies \xi(y \; \alpha^{-1} \; x)$, where $\alpha = \{r_1, ,..., r_n\}$.

$\mathsf{M} \models \xi(x \; \alpha \; y)[t]$ iff

   $\mathsf{M} \models \xi(x \; r_1 \; y) \vee ... \vee \xi(x \; r_n \; y)[t]$.

By definition of $\models$ there exists i such that $\mathsf{M} \models \xi(x \; r_i \; y)[t]$. It follows from the above proof that $\mathsf{M} \models \xi(y \; r_i^{-1} \; x)[t]$. On the other hand it follows from the definition of an inverse relation that $r_i^{-1} \in \alpha^{-1}$. And this already means that $\mathsf{M} \models \xi(y \; \alpha^{-1} \; x)[t]$.

Rule 4 is valid since it can be in fact reduced to the propositional calculus tautology $a \rightarrow (a \vee b)$.   ∎

The above theorem shows that in instant tense logic we are able to draw similar conclusions as in the point calculus. This indicates that the translation suggested here is sound. Reasoning is performed for formulas satisfied in a model, not in a structure—two axioms have been introduced that are not satisfied in any structure, as their validity depends on a valuation. This also concerns "data"—translations of specific axioms of the point calculus. On the other hand, satisfaction of these "data" at single time moments has only technical meaning—we cannot, after all, say that "p precedes q at a moment t", we can only say that "p precedes q in the considered model".

6.2 Translation of the point calculus for non-linear time into instant tense logic

In the description of point time structures in the first order predicate calculus as well as by means of instant tense logic, we differentiate linear and non-linear time by presence or absence of linearity axioms—no new axioms are introduced for non-linear time. In contrast, in the point calculus for non-linear time, a new relation *excludes* is added. To be sure, translations of "linear" primitive relations remain the same, but the formulation of translation for the relation *excludes* causes serious troubles, since we do not have at our disposal any operator showing that a formula is satisfied in another course of events. Moreover, we cannot include the axiom imposing non-emptiness of valuation $Pp \lor p \lor Fp$, as it need not be satisfied. The formula

$$\varrho(x) \;\rightarrow\; \mathsf{H}\neg\varrho(y) \;\&\; \neg\varrho(y) \;\&\; \mathsf{G}\neg\varrho(y)$$

could serve as a translation of the formula x *excludes* y only in models with single-element valuations. However, such a limitation introduced already on the level of translation seems to be exaggerated.

Thus in order to formulate a translation of the point calculus for non-linear time, we need additional operators, similar to those introduced in section 3.2.4 for interval time. We have not introduced such operators for point time, as there has been no need for this. A corresponding universal operator has the following semantics:

$\mathsf{M} \models \clubsuit\varphi[t]$ iff   for every t' such that $\neg(t < t' \lor t = t' \lor t' < t)$

$\qquad\qquad \mathsf{M} \models \varphi[j]$ holds,

and its existential counterpart is defined as $\spadesuit \equiv_{def} \neg\clubsuit\neg$.

Certainly, in this section we consider structures and models analogous to those in the previous section. Definitions of *compatible* and *weakly compatible* models are also the same as in the previous section. On the other hand, note that differentiation between partial and left linear order is made in an obvious way by the presence or absence of the left linearity axiom, whereas the right linearity axiom has been abandoned at all. Translations of the point calculus formulas are the same in both cases. Thus we are now able to formulate it.

DEFINITION

Let $\varrho: Z \longrightarrow X$ be a function transforming the set of variables of the point calculus onto the set of variables of instant tense logic. We define a function $\xi: \mathcal{F} \longrightarrow \mathcal{G}$ transforming formulas of the point calculus onto formulas of instant tense logic in the following way:

$$\xi(x \text{ before } y) \quad = \quad (\varrho(x) \rightarrow F\varrho(y)) \ \& \ (\varrho(y) \rightarrow P\varrho(x))$$

$$\xi(x \text{ equals } y) \quad = \quad \varrho(x) \leftrightarrow \varrho(y)$$

$$\xi(x \text{ after } y) \quad = \quad (\varrho(x) \rightarrow P\varrho(y)) \ \& \ (\varrho(y) \rightarrow F\varrho(x))$$

$$\xi(x \text{ excludes } y) \quad = \quad (\varrho(x) \rightarrow \spadesuit\varrho(y)) \ \& \ (\varrho(y) \rightarrow \spadesuit\varrho(x))$$

$$\xi(x \ \alpha \ y) \quad = \quad \xi(x \ r_1 \ y) \lor \dots \lor \xi(x \ r_n \ y), \text{ where } \alpha = \{ r_1, \dots, r_n \}$$

$$\xi(x \ \emptyset \ y) \quad = \quad p \ \& \ \neg p$$

where, as before, p is an arbitrary, fixed element of X.

For this translation we can formulate the following basic theorem.

Theorem 6.2.1. For any compatible models $\mathcal{M} = \langle T, <, W \rangle$ and $\mathsf{M} = \langle T, <, V \rangle$, and for every formula $f \in \mathcal{F}$ we have $\mathcal{M} \models f$ iff $\mathsf{M} \models f$.
Proof

- $f = x \text{ before } y$
  The reasoning is the same as in theorem 6.1.1.
- $f = x \text{ after } y$
  Similarly as in the proof of theorem 6.1.1, the reasoning is analogous to the previous one.
- $f = x \text{ equals } y$
  The reasoning is the same as in theorem 6.1.1.
- $f = x \text{ excludes } y$

$$\mathcal{M} \models f \qquad \text{iff} \quad \neg(W(x) < W(y) \lor W(x) = W(y) \lor W(y) < W(x)),$$

$$\mathsf{M} \models \xi(f)[t] \quad \text{iff} \quad \mathsf{M} \models (\varrho(x) \rightarrow \spadesuit\varrho(y)) \ \& \ (\varrho(y) \rightarrow \spadesuit\varrho(x))$$

$$\text{iff} \quad \text{if } \mathsf{M} \models \varrho(x)[t], \text{ then there exists } t' \text{ such that}$$

$$\neg(t < t' \lor t = t' \lor t' < t) \text{ and } \mathsf{M} \models \varrho(y)[t'] \quad \text{and}$$

$$\text{if } \mathsf{M} \models \varrho(y)[t], \text{ then there exists } t'' \text{ such that}$$

$$\neg(t < t'' \lor t = t'' \lor t'' < t) \text{ and } \mathsf{M} \models \varrho(y)[t'].$$

If $t = V(\varrho(x))$, then $\mathsf{M} \models \varrho(x)[t]$. Then there exists t' such that $\neg(t < t' \lor t = t' \lor t' < t)$ and $\mathsf{M} \models \varrho(y)[t']$. Otherwise, if $t \neq V(\varrho(x))$, then $\mathsf{M} \not\models \varrho(x)[t]$ and $\mathsf{M} \models (\varrho(x) \rightarrow \spadesuit\varrho(y))[t]$.
If $t = V(\varrho(y))$, then $\mathsf{M} \models \varrho(y)[t]$. Then there exists t'' such that $\neg(t < t'' \lor t = t'' \lor t'' < t)$ and $\mathsf{M} \models \varrho(y)[t'']$. Otherwise, if $t \neq V(\varrho(y))$, then $\mathsf{M} \not\models \varrho(y)[t]$ and $\mathsf{M} \models (\varrho(y) \rightarrow \spadesuit\varrho(x))[t]$.
But $V(\varrho(x)) = W(x)$ and $V(\varrho(y)) = W(y)$. Thus $\mathcal{M} \models f$ iff $\mathsf{M} \models \xi(f)$.

- $f = x\ \{r_1,\ ...,\ r_n\}\ y$

  The reasoning is the same as in theorem 6.1.1.

- For any models $\mathcal{M} = \langle T,\ <,\ W \rangle$ and $\mathtt{M} = \langle T,\ <,\ V \rangle$ and for any $x, y \in Z$, and $p \in X$ we have $\mathcal{M} \not\models x\ \emptyset\ y$ and $\mathtt{M} \not\models p\ \&\ \neg p$. Therefore also for $f = x\ \emptyset\ y$ we have $\mathcal{M} \models f$ iff $\mathtt{M} \models \xi(f)$.

Thus we have shown that for every $f \in \mathcal{F}$ we have $\mathcal{M} \models f$ iff $\mathtt{M} \models \xi(f)$. ∎

Corollary For any weakly compatible models $\mathcal{M} = \langle T,\ <,\ W \rangle$ and $\mathtt{M} = \langle T,\ <,\ V \rangle$, and for every formula $f \in \mathcal{F}$ if $\mathcal{M} \models f$, then $\mathtt{M} \models \xi(f)$.

As we have mentioned, the auxiliary axioms introduced in the previous section does not hold for non-linear time. However, as we have at our disposal the additional operators, we can modify them appropriately:

$$\text{P}p \lor p \lor \text{F}p \lor \clubsuit p,$$

$$p \rightarrow \text{H}\neg p\ \&\ \text{G}\neg p\ \&\ \clubsuit \neg p.$$

The above axioms enable proving a theorem analogous to theorem 6.1.2. However, we will not prove it here, the reasoning being very similar to the previous one.

6.3 Translation of the calculus of distances between points into metric tense logic

A translation of the point calculus with relative dates was suggested in [Hajnicz, 1991b]. The solution presented there has a hybrid character—qualitative relations between points were enriched by quantitative distances between the points, on condition that such a distance is exactly known. In this section we want to discuss a translation of the full calculus of distances between points, i.e. the one allowing for disjunctions of distances between points, into metric tense logic.

Recall that we deal with a metric point structure $\mathfrak{T} = \langle T,\ C,\ <,\ \delta \rangle$. Moreover, we consider a calculus of distances between points with a set of propositional variables Z, a set of formulas $\mathcal{F}$ and a model $\mathcal{M} = \langle T,\ C,\ <,\ \delta,\ S,\ W \rangle$ and a metric tense logic with a set of propositional variables X, a set of formulas $\mathcal{G}$ and a model $\mathtt{M} = \langle T,\ C,\ <,\ \delta,\ V \rangle$.

DEFINITION
Let $\mathfrak{T} = \langle T,\ C,\ <,\ \delta \rangle$ be a metric point structure, and $\varrho \colon Z \longrightarrow X$ be a function transforming the set of variables of the calculus of distances between points onto the set of variables of metric tense logic. The models $\mathcal{M} = \langle T,\ C,\ <,\ \delta,\ S,\ W \rangle$ and $\mathtt{M} = \langle T,\ C,\ <,\ \delta,\ V \rangle$ are *weakly compatible* if $W(x) \subseteq V(\varrho(x))$ holds for every $x \in Z$, and they are *compatible*, if $W(x) = V(\varrho(x))$ holds for every $x \in Z$.

We define a function $\xi : \mathcal{F} \longrightarrow \mathcal{G}$ transforming formulas of the calculus of distances between points onto formulas of metric tense logic in the following way:

$$\xi(x\ r_i\ y) = \begin{cases} (\varrho(x) \rightarrow F_{S(r_i)}\varrho(y)) \ \& \ (\varrho(y) \rightarrow P_{S(r_i)}\varrho(x)) & \text{for } i > 0 \\ \varrho(x) \leftrightarrow \varrho(y) & \text{for } i = 0 \\ (\varrho(x) \rightarrow P_{S(r_i)}\varrho(y)) \ \& \ (\varrho(y) \rightarrow F_{S(r_i)}\varrho(x)) & \text{for } i < 0 \end{cases}$$

$$\xi(x\ \alpha\ y) = \bigvee_{r_i \in \alpha} \xi(x\ r_i\ y)$$

$$\xi(x\ \emptyset\ y) = p\ \&\ \neg p$$

where p is an arbitrary, fixed element of X.

Also in this case we can formulate a basic theorem, showing the correctness of the translation.

Theorem 6.3.1. For any compatible models $\mathcal{M} = \langle T,\ \mathcal{C},\ <,\ \delta,\ S,\ W \rangle$ and $\mathsf{M} = \langle T,\ \mathcal{C},\ <,\ \delta,\ V \rangle$, and for every formula $f \in \mathcal{F}$ we have $\mathcal{M} \models f$ iff $\mathsf{M} \models f$.
Proof

- $f = x\ r_i\ y$ for $i > 0$

$$\begin{aligned} \mathcal{M} \models f \quad &\text{iff} \quad W(x) < W(y), \text{ and } \delta(W(x), W(y)) = S(r_i), \\ \mathsf{M} \models \xi(f)[t] \quad &\text{iff} \quad (\varrho(x) \rightarrow F_{S(r_i)}\varrho(y)) \ \& \ (\varrho(y) \rightarrow P_{S(r_i)}\varrho(x)) \\ &\text{iff} \quad \text{if } \mathsf{M} \models \varrho(x)[t], \text{ then there exists } t' \text{ such that } t < t' \text{ and} \\ & \qquad \delta(t, t') = S(r_i) \text{ and } \mathsf{M} \models \varrho(y)[t'] \text{ and if } \mathsf{M} \models \varrho(y)[t], \\ & \qquad \text{then there exists } t'' \text{ such that } t'' < t \text{ and} \\ & \qquad \delta(t, t'') = S(r_i) \text{ and } \mathsf{M} \models \varrho(x)[t'']. \end{aligned}$$

Let $\mathsf{M} \models \xi(f)[t]$. Consider $t = V(\varrho(x))$. Then $\mathsf{M} \models \varrho(x)[t]$, so there exists t' such that $t < t'$ and $\delta(t,t') = S(r_i)$ and $t' = V(\varrho(y))$. Since $V(\varrho(x)) = W(x)$ and $V(\varrho(y)) = W(y)$, we have $W(x) < W(y)$ and $\delta(W(x), W(y)) = S(r_i)$, hence $\mathcal{M} \models f$.

Let $\mathcal{M} \models f$. If $t = W(x) = V(\varrho(x))$, then for $t' = W(y) = V(\varrho(y))$ we have $t < t'$ and $\delta(t,t') = S(r_i)$, so $\mathsf{M} \models (\varrho(x) \rightarrow F_{S(r_i)}\varrho(y))[t]$. Otherwise, if $t \neq V(\varrho(x))$, then $\mathsf{M} \not\models \varrho(x)[t]$, so $\mathsf{M} \models (\varrho(x) \rightarrow F_{S(r_i)}\varrho(y))[t]$.

If $t = W(y) = V(\varrho(y))$, then for $t'' = W(x) = V(\varrho(x))$ we have $t'' < t$ and $\delta(t,t'') = S(r_i)$, i.e. $\mathsf{M} \models (\varrho(y) \rightarrow P_{S(r_i)}\varrho(x))[t]$. Otherwise, if $t \neq V(\varrho(y))$, then $\mathsf{M} \not\models \varrho(y)[t]$, hence $\mathsf{M} \models (\varrho(y) \rightarrow P_{S(r_i)}\varrho(x))[t]$. In all cases $\mathsf{M} \models \xi(f)[t]$.

Eventually, $\mathcal{M} \models f$ iff $\mathsf{M} \models \xi(f)$.

- $f = x \, r_i \, y$ for $i = 0$

$$\mathcal{M} \models f \qquad \text{iff} \qquad W(x) = W(y), \text{ and } \delta(W(x), W(y)) = S(r_0) = 0$$
$$\mathsf{M} \models \xi(f)[t] \quad \text{iff} \quad \mathsf{M} \models (\varrho(x) \leftrightarrow \varrho(y))[t]$$
$$\text{iff} \quad \text{if } \mathsf{M} \models \varrho(x)[t], \text{ then } \mathsf{M} \models \varrho(y)[t] \text{ and}$$
$$\text{if } \mathsf{M} \models \varrho(y)[t], \text{ then } \mathsf{M} \models \varrho(x)[t].$$

Let $\mathsf{M} \models \xi(f)[t]$. Consider $t = V(\varrho(x))$. Then $\mathsf{M} \models \varrho(x)[t]$, so $\mathsf{M} \models \varrho(y)[t]$, hence $t = V(\varrho(y))$. As $V(\varrho(x)) = W(x)$ and $V(\varrho(y)) = W(y)$, we have $W(x) = W(y)$ and $\delta(W(x), W(y)) = S(r_i)$, so $\mathcal{M} \models f$.

Let $\mathcal{M} \models f$. If $t = W(x) = V(\varrho(x))$, then $t = W(y) = V(\varrho(y))$, so $\mathsf{M} \models (\varrho(x) \rightarrow \varrho(y))[t]$. Otherwise, if $t \neq V(\varrho(x))$, then $\mathsf{M} \not\models \varrho(x)[t]$, hence $\mathsf{M} \models (\varrho(x) \rightarrow \varrho(y))[t]$. Analogously if $t = W(y) = V(\varrho(y))$, then $t = W(x) = V(\varrho(x))$, so $\mathsf{M} \models (\varrho(y) \rightarrow \varrho(x))[t]$, and if $t \neq V(\varrho(y))$, then $\mathsf{M} \not\models \varrho(y)[t]$, hence $\mathsf{M} \models (\varrho(y) \rightarrow \varrho(x))[t]$.

Eventually, $\mathcal{M} \models f$ iff $\mathsf{M} \models \xi(f)$.

- $f = x \, r_i \, y$ for $i < 0$

$$\mathcal{M} \models f \qquad \text{iff} \qquad W(y) < W(x), \text{ and } \delta(W(x), W(y)) = S(r_i)$$
$$\mathsf{M} \models \xi(f)[t] \quad \text{iff} \quad (\varrho(x) \rightarrow \mathsf{P}_{S(r_i)}\varrho(y)) \, \& \, (\varrho(y) \rightarrow \mathsf{F}_{S(r_i)}\varrho(x))$$
$$\text{iff} \quad \text{if } \mathsf{M} \models \varrho(x)[t], \text{ then there exists } t' \text{ such that } t' < t$$
$$\text{and } \delta(t, t') = S(r_i) \text{ and } \mathsf{M} \models \varrho(y)[t'] \quad \text{and}$$
$$\text{if } \mathsf{M} \models \varrho(y)[t], \text{ then there exists } t'' \text{ such that } t < t''$$
$$\text{and } \delta(t, t'') = S(r_i) \text{ and } \mathsf{M} \models \varrho(x)[t''].$$

The reasoning is analogous as for $i > 0$.

- $f = x \, \alpha \, y$

$$\mathcal{M} \models f \qquad \text{iff} \qquad \text{there exists } r_i \in \alpha \text{ such that } \mathcal{M} \models x \, r_i \, y,$$
$$\mathsf{M} \models \xi(f)[t] \quad \text{iff} \quad \mathsf{M} \models \bigvee_{r_i \in \alpha} \xi(x \, r_i \, y)[t]$$
$$\text{iff} \quad \text{there exists } r_i \in \alpha \text{ such that } \mathsf{M} \models \xi(x \, r_i \, y)[t].$$

Evidently, $\mathcal{M} \models x \, r_i \, y$ iff $\mathsf{M} \models \xi(x \, r_i \, y)[t]$. Therefore $\mathcal{M} \models f$ iff $\mathsf{M} \models \xi(f)$.

- For any models $\mathcal{M} = \langle T, \, \mathcal{C}, \, <, \, \delta, \, S, \, W \rangle$ and $\mathsf{M} = \langle T, \, \mathcal{C}, \, <, \, \delta, \, V \rangle$ and every $x, y \in Z$ and $p \in X$ we have $\mathcal{M} \not\models x \, \emptyset \, y$ and $\mathsf{M} \not\models p \, \& \, \neg p$. Thus also for $f = x \, \emptyset \, y$ we have $\mathcal{M} \models f$ iff $\mathsf{M} \models \xi(f)$.

Thus we have shown that for every $f \in \mathcal{F}$ we have $\mathcal{M} \models f$ iff $\mathsf{M} \models \xi(f)$. ∎

Corollary For any weakly compatible models $\mathcal{M} = \langle T, \, \mathcal{C}, \, <, \, \delta, \, S, \, W \rangle$ and $\mathsf{M} = \langle T, \, \mathcal{C}, \, <, \, \delta, \, V \rangle$ and for every formula $f \in \mathcal{F}$ if $\mathcal{M} \models f$, then $\mathsf{M} \models \xi(f)$.

Similarly as for "ordinary" linear time,, we can add the same two axioms for models satisfying the conditions of *weak compatibility* or *compatibility* (as operators G, H, F, P preserve their role):

$$Pp \lor p \lor Fp,$$

$$p \rightarrow H\neg p \ \& \ G\neg p$$

thus enabling adequate reasoning in metric tense logic.

Lemma 6.3.1. For any $x, y \in Z$ and $r_i, r_j \in \mathbf{P}$ we have $\mathsf{M} \models \xi(x \ r_i \ y)$ and $\mathsf{M} \models \xi(x \ r_j \ y)$ iff $i = j$.

Proof

Consider any model $\mathsf{M} = \langle T, C, <, \delta, V \rangle$, any $t \in T$ and any $x, y \in Z$. Evidently, if $t \notin V(\varrho(x))$ and $t \notin V(\varrho(y))$, then both formulas are satisfied at this time moment.

Consider any $t \in V(\varrho(x))$. Suppose that $\mathsf{M} \models \xi(x \ r_i \ y)$ and $\mathsf{M} \models \xi(x \ r_j \ y)$.

1. $i > 0, \ j > 0, \ i > j$

   This means that $\mathsf{M} \models F_{S(r_i)}\varrho(y)[t]$ and $\mathsf{M} \models F_{S(r_j)}\varrho(y)[t]$. Thus there exists t' such that $t < t'$ and $\delta(t, t') = S(r_i)$ and $\mathsf{M} \models \varrho(y)[t']$. Moreover, there exists t'' such that $t < t''$ and $\delta(t, t'') = S(r_j)$ and $\mathsf{M} \models \varrho(y)[t'']$. By definitions of δ and S we have $\delta(t', t'') = S(r_{i-j})$. On the other hand, we can infer from the axiom of consistency that $t'' < t'$. This means that $\mathsf{M} \models \varrho(y)[t'']$ and $\mathsf{M} \models F\varrho(y)[t'']$. We obtain contradiction with the axiom $p \rightarrow H\neg p \ \& \ G\neg p$.

2. $i > 0, \ j > 0, \ i = j$

   It is easy to show that in such a situation $\mathsf{M} \models \xi(x \ r_i \ y)$ and $\mathsf{M} \models \xi(x \ r_j \ y)$ really hold.

3. $i > 0, \ j > 0, \ i < j$

   The reasoning is analogous as in item 1.

4. $i > 0, \ j = 0$

   This means that $\mathsf{M} \models F_{S(r_i)}\varrho(y)[t]$ and $\mathsf{M} \models \varrho(y)[t]$. Thus there exists t' such that $t < t'$ and $\delta(t, t') = S(r_i)$ and $\mathsf{M} \models \varrho(y)[t']$. Therefore $\mathsf{M} \models F\varrho(y)[t]$, and we obtain contradiction with the axiom $p \rightarrow H\neg p \ \& \ G\neg p$.

5. $i > 0, \ j < 0$

   This means that $\mathsf{M} \models F_{S(r_i)}\varrho(y)[t]$ and $\mathsf{M} \models P_{S(r_j)}\varrho(y)[t]$. Thus there exists t' such that $t < t'$ and $\delta(t, t') = S(r_i)$ and $\mathsf{M} \models \varrho(y)[t']$. Moreover there exists t'' such that $t'' < t$ and $\delta(t, t'') = S(r_j)$ and $\mathsf{M} \models \varrho(y)[t'']$. Thus $\mathsf{M} \models FF\varrho(y)[t'']$, so by transitivity $\mathsf{M} \models F\varrho(y)[t'']$. On the other hand, $\mathsf{M} \models \varrho(y)[t'']$. We obtain contradiction with the axiom $p \rightarrow H\neg p \ \& \ G\neg p$.

6. $i = 0, \ j = 0$

   This evidently means that $i = j$. Also in this case we can show in a simple way that translations of both formulas are satisfied.

For the remaining cases the proof proceeds in a similar way.

Consider any $t \in V(\varrho(y))$. The reasoning is similar to the one performed for $t \in V(\varrho(x))$. The axiom $Pp \vee p \vee Fp$ guarantees that valuations are non-empty, hence there exists at least one t such that at most one of the considered formulas is satisfied in it. Thus also in the whole model only one such formula can be satisfied. Nevertheless it is possible that no such formula is satisfied in a model. ∎

Theorem 6.3.2. The translations of inference rules 1, 2 and 4 are tautologies of metric tense logic. The translation of rule 3 holds in it only under the assumption that both additional axioms considered above hold.

Proof

First we will show that the translation of rule 1 holds when its premises are atomic formulas.

$$x \, r_i \, y \, \& \, y \, r_j \, z \implies x \, r_{i+j} \, z.$$

$M \models \xi(x \, r_i \, y)[t]$ iff

  if $M \models \varrho(x)[t]$, then there exists t' such that $t < t'$ and $\delta(t, t') = S(r_i)$ and $M \models \varrho(y)[t']$ and if $M \models \varrho(y)[t]$, then there exists t'' such that $t'' < t$ and $\delta(t, t'') = S(r_i)$ and $M \models \varrho(x)[t'']$ for $i > 0$,

  if $M \models \varrho(x)[t]$, then $M \models \varrho(y)[t]$ and if $M \models \varrho(y)[t]$, then $M \models \varrho(x)[t]$ for $i = 0$,

  if $M \models \varrho(x)[t]$, then there exists t' such that $t' < t$ and $\delta(t, t') = S(r_i)$ and $M \models \varrho(y)[t']$ and if $M \models \varrho(y)[t]$, then there exists t'' such that $t < t''$ and $\delta(t, t'') = S(r_i)$ and $M \models \varrho(x)[t'']$ for $i < 0$,

$M \models \xi(y \, r_j \, z)[t]$ iff

  if $M \models \varrho(y)[t]$, then there exists t' such that $t < t'$ and $\delta(t, t') = S(r_j)$ and $M \models \varrho(z)[t']$ and if $M \models \varrho(z)[t]$, then there exists t'' such that $t'' < t$ and $\delta(t, t'') = S(r_j)$ and $M \models \varrho(y)[t'']$ for $i > 0$,

  if $M \models \varrho(y)[t]$, then $M \models \varrho(z)[t]$ and if $M \models \varrho(z)[t]$, then $M \models \varrho(y)[t]$ for $i = 0$,

  if $M \models \varrho(y)[t]$, then there exists t' such that $t' < t$ and $\delta(t, t') = S(r_j)$ and $M \models \varrho(z)[t']$ and if $M \models \varrho(z)[t]$, then there exists t'' such that $t < t''$ and $\delta(t, t'') = S(r_j)$ and $M \models \varrho(y)[t'']$ for $i < 0$.

  1. $i > 0, \ j > 0$

     Consider any t such that $M \models \varrho(x)[t]$, i.e. $t \in V(\varrho(x))$. Moreover there exists t' such that $t < t'$ and $\delta(t, t') = S(r_i)$ and $M \models \varrho(y)[t']$. Then there exists t'' such that $t' < t''$ and $\delta(t', t'') = S(r_j)$ and $M \models \varrho(z)[t'']$. But then $M \models F_{S(r_i)}F_{S(r_j)}\varrho(z)[t]$, so by the corresponding axiom $M \models F_{S(r_i)+S(r_j)}\varrho(z)[t]$. In section 5.6 $S(r_i)$ has been defined as $S(r_i) = |i| * S(r_1)$, hence $S(r_i) + S(r_j) = |i| * S(r_1) + |j| * S(r_1) = (|i| + |j|)S(r_1) = S(r_{i+j})$, as $i > 0$ and $j > 0$. Therefore $M \models F_{S(r_{i+j})}\varrho(z)[t]$. Thus $M \models (\varrho(x) \rightarrow F_{S(r_{i+j})}\varrho(z))[t]$ and $i + j > 0$.

For any t such that $t \notin V(\varrho(x))$ we have $M \not\models \varrho(x)[t]$, hence $M \models (\varrho(x) \rightarrow F_{S(r_{i+j})}\varrho(z))[t]$.

Consider any t such that $M \models \varrho(z)[t]$, i.e. $t \in V(\varrho(z))$. Then there exists t' such that $t' < t$ and $\delta(t, t') = S(r_j)$ and $M \models \varrho(y)[t']$. Then there exists t'' such that $t'' < t'$ and $\delta(t', t'') = S(r_i)$ and $M \models \varrho(x)[t'']$. But then $M \models P_{S(r_j)}P_{S(r_i)}\varrho(x)[t]$, so by the corresponding axiom $M \models P_{S(r_j)+S(r_i)}\varrho(x)[t]$. But $S(r_j) + S(r_i) = |j| * S(r_1) + |i| * S(r_1) = (|j| + |i|)S(r_1) = S(r_{i+j})$, as $i > 0$ and $j > 0$. Therefore $M \models P_{S(r_{i+j})}\varrho(x)[t]$. Thus $M \models (\varrho(z) \rightarrow P_{S(r_{i+j})}\varrho(x))[t]$ and $i + j > 0$.

For any t such that $t \notin V(\varrho(z))$ we have $M \not\models \varrho(z)[t]$, hence $M \models (\varrho(z) \rightarrow P_{S(r_{i+j})}\varrho(x))[t]$.

Eventually for every $t \in T$ we have $M \models \xi(x\ r_{i+j}\ z)[t]$.

2. $i > 0,\ \ j = 0$

Consider any t such that $M \models \varrho(x)[t]$, i.e. $t \in V(\varrho(x))$. Then there exists t' such that $t < t'$ and $\delta(t, t') = S(r_i)$ and $M \models \varrho(y)[t']$. Then $M \models \varrho(z)[t']$. This means that $M \models F_{S(r_i)}\varrho(y)[t]$. Since additionally $S(r_i) + S(r_0) = S(r_i)$, hence $M \models F_{S(r_{i+j})}\varrho(z)[t]$, so $M \models (\varrho(x) \rightarrow F_{S(r_{i+j})}\varrho(z))[t]$ and $i + j > 0$.

For any t such that $t \notin V(\varrho(x))$ we have $M \not\models \varrho(x)[t]$, hence $M \models (\varrho(x) \rightarrow F_{S(r_{i+j})}\varrho(z))[t]$.

Consider any t such that $M \models \varrho(z)[t]$, i.e. $t \in V(\varrho(z))$. Then $M \models \varrho(y)[t]$, i.e. $t \in V(\varrho(y))$, so there exists t' such that $t' < t$ and $\delta(t, t') = S(r_i)$ and $M \models \varrho(x)[t']$. This means that $M \models P_{S(r_i)}\varrho(x)[t]$. Since additionally $S(r_i) + S(r_0) = S(r_i)$, hence $M \models P_{S(r_{i+j})}\varrho(x)[t]$, so $M \models (\varrho(z) \rightarrow P_{S(r_{i+j})}\varrho(x))[t]$ and $i + j > 0$.

For any t such that $t \notin V(\varrho(z))$ we have $M \not\models \varrho(z)[t]$, i.e. $M \models (\varrho(z) \rightarrow P_{S(r_{i+j})}\varrho(x))[t]$.

Eventually for every $t \in T$ we have $M \models \xi(x\ r_{i+j}\ z)[t]$.

3. $i > 0,\ \ j < 0$

Consider any t such that $M \models \varrho(x)[t]$, i.e. $t \in V(\varrho(x))$. Then there exists t' such that $t < t'$ and $\delta(t, t') = S(r_i)$ and $M \models \varrho(y)[t']$, so there exists t'' such that $t'' < t'$ and $\delta(t', t'') = S(r_j)$ and $M \models \varrho(z)[t'']$. But then $M \models F_{S(r_i)}P_{S(r_j)}\varrho(z)[t]$.

If $|i| > |j|$, then $S(r_i) > S(r_j)$, hence by the corresponding axiom we have $M \models F_{S(r_i)-S(r_j)}\varrho(z)[t]$. But $S(r_i) - S(r_j) = |i| * S(r_1) - |j| * S(r_1) = (i + j)S(r_1) = S(r_{i+j})$, as $i > 0$ and $j < 0$. Therefore $M \models F_{S(r_{i+j})}\varrho(z)[t]$. Thus $M \models (\varrho(x) \rightarrow F_{S(r_{i+j})}\varrho(z))[t]$ and $i + j > 0$.

If $|i| < |j|$, then $S(r_i) < S(r_j)$, hence by the corresponding lemma we have $M \models P_{S(r_j)-S(r_i)}\varrho(z)[t]$. But $S(r_i) - S(r_j) = |j| * S(r_1) - |i| * S(r_1) =$

$(-i - j) * S(r_1) = |(i + j)| * S(r_{i+j})$, as $i > 0$ and $j < 0$. Therefore $M \models F_{S(r_{i+j})}\varrho(z)[t]$. Thus $M \models (\varrho(x) \rightarrow F_{S(r_{i+j})}\varrho(z))[t]$ and $i + j < 0$.

For every t such that $t \notin V(\varrho(x))$ we have $M \not\models \varrho(x)[t]$, hence $M \models (\varrho(x) \rightarrow F_{S(r_{i+j})}\varrho(z))[t]$ and $M \models (\varrho(x) \rightarrow P_{S(r_{i+j})}\varrho(z))[t]$. One of these formulas is necessary depending on whether $i + j > 0$ or $i + j < 0$ holds.

For every t such that $M \models \varrho(z)[t]$ the reasoning is analogous.

For every t such that $t \notin V(\varrho(z))$ we have $M \not\models \varrho(z)[t]$, hence $M \models (\varrho(z) \rightarrow P_{S(r_{i+j})}\varrho(x))[t]$ and $M \models (\varrho(z) \rightarrow F_{S(r_{i+j})}\varrho(x))[t]$ depending on whether $i + j > 0$ or $i + j < 0$ holds.

Eventually for every $t \in T$ we have $M \models \xi(x\ r_{i+j}\ z)[t]$.

4. $i = 0, \quad j = 0$

Consider any t such that $M \models \varrho(x)[t]$, i.e. $t \in V(\varrho(x))$. Then $M \models \varrho(y)[t]$, and then $M \models \varrho(z)[t]$. Therefore $M \models (\varrho(x) \rightarrow \varrho(z))[t]$ and $i + j = 0$.

For every t such that $t \notin V(\varrho(x))$ we have $M \not\models \varrho(x)[t]$, hence $M \models (\varrho(x) \rightarrow \varrho(z))[t]$.

For every t such that $M \models \varrho(z)[t]$ the reasoning is analogous.

For every t such that $t \notin V(\varrho(z))$ we have $M \not\models \varrho(z)[t]$, hence $M \models (\varrho(z) \rightarrow \varrho(x))[t]$.

Eventually, for every $t \in T$ we have $M \models \xi(x\ r_{i+j}\ z)[t]$.

For the remaining cases the reasoning is analogous.

We have shown that rule 1 is valid when its premises are atomic formulas. Now we will show that it is valid in the general case, for arbitrary formulas, i.e. for $x\ \alpha\ y\ \&\ y\ \beta\ z \implies x\ \alpha \circ \beta\ z$.

$$M \models \xi(x\ \alpha\ y)[t] \quad \text{iff} \quad \bigvee_{r_i \in \alpha} \xi(x\ r_i\ y)$$

$$M \models \xi(y\ \beta\ z)[t] \quad \text{iff} \quad \bigvee_{r_j \in \beta} \xi(y\ r_j\ z)$$

By definition of $\models$ there exist i, j, such that $M \models \xi(x\ r_i\ y)[t]$ and $M \models \xi(y\ r_j\ z)[t]$. It follows from the proof above that $M \models \xi(x\ r_i \circ r_j\ z)[t]$. On the other hand, it follows by definition of $\circ$ that $r_i \circ r_j \subseteq \alpha \circ \beta$. And this means that $M \models \xi(x\ \alpha \circ \beta\ z)[t]$.

Now we must show that rule 2 is valid, i.e. $\xi(x\ \alpha\ y\ \&\ x\beta\ y) \implies \xi(x\ \alpha \cap \beta\ y)$.

$$M \models \xi(x\ \alpha\ y)[t] \quad \text{iff} \quad \bigvee_{r_i \in \alpha} \xi(x\ r_i\ y)$$

$$M \models \xi(x\ \beta\ y)[t] \quad \text{iff} \quad \bigvee_{r_j \in \beta} \xi(x\ r_j\ y)$$

By definition of $\models$ there exist i, j such that $M \models \xi(x\ r_i\ y)[t]$ and $M \models \xi(x\ r_j\ y)[t]$. On the other hand, it follows from lemma 6.3.1 that only one such formula can be satisfied at any particular moment t, i.e. $r_i = r_j$. And this means that $r_i \in \alpha \cap \beta$, hence $M \models \xi(x\ \alpha \cap \beta\ y)[t]$.

The fact that the translation of rule 3 is valid when its premises are atomic formulas is straightforward—the translations of the formulas $x\ r_i\ y$ and $y\ r_{-i}\ x$ are identical. So we must show that this rule is valid in the general case, i.e. that $\xi(x\ \alpha\ y) \implies \xi(y\ \alpha^{-1}\ x)$, where $\alpha = \{r_1,\ ,...,\ r_n\}$.

$$M \models \xi(x\ \alpha\ y)[t] \quad \text{iff} \quad \bigvee_{r_i \in \alpha} \xi(x\ r_i\ y)$$

By definition of $\models$ there exists i such that $M \models \xi(x\ r_i\ y)[t]$. It follows from the above proof that $M \models \xi(y\ r_i^{-1}\ x)[t]$. On the other hand, it follows from the definition of an inverse relation that $r_i^{-1} \in \alpha^{-1}$. And this already means that $M \models \xi(y\ \alpha^{-1}\ x)[t]$.

Rule 4 is valid since it can be in fact reduced to the propositional calculus tautology $a \rightarrow (a \vee b)$.   ∎

6.4 Translation of the interval calculus for linear time into extended tense logic

After considering various cases of point time, we shall now concentrate on interval time. We will only consider linear time. Recall that we have a linear interval structure $\Im = \langle I, <, \subseteq \rangle$. Moreover, we consider an interval calculus with a set of propositional variables Z, a set of formulas $\mathcal{F}$ and a model $\mathcal{M} = \langle I, <, \subseteq, W \rangle$, and an extended tense logic with a set of propositional variables X, a set of formulas $\mathcal{G}$ and a model $M = \langle I, <, \subseteq, V \rangle$.

As before, we can consider *compatible* and *weakly compatible* models.

DEFINITION
Let $\Im = \langle I, <, \subseteq \rangle$ be an interval structure, and $\varrho: Z \longrightarrow X$ be a function transforming the set of variables of the interval calculus onto the set of variables of extended tense logic. The models $\mathcal{M} = \langle I, <, \subseteq, W \rangle$ and $M = \langle I, <, \subseteq, V \rangle$ are *weakly compatible* if $W(x) \subseteq V(\varrho(x))$ holds for every $x \in Z$, and they are *compatible*, if $W(x) = V(\varrho(x))$ holds for every $x \in Z$. Now, too we can write for compatible models $i = V(\varrho(x))$ instead of $i \in V(\varrho(x))$.

Similarly as in the case of points, also in this situation two translations can be defined—a simpler one and a more complicated one. This time we limit ourselves to the latter. Knowing it, one can easily imagine the simpler one.

DEFINITION
We define a function $\xi: \mathcal{F} \longrightarrow \mathcal{G}$ transforming formulas of the interval calculus onto formulas of extended tense logic in the following way:

$$\xi(x\ b\ y)\ =\ (\varrho(x)\ \rightarrow\ FF\varrho(y))\ \&\ (\varrho(y)\ \rightarrow\ PP\varrho(x))$$

$$\xi(x\ m\ y)\ =\ (\varrho(x)\ \rightarrow\ F\varrho(y)\ \&\ \neg FF\varrho(y))\ \&\ (\varrho(y)\ \rightarrow\ P\varrho(x))\ \&\ \neg PP\varrho(x))$$

$$\xi(x\ o\ y)\ =\ (\varrho(x)\ \rightarrow\ \Diamond F\varrho(y)\ \&\ \neg F\varrho(y))\ \&$$
$$(\varrho(y)\ \rightarrow\ \Diamond P\varrho(x))\ \&\ \neg P\varrho(x))$$

$$\xi(x\ fi\ y)\ =\ (\varrho(x)\ \rightarrow\ \Diamond F\varrho(y)\ \&\ \neg\Diamond P\varrho(y))\ \&\ (\varrho(y)\ \rightarrow\ \neg\Diamond P\varrho(x))$$

$$\xi(x\ di\ y)\ =\ \varrho(x)\ \rightarrow\ \Diamond F\varrho(y)\ \&\ \Diamond P\varrho(y)\ \&\ \neg F\varrho(y)\ \&\ \neg P\varrho(y)$$

$$\xi(x\ s\ y)\ =\ (\varrho(y)\ \rightarrow\ \Diamond P\varrho(x)\ \&\ \neg\Diamond F\varrho(x))\ \&\ (\varrho(x)\ \rightarrow\ \neg\Diamond F\varrho(y))$$

$$\xi(x\ eq\ y)\ =\ \varrho(x)\ \leftrightarrow\ \varrho(y)$$

$$\xi(x\ si\ y)\ =\ (\varrho(x)\ \rightarrow\ \Diamond P\varrho(y)\ \&\ \neg\Diamond F\varrho(y))\ \&\ (\varrho(y)\ \rightarrow\ \neg\Diamond F\varrho(x))$$

$$\xi(x\ d\ y)\ =\ \varrho(y)\ \rightarrow\ \Diamond F\varrho(x)\ \&\ \Diamond P\varrho(x)\ \&\ \neg F\varrho(x)\ \&\ \neg P\varrho(x)$$

$$\xi(x\ f\ y)\ =\ (\varrho(y)\ \rightarrow\ \Diamond F\varrho(x)\ \&\ \neg\Diamond P\varrho(x))\ \&\ (\varrho(x)\ \rightarrow\ \neg\Diamond P\varrho(y))$$

$$\xi(x\ oi\ y)\ =\ (\varrho(x)\ \rightarrow\ \Diamond P\varrho(y)\ \&\ \neg P\varrho(y))\ \&$$
$$(\varrho(y)\ \rightarrow\ \Diamond F\varrho(x))\ \&\ \neg F\varrho(x))$$

$$\xi(x\ mi\ y)\ =\ (\varrho(x)\ \rightarrow\ P\varrho(y)\ \&\ \neg PP\varrho(y))\ \&\ (\varrho(y)\ \rightarrow\ F\varrho(x))\ \&\ \neg FF\varrho(x))$$

$$\xi(x\ bi\ y)\ =\ (\varrho(x)\ \rightarrow\ PP\varrho(y))\ \&\ (\varrho(y)\ \rightarrow\ FF\varrho(x))$$

$$\xi(x\ \alpha\ y)\ =\ \xi(x\ r_1\ y)\ \vee\ ...\ \vee\ \xi(x\ r_n\ y),\quad\text{where }\alpha=\{\,r_1,\ ...,\ r_n\,\}$$

$$\xi(x\ \emptyset\ y)\ =\ p\ \&\ \neg p$$

where, as before, p is an arbitrary, fixed element of X.

Note, that the above translation depends much more on the implicit assumption that in the model M valuations are singletons than it was in the case of points. Some translations, e.g. $\xi(x\ m\ y)$, impose additional constraints on models. Similarly as in the case of points, such constraints can be introduced by means of auxiliary axioms, similar to the ones used before:

$$Pp\ \vee\ \Diamond\varoplus p\ \vee\ Fp$$
$$p\ \rightarrow\ H\boxtimes\neg p\ \&\ G\boxtimes\neg p$$

Unfortunately, the latter axiom has much less expressive power than it was in the case of points. Namely, we are not able to forbid occurrence of a propositional variable p in subintervals of a certain interval because of the reflexivity of the relation $\subseteq$. Nevertheless we have managed to exclude p from superintervals of an interval. Note, that the use of additional operators $\boxtimes$ and $\varoplus$ is indispensable.

In the case of points, the translations themselves did not contain constraints on multiple occurrences of some $\varrho(x)$ in a model—such constraints were needed only to obtain Allen-like reasoning, while the translations themselves could be used for an analysis of multiple dependencies, which are suitable for describing occurrences of events or facts. Unfortunately, we have not managed to find such "universal" translations for intervals.

For models of extended tense logic compatible with models of the interval calculus the translation presented above is correct, i.e. the following theorem holds:

Theorem 6.4.1. For any compatible models $\mathcal{M} = \langle I, <, \subseteq, W \rangle$ and $\mathsf{M} = \langle I, <, \subseteq, V \rangle$ and for every formula $f \in \mathcal{F}$ we have $\mathcal{M} \models f$ iff $\mathsf{M} \models f$.

Proof

- $f = x \; b \; y$

$$
\begin{array}{lll}
\mathcal{M} \models f & \text{iff} & \exists i \; (W(x) < i \; \& \; i < W(y)), \\
\mathsf{M} \models \xi(f)[i] & \text{iff} & (\varrho(x) \rightarrow \mathrm{FF}\varrho(y)) \; \& \; (\varrho(y) \rightarrow \mathrm{PP}\varrho(x)) \\
& \text{iff} & \text{if } \mathsf{M} \models \varrho(x)[i], \text{ then there exists } i_1 \text{ such that } i < i_1 \\
& & \text{and there exists } i_2 \text{ such that } i_1 < i_2 \text{ and } \mathsf{M} \models \varrho(y)[i_2] \\
& & \text{and if } \mathsf{M} \models \varrho(y)[i], \text{ then there exists } j_1 \text{ such that } j_1 < i \\
& & \text{and there exists } j_2 \text{ such that } j_2 < j_1 \text{ and } \mathsf{M} \models \varrho(x)[j_2].
\end{array}
$$

If $i = V(\varrho(x))$, then $\mathsf{M} \models \varrho(x)[i]$, and then there exist i_1, i_2 such that $i < i_1$ and $i_1 < i_2$ and $\mathsf{M} \models \varrho(y)[i_2]$, so $i_2 = V(\varrho(y))$. Thus $\mathsf{M} \models \varrho(x) \rightarrow \mathrm{FF}\varrho(y)[i]$. Otherwise, if $i \neq V(\varrho(x))$, then $\mathsf{M} \not\models \varrho(x)[i]$, and then also $\mathsf{M} \models \varrho(x) \rightarrow \mathrm{FF}\varrho(y)[i]$.

If $i = V(\varrho(y))$, then $\mathsf{M} \models \varrho(y)[i]$, so there exist j_1, j_2 such that $j_1 < i$ and $j_2 < j_1$ and $\mathsf{M} \models \varrho(x)[j_2]$, hence $j_2 = V(\varrho(x))$. Thus $\mathsf{M} \models \varrho(y) \rightarrow \mathrm{PP}\varrho(x)[i]$. Otherwise, if $i \neq V(\varrho(y))$, then $\mathsf{M} \not\models \varrho(y)[i]$, and then also $\mathsf{M} \models \varrho(y) \rightarrow \mathrm{PP}\varrho(x)[i]$.

Thus $\mathsf{M} \models \xi(f)[i]$ iff there exists i such that $V(\varrho(x)) < i$ and $i < V(\varrho(y))$. But $V(\varrho(x)) = W(x)$ and $V(\varrho(y)) = W(y)$. Therefore $\mathcal{M} \models x \; b \; y$ iff $\mathsf{M} \models \xi(x \; b \; y)$.

- $f = x \; m \; y$

$$
\begin{array}{lll}
\mathcal{M} \models f & \text{iff} & W(x) < W(y) \; \& \; \forall i \; \neg(W(x) < i \; \& \; i < W(y)), \\
\mathsf{M} \models \xi(f)[i] & \text{iff} & (\varrho(x) \rightarrow \mathrm{F}\varrho(y) \; \& \; \neg\mathrm{FF}\varrho(y)) \; \& \\
& & (\varrho(y) \rightarrow \mathrm{P}\varrho(x)) \; \& \; \neg\mathrm{PP}\varrho(x)) \\
& \text{iff} & \text{if } \mathsf{M} \models \varrho(x)[i], \text{ then there exists } j \text{ such that } i < j \text{ and} \\
& & \mathsf{M} \models \varrho(y)[j] \text{ and for every } i_1 \text{ such that } i < i_1 \text{ and} \\
& & \text{every } i_2 \text{ such that } i_1 < i_2, \; \mathsf{M} \not\models \varrho(y)[i_2] \qquad \text{and} \\
& & \text{if } \mathsf{M} \models \varrho(y)[i], \text{ then there exists } j \text{ such that } j < i \text{ and} \\
& & \mathsf{M} \models \varrho(y)[j] \text{ and for every } j_1 \text{ such that } j_1 < j \text{ and} \\
& & \text{every } j_2 \text{ such that } j_2 < j_1 \; \mathsf{M} \not\models \varrho(x)[j_2].
\end{array}
$$

If $i = V(\varrho(x))$, then $M \models \varrho(x)[i]$, and then there exists j such that $i < j$ and $M \models \varrho(y)[j]$, so $i = V(\varrho(x))$. On the other hand, for every i_1, i_2 such that $i < i_1$ and $i_1 < i_2$ we have $M \not\models \varrho(x)[i]$, so $i_2 \neq V(\varrho(x))$. This means that for every i_1 such that $V(\varrho(x)) < i_1$ we have $\neg(i_1 < V(\varrho(y)))$.

Otherwise, if $i \neq V(\varrho(x))$, then $M \not\models \varrho(x)[i]$, hence $M \models (\varrho(x) \rightarrow F\varrho(y) \& \neg FF\varrho(y))[i]$.

For $i = V(\varrho(y))$ and $i \neq V(\varrho(y))$ the reasoning is analogous—due to the symmetry w.r.t. the time arrow.

Therefore we have $M \models \xi(f)[i]$ iff $V(\varrho(x)) < V(\varrho(y))$ and for every i_1, if $V(\varrho(x)) < i_1$, then $\neg(i_1 < V(\varrho(x)))$ and for every i_2, if $i_2 < V(\varrho(y))$, then $\neg(V(\varrho(x)) < i_2)$. But $V(\varrho(x)) = W(x)$ and $V(\varrho(y)) = W(y)$. Thus $\mathcal{M} \models x \, m \, y$ iff $M \models \xi(x \, m \, y)$.

- $f = x \, o \, y$

$$
\begin{aligned}
\mathcal{M} \models f \quad &\text{iff} \quad \exists i \, (i \subseteq W(x) \& i < W(y)) \ \& \\
&\qquad \exists i \, (i \subseteq W(x) \& i \subseteq W(y)) \ \& \\
&\qquad \exists i \, (W(x) < i \& i \subseteq W(y)), \\
M \models \xi(f)[i] \quad &\text{iff} \quad (\varrho(x) \rightarrow \Diamond F\varrho(y) \& \neg F\varrho(y)) \ \& \\
&\qquad (\varrho(y) \rightarrow \Diamond P\varrho(x)) \& \neg P\varrho(x)) \\
&\text{iff} \quad \text{if } M \models \varrho(x)[i], \text{ then there exists } i_1 \text{ such that } i_1 \subseteq i \text{ and} \\
&\qquad \text{there exists } j \text{ such that } i_1 < j \text{ and } M \models \varrho(y)[j] \text{ and for} \\
&\qquad \text{every } k \text{ such that } i < k \text{ we have } M \not\models \varrho(y)[k] \quad \text{and} \\
&\qquad \text{if } M \models \varrho(y)[i], \text{ then there exists } j_1 \text{ such that } j_1 \subseteq i \text{ and} \\
&\qquad \text{there exists } j \text{ such that } j < j_1 \text{ and } M \models \varrho(x)[j] \text{ and} \\
&\qquad \text{for every } k \text{ such that } k < i \text{ we have } M \not\models \varrho(x)[k].
\end{aligned}
$$

If $i = V(\varrho(x))$, then $M \models \varrho(x)[i]$, and then there exists i_1 such that $i_1 \subseteq i$ and there exists j such that $i_1 < j$ and $M \models \varrho(y)[j]$, so $j = V(\varrho(y))$. Moreover, $M \not\models F\varrho(y)[i]$, i.e. for every k such that $i < k$ we have $M \not\models \varrho(y)[k]$, so $k \neq V(\varrho(y))$. Suppose that $M \models P\varrho(y)[i]$. Then by *MON* we have $M \models \Box P\varrho(y)[i]$, hence $M \models P\varrho(y)[i_1]$. This is a contradiction with $i_1 < j = V(\varrho(y))$. Therefore $M \models \Diamond \Diamond \varrho(y)[i]$, i.e. there exists k_1 such that $k_1 \subseteq i$ and there exists k_2 such that $k_1 \subseteq k_2$ and $M \models \varrho(y)[k_2]$. Thus eventually we can say that $i_1 \subseteq V(\varrho(x)) \& i_1 < V(\varrho(y))$ and $k_1 \subseteq V(\varrho(x)) \& k_1 \subseteq V(\varrho(y))$. On the other hand, compatibility of the models guarantees that since $\exists i' \, (i' \subseteq W(x) \& i' \subseteq W(y))$, also $M \not\models F\varrho(y)[i]$.

Otherwise, if $i \neq V(\varrho(x))$, then $M \not\models \varrho(x)[i]$, hence $M \models (\varrho(x) \rightarrow \Diamond F\varrho(y) \& \neg F\varrho(y))[i]$.

If $i = V(\varrho(y))$, then $M \models \varrho(y)[i]$, and then there exists j_1 such that $j_1 \subseteq i$ and there exists j such that $j < j_1$ and $M \models \varrho(x)[j]$, so $j = V(\varrho(x))$. This means that there exists j_1 such that $V(\varrho(x)) < j_1 \& j_1 \subseteq V(\varrho(y))$.

On the other hand, compatibility of the models guarantees that since $\exists i'\ (i' \subseteq W(x)\ \&\ i' \subseteq W(y))$, then $M \not\models P\varrho(x)[i]$.

Otherwise, if $i \neq V(\varrho(y))$, then $M \not\models \varrho(y)[i]$, hence $M \models (\varrho(y) \rightarrow \Diamond F\varrho(x)\ \&\ \neg F\varrho(x))[i]$.

But $V(\varrho(x)) = W(x)$ and $V(\varrho(y)) = W(y)$. Therefore $\mathcal{M} \models x\ o\ y$ iff $M \models \xi(x\ o\ y)$.

- $f = x\ fi\ y$

$$\mathcal{M} \models f \quad \text{iff} \quad \exists i\ (i \subseteq W(x)\ \&\ i < W(y))\ \&$$
$$\forall i\ (W(x) < i\ \leftrightarrow\ W(y) < i),$$

$M \models \xi(f)[i]$ iff $(\varrho(x) \rightarrow \Diamond F\varrho(y)\ \&\ \neg\Diamond P\varrho(y))\ \&\ (\varrho(y) \rightarrow \neg\Diamond P\varrho(x))$

iff if $M \models \varrho(x)[i]$, then there exists i_1 such that $i_1 \subseteq i$ and there exists j such that $i_1 < j$ and $M \models \varrho(y)[j]$ and for every i_2 such that $i_2 \subseteq i$ and every i_3 such that $i_3 < i_2$ we have $M \not\models \varrho(x)[i_3]$ and   if $M \models \varrho(y)[i]$, then for every j_2 such that $j_2 \subseteq i$ and every j_3 such that $j_3 < j_2$ we have $M \not\models \varrho(x)[j_3]$.

If $i = V(\varrho(x))$, then $M \models \varrho(x)[i]$ and then there exists i_1 such that $i_1 \subseteq i$ and there exists j such that $i_1 < j$ and $M \models \varrho(y)[j]$, so $j = V(\varrho(y))$. This means that $\exists i_1\ (i_1 \subseteq V(\varrho(x))\ \&\ i_1 < V(\varrho(y)))$.

Consider any k such that $V(\varrho(x)) = i < k$. Suppose that $M \models F\varrho(y)[k]$. This means that there exists i_2 such that $k < i_2$ and $M \models \varrho(y)[i_2]$. Then $M \models PP\varrho(x)[i_2]$, and by P_TRANS we have $M \models P\varrho(x)[i_2]$. This means that $M \models (\varrho(y) \rightarrow P\varrho(x))[i_2]$. We obtain contradiction with the assumption that $\varrho(y) \rightarrow \neg\Diamond P\varrho(x)$. Suppose that $M \models \Diamond\Phi\varrho(y)[k]$. This means that there exist j_1, j_2 such that $j_1 \subseteq k$ and $j_1 \subseteq j_2$ and $M \models \varrho(y)[j_2]$. On the other hand, $M \models P\varrho(x)[k]$, so by MON $M \models \Box P\varrho(x)[k]$, hence $M \models P\varrho(x)[j_1]$. But $M \models \neg\Diamond P\varrho(x)[j_2]$, so $M \models \neg P\varrho(x)[j_1]$. Contradiction. Therefore $M \models G\neg\varrho(x)[k]$ and $M \models \Box\boxtimes\varrho(x)[k]$. Thus $V(\varrho(y)) = j < k$.

Consider any k such that $V(\varrho(y)) = j < k$. An analogous reasoning using $\varrho(x) \rightarrow \neg\Diamond P\varrho(y)$ leads to the conclusion that $V(\varrho(x)) = i < k$. This means that $\forall i\ (V(\varrho(x)) < i\ \leftrightarrow\ V(\varrho(y)) < i)$. But $V(\varrho(x)) = W(x)$ and $V(\varrho(y)) = W(y)$, and this implies $\mathcal{M} \models x\ fi\ y$.

If $i = W(x) = V(\varrho(x))$, then $\exists i'\ (i' \subseteq W(x)\ \&\ i' < W(y))$. This means that $M \models \varrho(x)[i]$ and $M \models \Diamond F\varrho(y)[i]$. Consider any i_1, i_2 such that $i_1 \subseteq i$ and $i_2 < i_1$. Suppose that $M \models \varrho(y)[i_2]$. Because of compatibility of models this means that $i_2 = V(\varrho(y)) = W(y)$. Therefore $W(y) < i_1$, hence $W(x) < i_1$, so $i < i_1$. We obtain contradiction with the fact that $i_1 \subseteq i$. Thus $M \models \neg\Diamond P\varrho(y)[i]$, hence $M \models (\varrho(x) \rightarrow \Diamond F\varrho(y)\ \&\ \neg\Diamond P\varrho(y))$.

Otherwise, if $i \neq W(x) \neq V(\varrho(x))$, then $\mathsf{M} \not\models \varrho(x)[i]$, hence $\mathsf{M} \models (\varrho(x) \rightarrow \Diamond \mathsf{F}\varrho(y) \,\&\, \neg\Diamond \mathsf{P}\varrho(y))[i]$.

If $i = W(y) = V(\varrho(y))$, then $\mathsf{M} \models \varrho(y)[i]$. Consider any i_1, i_2 such that $i_1 \subseteq i$ and $i_2 < i_1$. Suppose that $\mathsf{M} \models \varrho(x)[i_2]$. Because of compatibility of models this means that $i_2 = V(\varrho(x)) = W(x)$. Therefore $W(x) < i_1$, hence $W(y) < i_1$, so $i < i_1$. Contradiction with the fact that $i_1 \subseteq i$. Thus $\mathsf{M} \models \neg\Diamond \mathsf{P}\varrho(x)[i]$, hence $\mathsf{M} \models (\varrho(y) \rightarrow \neg\Diamond \mathsf{P}\varrho(x))$. Otherwise, if $i \neq W(y) \neq V(\varrho(y))$, then $\mathsf{M} \not\models \varrho(y)[i]$, hence $\mathsf{M} \models (\varrho(y) \rightarrow \neg\Diamond \mathsf{P}\varrho(x))[i]$. Thus eventually $\mathcal{M} \models x$ fi y iff $\mathsf{M} \models \xi(x$ fi $y)$.

- $f = x$ di y

$$\mathcal{M} \models f \qquad \text{iff} \quad \exists i \,(i \subseteq W(x) \,\&\, i < W(y)) \,\&\,$$
$$\exists i \,(i \subseteq W(x) \,\&\, W(y) < i),$$

$\mathsf{M} \models \xi(f)[i]$ iff $\varrho(x) \rightarrow \Diamond \mathsf{F}\varrho(y) \,\&\, \Diamond \mathsf{P}\varrho(y) \,\&\, \neg \mathsf{F}\varrho(y) \,\&\, \neg \mathsf{P}\varrho(y)$

          iff   if $\mathsf{M} \models \varrho(x)[i]$, then there exists i_1 such that $i_1 \subseteq i$ and there exists j_1 such that $i_1 < j_1$ and $\mathsf{M} \models \varrho(y)[j_1]$ and there exists i_2 such that $i_2 \subseteq i$ and there exists j_2 such that $i_2 < j_2$ and $\mathsf{M} \models \varrho(y)[j_2]$ and for every k such that $k < i$, $\mathsf{M} \not\models \varrho(y)[k]$ and for every k such that $i < k$ we have $\mathsf{M} \not\models \varrho(y)[k]$.

If $i = V(\varrho(x))$, then $\mathsf{M} \models \varrho(x)[i]$, and then there exists i_1 such that $i_1 \subseteq i$ and there exists j_1 such that $i_1 < j_1$ and $\mathsf{M} \models \varrho(y)[j_1]$, so $j_1 = V(\varrho(y))$. On the other hand, there exists i_2 such that $i_2 \subseteq i$ and there exists j_2 such that $j_2 < i_2$ and $\mathsf{M} \models \varrho(y)[j_2]$, so $j_2 = V(\varrho(y))$. Therefore we have $\exists i_1 \,(i_1 \subseteq V(\varrho(x)) \,\&\, i_1 < V(\varrho(y)))$ and $\exists i_2 \,(i_2 \subseteq V(\varrho(x)) \,\&\, V(\varrho(y)) < i_2))$. Moreover, compatibility of models guarantees that $\exists i' \,(i' \subseteq W(x) \,\&\, i' \subseteq W(y))$ entails $\mathsf{M} \not\models \mathsf{F}\varrho(y)[i]$ and $\mathsf{M} \not\models \mathsf{P}\varrho(y)[i]$.

Otherwise, if $i \neq V(\varrho(x))$, then $\mathsf{M} \not\models \varrho(x)[i]$, hence $\mathsf{M} \models \varrho(x) \rightarrow \Diamond \mathsf{F}\varrho(y) \,\&\, \Diamond \mathsf{P}\varrho(y) \,\&\, \neg \mathsf{F}\varrho(y) \,\&\, \neg \mathsf{P}\varrho(y)$.

But $V(\varrho(x)) = W(x)$ and $V(\varrho(y)) = W(y)$. Thus $\mathcal{M} \models x$ di y iff $\mathsf{M} \models \xi(x$ di $y)$.

- $f = x$ s y

$$\mathcal{M} \models f \qquad \text{iff} \quad \exists i \,(W(x) < i \,\&\, i \subseteq W(y)) \,\&\,$$
$$\forall i \,(i < W(x) < i \,\leftrightarrow\, i < W(y)),$$

$\mathsf{M} \models \xi(f)[i]$ iff $(\varrho(y) \rightarrow \Diamond \mathsf{P}\varrho(x) \,\&\, \neg\Diamond \mathsf{F}\varrho(x)) \,\&\, (\varrho(x) \rightarrow \neg\Diamond \mathsf{F}\varrho(y))$

          iff   if $\mathsf{M} \models \varrho(y)[i]$, then there exists i_1 such that $i_1 \subseteq i$ and there exists j such that $j < i_1$ and $\mathsf{M} \models \varrho(x)[j]$ and for every i_2 such that $i_2 \subseteq i$ and every i_3 such that $i_2 < i_3$ we have $M \not\models \varrho(y)[i_3]$ and   if $M \models \varrho(x)[i]$, then for every j_2 such that $j_2 \subseteq i$ and every j_3 such that $j_2 < j_3$ we have $M \not\models \varrho(y)[j_3]$.

The reasoning is analogous as for $f = x$ fi y—we must replace x by y and *vice versa* and make use of symmetry w.r.t. the time arrow.

- $f = x$ eq y

$$\mathcal{M} \models f \qquad \text{iff} \quad W(x) = W(y),$$
$$M \models \xi(f)[i] \quad \text{iff} \quad M \models (\varrho(x) \leftrightarrow \varrho(y))[i]$$
$$\text{iff} \quad \text{if } M \models \varrho(x)[i], \text{ then } M \models \varrho(y)[i] \text{ and}$$
$$\text{if } M \models \varrho(y)[i], \text{ then } M \models \varrho(x)[i].$$

If $i = V(\varrho(x))$, then $M \models \varrho(x)[i]$, hence $M \models \varrho(y)[i]$, so $i = V(\varrho(y))$. Otherwise, if $t \neq V(\varrho(i))$, then $M \not\models \varrho(x)[i]$, hence $M \models (\varrho(x) \rightarrow \varrho(y))[i]$. Analogously if $i = V(\varrho(y))$, then $M \models \varrho(y)[i]$, hence $M \models \varrho(x)[i]$, so $i = V(\varrho(x))$. Conversely, if $i \neq V(\varrho(y))$, then $M \not\models \varrho(y)[i]$, hence we have $M \models (\varrho(y) \rightarrow \varrho(x))[i]$.
Therefore $M \models \xi(f)[i]$ holds for $V(\varrho(x)) = V(\varrho(y))$. But $V(\varrho(x)) = W(x)$ and $V(\varrho(y)) = W(y)$. Eventually $\mathcal{M} \models x$ eq y iff $M \models \xi(x$ eq $y)$.

- $f = x$ si y
The reasoning is analogous as for $f = x$ fi y—due to the symmetry w.r.t. the time arrow.

- $f = x$ d y
The reasoning is analogous as for $f = x$ di y—we must replace x by y and *vice versa*.

- $f = x$ f y
The reasoning is analogous as for $f = x$ fi y—we must replace x by y and *vice versa*.

- $f = x$ oi y
The reasoning is analogous as for $f = x$ o y—we must replace x by y and *vice versa*.

- $f = x$ mi y
The reasoning is analogous as for $f = x$ m y—we must replace x by y and *vice versa*.

- $f = x$ bi y
The reasoning is analogous as for $f = x$ b y—we must replace x by y and *vice versa*.

- $f = x \{r_1, ..., r_n\} y$

  $\mathcal{M} \models f$ iff $\mathcal{M} \models x \, r_1 \, y$ or ... or $\mathcal{M} \models x \, r_n \, y$,

  $\mathsf{M} \models \xi(f)[t]$ iff $\mathsf{M} \models (\xi(x \, r_1 \, y \lor ... \lor x \, r_n \, y)[i]$

              iff $\mathsf{M} \models \xi(x \, r_1 \, y)[i]$ or ... or $\mathsf{M} \models \xi(x \, r_n \, y)[i]$.

  Evidently, $\mathcal{M} \models x \, r_i \, y$ iff $\mathsf{M} \models \xi(x \, r_i \, y)[i]$. Therefore $\mathcal{M} \models f$ iff $\mathsf{M} \models \xi(f)$.
- For any models $\mathcal{M} = \langle I, <, \subseteq, W \rangle$ and $\mathsf{M} = \langle I, <, \subseteq, V \rangle$ and every $x, y \in Z$, $p \in X$ we have $\mathcal{M} \not\models x \, \emptyset \, y$ and $\mathsf{M} \not\models p \,\&\, \neg p$. Therefore also for $f = x \, \emptyset \, y$ we have $\mathcal{M} \models f$ iff $\mathsf{M} \models \xi(f)$.

Thus we have shown that for every $f \in \mathcal{F}$ we have $\mathcal{M} \models f$ iff $\mathsf{M} \models \xi(f)$. ∎

In this proof we make very strong use of the compatibility of models, and actually rather of its consequence—the fact that the valuation V has single-element values. This puts into doubt the validity of the counterpart of the above theorem for weakly compatible models (where V need not have single-element values, which theorem is in the case of points a consequence of the theorem for compatible models. Nevertheless such a theorem is valid, since the fact that a valuation yields singletons was used when axioms concerning the whole structure (e.g. *MON*) where applied, and such axioms must also hold when there are no other occurrences of a given propositional variable. In a proof of this theorem we would have to use first order axioms (from section 2) applied directly to intervals. On the other hand, exactly for this reason, the translation $\xi(x \text{ fi } y) = (\varrho(x) \rightarrow \Diamond F \varrho(y) \,\&\, \neg F \varrho(y)) \,\&\, (P \varrho(x) \leftrightarrow P \varrho(y))$ (and the ones similar to it, concerning primitive relations s, si, f) that were introduced in [Hajnicz, 1989b; 1991a], have been substituted by considerably less natural translations presented in this book. In fig. 6.2 two different models are presented, in which the above formula is satisfied, even though there is no dependency of finishing one interval by another.

a)   b)

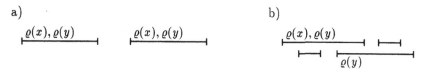

Fig. 6.2. Models, in which the "old" translation for x fi y is not satisfied

<u>Corollary</u> For any weakly compatible models $\mathcal{M} = \langle I, <, \subseteq, W \rangle$ and $\mathsf{M} = \langle I, <, \subseteq, V \rangle$, and for every formula $f \in \mathcal{F}$ if $\mathcal{M} \models f$, then $\mathsf{M} \models \xi(f)$.

Now we could to attempt to perform an analysis of the adequacy of the above translation by examining whether the corresponding inference mechanism is preserved, as it has been done for points. However, because of a much greater degree of complexity of this case (the necessity of considering 125 inference rules after omitting the "trivial" relation *equals*), we shall not enter into such an analysis.

6.5 Translation of the interval calculus for linear time into Halpern & Shoham's logic

In the previous section we have presented a translation of the interval calculus (for linear time) into extended tense logic. This translation is much less "natural" than it has been in the case of points—we have to forbid occurrence of propositional variables in certain intervals. It seems that Halpern & Shoham's logic is much closer to the interval calculus and that in this case a more "natural" translation could be obtained.

Unfortunately, there is a very serious obstacle to this task, namely the semantics of the interval calculus is based on the classic theory of interval time, whereas we have at our disposal two semantics of Halpern & Shoham's logic: one of them is based on interval-point structure, and the second is based on Allen & Hayes's (or Venema's) theory of interval structure. Thus we would need two translations to compare the logics: first, to translate the interval calculus into Halpern & Shoham's logic, and next, to translate a semantic description of an interval calculus formula into the corresponding theory.

However, we should remember that Allen & Hayes have formalized the interval relation constraint propagation algorithm by means of their theory. As a matter of fact, their formalization cannot be used directly to achieve our goal (as we do not want to translate their first order theory), but one can imagine a formalization of the algorithm with semantics based on Allen & Hayes's theory exactly in the same way, as primitive relations between intervals have been defined in this theory. And this makes a translation of a calculus defined in such a way into Halpern & Shoham's logic (with corresponding semantics) possible.

Hence recall that we have a linear interval structure $\mathfrak{J} = \langle J, \| \rangle$. Moreover, we consider an interval calculus with a set of propositional variables Z, a set of formulas $\mathcal{F}$ and a model $\mathcal{M} = \langle J, \|, W \rangle$, and Halpern & Shoham's logic with a set of propositional variables X, a set of formulas $\mathcal{H}$ and a model $\mathfrak{M} = \langle J, \|, U \rangle$.

As in all the previous cases, we can consider *compatible* and *weakly compatible* models.

DEFINITION
Let $\mathfrak{J} = \langle J, \| \rangle$ be an interval structure, and $\varrho : Z \longrightarrow Y$ be a function transforming the set of variables of the interval calculus onto the set of variables of Halpern & Shoham's logic. The models $\mathcal{M} = \langle I, \|, W \rangle$ and $\mathfrak{M} = \langle J, \|, U \rangle$ are *weakly compatible* if $W(x) \subseteq U(\varrho(x))$ holds for every $x \in Z$, and they are *compatible*, if $W(x) = U(\varrho(x))$ holds for every $x \in Z$. Now, too we can write for compatible models $i = U(\varrho(x))$ instead of $i \in U(\varrho(x))$.

As always before, also now two translations can be defined—a simpler one and a more complicated one. This time we again restrict ourselves to the latter. Knowing, it one can easily imagine the simpler one.

DEFINITION

We define a function $\xi: \mathcal{F} \longrightarrow \mathcal{H}$ transforming formulas of the interval calculus onto formulas of Halpern & Shoham's logic in the following way:

$$\xi(x \ b \ y) \ = \ (\varrho(x) \ \rightarrow \ \langle A \rangle \langle A \rangle \varrho(y)) \ \& \ (\varrho(y) \ \rightarrow \ \langle \bar{A} \rangle \langle \bar{A} \rangle \varrho(x))$$

$$\xi(x \ m \ y) \ = \ (\varrho(x) \ \rightarrow \ \langle A \rangle \varrho(y)) \ \& \ (\varrho(y) \ \rightarrow \ \langle \bar{A} \rangle \varrho(x))$$

$$\xi(x \ o \ y) \ = \ (\varrho(x) \ \rightarrow \ \langle E \rangle \langle \bar{B} \rangle \varrho(y)) \ \& \ (\varrho(y) \ \rightarrow \ \langle B \rangle \langle \bar{E} \rangle \varrho(x))$$

$$\xi(x \ fi \ y) \ = \ (\varrho(x) \ \rightarrow \ \langle E \rangle \varrho(y)) \ \& \ (\varrho(y) \ \rightarrow \ \langle \bar{E} \rangle \varrho(x))$$

$$\xi(x \ di \ y) \ = \ (\varrho(x) \ \rightarrow \ \langle B \rangle \langle E \rangle \varrho(y)) \ \& \ (\varrho(y) \ \rightarrow \ \langle \bar{B} \rangle \langle \bar{E} \rangle \varrho(x))$$

$$\xi(x \ s \ y) \ = \ (\varrho(x) \ \rightarrow \ \langle \bar{B} \rangle \varrho(y)) \ \& \ (\varrho(y) \ \rightarrow \ \langle B \rangle \varrho(x))$$

$$\xi(x \ eq \ y) \ = \ \varrho(x) \ \leftrightarrow \ \varrho(y)$$

$$\xi(x \ si \ y) \ = \ \xi(y \ s \ x)$$

$$\xi(x \ d \ y) \ = \ \xi(y \ di \ x)$$

$$\xi(x \ f \ y) \ = \ \xi(y \ fi \ x)$$

$$\xi(x \ oi \ y) \ = \ \xi(y \ o \ x)$$

$$\xi(x \ mi \ y) \ = \ \xi(y \ m \ x)$$

$$\xi(x \ bi \ y) \ = \ \xi(y \ b \ x)$$

$$\xi(x \ \alpha \ y) \ = \ \xi(x \ r_1 \ y) \ \vee \ ... \ \vee \ \xi(x \ r_n \ y), \quad \text{where } \alpha = \{ r_1, \ ..., \ r_n \}$$

$$\xi(x \ \emptyset \ y) \ = \ p \ \& \ \neg p$$

where, as before, p is an arbitrary, fixed element of X.

In this case, the translations themselves do not impose any additional constraints on multiple occurrences of some $\varrho(x)$ in a model, as expected. Such constraints can be introduced into the logic by adding auxiliary axioms, similar to those introduced in the previous sections:

$$p \vee \langle B \rangle p \vee \langle \bar{B} \rangle p \vee \langle E \rangle p \vee \langle \bar{E} \rangle p \vee \langle B \rangle \langle E \rangle p \vee \langle \bar{B} \rangle \langle \bar{E} \rangle p \vee \langle \bar{B} \rangle \langle E \rangle p \vee \langle \bar{E} \rangle \langle B \rangle p$$

$$p \ \rightarrow \ ([B] \neg p \ \& \ [\bar{B}] \neg p \ \& \ [E] \neg p \ \& \ [\bar{E}] \neg p \ \& \ [B][E] \neg p \ \& \ [\bar{B}][\bar{E}] \neg p \ \&$$
$$[\bar{B}][E] \neg p \ \& \ [\bar{E}][B] \neg p)$$

For models of Halpern & Shoham's logic compatible with models of the interval calculus the above translation is correct, i.e. the following theorem holds:

Theorem 6.5.1. For compatible models $\mathcal{M} = \langle J, \|, W \rangle$ and $\mathfrak{M} = \langle J, \|, U \rangle$, and for every formula $f \in \mathcal{F}$ we have $\mathcal{M} \models f$ iff $\mathfrak{M} \models f$.
Proof

- $f = x \ b \ y$

    $\mathcal{M} \models f$ iff $\exists k \ (W(x) \ \| \ k \ \& \ k \ \| \ W(y))$,

$\mathfrak{M} \models \xi(f)[i]$ iff $\mathfrak{M} \models (\varrho(x) \rightarrow \langle A \rangle \langle A \rangle \varrho(y))$ &
$\qquad\qquad\qquad\qquad (\varrho(y) \rightarrow \langle \bar{A} \rangle \langle \bar{A} \rangle \varrho(x))[i]$

$\qquad\qquad$ iff   if $\mathfrak{M} \models \varrho(x)[i]$, then there exists i_1 such that $i \parallel i_1$
$\qquad\qquad\qquad$ and there exists i_2 such that $i_1 \parallel i_2$ and $M \models \varrho(y)[i_2]$
$\qquad\qquad\qquad$ and if $\mathfrak{M} \models \varrho(y)[i]$, then there exists j_1 such that
$\qquad\qquad\qquad$ $j_1 \parallel i$ and there exists j_2 such that $j_2 \parallel j_1$
$\qquad\qquad\qquad$ and $M \models \varrho(x)[j_2]$.

If $i = U(\varrho(x))$, then $\mathfrak{M} \models \varrho(x)[i]$, and then there exist i_1, i_2 such that
$i \parallel i_1$ and $i_1 \parallel i_2$ and $\mathfrak{M} \models \varrho(y)[i_2]$, so $i_2 = U(\varrho(y))$. If $i = U(\varrho(y))$,
then $\mathfrak{M} \models \varrho(y)[i]$, and then there exist j_1, j_2 such that $j_1 \parallel i$ and $j_2 \parallel j_1$
and $\mathfrak{M} \models \varrho(x)[j_2]$, hence $j_2 = U(\varrho(x))$. Thus there exists k such that
$U(\varrho(x)) \parallel k$ & $k \parallel U(\varrho(y))$.

On the other hand, if there exists k such that $U(\varrho(x)) \parallel k$ & $k \parallel U(\varrho(x))$,
then evidently $\mathfrak{M} \models (\varrho(x) \rightarrow \langle A \rangle \langle A \rangle \varrho(y))$ & $(\varrho(y) \rightarrow \langle \bar{A} \rangle \langle \bar{A} \rangle \varrho(x))[i]$.
But $U(\varrho(x)) = W(x)$ and $U(\varrho(y)) = W(y)$. Therefore $\mathcal{M} \models x \; b \; y$ iff
$\mathfrak{M} \models \xi(x \; b \; y)[i]$.

- $f = x \; m \; y$

$\mathcal{M} \models f$ iff $W(x) \parallel W(y)$,
$\mathfrak{M} \models \xi(f)[i]$ iff $\mathfrak{M} \models (\varrho(x) \rightarrow \langle A \rangle \varrho(y))$ & $(\varrho(y) \rightarrow \langle \bar{A} \rangle \varrho(x))[i]$
$\qquad\qquad$ iff   if $\mathfrak{M} \models \varrho(x)[i]$, then there exists j such that $i \parallel j$
$\qquad\qquad\qquad$ and $\mathfrak{M} \models \varrho(y)[j]$ and
$\qquad\qquad\qquad$ if $\mathfrak{M} \models \varrho(y)[i]$, then there exists j such that $j \parallel i$
$\qquad\qquad\qquad$ and $\mathfrak{M} \models \varrho(x)[j]$.

If $i = U(\varrho(x))$, then $\mathfrak{M} \models \varrho(x)[i]$, and then there exists j such that $i \parallel j$
and $\mathfrak{M} \models \varrho(y)[j]$, hence $j = U(\varrho(y))$. If $i = U(\varrho(y))$, then $\mathfrak{M} \models \varrho(y)[i]$, so
there exists j such that $j \parallel i$ and $\mathfrak{M} \models \varrho(x)[j]$, so $j = U(\varrho(x))$. Therefore
$U(\varrho(x)) \parallel U(\varrho(y))$.

Conversely, if $U(\varrho(x)) \parallel U(\varrho(y))$, then evidently we have $\mathfrak{M} \models (\varrho(x) \rightarrow$
$\langle A \rangle \varrho(y))$ & $(\varrho(y) \rightarrow \langle \bar{A} \rangle \varrho(x))[i]$. But $U(\varrho(x)) = W(x)$ and $U(\varrho(y)) =$
$W(y)$. Thus $\mathcal{M} \models x \; m \; y$ iff $\mathfrak{M} \models \xi(x \; m \; y)[i]$.

- $f = x \; o \; y$

$\mathcal{M} \models f$ iff $\exists p, q, k, l, m \; ((p \parallel W(x) \; \& \; W(x) \parallel l \; \& \; l \parallel m) \;$ &
$\qquad\qquad\qquad\qquad (p \parallel q \; \& \; q \parallel W(y) \; \& \; W(y) \parallel m) \;$ &
$\qquad\qquad\qquad\qquad (q \parallel k \; \& \; k \parallel l)),$
$\mathfrak{M} \models \xi(f)[i]$ iff $\mathfrak{M} \models (\varrho(x) \rightarrow \langle E \rangle \langle \bar{B} \rangle \varrho(y))$ &
$\qquad\qquad\qquad\qquad (\varrho(y) \rightarrow \langle B \rangle \langle \bar{E} \rangle \varrho(x))[i]$

iff   if $\mathfrak{M} \models \varrho(x)[i]$, then for some j there
exist k, l, m such that $(k \parallel i \ \& \ i \parallel m) \ \& \ (k \parallel l \ \&$
$l \parallel j \ \& \ j \parallel m)$ and for some j_1 there
exist k_1, l_1, m_1 such that $(k_1 \parallel j \ \& \ j \parallel l_1 \ \& \ l_1 \parallel m_1) \ \&$
$(k_1 \parallel j_1 \ \& \ j_1 \parallel m_1)$ and $\mathfrak{M} \models \varrho(y)[j_1]$ and
if $\mathfrak{M} \models \varrho(y)[i]$, then for some j there
exist k, l, m such that $(k \parallel i \ \& \ i \parallel m) \ \& \ (k \parallel j \ \&$
$j \parallel l \ \& \ l \parallel m)$ and for some j_1 there exist
k_1, l_1, m_1 such that $(k_1 \parallel l_1 \ \& \ l_1 \parallel j \ \& \ j \parallel m_1) \ \&$
$(k_1 \parallel j_1 \ \& \ j_1 \parallel m_1)$ and $\mathfrak{M} \models \varrho(x)[j_1]$.

If $i = U(\varrho(x))$, then $\mathfrak{M} \models \varrho(x)[i]$, and then for some j there exist k, l, m such that $(k \parallel i \parallel m) \ \& \ (k \parallel ll \parallel j \parallel m)$ and for some j_1 there exist k_1, l_1, m_1 such that $(k_1 \parallel j \parallel l_1 \parallel m_1) \ \& \ (k_1 \parallel j_1 \parallel m_1)$ and $\mathfrak{M} \models \varrho(y)[j_1]$, so $j_1 = U(\varrho(y))$. Since $l \parallel j$ and $k_1 \parallel j$ and $k_1 \parallel j_1$, for every φ such that $\mathfrak{M} \models \varphi[j_1]$ we have $\mathfrak{M} \models \langle A \rangle \langle \bar{A} \rangle \langle A \rangle \varphi[l]$, hence by S14 $\mathfrak{M} \models \langle A \rangle \varphi[l]$, so $l \parallel j_1$. Since $i \parallel m$ and $j \parallel m$ and $j \parallel l_1$, then we can show in an analogous way that $i \parallel l_1$. Therefore $\exists k, l, j, l_1, m_1 \ ((k \parallel U(\varrho(x)) \parallel l_1 \parallel m_1) \ \& \ (k \parallel l \parallel U(\varrho(y)) \parallel m_1) \ \& \ (l \parallel j \parallel l_1))$.

Conversely, if $\exists p, q, k, l, m \ ((p \parallel U(\varrho(x)) \parallel l \parallel m) \ \& \ (p \parallel q \parallel U(\varrho(y)) \parallel m) \ \& \ (q \parallel k \parallel l))$, then there exist k, p, q, l such that $(p \parallel U(\varrho(x)) \parallel l) \ \& \ (p \parallel q \parallel k \parallel l)$ and there exist q, l, m such that $(q \parallel k \parallel l \parallel m) \ \& \ (q \parallel U(\varrho(y)) \parallel m)$, hence $\mathfrak{M} \models \langle \bar{B} \rangle \varrho(y))[k]$ and $\mathfrak{M} \models E \rangle \langle \bar{B} \rangle \varrho(y))[i]$, so $\mathfrak{M} \models (\varrho(x) \rightarrow \langle E \rangle \langle \bar{B} \rangle \varrho(y))$.

If $i = U(\varrho(y))$, then the reasoning proceeds in an analogous way. But we have $U(\varrho(x)) = W(x)$ and $U(\varrho(y)) = W(y)$. Thus $\mathcal{M} \models x \circ y$ iff $\mathfrak{M} \models \xi(x \circ y)[i]$.

- $f = x \text{ fi } y$

$\mathcal{M} \models f$ iff $\exists k, l, m \ ((k \parallel l \ \& \ l \parallel W(y) \ \& \ W(y) \parallel m) \ \&$
$(k \parallel W(x) \ \& \ W(x) \parallel m))$,

$\mathfrak{M} \models \xi(f)[i]$ iff $\mathfrak{M} \models (\varrho(x) \rightarrow \langle E \rangle \varrho(y)) \ \& \ (\varrho(y) \rightarrow \langle \bar{E} \rangle \varrho(x))[i]$
iff   if $\mathfrak{M} \models \varrho(x)[i]$, then for some j there
exist k, l, m such that $(k \parallel l \ \& \ l \parallel j \ \& \ j \parallel m) \ \&$
$(k \parallel i \ \& \ i \parallel m)$ and $\mathfrak{M} \models \varrho(y)[j]$ and
if $\mathfrak{M} \models \varrho(y)[i]$, then for some j there
exist k, l, m such that $(k \parallel j \ \& \ j \parallel m) \ \&$
$(k \parallel l \ \& \ l \parallel i \ \& \ i \parallel m)$ and $\mathrm{M} \models \varrho(x)[j]$.

If $i = U(\varrho(x))$, then $\mathfrak{M} \models \varrho(x)[i]$, and then for some j there exist k, l, m such that $(k \parallel l \parallel i \parallel m)$ & $(k \parallel j \parallel m)$ and $\mathfrak{M} \models \varrho(y)[j]$, so $j = U(\varrho(y))$. This means that there exist k, l, m such that $(k \parallel l \parallel U(\varrho(y)) \parallel m)$ & $(k \parallel U(\varrho(x)) \parallel m)$.

Conversely, if $\exists k, l, m \ ((k \parallel l \parallel U(\varrho(y)) \parallel m)$ & $(k \parallel U(\varrho(x)) \parallel m))$, then evidently $\mathfrak{M} \models (\varrho(x) \rightarrow \langle E \rangle \varrho(y))$.

If $i = U(\varrho(y))$, then the reasoning proceeds in an analogous way. But $U(\varrho(x)) = W(x)$ and $U(\varrho(y)) = W(y)$. Thus eventually $\mathcal{M} \models x \text{ fi } y$ iff $\mathfrak{M} \models \xi(x \text{ fi } y)[i]$.

- $f = x \text{ di } y$

$$\mathcal{M} \models f \qquad \text{iff} \qquad \exists k, l, m, p \ ((k \parallel l \ \& \ l \parallel W(y) \ \& \ W(y) \parallel m \ \& \ m \parallel p) \ \& \ (k \parallel W(x) \ \& \ W(x) \parallel p)),$$

$$\mathfrak{M} \models \xi(f)[i] \qquad \text{iff} \qquad \mathfrak{M} \models (\varrho(x) \rightarrow \langle B \rangle \langle E \rangle \varrho(y)) \ \&$$
$$(\varrho(y) \rightarrow \langle \bar{B} \rangle \langle \bar{E} \rangle \varrho(x))[i]$$

iff   if $\mathfrak{M} \models \varrho(x)[i]$, then for some j there exist k, l, m such that $(k \parallel j \ \& \ j \parallel l \ \& \ l \parallel m)$ & $(k \parallel i \ \& \ i \parallel m)$ and for some j_1 there exist k_1, l_1, m_1 such that $(k_1 \parallel l_1 \ \& \ l_1 \parallel j_1 \ \& \ j_1 \parallel m_1)$ & $(k_1 \parallel j \ \& \ j \parallel m_1)$ and $\mathfrak{M} \models \varrho(y)[j_1]$ and if $\mathfrak{M} \models \varrho(y)[i]$, then for some j there exist k, l, m such that $(k \parallel j \ \& \ j \parallel m)$ & $(k \parallel i \ \& \ i \parallel l \ \& \ l \parallel m)$ and for some j_1 there exist k_1, l_1, m_1 such that $(k_1 \parallel j_1 \ \& \ j_1 \parallel m_1)$ & $(k_1 \parallel l_1 \ \& \ l_1 \parallel j \ \& \ j \parallel m_1)$ and $\mathfrak{M} \models \varrho(x)[j_1]$.

If $i = U(\varrho(x))$, then $\mathfrak{M} \models \varrho(x)[i]$, and then for some j there exist k, l, m such that $(k \parallel j \parallel l \parallel m)$ & $(k \parallel i \parallel m)$ and for some j_1 there exist k_1, l_1, m_1 such that $(k_1 \parallel l_1 \parallel j_1 \parallel m_1)$ & $(k_1 \parallel j \parallel m_1)$ and $\mathfrak{M} \models \varrho(y)[j_1]$, so $j_1 = U(\varrho(y))$. Since $k \parallel j$ and $k_1 \parallel j$ and $k_1 \parallel l_1$, then for every φ such that $\mathfrak{M} \models \varphi[l_1]$ we have $\mathfrak{M} \models \langle A \rangle \langle \bar{A} \rangle \langle A \rangle \varphi[k]$, hence by S14 $\mathfrak{M} \models \langle A \rangle \varphi[k]$, so $k \parallel l_1$. Since $j_1 \parallel m_1$ and $j \parallel m_1$ and $j \parallel l$, then we can prove in an analogous way that $j_1 \parallel l$. Thus $\exists k, l_1, l, m \ ((k \parallel l_1 \parallel U(\varrho(y)) \parallel l \parallel m)$ & $(k \parallel U(\varrho(x)) \parallel m)$.

Conversely, if $\exists k, l, m, p \ ((k \parallel l \parallel U(\varrho(y)) \parallel m \parallel p)$ & $(k \parallel U(\varrho(x)) \parallel p))$, then we can say that $U(\varrho(x)) = i$ and $U(\varrho(y)) = j$. Then $\mathfrak{M} \models \langle A \rangle \varrho(y)[l]$. Since $k \parallel l \parallel j \parallel m \parallel p$, by S19' we get $\mathfrak{M} \models \langle \bar{B} \rangle \langle E \rangle \varrho(y)[l]$. This means that there exists j' such that $k \parallel j' \parallel m$ and $\mathfrak{M} \models \langle E \rangle \varrho(y)[j']$. But moreover $k \parallel i \parallel p$ and $m \parallel p$, hence $\mathfrak{M} \models \langle B \rangle \langle E \rangle \varrho(y)[i]$, so $\mathfrak{M} \models (\varrho(x) \rightarrow \langle B \rangle \langle E \rangle \varrho(y))$.

If $i = U(\varrho(y))$, then the reasoning proceeds in an analogous way. But we have $U(\varrho(x)) = W(x)$ and $U(\varrho(y)) = W(y)$. Therefore $\mathcal{M} \models x \; di \; y$ iff $\mathfrak{M} \models \xi(x \; di \; y)[i]$.

- $f = x \; s \; y$

  $\mathcal{M} \models f$ iff $\exists k, l, m \; ((k \parallel W(x) \;\&\; W(x) \parallel l \;\&\; l \parallel m) \;\&$
  $(k \parallel W(y) \;\&\; W(y) \parallel l)),$

  $\mathfrak{M} \models \xi(f)[i]$ iff $\mathfrak{M} \models (\varrho(x) \rightarrow \langle \bar{B} \rangle \varrho(y)) \;\&\; (\varrho(y) \rightarrow \langle B \rangle \varrho(x))[i]$
            iff   if $\mathfrak{M} \models \varrho(x)[i]$, then for some j there
                 exist k, l, m such that $(k \parallel j \;\&\; j \parallel m) \;\&\; (k \parallel i \;\&$
                 $i \parallel l \;\&\; l \parallel m)$ and $\mathfrak{M} \models \varrho(x)[j]$ and
                 if $\mathfrak{M} \models \varrho(y)[i]$, then for some j there
                 exist k, l, m such that $(k \parallel i \;\&\; i \parallel m) \;\&$
                 $(k \parallel j \;\&\; j \parallel l \;\&\; l \parallel m)$ and $\mathtt{M} \models \varrho(x)[j]$.

The reasoning is analogous as for $f = x \; fi \; y$—we must replace x by y and *vice versa* and consider symmetry w.r.t. the time arrow.

- $f = x \; eq \; y$

  $\mathcal{M} \models f$ iff $\exists k, l \; ((k \parallel W(x) \;\&\; W(x) \parallel l) \;\&$
  $(k \parallel W(y) \;\&\; W(y) \parallel l)),$

  $\mathfrak{M} \models \xi(f)[i]$ iff $\mathfrak{M} \models (\varrho(x) \leftrightarrow \varrho(y))[i]$
            iff   if $\mathfrak{M} \models \varrho(x)[i]$, then $\mathfrak{M} \models \varrho(y)[i]$ and
                 if $\mathfrak{M} \models \varrho(y)[i]$, then $\mathfrak{M} \models \varrho(x)[i]$.

If $i = U(\varrho(x))$, then $\mathfrak{M} \models \varrho(x)[i]$, hence $\mathfrak{M} \models \varrho(y)[i]$, so $i = U(\varrho(y))$. Therefore $\mathfrak{M} \models (\varrho(x) \;\&\; \varrho(y))[i]$. Thus, by S7, $\mathfrak{M} \models [\bar{A}] \langle A \rangle (\varrho(x) \;\&\; \varrho(y))[i]$ and by S6, $\mathfrak{M} \models [A] \langle \bar{A} \rangle (\varrho(x) \;\&\; \varrho(y))[i]$. Due to $SSUCC$ this means that $\mathfrak{M} \models \langle \bar{A} \rangle \langle A \rangle (\varrho(x) \;\&\; \varrho(y))[i]$ and $\mathfrak{M} \models \langle A \rangle \langle \bar{A} \rangle (\varrho(x) \;\&\; \varrho(y))[i]$. Thus there exist k, l such that $k \parallel i \parallel l$ and $\mathfrak{M} \models \langle A \rangle (\varrho(x) \;\&\; \varrho(y)) [k]$ and $\mathfrak{M} \models \langle \bar{A} \rangle (\varrho(x) \;\&\; \varrho(y)) [l]$. Therefore $\exists k, l \; ((k \parallel U(\varrho(x)) \parallel l) \;\&$ $(k \parallel U(\varrho(y)) \parallel l))$.

Suppose that $\exists k, l \; ((k \parallel U(\varrho(x)) \parallel l) \;\&\; (k \parallel U(\varrho(y)) \parallel l))$. Let $U(\varrho(x)) = i$ and $U(\varrho(y)) = j$. Then $\mathfrak{M} \models (\langle A \rangle \langle \bar{A} \rangle \varrho(y)) [i]$. Thus, by SL_LIN, $\mathfrak{M} \models (\varrho(y) \vee \langle B \rangle \varrho(y) \vee \langle \bar{B} \rangle \varrho(y))[i]$. Suppose that $\mathfrak{M} \models \langle B \rangle \varrho(y)[i]$. This means that there exist k', l', m' such that $(k' \parallel i \parallel m') \;\&\; (k' \parallel j \parallel l' \parallel m')$. Since $i \parallel l \;\&\; i \parallel m' \;\&\; l' \parallel m'$, it can be proved in a similar way as before that $l' \parallel l$. Therefore $j \parallel l' \parallel l$. This is contrary to the fact that $j \parallel l$. Suppose that $\mathfrak{M} \models \langle \bar{B} \rangle \varrho(y)[i]$. This means that there exist k', l', m' such that $(k' \parallel i \parallel l' \parallel m') \;\&\; (k' \parallel j \parallel m')$. As $j \parallel l \;\&\; i \parallel l \;\&\; i \parallel l'$, then as before we can prove that $j \parallel l'$. Hence $j \parallel l' \parallel m'$. This is contrary to the fact that $j \parallel m'$. Therefore $\mathfrak{M} \models \varrho(y)[i]$. And this means that $\mathfrak{M} \models (\varrho(x) \rightarrow \varrho(y))[i]$.

If $i = U(\varrho(y))$, then the reasoning is analogous. But $U(\varrho(x)) = W(x)$ and $U(\varrho(y)) = W(y)$. Eventually $\mathcal{M} \models f$ iff $\mathfrak{M} \models \xi(f)$.

Comment: The use of the linearity axiom in the above reasoning is justified, since the semantics of the relation *equals* suggested by Allen & Hayes makes sense only for linear structures (One can imagine two non-collinear intervals with common predecessor and successor). Nevertheless, the use of the axiom *SSUCC* is less justified and follows from the fact that Allen & Hayes consider only infinite structures. However, a weaker definition can be suggested for the relation *equals*: $\forall k,l \; ((k \parallel W(x) \; \& \; W(x) \parallel l) \rightarrow (k \parallel W(y) \; \& \; W(y) \parallel l))$. It is equivalent to the original one when *SSUCC* holds.

- $f = x \; si \; y$
  The reasoning is analogous as for $f = x \; fi \; y$—due to the symmetry w.r.t. the time arrow.

- $f = x \; d \; y$
  The reasoning is analogous as for $f = x \; di \; y$—we must replace x by y and *vice versa*.

- $f = x \; f \; y$
  The reasoning is analogous as for $f = x \; fi \; y$—we must replace x by y and *vice versa*.

- $f = x \; oi \; y$
  The reasoning is analogous as for $f = x \; o \; y$—we must replace x by y and *vice versa*.

- $f = x \; mi \; y$
  The reasoning is analogous as for $f = x \; m \; y$—we must replace x by y and *vice versa*.

- $f = x \; bi \; y$
  The reasoning is analogous as for $f = x \; b \; y$—we must replace x by y and *vice versa*.

- $f = x \; \{r_1, ..., r_n\} \; y$

  $\mathcal{M} \models f$ iff $\mathcal{M} \models x \; r_1 \; y$ or ... or $\mathcal{M} \models x \; r_n \; y$

  $\mathfrak{M} \models \xi(f)[t]$ iff $\mathfrak{M} \models (\xi(x \; r_1 \; y \; \vee \; ... \; \vee \; x \; r_n \; y)[i]$

                 iff $\mathfrak{M} \models \xi(x \; r_1 \; y)[i]$ or ... or $\mathfrak{M} \models \xi(x \; r_n \; y)[i]$

  Evidently $\mathcal{M} \models x \; r_i \; y$ iff $\mathfrak{M} \models \xi(x \; r_i \; y)[i]$. Therefore $\mathcal{M} \models f$ iff $\mathfrak{M} \models \xi(f)$.

- For any models $\mathcal{M} = \langle J, \|, W \rangle$ and $\mathfrak{M} = \langle J, \|, U \rangle$ and every $x, y \in Z$, $p \in X$ we have $\mathcal{M} \not\models x \, \emptyset \, y$ and $\mathfrak{M} \not\models p \, \& \, \neg p$. Therefore also for $f = x \, \emptyset \, y$ we have $\mathcal{M} \models f$ iff $\mathfrak{M} \models \xi(f)$.

Thus we have shown that for every $f \in \mathcal{F}$ we have $\mathcal{M} \models f$ iff $\mathfrak{M} \models \xi(f)$. ∎

Corollary For weakly compatible models $\mathcal{M} = \langle J, \|, W \rangle$ and $\mathfrak{M} = \langle J, \|, U \rangle$, and for every formula $f \in \mathcal{F}$ if $\mathcal{M} \models f$, then $\mathfrak{M} \models \xi(f)$.

Bibliography

Abadi, M. & Lamport, L. (1991) An old-fashioned recipe for real time, in Bakker, J.W., Huizing, C., Roever, W.P. & Rozenberg, G. (eds.) *Proceedings on REX Workshop on Real Time: Theory in Practice*, Mook, The Netherlands LNCS 600, Springer Verlag, pp. 1-27

Abadi, M. & Manna, Z. (1985) Nonclausal Temporal Deduction, in Parikh, R. (ed.) *Proceedings of the Conference on Logics of Programs*, Brooklyn, NY, USA, LNCS 193, Springer Verlag pp. 1-15

Allen, J. F. (1983) Maintaining Knowledge about Temporal Intervals, *Communications of ACM* **26** (11), pp. 832-843.

Allen, J. F. (1984) Towards a General Theory of Action and Time, *Artificial Intelligence* **23** (2), pp. 123-154

Allen, J. & Hayes, P. J. (1985) A Common-Sense Theory of Time, *Proceedings of the Ninth International Joint Conference on Artificial Intelligence*, Los Angeles, CA, USA, Morgan Kaufmann Publishers, pp. 528-531

Allen, J.F. & Koomen, J. (1983) Planning Using a Temporal World Model, *Proceedings of the Eighth International Joint Conference on Artificial Intelligence*, Karlsruhe, Germany, Morgan Kaufmann Publishers, pp. 741-746

Alur, R., Cowrcoubetis, C. & Dill, D. (1991) Logics and Models of Real Time: A Survey, in Bakker, J.W., Huizing, C., Roever, W.P. & Rozenberg, G. (eds.) *Proceedings on REX Workshop on Real Time: Theory in Practice*, Mook, The Netherlands LNCS 600, Springer Verlag, pp. 28-44

Andre, E., Herzog, G. & Rist, Th. (1988) On the Simultaneous Interpretation of Real World Image Sequences and their Natural Language Description: the System SOCCER, *Proceedings of the Eighth European Conference on Artificial Intelligence*, Munich, Germany, Pitman Publishing, pp. 188-200

Andréka, H., Gornako, V., Mikulás, S., Németi, I. & Sain, I. (1995) Effective Temporal Logics of Programs, in L. Bolc, A. Szalas (eds.) *Logic and Time*, UCL Press, pp. 51-129

Asada, M. & Tsuji, S. (1985) Utilization of a Stripe Pattern for Dynamic Scene Analysis, *Proceedings of the Ninth International Joint Conference on Artificial Intelligence*, Los Angeles, CA, USA, Morgan Kaufmann Publishers, pp. 895-897

Augustynek, Z. (1972) *Własności Czasu (Time Properties)* (in Polish), PWN, Warsaw, Poland

Augustynek, Z. (1979) *Przeszłość, Teraźniejszość, Przyszłość. Studium Filozoficzne (Past, Present, Future. A Philosophical Study)*, (in Polish) PWN, Warsaw, Poland

Ayache, N. & Faugeras, O.D. (1987) Building a Consistent 3d Representation of a Mobile Robot Environment by Combining Multiple Stereo Vision Views, *Proceedings of the Tenth International Joint Conference on Artificial Intelligence*, Milan, Italy, Morgan Kaufmann Publishers, pp. 808-810

Ayache, N. & Lustman F. (1987) Trinocular Stereovision, *Proceedings of the Tenth International Joint Conference on Artificial Intelligence*, Milan, Italy, Morgan Kaufmann Publishers, pp. 826–828

Bajcsy, R., Joshi, A., Krotkov, E. & Zwarico, A. (1985) LandScan: A Natural Language and Computer Vision System for Analyzing Aerial Images, *Proceedings of the Ninth International Joint Conference on Artificial Intelligence*, Los Angeles, CA, USA, Morgan Kaufmann Publishers, pp. 919–921

Badaloni, S. & Berati, M. (1994) Dealing with Time Granularity in a Temporal Planning System, in Gabbay, D.M. & Ohlbah, H.J. (eds.) *Proceedings of the First International Conference on Temporal Logic*, Bonn, Germany, LNAI 827, Springer Verlag, pp. 101–116

Barron, J.L., Jepson, A.D. & Tsotsos, T.K. (1987) Determination of Egomotion and Environmental Layout from Noisy Time-Varying Sequences, *Proceedings of the Tenth International Joint Conference on Artificial Intelligence*, Milan, Italy, Morgan Kaufmann Publishers, pp. 822–825

Baudinet, M., Chomicki, J. & Wolper, P. (1993) Temporal Deductive Databases, in Tansel, A., Clifford, J., Gadia, S., Jajodia, S., Segev, A. & Snodgrass, R. (eds.) *Temporal Databases: Theory, Design, and Implementation*, Benjamin/Cummings, pp. 294–320

van Beek, P. (1989) Approximation Algorithms for Temporal Reasoning, *Proceedings of the Eleventh International Joint Conference on Artificial Intelligence*, Detroit, MI, USA, Morgan Kaufmann Publishers, pp. 1291–1296

van Beek, P. (1990) Reasoning about Qualitative Temporal Information, *Proceedings of the Eighth AAAI Conference*, Boston, MA, USA, MIT Press, pp. 728–734

van Beek, P. & Cohen, R. (1990) Exact and Approximate Reasoning about Temporal Relations, *Computational Intelligence* 6 (3), pp. 132–144

Ben-Ari, M., Manna, Z. & Pnueli, A. (1983) The Temporal Logic of Branching Time, *Acta Informatica* 20 (3), pp. 207–226

van Benthem, J.F.A.K. (1983) *The Logic of Time*, D. Reidel Publishing Company

Blackburn, P., Gardent, C. & de Rijke, M. (1994) Back and Forth through Time and Events, in Gabbay, D.M. & Ohlbah, H.J. (eds.) *Proceedings of the First International Conference on Temporal Logic*, Bonn, Germany, LNAI 827, Springer Verlag, pp. 225–237

Böhlen, M. & Marti, R. (1994) On the Completeness of Temporal Database Query Languages, in Gabbay, D.M. & Ohlbah, H.J. (eds.) *Proceedings of the First International Conference on Temporal Logic*, Bonn, Germany, LNAI 827, Springer Verlag, pp. 283–300

Burger, W. & Bhanu, B. (1987) Qualitative Model Understanding, *Proceedings of the Tenth International Joint Conference on Artificial Intelligence*, Milan, Italy, Morgan Kaufmann Publishers, pp. 819–821

Burgess, J.P. (1982a) Axioms for Tense Logic I. "Since" and "Until", *Notre Dame Journal of Formal Logic* 23 (4), pp. 367–374

Burgess, J.P. (1982b) Axioms for Tense Logic II. Time Periods, *Notre Dame Journal of Formal Logic* 23 (4), pp. 375–383

Burns, J.B. & Kitchen, L.J. (1987) Recognition in 2D Images of 3D Images from Large Model bases Using Prediction Hierarchies, *Proceedings of the Tenth International Joint Conference on Artificial Intelligence*, Milan, Italy, Morgan Kaufmann Publishers, pp. 763–766

Cheng, J. & Irani, K.B. (1987) Subgoal Ordering and Goal Augmentation for Heuristic Problem Solving, *Proceedings of the Tenth International Joint Conference on Artificial Intelligence*, Milan, Italy, Morgan Kaufmann Publishers, pp. 1018–1024

Cheng, J. & Irani, K.B. (1989) Ordering Problem Subgoals, *Proceedings of the Ninth International Joint Conference on Artificial Intelligence*, Los Angeles, CA, USA, Morgan Kaufmann Publishers, pp. 931–936

Chomicki, J. (1994) Temporal Query Languages: a Survey, in Gabbay, D.M. & Ohlbah, H.J. (eds.) *Proceedings of the First International Conference on Temporal Logic*, Bonn, Germany, LNAI 827, Springer Verlag, pp. 506–532

Dean, Th. (1985) Temporal Reasoning Involving Counterfactuals and Disjunction, *Proceedings of the Ninth International Joint Conference on Artificial Intelligence*, Los Angeles, CA, USA, Morgan Kaufmann Publishers, pp. 1060–1062

Dechter, R., Meiri, I. & Pearl, J. (1989) Temporal Constraint Networks, *Proceedings of the First International Conference on Principles of Knowledge Representation and Reasoning*, Toronto, Canada, Morgan Kaufmann Publishers, pp. 83–93

Dechter, R., Meiri, I. & Pearl, J. (1991) Temporal Constraint Networks, *Artificial Intelligence* **49**, pp. 61–95

Denbigh, K.G. (1975) *An Inventive Universe*, Hutchinson & Co. Publishers

Doyle, J. (1978) *Truth Maintenance Systems for Problem Solving*, Technical Report 419, Massachusetts Institute of Technology, Artificial Intelligence Laboratory, Cambridge, MA, USA

Doyle, R.J. Atkinson, D.J. & Joshi, R.S. (1986) Generating Perception Requests and Expectations to Verify the Executions of Plans, *Proceedings of the Fifth AAAI Conference*, Philadelphia, PA, USA, Morgan Kaufmann Publishers, pp. 81–88

Eberle, K. (1988) Partial Orderings and Aktionsarten in Discourse Representing Theory, *Proceedings of the 12th International Conference on Computational Linguistics*, Budapest, Hungary, pp. 160–165

Emerson, E.A. & Halpern, J.Y. (1986) "Sometimes" and "Not Never" Revisited: On Branching Time versus Linear Time, *Journal of the ACM* **33**, pp. 151–178

Emerson, E.A. (1991) Real Time and Mu-Calculus, in Bakker, J.W., Huizing, C., Roever, W.P. & Rozenberg, G. (eds.) *Proceedings on REX Workshop on Real Time: Theory in Practice*, Mook, The Netherlands LNCS 600, Springer Verlag, pp. 176–194

van Eynde, F. (1988) The Analysis if Tense and Aspect in Eurotra, *Proceedings of the 12th International Conference on Computational Linguistics*, Budapest, Hungary, pp. 699–704

Fiadero, J.L. & Maibaum, T. (1994) Sometimes "Tomorrow' Is "Sometime": Action Refinement in a Temporal Logic of Programs, in Gabbay, D.M. & Ohlbah, H.J. (eds.) *Proceedings of the First International Conference on Temporal Logic*, Bonn, Germany, LNAI 827, Springer Verlag, pp. 48–66

Fikes, R. & Nilsson N.J. (1971) STRIPS: A New Approach to Application of Theorem Proving to Problem Solving, *Artificial Intelligence* **2**, pp. 189–208

Firby, R.J. (1987) An Investigation into Reactive Planning in Complex Domain, *Proceedings of the Sixth AAAI Conference*, Seattle, WA, USA, Morgan Kaufmann Publishers, pp. 202–206

Fisher, R.B. (1987) Invocation for Three Dimensional Scene Understanding, *Proceedings of the Tenth International Joint Conference on Artificial Intelligence*, Milan, Italy, Morgan Kaufmann Publishers, pp. 805–807

Forbus, K.D. (1984) Qualitative Process Theory, *Artificial Intelligence* **24**, pp. 85–165

Forbus, K.D. (1989) Introducing actions into Qualitative Simulation, *Proceedings of the Eleventh International Joint Conference on Artificial Intelligence*, Detroit, MI, USA, Morgan Kaufmann Publishers, pp. 1273–1278

Freksa, C. (1992) Temporal Reasoning Based on Semi-Intervals, *Artificial Intelligence* **54** (1–2), pp. 199–227

Gabbay, D.M., Hodkinson, I.M. & Reynolds, M.A. (1994) *Temporal Logic* vol. 1: *Mathematical Foundations*, Oxford University Press

Gabbay, D.M., Pnueli, A., Shelah, S., & Stavi, J. (1980) On the Temporal Analysis of Fairness, *Seventh Annual ACM Symposium on Principles of Programming Languages*, Las Vegas, NV, USA, pp. 163–173

Georgeff, M.P. (1986) Representation of Events in Multi-Agent Planning, *Proceedings of the Fifth AAAI Conference*, Philadelphia, PA, USA, Morgan Kaufmann Publishers, pp. 70–75

Georgeff. M.P. (1987) Actions, Processes and Causality, *Proceedings of the Workshop of Reasoning about Action and Plans*, Timberline, OR, USA, Morgan Kaufmann Publishers, pp. 99–122

Georgeff, M.P. & Lansky, A.L. (1987) Reactive Reasoning and Planning, *Proceedings of the Sixth AAAI Conference*, Seattle, WA, USA, Morgan Kaufmann Publishers, pp. 677–682

Ghallab, M. & Alaoui, A.M. (1989) Managing Efficiently Temporal Relations Through Indexing Spanning Trees, *Proceedings of the Eleventh International Joint Conference on Artificial Intelligence*, Detroit, MI, USA, Morgan Kaufmann Publishers, pp. 1297–1303

Grumberg, O. & Kurshan, R.P. (1994) How Linear Can branching-time Be?, in Gabbay, D.M. & Ohlbah, H.J. (eds.) *Proceedings of the First International Conference on Temporal Logic*, Bonn, Germany, LNAI 827, Springer Verlag, pp. 180–194

Haas, A.R. (1992) A Reactive Planner that Uses Explanation Closure, *Proceedings of the Third International Conference on Principles of Knowledge Representation and Reasoning*, Cambridge, MA, USA, Morgan Kaufmann Publishers, pp. 93–102

Hajnicz, E. (1987) *System wnioskowania o zależnościach czasowych między zdarzeniami. Koncepcja i implementacja (An Inferential System on Temporal Dependencies between Events. Conception and Implementation* (in Polish), ICS PAS Reports 603, Warsaw, Poland

Hajnicz, E. (1988) *Implementacja dat względnych w systemie wnioskowania o zależnościach czasowych między zdarzeniami (Implementation of Relative Dates in Inferential System on Temporal Dependencies between Events)* (in Polish), ICS PAS Reports 628, Warsaw, Poland

Hajnicz, E. (1989a) Absolute Dates and Relative Dates in an Inferential System on Temporal Dependencies between Events, *International Journal of Man-Machine Studies* **30**, pp. 537–549

Hajnicz, E. (1989b) *Formalizacja systemu wnioskowania o zależnościach czasowych między zdarzeniami (Formalization of Inferential System on Temporal Dependencies between Events)* (in Polish), ICS PAS Reports 658, Warsaw, Poland

Hajnicz, E. (1990) Role of the Present in Temporal Representation in Artificial Intelligence, *International Journal of Man-Machine Studies* **30**, pp. 263–274

Hajnicz, E. (1991a) Another Approach to Formalizing the Point and Interval Calculi, *International Journal of Man-Machine Studies* **34**, pp. 703–716

Hajnicz, E. (1991b) A Formalization of Absolute Dates and Relative Dates Based on the Point Calculus, *International Journal of Man-Machine Studies* **34**, pp. 717–730

Hajnicz, E. (1991c) *Reprezentacja i opis formalny struktur czasu nieliniowego na potrzeby sztucznej inteligencji (Representation and Formal Description of Nonlinear Time Structures for Artificial Intelligence)* (in Polish), Ph.D. Dissertation, Institute of Computer Science, Polish Academy of Sciences, Warsaw, Poland

Hajnicz, E. (1995a) *An Analysis of Structure of Time in the First Order Predicate Calculus*, in L. Bolc, A. Szałas (eds.) *Logic and Time*, UCL Press, pp. 279–322

Hajnicz, E. (1995b) Some Considerations on Non-linear Time Intervals, forthcoming in *Journal of Logic, Language and Information*

Hajnicz, E. (1995c) Applying Allen's Constraint Propagation Algorithm for Non-linear Time Intervals, forthcoming in *Journal of Logic, Language and Information*

Hajnicz, E. (1996) Some considerations on branching area of time, in preparation

Halpern, J.Y. & Shoham, Y. (1991) A propositional Modal Logic of Time Intervals, *Journal of the Association for Computing Machinery* **38** (4), pp. 935–962

Hansen, M.R. & Chaochen, Z. (1991) Semantics and Completeness of Duration Calculus, in Bakker, J.W., Huizing, C., Roever, W.P. & Rozenberg, G. (eds.) *Proceedings on REX Workshop on Real Time: Theory in Practice*, Mook, The Netherlands, LNCS 600, Springer Verlag, pp. 209–225

Haugh, B. A. (1987) Non-Standard Semantics for the Method of Temporal Arguments, *Proceedings of the Tenth International Joint Conference on Artificial Intelligence*, Milan, Italy, Morgan Kaufmann Publishers, pp. 449–455

Hayes, C.C. (1989) A Model of Planning for Plan Efficiency: Taking Advantage of Operator Overlap, *Proceedings of the Eleventh International Joint Conference on Artificial Intelligence*, Detroit, MI, USA, Morgan Kaufmann Publishers, pp. 949–953

Hayes, P.J. & Allen, J.F. (1987) Short Time Periods, *Proceedings of the Tenth International Joint Conference on Artificial Intelligence*, Milan, Italy, Morgan Kaufmann Publishers, pp. 981–983

Hendrix, G.C. (1973) Modeling Simultaneous Actions and Continuous Processes, *Artificial Intelligence* 4, pp. 145–180

Hertzberg, J. & Horz, A. (1989) Towards a Theory of Conflict Detection and Resolution in Nonlinear Plans, *Proceedings of the Eleventh International Joint Conference on Artificial Intelligence*, Detroit, MI, USA, Morgan Kaufmann Publishers, pp. 937–942

Hirschman, L. & Story, G. (1981) Representing Implicit and Explicit Time Relations in Narrative, *Proceedings of the Seventh International Joint Conference on Artificial Intelligence*, Vancouver, Canada, Morgan Kaufmann Publishers, pp. 289–295

Hobbs, J.R. & Agar, M. (1981) Text Plans and World Plans in Natural Discourse, *Proceedings of the Seventh International Joint Conference on Artificial Intelligence*, Vancouver, Canada, Morgan Kaufmann Publishers, pp. 190–196

Hogge, J.C. (1987) Compiling Plan Operators From Domains Expressed in Qualitative Process Theory, *Proceedings of the Sixth AAAI Conference*, Seattle, WA, USA, Morgan Kaufmann Publishers, pp. 229–233

Hogge, J.C. (1988) Prevention Techniques for a Temporal Planner, *Proceedings of the Seventh AAAI Conference*, Saint Paul, MN, USA, Morgan Kaufmann Publishers, pp. 43–48

Hornstein, N. (1977) Towards a Theory of Tense, *Linguistic Theory* 8 (3)

Hrycej, T. (1986) *A Transitivity-Based Algorithm for Temporal Constraint Propagation*, Technical Report TEX-B Memo 13–86, Munich, Germany

Hrycej, T. (1988) *A Comparative Evaluation of Transitivity-Based Temporal Constraint Propagation*, Technical Report TEX-B Memo 28–88, Munich, Germany

Huber, A. & Becker, S. (1988) Production Planning Using a Temporal Planning Component, *Proceedings of the Eighth European Conference on Artificial Intelligence*, Munich, Germany, Pitman Publishing, pp. 188–200

Hwang, C.H., & Schubert, L.K. (1994) Interpreting Tense, Aspect and Time Adverbials: A Compositional, Unifying Approach, in Gabbay, D.M. & Ohlbah, H.J. (eds.) *Proceedings of the First International Conference on Temporal Logic*, Bonn, Germany, LNAI 827, Springer Verlag, pp. 238–264

Kabanza, F., Stevenne, J.M. & Wolper, P. (1990) Handling Infinite Temporal Data, in *Proceedings on the Ninth Annual ACM SIGACT-SIGMOND-SIGART Symposium on Principles of Database Systems*, Nashville, TN, USA

Kahn, K. & Gorry, G.A. (1977) Mechanizing Temporal Knowledge, *Artificial Intelligence* 9, pp. 87–108

Kamp, H. (1979) Instants and Temporal Reference, in von Stechow (ed.) *Semantics from different points of view*, Springer Series in Language and Communication 6, Springer Verlag, pp. 376–417

Kamp, H. (1980) Some Remarks on the Logic of Change. Part I, in Guenthner, F. (ed.) *Proceedings of the Stuttgart Conference on the Logic of Tense and Quantification*, North Holland, pp. 135–179

Katsuno, H. & Mendelzon, A.O. (1991) On the Difference between Updating Knowledge Base and Revising it, *Proceedings of the Second International Conference on Principles of Knowledge Representation and Reasoning*, Cambridge, MA, USA, Morgan Kaufmann Publishers, pp. 387–394

Katz, S. (1994) Global Equivalence Proofs for ISTL, in Gabbay, D.M. & Ohlbah, H.J. (eds.) *Proceedings of the First International Conference on Temporal Logic*, Bonn, Germany, LNAI 827, Springer Verlag, pp. 17–29

Kautz, H.A. (1987) *A Formal Theory of Plan Recognition*, Ph.D. Thesis, Department of Computer Science, University of Rochester, Rochester, NY, USA

Kautz, H.A. & Allen, J.F. (1986) Generalized Plan Recognition, *Proceedings of the Fifth AAAI Conference*, Philadelphia, PA, USA, Morgan Kaufmann Publishers, pp. 32–37

Kautz, H.A. & Ladkin, P.B. (1991) *Integrating Metric and Qualitative Temporal Reasoning*, Proceedings of the Ninth AAAI Conference, Anaheim, CA, USA, MIT Press, pp. 241–246

Keretho, S. & Loganantharaj, R. (1993) Reasoning about Networks of Temporal Relations and Its Applications to Problem Solving, *Applied Intelligence* 3 (1), pp. 47–70

Koomen, J.A.G.M. (1987) *The TIMELOGIC Temporal Reasoning System in Common Lisp*, Technical Report TR 231, University of Rochester, Rochester, NY, USA

Koomen, J.A.G.M. (1989) Localizing Temporal Constraint Propagation, *Proceedings of the First International Conference on Principles of Knowledge Representation and Reasoning*, Toronto, Canada, Morgan Kaufmann Publishers, pp. 198–202

Kornatzky, Y. & Pinter, S.S. (1986) $POTL[u, \bar{U}]$ an Extention to Partial Order Temporal Logic (POTL), EE Publication 596, Department of Electrical Engineering, Technion, Haifa, Israel

Koubarakis, M. (1992) Dense Time and Temporal Constraints with $\neq$, *Proceedings of the Third International Conference on Principles of Knowledge Representation and Reasoning*, Cambridge, MA, USA, Morgan Kaufmann Publishers, pp. 24–35

Kowalski, R. & Sergot, M. (1986) A Logic-Based Calculus of Events, *New Generation Computing* 4, pp. 67–95

Kripke, S. (1959) A completeness theorem in modal logic, *Journal of Symbolic Logic* 24, pp. 1–14

Kripke, S. (1963) Semantical Analysis of modal logic I: normal modal propositional calculi, *Zeitschrift für Math. Logic und Grundlagen der Math.* 9, pp. 67–96

Kröger, F. (1985) *Temporal Logic of Programs, Lecture Notes*, Technical Report TUM-I8521, Institut für Informatik, Technische Universität, München

Kutty, G., Moser, L.E., Melliar-Smith, P.M., Dillon, L.K. & Ramakrishna, Y.S. (1994) First-Order Future Interval Logic, in Gabbay, D.M. & Ohlbah, H.J. (eds.) *Proceedings of the First International Conference on Temporal Logic*, Bonn, Germany, LNAI 827, Springer Verlag, pp. 195–209

Kwiatkowska, M., Peled, D. & Penczek, W. (1994) A Hierarchy of Partial Order Temporal Properties, in Gabbay, D.M. & Ohlbah, H.J. (eds.) *Proceedings of the First International Conference on Temporal Logic*, Bonn, Germany, LNAI 827, Springer Verlag, pp. 398–414

Lâasri, H., Maître, B., Mondot, T., Charpillet, F. & Haton, J.P. (1988) ATOME: a blackboard architecture with temporal and hypothetical reasoning, *Proceedings of the Eighth European Conference on Artificial Intelligence*, Munich, Germany, Pitman Publishing, pp. 5–10

Ladkin, P. (1986a) Time Representation: A Taxonomy of Interval Relations, *Proceedings of the Fifth AAAI Conference*, Philadelphia, PA, USA, Morgan Kaufmann Publishers, pp. 360–366

Ladkin, P.(1986b) Primitives and Units for Time Specification, *Proceedings of the Fifth AAAI Conference*, Philadelphia, PA, USA, Morgan Kaufmann Publishers, pp. 354–359

Ladkin, P. B. (1987) Models of Axioms for Time Intervals, *Proceedings of the Sixth AAAI Conference*, Seattle, WA, USA, Morgan Kaufmann Publishers, pp. 234–239

Ladkin, P.B. & Maddux, R.D. (1987) *The Algebra of Convex Time Intervals*, Kestrel Institute Technical Report KES.U.87.2, Palo Alto, CA, USA

Ladkin, P.B. & Reinefeld, A. (1992) Effective Solution of Qualitative Interval Constraint Problems, *Artificial Intelligence* **57** (1), pp. 105–124

Lamport, L. (1980) "Sometime" is Sometimes "Not Never", *Seventh Annual ACM Symposium on Principles of Programming Languages*, Las Vegas, NV, USA, pp. 174–184

Leban, B., McDonald, D.D. & Forster, D.R. (1986) A representation for Collection of Temporal Intervals, *Proceedings of the Fifth AAAI Conference*, Philadelphia, PA, USA, Morgan Kaufmann Publishers, pp. 367–371

Lee, R.M., Coelho, H. & Cotta, J.C. (1985) Temporal Inferencing on Administrative Databases, *Information Systems* **10** (2), pp. 197–206

Levi, P. (1988) TOPAS: A Task-Oriented Planner for Optimized Assembly Sequences, *Proceedings of the Eighth European Conference on Artificial Intelligence*, Munich, Germany, Pitman Publishing, pp. 638–643

Lichtenstein, O., Pnueli, A. & Zuck, L. (1985) The glory of the past, in Parikh, R. (ed.) *Proceedings of the Conference on Logics of Programs*, Brooklyn, NY, LNCS 193, Springer Verlag

Lin, Y. (1991) Two Theories of Time, *Journal of Applied Non-Classical Logics* **1**, pp. 37–63

Lucas, B.D. & Kanade, T. (1985) Optical Navigation by the Method of Differences, *Proceedings of the Ninth International Joint Conference on Artificial Intelligence*, Los Angeles, CA, USA, Morgan Kaufmann Publishers, pp. 981–983

Lyndon, G.C. (1966) *Notes on Logic*, Van Nostrand Comp.

Man-Kam Yip, K. (1985) Tense, Aspect and the Cognitive Representation of Time, *Proceedings of the Ninth International Joint Conference on Artificial Intelligence*, Los Angeles, CA, USA, Morgan Kaufmann Publishers, pp. 807–814

Manna, Z. & Pnueli, A. (1981) Verification of Concurrent Programs: The Temporal Framework, in Boyer, R.S. & Moore, J.S. (eds.) *The Correctness Problems in Computer Science*

Manna, Z. & Pnueli, A. (1982) Verification of Concurrent Programs: Temporal Proof Principles, in Kozen, D. (ed.) *Proceedings of the Workshop on Logics of Programs*, Yorktown Heights, NY, USA, LNCS 131, Springer Verlag, pp. 200–252

Matsujama, T. & Hwang, V. (1985) SIGMA: A Framework for Image Understanding— Integration of Bottom-Up and Top-Down Analysis, *Proceedings of the Ninth International Joint Conference on Artificial Intelligence*, Los Angeles, CA, USA, Morgan Kaufmann Publishers, pp. 908–915

di Maio, M.C. & Zanardo, A. (1994) Synchronized Histories in Prior-Thomason Representation of Branching Time, in Gabbay, D.M. & Ohlbah, H.J. (eds.) *Proceedings of the First International Conference on Temporal Logic*, Bonn, Germany, LNAI 827, Springer Verlag, pp. 265–282

Mays, E. Lanka, S. Joshi, A.K. & Vebber, B. (1981) Natural Language Interaction with Dynamic Knowledge Bases: Monitoring as Response, *Proceedings of the Seventh International Joint Conference on Artificial Intelligence*, Vancouver, Canada, Morgan Kaufmann Publishers, pp. 61–63

Mays, E. (1983) A Modal Temporal Logic for Reasoning About Change, *Proceedings of the 21st Meeting of Association for Computational Linguistics*, MIT, Cambridge, MA, USA

McCarthy, J. & Hayes, P. J. (1969) Some Philosophical Problems from the Standpoint of Artificial Intelligence, in Meltzer, B. & Mitchie, D. (eds.), *Machine Intelligence 4*, Edinburgh University Press, pp. 463–502

McDermott, D. (1982) A Temporal Logic for Reasoning about Processes and Plans, *Cognitive Science 6*, pp. 101–155

McKenzie, L.E., Jr. & Snodgrass, R.T. (1991) Evaluation of Relational Algebras Incorporating the Time Dimension in Databases, *ACM Computing Surveys 23* (4), pp. 501–543

McTaggart, J.M.E. (1908) The unreality of Time, *Mind*, pp. 457–474

McTaggart, J.M.E. (1927) *The Nature of Existence*, Cambridge, Great Britain

Merkel, M. (1988) A Novel Analysis of Temporal Frame Adverbials, *Proceedings of the 12th International Conference on Computational Linguistics*, Budapest, Hungary, pp. 426–430

Meya, M. & Vidal, J. (1988) An Integrated Model for the Treatment of Time in MT-Systems, *Proceedings of the 12th International Conference on Computational Linguistics*, Budapest, Hungary, pp. 437–441

Miller, D. Firby, R. A. & Dean, Th. (1985) Deadlines, Travel Time and Robot Problem Solving, *Proceedings of the Ninth International Joint Conference on Artificial Intelligence*, Los Angeles, CA, USA, Morgan Kaufmann Publishers, pp. 1052–1054

Minton, S., Drummond, M., Beresina, J.L. & Philips, A.B. (1992) bf Total orders *vs*. Partial Order Planning Factors Influencing Performance, *Proceedings of the Third International Conference on Principles of Knowledge Representation and Reasoning*, Cambridge, MA, USA, Morgan Kaufmann Publishers, pp. 83–92

Moens, M. & Steedman, J. (1988) Temporal Ontology and Temporal Reference, *Computational Linguistics* **14**, pp. 15–28

Mokkedem, A. & Méry, D. (1994) A Stuttering Closed Temporal Logic for Modular Reasoning about Concurrent Programs, in Gabbay, D.M. & Ohlbah, H.J. (eds.) *Proceedings of the First International Conference on Temporal Logic*, Bonn, Germany, LNAI 827, Springer Verlag, pp. 382–397

Morgenstern, L. (1987) Knowledge Preconditions for Actions and Plans, *Proceedings of the Tenth International Joint Conference on Artificial Intelligence*, Milan, Italy, Morgan Kaufmann Publishers, pp. 867–874

Moszkowski, B. & Manna, Z. (1984) Reasoning in Interval Temporal Logic, in Clarke, E. & Kozen, D. (eds.) *Proceedings the Workshop on Logics of Programs*, Pittsburgh, PA, USA, LNCS 164, Springer Verlag, pp. 371–382

Nebel, B. & Bürckert, H.-J. (1993) *Reasoning about Temporal Relations: A Maximal Tractable Subclass of Allen's Interval Algebra*, Research report DFKi-RR-93-11, Deutsches Forschungszentrum für Künstliche Inteligenz GmBH, Saarbrücken, Germany

Neumann, B. (1984a) *Natural language Description of Time Varying Scenes*, Report 105, Fachbereich Informatik, Universitat Hamburg, Germany

Neumann, B. (1984b) *Natural Language Access to Image Sequences: Event Recognition and Verbalization*, Report 125, Fachbereich Informatik, Universitat Hamburg, Germany

Novak, H-J. (1985) *A Relational matching Strategy for Temporal Event Recognition*, Report 131, Fachbereich Informatik, Universitat Hamburg, Germany

Orłowska, E. (1981) *Dynamic Information Systems*, ICS PAS Reports 434, Warsaw, Poland

Orłowska, E. (1982) *Representation of Temporal Information*, ICS PAS Reports 484, Warsaw, Poland

Pednault, E.P.D. (1988) Extending Conventional Planning Techniques to handle Actions with Context-Dependent Effects, *Proceedings of the Seventh AAAI Conference*, Saint Paul, MN, USA, Morgan Kaufmann Publishers, pp. 55–59

Penberthy, J.S. & Weld, D.S. (1992) UCPOP: A Sound, Complete, Partial Order Planner for ADL, *Proceedings of the Third International Conference on Principles of Knowledge Representation and Reasoning*, Cambridge, MA, USA, Morgan Kaufmann Publishers, pp. 103–114

Penczek, W. (1995) Branching Time and Partial Order in Temporal Logics, in L. Bolc, A. Szalas (eds.) *Logic and Time*, UCL Press, pp. 179–228

Pinter, S.S. & Wolper, P. (1984) A Temporal Logic for Reasoning about Partialy Ordered Computations, *Proceedings of the Third Symposium on Principles of Distributed Computing*, pp. 28–37

Poesio, M. & Brachman, R.J. (1991) Metric Constraints for Maintaining Appointments: Dates and Repeated Actions, *Proceedings of the Ninth AAAI Conference*, Anaheim, CA, USA, MIT Press, pp. 241–246

Prior, A.N. (1957) *Time and Modality*, Clarendon Press

Prior, A.N. (1967) *Past, Present and Future*, Clarendon Press

Rasiowa, H. (1968) *Wstęp do matematyki współczesnej, (Introduction to Contemporary mathematics)*, Biblioteka Matematyczna, (Mathematics Library) (in Polish), PWN, Warsaw, Poland

Raulefs, P. (1987) A Representational Framework for Continuous Dynamic Systems, *Proceedings of the Tenth International Joint Conference on Artificial Intelligence*, Milan, Italy, Morgan Kaufmann Publishers, pp. 468–471

Reichenbach, H. (1966) *Elements of Symbolic Logic*, The Free Press

Rescher, N. & Urquhart, A. (1971) *Temporal Logic*, Library of Exact Philosophy, Springer Verlag

Reynolds, M. (1994) Axiomatizing U and S over Integer Time, in Gabbay, D.M. & Ohlbah, H.J. (eds.) *Proceedings of the First International Conference on Temporal Logic*, Bonn, Germany, LNAI 827, Springer Verlag, pp. 117–132

Richards, B., Bethke, I., van der Does, J. & Oberlander, J. (1989) *Temporal Representation and Inference*, Academic Press

Rodriguez, R., Anger, F. & Ford, K. (1991) Temporal Reasoning: a relativistic model, *International Journal of Intelligent Systems* **6**, pp. 237–254

Rodriguez, R.V. (1993) A Relativistic Temporal Algebra for Efficient Design of Distributed Systems, *Applied Intelligence: The International Journal of Artificial Intelligence, Neural Networks and Complex Problem-Solving Technologies* **3**, pp. 31–45

Sacerdoti, E.D. (1977) *A Structure for Time and Behaviour*, Elsevier North Holland

Sandewall, E. & Ronnquist, R. (1986) A Representation of Action Structures, *Proceedings of the Fifth AAAI Conference*, Philadelphia, PA, USA, Morgan Kaufmann Publishers, pp. 89–97

Shmolze, J. (1986) Physics for Robots, *Proceedings of the Fifth AAAI Conference*, Philadelphia, PA, USA, Morgan Kaufmann Publishers, pp. 44–50

Schoppers, M.J. (1987) Universal Plans for Reactive Robots in Unpredictable Environment, *Proceedings of the Tenth International Joint Conference on Artificial Intelligence*, Milan, Italy, Morgan Kaufmann Publishers, pp. 1039–1046

Schwartz, R.L., Melliar-Smith, P.M. & Vogt, F.H. (1984) On Interval-Based Temporal Logic, in Clarke, E. & Kozen, D. (eds.) *Proceedings the Workshop on Logics of Programs*, Pittsburgh, PA, USA, LNCS 164, Springer Verlag, pp. 443–457

Shoham, Y. (1987) *Reasoning about Change: Time and Causation from the Standpoint of Artificial Intelligence*, Ph.D. Thesis, Yale University, New Haven, CT, USA

Shoham, Y (1989) Time for Action: On the Relation between Time, Knowledge and Action, *Proceedings of the Eleventh International Joint Conference on Artificial Intelligence*, Detroit, MI, USA, Morgan Kaufmann Publishers, pp. 954–959

Snodgrass, R.T. (1992) Temporal Databases, in Frank, A.U., Campari, I. & Formentini, U. (eds.) *Theories and Methods of Spatio-Temporal Reasoning in Geographic Space*, LNCS 639, Springer Verlag, pp. 22–64

Song, F. (1994) Combining Temporal and Hierarchical Constraints for Temporal Reasoning, in Ohlbah, (ed.), *Proceedings of the Workshop on Temporal Logic*, Bonn, Germany, Report MPI-I-94-230, Max-Planck-Institute für Informatik, pp. 91–98

Song, F. & Cohen R. (1988) The Interpretation of Temporal Relations in Narratives, *Proceedings of the Seventh AAAI Conference*, Saint Paul, MN, USA, Morgan Kaufmann Publishers, pp. 745–750

Song, F. & Cohen R. (1991) Temporal Reasoning during plan recognition, *Proceedings of the Ninth AAAI Conference*, Anaheim, CA, USA, MIT Press, pp. 247–252

Sørensen, M.U., Hansen, O.E. & Løvengreen, H.H. (1994) Combining Temporal Specification Techniques, in Gabbay, D.M. & Ohlbah, H.J. (eds.) *Proceedings of the First International Conference on Temporal Logic*, Bonn, Germany, LNAI 827, Springer Verlag, pp. 1–16

Song, F. & Cohen R. (1991) Temporal Reasoning during Plan Recognition, *Proceedings of the Ninth AAAI Conference*, Anaheim, CA, USA, MIT Press, pp. 247–252

Tsang, E.P.K. (1986) *The Interval Structure of Allen's Logic*, Technical Report CSCM-24, University of Essex, Great Britain

Tsang, E.P.K. (1987a) Time Structures for AI, *Proceedings of the Tenth International Joint Conference on Artificial Intelligence*, Milan, Italy, Morgan Kaufmann Publishers, pp. 456–461

Tsang, E.P.K. (1987b) The Consistent Labeling Problem in Temporal Reasoning, *Proceedings of the Sixth AAAI Conference*, Seattle, WA, USA, Morgan Kaufmann Publishers, pp. 251–256

Tychonievitch, L., Zaret, D., Mantegna, J., Evans, R. Muehle, E. & Martin, S. (1989) A Maneuvering-Board Approach to Path Planning with Moving Obstacles, *Proceedings of the Eleventh International Joint Conference on Artificial Intelligence*, Detroit, MI, USA, Morgan Kaufmann Publishers, pp. 1017–1021

Valdés-Péres, R.E. (1987) The satisfiability of Temporal Constraint Networks, *Proceedings of the Sixth AAAI Conference*, Seattle, WA, USA, Morgan Kaufmann Publishers, pp. 256–260

Venema, Y. (1988) *Expressiveness and Completeness of an Interval Tense Logic—longer version*, ITLI Prepublication Series 88-02, Institute For Language, Logic and Information, University of Amsterdam, The Netherlands

Venema, Y. (1990) Expressiveness and Completeness of an Interval Tense Logic, *Notre Dame Journal of Formal Logic* **31** (4), pp. 529–547

Venema, Y. (1991) Completeness via Completeness, in de Rijke, M. (ed.) *Collegium on Modal Logic*, ITLI-Network Publication, Institute For Language, Logic and Information, University of Amsterdam, The Netherlands

Vilain, M.B. (1982) A System for Reasoning about Time, *Proceedings of the First AAAI Conference*, Pittsburgh, PA, Morgan Kaufmann Publishers, pp. 197–201

Vilain, M. B. & Kautz, H. (1986) Constraint Propagation Algorithms for Temporal Reasoning, *Proceedings of the Fifth AAAI Conference*, Philadelphia, PA, Morgan Kaufmann Publishers, pp. 377–392

Lecture Notes in Artificial Intelligence (LNAI)

Lecture Notes in Computer Science